ABS Tax Service

# The Self Employed Taxpayer

## Based on 2011 Tax Law

By:

**Mary W. Adams, EA**

**Edited By:**
**D.Blake**
**Linda Williams**
**Jaimie Sanford**

*AuthorHouse™*
*1663 Liberty Drive*
*Bloomington, IN 47403*
*www.authorhouse.com*
*Phone: 1-800-839-8640*

*Published by AuthorHouse   06/19/12*

*ISBN: 978-1-4772-2085-6 (sc)*

*Library of Congress Control Number: 2012910939*

*Any people depicted in stock imagery provided by Thinkstock are models, and such images are being used for illustrative purposes only. Certain stock imagery © Thinkstock.*

*This book is printed on acid-free paper.*

# Table of Contents

# Introduction

When a taxpayer chooses to start his or her own business, they often don't think about the tax consequences of the venture. If the taxpayer is the sole owner of the business, and he or she has not formed a separate entity, such as a corporation or a Limited Liability Company, the taxpayer becomes a sole proprietor. A sole proprietor is liable for income taxes, as well as self employment taxes on the net income of the business. The sole proprietor will report the income of the business and pay taxes on that business with his or her individual income tax return.

In this course, we will cover many aspects of a sole proprietorship from beginning to end. We will discuss start-up expenses and the basis of property purchased or acquired by other means for use in the business. We will discuss preparing the return and what expenses are allowable. We will discuss depreciation and expensing assets used in the business. We will also discuss the consequences of disposing of the property used in the business.

# Chapter 1 – The Beginning

In this chapter, we will be discussing the basis of property acquired in many different ways for business use. We will, also, learn what start-up expenses are and how they are deducted.

## Terms

**Adjusted basis** – the cost or other basis increased by improvements and other adjustments, and decreased by deductions taken, such as depreciation or depletion.

**Amortize** – to deduct expenses allowed by spreading the cost over a period of time.

**Basis** – the amount of investment the taxpayer has in an asset.

**Capitalize** – to add an expense to the basis of an asset instead of deducting it in the current tax year.

**Exchange** – a transfer of property for other property or services.

**Fair market value** – the price an item would sell for, assuming the buyer and a seller both have reasonable knowledge and are not under undue pressure.

**Sole proprietor** – an individual who is the sole owner of his or her trade or business. The income or loss incurred in a sole proprietorship is carried to the sole proprietor's individual tax return.

**Start-up expenses** – nonrecurring costs associated with setting up a business, such as accountant's fees, legal fees, or registration charges.

## *Basis*

The basis of property is usually its cost. The cost is the amount paid in cash, debt obligations, other property, or services. The taxpayer's cost also includes amounts paid for the following items:

- Sales tax
- Freight
- Installation and testing
- Excise taxes
- Legal and accounting fees that must be capitalized (added to the basis)
- Revenue stamps
- Recording fees
- Real estate taxes that were assumed for the seller

### Real Property

If the taxpayer buys real property, certain fees and other expenses will become part of the basis. If the taxpayer paid real estate taxes the seller owed on real property the taxpayer purchased, and the taxpayer was not reimbursed, the real estate taxes will be added to the basis. If the taxpayer reimburses the seller for taxes the seller paid for the taxpayer, the taxpayer may deduct the taxes as an expense in the year paid. Do not add this amount to the basis. If the seller was not reimbursed, the taxpayer's basis must be reduced by the amount of the real estate taxes.

Settlement fees the taxpayer paid when purchasing the property can be added to the basis. Fees and costs for getting a loan on the property cannot be added to the basis. The following are some of the settlement fees or closing costs that can be included in the basis of the property:

- Abstract fees (abstract of title fees)
- Charges for installing utility services.
- Legal fees (including title search and preparation of the sales contract and deed).
- Recording fees
- Surveys
- Transfer fees
- Owner's title insurance
- Any amounts the seller owes that the taxpayer agreed to pay, such as back taxes or interest, recording or mortgage fees, changes for improvements or repairs, and sales commissions.

Amounts placed in escrow for future payment of items such as taxes and insurance are not included in the settlement costs. The following settlement fees and closing costs are not included in the basis:

- Fire insurance premiums
- Rent for occupancy of the property before closing
- Charges for utilities or other services related to occupancy of the property before closing
- Charges connected with getting a loan
- Fees for refinancing a mortgage

For real property purchases, the basis includes the land and any building on the land. When calculating the basis for depreciation, the land is not included because land is not depreciable. If this is the case, any settlement fees included in the basis must be allocated between the land and buildings.

**Example:** Betty Jones purchased a lot and a building to be used in her business for $175,000. She paid $8,000 in settlement fees. The fair market value of the land was $35,000 on the date of purchase. The percentage of the purchase price allocated to the building is 80%: $140,000 ÷ $175,000 = 0.80
The settlement fees allocated to the building are $6,400: $8,000 x 80% = $6,400
The basis of the building is $146,400: $140,000 + $6,400 = $146,400
The settlement fees allocated to the land are $1,600: $8,000 - $6,400 = $1,600
Betty's basis in the land is $36,600: $35,000 + $1,600 = $36,600

## Constructed property

If the taxpayer builds the property or has it built for him or her, the expenses for construction are included in the basis. These expenses include the following:
- The cost of the land
- Cost of labor and materials
- Architect's fees
- Building permit charges
- Payments to contractors
- Payments for rental equipment
- Inspection fees

If the taxpayer uses their own employees, materials, and equipment to build an asset, their basis would also include the following costs:

- Employee wages paid for the construction work.
- Depreciation on equipment the taxpayer owns while it is used in construction.
- Operating and maintenance costs for equipment used in the construction.
- The cost of business supplies and materials used in the construction.

These expenses are not deducted in the year paid; instead, they are capitalized (added to the basis).

## *Adjusted Basis*

The adjusted basis of property is its cost or other basis increased by improvements and other adjustments, and decreased by deductions taken, such as depreciation or depletion. The following table illustrates different factors that affect the adjusted basis.

## Examples of Increases and Decreases to Basis

| Increases to Basis | Decreases to Basis |
| --- | --- |
| Capital improvements:<br>• Putting an addition on your office<br>• Replacing an entire roof<br>• Paving your parking lot<br>• Installing central air conditioning<br>• Rewiring your office<br><br>Assessments for local improvements:<br>• Water connections<br>• Sidewalks<br>• Roads<br><br>Casualty losses:<br>• Restoring damaged property<br><br>Legal fees:<br>• Cost of defending and perfecting a title<br><br>Zoning costs | Exclusion from income of subsidies for energy conservation measures<br><br>Casualty or theft loss deductions and insurance reimbursements<br><br>Credit for qualified electric vehicles<br><br>Section 179 deduction<br><br>Deduction for clean-fuel vehicles and clean-fuel vehicle refueling property<br><br>Depreciation or Amortization<br><br>Nontaxable corporate distributions<br><br>Deferred gains<br><br>Investment credit<br><br>Rebates from a manufacturer or seller<br><br>Easements |

# Basis of Converted Property

If the taxpayer holds property for personal use, then changes it to business use or to produce rent, there are different factors to consider when figuring the basis.

## *Depreciation*

The basis for depreciation is the lesser of the fair market value of the property on the date of the conversion, or the adjusted basis on the date of the conversion.

**Example:** Marvin Johnson paid $185,000 for his home several years ago. $25,000 was for the land. He's paid $15,000 for improvements since he purchased it. He's started renting the house out and wants to know his basis for depreciation. The FMV on the date he changed its use was $180,000 with $15,000 for the land. His adjusted basis is $175,000 ($185,000 – $25,000 + $15,000). The FMV is $165,000 ($180,000 - $15,000). The lesser of the two is the FMV of $165,000.

## *Gain or Loss*

If the taxpayer sells the property, he or she would determine the basis based on whether it was being sold at a gain or loss. If the property is sold at a gain, the basis for determining the gain is the taxpayer's adjusted basis. Remember, any depreciation deductions allowed, or allowable, are deducted to determine the basis.

**Example:** Using the facts from the previous example, assume Mr. Johnson sold the house at a gain after being allowed depreciation deductions of $37,500. His adjusted basis for figuring the gain is $162,500 ($175,000 + $25,000 - $37,500).

If the taxpayer sells the property at a loss, figure the basis starting with the smaller of the adjusted basis or the FMV on the date of conversion, then adjust this amount for the period after the change in the property's use.

**Example:** Assume the same facts as the previous example, except Mr. Johnson sold the property at a loss after being allowed depreciation deductions of $37,500. In this case, start with the FMV of $180,000 because it's the lesser amount. Then, deduct the depreciation of $37,500 to arrive at the basis for loss of $142,500.

If the taxpayer sells the property for an amount between the basis for gain and the basis for loss, there will be no gain or loss on the sale.

# Basis of Gifts

To determine the basis of property received as a gift, the taxpayer must know the adjusted basis to the donor right before it was given to the taxpayer, and the FMV on the date it was given to the taxpayer. The taxpayer's basis in the property for depreciation is the donor's adjusted basis, plus or minus any required adjustments while the taxpayer holds the property.

## *FMV less than the donor's adjusted basis*

If the FMV of the property is less than the donor's adjusted basis, the taxpayer's basis depends on whether the property is sold at a gain or a loss. If the property is sold at a gain, the basis is the same as the donor's adjusted basis, plus or minus any required adjustments. The basis for figuring a loss is the FMV, plus or minus any required adjustments. If the property is sold for an amount between the FMV and adjusted basis, neither a gain nor a loss is recognized.

### *FMV Equal to or more than the donor's adjusted basis*

If the FMV of the property is equal to or greater than the donor's adjusted basis, the taxpayer's basis is the donor's adjusted basis, plus or minus any required adjustments.

## Basis of Exchanges

### *Taxable Exchanges*

A taxable exchange is as it sounds. It is an exchange of property in which the gain is taxable and the loss is deductible. This usually happens when the taxpayer receives cash or property not similar or related in use to the property exchanged. The basis of the property received is the FMV at the time of the exchange

> **Example:** Matthew Stone receives a piece of land with a FMV of $6,500 in exchange for a truck with a FMV of $3,800. Mr. Stone will recognize a gain of $2,700 and his basis in the land is $6,500.

### *Nontaxable exchanges*

A nontaxable exchange is an exchange in which the taxpayer is not taxed on any gain, and cannot deduct the loss. The most common nontaxable exchange is an exchange of like-kind property. Like-kind property is items of property with the same nature or character. To qualify as a like-kind exchange, the taxpayer must hold both the property received and the property given up for business or investment purposes. The taxpayer's basis in the property received is the same as the property traded.

> **Example:** The taxpayer holds a plot of land for investment purposes. The adjusted basis of the land is $46,000 and the FMV is $75,000. The taxpayer traded this property for another plot of land held for investment with a FMV of $82,000. The taxpayer's basis in the new property is $46,000.

### *Partially nontaxable exchanges*

A partially nontaxable exchange is an exchange in which unlike property or money is received, as well as like property. The basis, in this case, will take some calculations. The basis of the property received is the same as the property given up with the following calculations:

- Decrease the basis by
  - o Any money received
  - o Any loss recognized on the exchange
- Increase the basis by
  - o Any additional costs incurred
  - o Any gain recognized on the exchange.

**Example:** Bethany Harris traded a piece of land held for investment use for a smaller piece of land and $23,000 cash. The piece of land she gave up had an adjusted basis of $55,000 and a FMV of $85,000. The piece of land she received had a FMV of $61,000.

> She realized a gain on the exchange: She received $61,000 + $23,000 for property with a basis of $55,000 giving her a gain of $84,000 - $55,000 = $29,000. The unlike property she received was the cash of $23,000. Therefore, she will only recognize a taxable gain of $23,000 because the exchange of the land qualifies as a nontaxable gain. If the gain had been less than the amount of cash received, the recognized gain would have been limited to the amount of the gain.

Her basis in the property received is her adjusted basis in the property of $55,000 minus the cash received of $23,000, plus the gain recognized of $23,000. Her basis is $55,000.

## Allocation of basis

If the taxpayer buys a group of assets for one lump sum, the taxpayer must allocate the basis to each asset for depreciation and disposition purposes. At the time of the transaction, the taxpayer and the seller may agree to a specific allocation of the purchase price among the assets in the sales contract. If the taxpayer acquired a trade or business in the sale, the allocation must be made in a specific order. First, reduce the amount paid by any cash and general deposit accounts received. The remaining consideration will be allocated in proportion to their FMV in the following order:

1.  Certificates of deposit, U.S. Government securities, foreign currency, and actively traded personal property, including stock and securities.
2.  Accounts receivable, other debt instruments, and assets marked to market at least annually for federal income tax purposes.
3.  Property of a kind that would properly be included in inventory, if on hand at the end of the tax year, or property held primarily for sale to customers in the ordinary course of business.
4.  All other assets except section 197 intangibles, goodwill, and going concern value.
5.  Section 197 intangibles except goodwill and going concern value.
6.  Goodwill and going concern value (whether or not they qualify as section 197 intangibles).

# *Start-up expenses*

When a taxpayer chooses to start a business, the initial cost can be pretty substantial. Many of the expenses that occur before the taxpayer begins operating the business must be treated as start-up costs. Start-up costs are amounts paid or incurred for creating an active trade or business. Start-up costs include amounts paid or incurred in connection with existing activity engaged in for profit; and for the production of income in anticipation of the activity becoming an active trade or business.

Business start-up costs are generally amortized over a period of time. However, the taxpayer can elect to deduct up to $5,000 of start-up costs. If the taxpayer has more than $50,000 in start-up costs, the $5,000 is reduced by the amount that exceeds $50,000. The remaining costs must be amortized over 180 months beginning the month the taxpayer's active trade or business begins operation. To qualify as a start-up cost, it must meet both of the following tests:

*   It is a cost that could be deducted if it is paid or incurred to operate an existing active trade or business (in the same field as the one the taxpayer entered into).
*   It is a cost paid or incurred before the day the active trade or business begins.

Start-up costs include amounts paid for the following:

*   An analysis or survey of potential markets, products, labor supply, transportation facilities, etc.
*   Advertisements for the opening of the business.
*   Salaries and wages for employees who are being trained, and their instructors.

- Travel and other necessary costs for securing prospective distributors, suppliers, or customers.
- Salaries and fees for executives and consultants, or for similar professional services.

# Chapter Review

1) List three things that are added to the basis of a property.

2) List three types of settlement fees that are not added to the basis.

3) List three things that decrease a property's basis.

4) What is the depreciable basis of converted property?

5) What is the depreciable basis of a gift?

6) What are the two qualifications that have to be met for an expense to be classified as a start-up cost?

## *Exercises*

1) Find the adjusted basis. Eddie Miller bought an office building for $67,000 in 2005. The land was $12,500 and the building was $54,500. His settlement costs, at the time of the purchase, were $3,824. He made some major improvements to the interior of the building in 2007, for a total cost of $5,676. He has claimed the allowable depreciation deduction of $12,322. What is the adjusted basis for the building and the land separately?

2) Jenny Monroe bought a house on a lot in 1996 for a total of $74,000. The land was $11,750. She put a new roof on the house in 2000 for $3,200 and repainted some of the rooms for $325. She moved out of the house and began renting it out in 2004. The FMV at that time was $83,000 for the house and $17,500 for the land. She has since added on a room for $4,250 and claimed depreciation deductions in the amount of $13,900. What is her basis for depreciation? Her basis if she sold it at a gain? Her basis if she sold it at a loss?

3) Billy Martin's dad gave him a truck. Billy's dad had an adjusted basis of $22,000. The FMV of the truck when he gave it to Billy was $14,300. What is Billy's basis for depreciation, gain, and loss?

4) Billy's dad also gave him a piece of land. Billy's dad had an adjusted basis of $13,000. The FMV of the land when he gave it to Billy was $26,000. What is Billy's basis for depreciation, gain, and loss?

# Chapter 2 – The Tax Return

In this chapter, we will discuss the filing of the sole proprietor's tax return. A self employed taxpayer's income and expenses will be filed on a Schedule C, and the net income or loss will be carried to the taxpayer's individual income tax return.

## Terms

**At-risk amount** – The money and adjusted basis of property the taxpayer contributed to the activity, plus any debts for which the taxpayer is personally liable.

**Business-use-of-home deduction** – A tax deduction allowed for operating expenses and depreciation on the portion of a home used for business purposes.

**Capital expenditures** – Money spent to acquire or upgrade physical assets such as buildings and machinery with a useful life of greater than one year.

**Cost of goods sold** – The direct costs attributable to the production of the goods sold by a company. This amount includes the cost of the materials used in creating the good, along with the direct labor costs used to produce the goods.

**Gross income** – The gross profit plus any other income from the business.

**Gross profit** – Total revenue of the business minus the cost of goods sold and any returns and allowances.

**Inventory** – items held for sale to customers in the due course of business.

**Necessary expense** – An expense that is helpful and appropriate, although not necessarily required for your business.

**Net operating loss (NOL)** – A net operating loss occurs when the net deductions exceed the income for the year, usually attributable to a loss from operating a business.

**Ordinary expense** – An expense that is common and accepted in the taxpayer's field of business, trade, or profession.

**Sole proprietor** – an individual who is the sole owner of his or her trade or business. The income or loss incurred in a sole proprietorship is carried to the sole proprietor's individual tax return.

**Statutory employee** – A taxpayer that is treated as self-employed for income tax purposes, but as an employee for social security and Medicare purposes.

**Tax home** – The taxpayer's regular place of business.

**Transportation expense** – The cost of transportation incurred in the normal course of business, such as going to meetings away from the workplace, running errands for the job, or visiting clients or customers.

**Travel expenses** – Ordinary and necessary expenses of traveling away from home for business purposes.

# Business Income and Expenses

A taxpayer is self employed if they carry on a trade or business as a sole proprietor or an independent contractor. A sole proprietor is the sole owner of a business. An independent contractor is generally someone who has the right to control, or to direct, only the result of the work and not how it will be done.

A self employed taxpayer must file a tax return if net earnings from self employment are $400 or more. Schedule C (Illustration 2) is used to report income and expenses, and Schedule SE is also completed to pay self employment taxes on the income. The self employment tax consists of Medicare and social security tax.

There are many cases when the line between an employee and a self employed taxpayer is a bit blurry. To determine whether the taxpayer is an employee or is an independent contractor, many things must be considered. Generally, an employee will be told by the employer:

- When and where to do the work.
- What tools or equipment to use.
- What workers to hire or to assist with the work.
- Where to purchase supplies and services.
- What work must be performed by a specified individual.
- What order or sequence to follow.

Ultimately, as a tax preparer, the decision is already made when the taxpayer comes to us. If the taxpayer's income is reported on a Form W-2, they are considered an employee. If the taxpayer's income is reported on a Form 1099-MISC (Illustration 1) as nonemployee compensation (box 7), they are considered self employed. Also, if the taxpayer is paid cash for their work and it's not reported by the payer, they are still considered self employed and must file a tax return claiming their earnings. If the taxpayer believes they were an employee, but the employer reported their earnings on a Form 1099-MISC instead of a Form W-2, refer the taxpayer to IRS Pub. 1779 for more information.

There are many husband and wife teams that own and operate a business together. If one of them is the primary owner, they may file a Schedule C to report their income and expenses. If they own the business together and share in the profit or losses, they generally must file a partnership return. However, there are two exceptions to this rule. The first is for taxpayers that own and operate their business in a community property state. They may treat the business as a sole proprietorship or a partnership. The second exception is a "Qualified Joint Venture". If the taxpayer and spouse materially participate as the only owners of a jointly owned and operated business, and they file a joint return, they may each divide the income and expenses in accordance with their respective interests. They will each file a separate Schedule C for their portion of the income and expenses.

If the taxpayer has employees, they are required to report employment taxes. Most employers must withhold and pay income tax, social security tax, and Medicare tax. The taxpayer must also pay FUTA (federal unemployment tax). The taxpayer must also file a Form W-2 for each employee at the end of the tax year.

## Filing Requirement for the Self Employed

If the taxpayer's net earnings from self employment are $400 or more, they are required to file a return. If the taxpayer's net earnings from self employment are less than $400 and they meet any of the other filing requirements, they will still be required to file a tax return.

# *Schedule C*

If the taxpayer has self employment income, a Schedule C will need to be filed. If the taxpayer owns more than one business, a separate Schedule C must be filed for each business.

**Line A:** The taxpayer's business or professional activity that provided the main source of income reported on the Schedule C is reported here. Enter the general field or activity and the type of product or service. If the taxpayer is in wholesale or retail trade, or services connected with production services, also enter the type of customer or client the taxpayer targets.

**Line B:** The principal business or professional activity code is entered on this line. Illustration 2 is a sample of the table. The table in its entirety can be found in the appendix. Select the category that best describes the principal business and enter the six digit code. For example, someone whose principal business is Drywall installation will enter 238310 as their six digit code.

**Line D:** The taxpayer will need an employer ID number if they had a qualified retirement plan, or were required to file an employment, excise, estate, trust, or alcohol, tobacco, and firearms tax return. If the taxpayer has an EIN it will be entered here. If the taxpayer does not, leave this line blank. Do not enter the SSN on this line.

**Line E:** Enter the address at which the business is located. If the business is located at the home address reported on the Form 1040, this line may be left blank.

**Line F:** The accounting method the taxpayer used in their business must be specified here.

## Cash Method
This is the most widely used method. The cash method of accounting requires the taxpayer to include income when it is actually or constructively received. The expenses are deducted when they are paid.

## Accrual Method
The accrual method requires the taxpayer to include income when it is earned, and to deduct expenses when they are incurred. If the taxpayer has inventory, they must generally use the accrual method for the sales and purchases.

## Hybrid Method
The hybrid method is a combination of both accounting methods. It is especially used when the taxpayer has inventory, and the taxpayer must use the accrual method of accounting for the inventory, but uses the cash method of accounting for everything else. **Note:** The taxpayer can use the cash method of accounting if they have inventory and they meet one of the following requirements:

- The taxpayer had average gross receipts of less than $1 million over the previous three years.
- The taxpayer does not qualify as a tax shelter.

In this case, the inventory expense is treated as a current year tax deduction.

**Line G:** The question asks if the taxpayer materially participated in the business. If the taxpayer answers no and has a net loss from the business, it is deemed a passive loss, and is subject to certain limits. Generally, the taxpayer materially participated in the business if they did any work regularly in connection with the business. If the taxpayer meets any one of the following seven tests, they materially participated in the business:

- The taxpayer participated in the activity for more than 500 hours during the tax year.
- The taxpayer's participation in the activity for the tax year was substantially all of the activity of all individuals (including individuals who did not own any interest in the activity).

- The taxpayer participated in the activity for more than 100 hours, and at least as much as any other person for the tax year. This includes any individuals who did not own any interest in the activity.
- The activity is a significant participation activity for the tax year, and the taxpayer participated in all significant participation activities for more than 500 hours during the year. An activity is a "significant participation activity" if it involves the conduct of a trade or business, the taxpayer participated in the activity for more than 100 hours during the tax year, and they did not materially participate under any of the other material participation tests.
- The taxpayer materially participated in the activity for any 5 of the prior 10 years.
- The activity is a personal service activity in which the taxpayer materially participated for any 3 prior tax years. A personal service activity is an activity that involves performing personal services in the fields of health, law, engineering, architecture, accounting, actuarial science, performing arts, consulting, or any other trade or business in which capital is not a material income producing factor.
- Based on all the facts and circumstances, the taxpayer participated in the activity on a regular, continuous, and substantial basis for more than 100 hours during the tax year. The taxpayer's participation in managing the activity does not count in determining if the taxpayer meets this test if any person (except the taxpayer); a) received compensation for performing management services in connection with the activity; b) spent more hours during the tax year than the taxpayer spent performing management services in connection with the activity (regardless of whether the person was compensated for the services).

**Line I:** If the taxpayer pays anyone $600 or more for contract labor, a Form-MISC must be filed.

**Part I – Income**

If the taxpayer receives a Form W-2 that has the statutory box in box 13 of their Form W-2 marked, the income will be reported on line 1 of the Schedule C. However, their employer withholds and pays the social security and Medicare tax, so a Schedule SE is not needed. The statutory box applies only to certain occupations, such as life insurance salespersons, certain agent or commission drivers, traveling salespersons, and certain home workers.

**Line 1:** Enter the amount for gross income attributable to the business.
> **Line1a:** If the taxpayer received merchant card payments (for example: Visa or Mastercard), or third party payments (for example: Paypal or Google Checkout), they should receive a Form 1099-K (Illustration 3).
> **Line 1b:** Enter all other amounts the taxpayer received from trade or business. Any amounts that are reported to the taxpayer in box 7 of Form 1099-MISC should be included here.
> **Line 1c:** If the taxpayer received a Form W-2 with the statutory employee box marked, enter the statutory income from box 1 of the Form W-2.

**Line 2:** Returns and allowances are any cash and credit refunds, rebates, and other allowances given to the customer, if they were included in line 1. If the amounts were not included in income, there is no need to report them. They are not deductible.

**Line 4: Cost of Goods Sold**
The taxpayer will only have an amount on this line if they keep inventory. Generally, a taxpayer will keep an inventory if they produce, purchase, or sell merchandise in the business. This amount will come from Schedule C, page 2, part III.

## Illustration 1

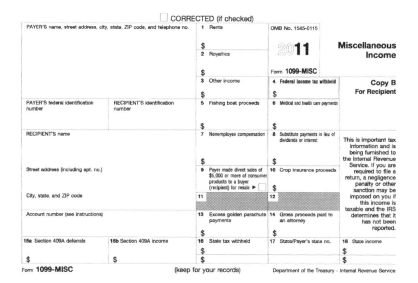

## Illustration 2

**Principal Business or Professional Activity Codes** *(continued)*

| | | | |
|---|---|---|---|
| 238110 | Poured concrete foundation & structure contractors | 621900 | Other ambulatory health care services (including ambulance services, blood, & organ banks) |
| 238160 | Roofing contractors | | |
| 238170 | Siding contractors | | |
| 238910 | Site preparation contractors | **Hospitals** | |
| 238120 | Structural steel & precast concrete construction contractors | 622000 | Hospitals |
| | | **Nursing & Residential Care Facilities** | |
| 238340 | Tile & terrazzo contractors | 623000 | Nursing & residential care facilities |
| 238290 | Other building equipment contractors | **Social Assistance** | |
| | | 624410 | Child day care services |

| **Food Manufacturing** | | | |
|---|---|---|---|
| 311110 | Animal food mfg. | 811210 | Electronic & precision equipment repair & maintenance |
| 311800 | Bakeries & tortilla mfg. | | |
| 311500 | Dairy product mfg. | 811430 | Footwear & leather goods repair |
| 311400 | Fruit & vegetable preserving & speciality food mfg. | 811410 | Home & garden equipment & appliance repair & maintenance |
| 311200 | Grain & oilseed milling | | |
| 311610 | Animal slaughtering & processing | 811420 | Reupholstery & furniture repair |
| 311710 | Seafood product preparation & packaging | 811490 | Other personal & household goods repair & maintenance |

## Illustration 3

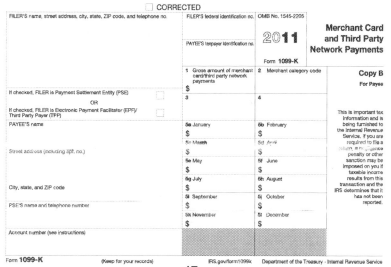

Illustration 4

<table>
<tr><td colspan="2">**SCHEDULE C**<br>**(Form 1040)**<br><br>Department of the Treasury<br>Internal Revenue Service (99)</td><td>**Profit or Loss From Business**<br>(Sole Proprietorship)<br><br>▶ **For information on Schedule C and its instructions, go to** *www.irs.gov/schedulec*<br>▶ **Attach to Form 1040, 1040NR, or 1041; partnerships generally must file Form 1065.**</td><td>OMB No. 1545-0074<br><br>20**11**<br>Attachment<br>Sequence No. **09**</td></tr>
</table>

| Name of proprietor | Social security number (SSN) |
|---|---|

| A | Principal business or profession, including product or service (see instructions) | | B  Enter code from instructions ▶ |
|---|---|---|---|
| C | Business name. If no separate business name, leave blank. | | D  Employer ID number (EIN), (see instr.) |

E   Business address (including suite or room no.) ▶
    City, town or post office, state, and ZIP code

F   Accounting method:   **(1)** ☐ Cash   **(2)** ☐ Accrual   **(3)** ☐ Other (specify) ▶

G   Did you "materially participate" in the operation of this business during 2011? If "No," see instructions for limit on losses   ☐ Yes   ☐ No

H   If you started or acquired this business during 2011, check here   ▶ ☐

I   Did you make any payments in 2011 that would require you to file Form(s) 1099? (see instructions)   ☐ Yes   ☐ No

J   If "Yes," did you or will you file all required Forms 1099?   ☐ Yes   ☐ No

## Part I   Income

| | | | |
|---|---|---|---|
| 1a | Merchant card and third party payments. For 2011, enter -0- | 1a | |
| b | Gross receipts or sales not entered on line 1a (see instructions) | 1b | |
| c | Income reported to you on Form W-2 if the "Statutory Employee" box on that form was checked. **Caution.** See instr. before completing this line | 1c | |
| d | **Total gross receipts.** Add lines 1a through 1c | 1d | |
| 2 | Returns and allowances plus any other adjustments (see instructions) | 2 | |
| 3 | Subtract line 2 from line 1d | 3 | |
| 4 | Cost of goods sold (from line 42) | 4 | |
| 5 | **Gross profit.** Subtract line 4 from line 3 | 5 | |
| 6 | Other income, including federal and state gasoline or fuel tax credit or refund (see instructions) | 6 | |
| 7 | **Gross income.** Add lines 5 and 6 ▶ | 7 | |

## Part II   Expenses          Enter expenses for business use of your home only on line 30.

| | | | | | | | |
|---|---|---|---|---|---|---|---|
| 8 | Advertising | 8 | | 18 | Office expense (see instructions) | 18 | |
| 9 | Car and truck expenses (see instructions) | 9 | | 19 | Pension and profit-sharing plans | 19 | |
| 10 | Commissions and fees | 10 | | 20 | Rent or lease (see instructions): | | |
| 11 | Contract labor (see instructions) | 11 | | a | Vehicles, machinery, and equipment | 20a | |
| 12 | Depletion | 12 | | b | Other business property | 20b | |
| 13 | Depreciation and section 179 expense deduction (not included in Part III) (see instructions) | 13 | | 21 | Repairs and maintenance | 21 | |
| | | | | 22 | Supplies (not included in Part III) | 22 | |
| | | | | 23 | Taxes and licenses | 23 | |
| | | | | 24 | Travel, meals, and entertainment: | | |
| 14 | Employee benefit programs (other than on line 19) | 14 | | a | Travel | 24a | |
| 15 | Insurance (other than health) | 15 | | b | Deductible meals and entertainment (see instructions) | 24b | |
| 16 | Interest: | | | 25 | Utilities | 25 | |
| a | Mortgage (paid to banks, etc.) | 16a | | 26 | Wages (less employment credits) | 26 | |
| b | Other | 16b | | 27a | Other expenses (from line 48) | 27a | |
| 17 | Legal and professional services | 17 | | b | **Reserved for future use** | 27b | |

| | | | |
|---|---|---|---|
| 28 | **Total expenses** before expenses for business use of home. Add lines 8 through 27a ▶ | 28 | |
| 29 | Tentative profit or (loss). Subtract line 28 from line 7 | 29 | |
| 30 | Expenses for business use of your home. Attach **Form 8829**. Do **not** report such expenses elsewhere | 30 | |
| 31 | **Net profit or (loss).** Subtract line 30 from line 29.<br><br>• If a profit, enter on both **Form 1040, line 12** (or **Form 1040NR, line 13**) and on **Schedule SE, line 2.** If you entered an amount on line 1c, see instr. Estates and trusts, enter on **Form 1041, line 3.**<br>• If a loss, you **must** go to line 32. | 31 | |
| 32 | If you have a loss, check the box that describes your investment in this activity (see instructions).<br><br>• If you checked 32a, enter the loss on both **Form 1040, line 12, (or Form 1040NR, line 13**) and on **Schedule SE, line 2.** If you entered an amount on line 1c, see the instructions for line 31. Estates and trusts, enter on **Form 1041, line 3.**<br>• If you checked 32b, you **must** attach **Form 6198.** Your loss may be limited. | 32a ☐ All investment is at risk.<br>32b ☐ Some investment is not at risk. | |

**For Paperwork Reduction Act Notice, see your tax return instructions.**     Cat. No. 11334P     Schedule C (Form 1040) 2011

Illustration 4 continued

**Part III**    **Cost of Goods Sold** (see instructions)

**33**   Method(s) used to
value closing inventory:    **a** ☐ Cost     **b** ☐ Lower of cost or market     **c** ☐ Other (attach explanation)

**34**   Was there any change in determining quantities, costs, or valuations between opening and closing inventory?
If "Yes," attach explanation . . . . . . . . . . . . . . . . . . . . . . . . . . ☐ **Yes**     ☐ **No**

| | | | |
|---|---|---|---|
| **35** | Inventory at beginning of year. If different from last year's closing inventory, attach explanation . . . | **35** | |
| **36** | Purchases less cost of items withdrawn for personal use . . . . . . . . | **36** | |
| **37** | Cost of labor. Do not include any amounts paid to yourself . . . . . . . . | **37** | |
| **38** | Materials and supplies . . . . . . . . . . . . . . | **38** | |
| **39** | Other costs . . . . . . . . . . . . . . . . . . | **39** | |
| **40** | Add lines 35 through 39 . . . . . . . . . . . . . . | **40** | |
| **41** | Inventory at end of year . . . . . . . . . . . . . . | **41** | |
| **42** | **Cost of goods sold.** Subtract line 41 from line 40. Enter the result here and on line 4 . . . . . . | **42** | |

**Part IV**    **Information on Your Vehicle.** Complete this part **only** if you are claiming car or truck expenses on line 9 and are not required to file Form 4562 for this business. See the instructions for line 13 to find out if you must file Form 4562.

**43**   When did you place your vehicle in service for business purposes? (month, day, year)   ▶   /   /

**44**   Of the total number of miles you drove your vehicle during 2011, enter the number of miles you used your vehicle for:

**a** Business _____    **b** Commuting (see instructions) _____    **c** Other _____

**45**   Was your vehicle available for personal use during off-duty hours? . . . . . . . . . . ☐ **Yes**    ☐ **No**

**46**   Do you (or your spouse) have another vehicle available for personal use?. . . . . . . . . ☐ **Yes**    ☐ **No**

**47a**   Do you have evidence to support your deduction? . . . . . . . . . . . . . ☐ **Yes**    ☐ **No**

**b**   If "Yes," is the evidence written? . . . . . . . . . . . . . . . . . . . ☐ **Yes**    ☐ **No**

**Part V**    **Other Expenses.** List below business expenses not included on lines 8–26 or line 30.

| | | |
|---|---|---|
| | | |
| | | |
| | | |
| | | |
| | | |
| | | |
| | | |
| | | |
| | | |
| **48** | **Total other expenses.** Enter here and on line 27a . . . . . . . . . . . . . . . | **48** | |

**Line 33:** Enter the method of inventory valuation on this line.

**Cost method:** To value the inventory at cost, all direct and indirect costs associated with the item must be included. The following rules apply:

- For merchandise on hand at the beginning of the tax year, cost means the ending inventory price of the goods.
- For merchandise purchased during the year, cost means the invoice price, minus appropriate discounts, plus transportation or other charges incurred in acquiring the goods. It can also include other costs that have to be capitalized under the uniform capitalization rules of section 263A.
- For merchandise produced during the year, cost means all direct and indirect costs that have to be capitalized under the uniform capitalization rules.

*Uniform capitalization rules* – Direct and indirect costs for production or resale activities must be capitalized. The costs should be included in the basis of property produced or acquired for resale, rather than claimed as a current deduction.

*Discounts* – There are two types of discounts:

- Trade discount – a discount given regardless of when payment is made. Trade discounts are usually allowed for volume or quantity purchases. The cost of the inventory must be reduced by the discount.
- Cash discount – a reduction in the purchase price if the payment is made within a certain time period. The taxpayer can either reduce the cost of the inventory, or treat the cash discount as income, but they must be treated the same from year to year.

**Lower of cost or market method:** The market value of each item on hand must be compared with the cost and the lower of the two amounts will be used to value the inventory.

**Line 35:** On this line, enter the value of the inventory at the beginning of the tax year. If a Schedule C was filed for this business in the previous year, this amount should be the same as the ending inventory on last year's return. If the amount is different than the ending inventory from last year's return, a statement must be attached explaining why.

**Line 36:** If the taxpayer purchases items for sale, use the cost of what was purchased during the year. If the taxpayer manufactures or produces property for sale, the cost of raw materials or parts purchased to manufacture the finished product will be entered on this line. Any purchases made that were withdrawn for personal use are deducted from this amount.

**Line 37:** This is the cost of labor associated with the cost of goods sold. It only includes the labor cost allocable to the direct and indirect labor used in fabricating the raw material into a finished, saleable product. Generally, only manufacturing and mining businesses will have an amount to enter on this line.

**Line 38:** Only materials and supplies used in manufacturing goods are entered on this line.

**Line 39:** Other costs incurred in the manufacturing or mining process, such as containers, freight, and overhead expenses directly related to the manufacturing of the product, will be entered here.

**Line 41:** The value of the inventory at the close of the tax year is entered on this line. One of the following two methods must be used to value the inventory:

**FIFO (First in first out)** – This is a method of valuing inventory in which the first items purchased or produced are the first items sold.

**LIFO (Last in first out)** – This is a method of valuing inventory in which the last items purchased or produced are the first items sold.

**Line 42:** This is the cost of goods sold and is carried to Schedule C, page 1, line 4.

**Line 6:** This is where income from a source other than the regular operation of the business is located. This includes income such as interest on notes and accounts receivable, prizes and awards, and income from scrap sales.

**Line 7:** This is the gross income from the operation of the business.

# Part II – Expenses:

Lines 8 through 27 pertain to expenses from the operation of the business. A sole proprietor may deduct ordinary and necessary business expenses from their gross business income. An ordinary expense is an expense that is common and accepted in the taxpayer's field of business, trade, or profession. A necessary expense is an expense that is helpful and appropriate, although not necessarily required for the taxpayer's business. In this section, we will only discuss the expenses that may need additional explanation.

**Line 9:** The car and truck expenses for the business use of the vehicle are reported here. These expenses are the cost of driving and maintaining the car. If the transportation expenses are incurred while traveling, they must be deducted as a travel expense. Deductible car and truck expenses, first of all, do **not** include the expense of getting from the taxpayer's home to their regular workplace. These are commuting expenses, and are never deductible. If the taxpayer has a second job, they may deduct the cost of getting from one workplace to the other. If the taxpayer has a temporary assignment or job, they may deduct the expense of getting from home to the temporary assignment or job, as well as the cost of getting from the regular workplace to the temporary assignment or job. If the taxpayer visits clients or customers, goes to business meetings away from the workplace, or runs errands for the job, they may deduct the cost of transportation for these purposes. Illustration 5 shows when car and truck expenses are deductible.

The taxpayer may generally deduct the expenses one of two ways; actual auto expenses or standard mileage rate. In most cases, the method that will provide the biggest deduction should be used. However, if the taxpayer uses actual auto expenses the first year the vehicle is used for business purposes, actual auto expenses must always be used for that vehicle. If the taxpayer uses standard mileage in the first year, they can choose either the actual auto expenses, or standard mileage in the later years. Any parking fees and tolls paid while incurring deductible transportation expenses are fully deductible with either method.

## Actual Auto Expenses

The taxpayer may use the actual car expenses to claim their transportation expense deduction. Actual Expenses must be used if:

- The vehicle was used for hire,
- Five or more vehicles were used at the same time.

There are also many stipulations put on vehicles that have been depreciated. We will cover this deeper in Chapter 3.

Actual expenses include:

- Depreciation (This will be explained in the next chapter)
- Licenses

- Gas
- Lease Payments
- Insurance
- Garage Rent
- Registration Fees
- Repairs
- Tires

If the taxpayer uses their vehicle partly for business use and partly for personal use, they may only deduct the business portion of these expenses. To determine the business portion, the taxpayer must divide the business mileage by the total mileage the vehicle was driven for the year. That percentage will then be multiplied by the total of the above expenses.

## Standard Mileage

The standard mileage rate varies from year to year and is generally adjusted for inflation. The standard mileage will give the taxpayer a deduction of 51 cents per business mile driven before July $1^{st}$, 2011, and 55.5 cents per business mile driven after June $30^{th}$, 2011. To claim car and truck expenses, Part IV of page 2 on the Schedule C must be filled out. If the taxpayer claims actual auto expenses, enter the business expenses on line 9, and enter any depreciation taken for the vehicle on line 13 of the Schedule C.

**Line 11:** Enter the amounts paid for work done by persons the taxpayer does not consider employees on this line. If the taxpayer pays anyone $600 or more, the taxpayer must file a Form 1099-MISC with the IRS, as well as the payee.

**Line 12:** If the taxpayer has an economic interest in mineral property, they may be able to take a deduction for depletion.

**Line 13:** We'll discuss depreciation in detail in Chapter 3. If a Form 4562 is needed to be filed with the return, carry the amounts from that form to this line of the Schedule C. If no Form 4562 is needed, carry the amounts directly from the depreciation worksheet.

**Line 14:** Enter any amounts that were paid on behalf of the taxpayer's employees to benefit programs, other than pension and profit-sharing plans, on this line. This includes amounts paid for health and accident insurance, group term life insurance, and dependent care programs. Any amounts paid on behalf of the self-employed person are not included on this line.

If the taxpayer pays premiums for health insurance for themselves or their families, the premiums may be deductible on line 29 of the Form 1040. For the premiums to be deductible, they cannot be paid for any month in which the self employed person is eligible to be covered under their employer's plan, if they work as an employee in addition to being self employed, or any month in which the self employed person is eligible to be covered under a spouse's health insurance plan. In either of these cases, it doesn't matter whether the self employed person is actually covered or not, only that they're eligible to be covered. To deduct self employed health insurance premiums the taxpayer:

- Must have been self employed and had a net profit for the year,

- Must have used one of the optional methods to figure their net earnings from self-employment on Schedule SE, or
- Must have received wages for the tax year from an S corporation, in which the taxpayer was a more than 2% shareholder.

A worksheet to calculate the deduction is in the Form 1040 instructions.

**Line 15:** Any insurance premiums paid for the purpose of the business, other than health insurance, are entered here. This includes liability insurance, insurance on the business property and assets, and worker's compensation insurance.

**Line 16:** Interest expense is entered on this line. Mortgage interest goes on line 16a, and interest on any other business accounts is entered on line 16b.

Illustration 5

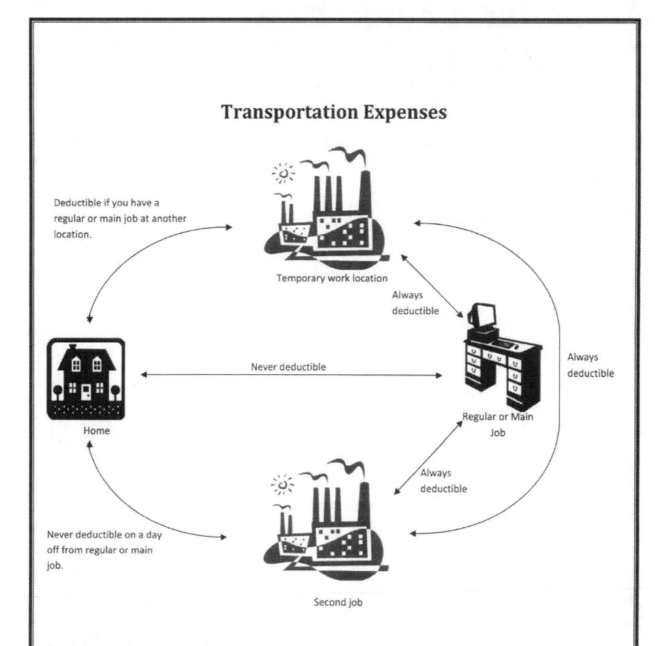

## Transportation Expenses

Deductible if you have a regular or main job at another location.

Temporary work location

Always deductible

Never deductible

Home

Always deductible

Regular or Main Job

Never deductible on a day off from regular or main job.

Always deductible

Second job

**Home:** The place where you reside. Transportation expenses between your home and your main or regular place of work are personal commuting expenses.

**Regular or main job:** your principal place of business. If you have more than one job, you must determine which one is your regular or main job. Consider the time you spend at each, the activity you have at each, and the income you earn at each.

**Temporary work location:** A place where your work assignment is realistically expected to last (and does in fact last) one year or less. Unless you have a regular place of business, you can only deduct your transportation expenses to a temporary work location <u>outside</u> your metropolitan area.

**Second job:** If you regularly work at two or more places in one day, whether or not for the same employer, you can deduct your transportation expenses of getting from one workplace to another. You cannot deduct your transportation costs between your home and a second job on a day off from your main job.

**Line17:** Legal and professional services include attorney and accounting fees. Remember to deduct the portion of the tax preparation fee attributable to the business portion of the tax return, paid in the current year, on this line. For example, when the taxpayer filed his 2010 return, he or she paid to have his taxes prepared in 2011. The amount he or she paid in 2011 is deductible on his or her 2011 tax return.

**Line 19:** Enter any contributions to pension or profit-sharing plans for the employees on this line. Do not include any amounts paid on behalf of the self-employed person. If the taxpayer makes any contributions to a self employed SEP, SIMPLE, or qualified plan on behalf of themselves, it is deducted on Form 1040, line 28.

**Line 21:** Costs for the repairs and maintenance of business property are included on this line. Remember to distinguish the difference between repair expense and improvement expense.

**Line 22:** Supplies that are not considered a part of the cost of goods sold are included on this line. The supplies that are a part of the cost of goods sold are entered on Schedule C, part III, line 38.

**Line 23:** The taxes and cost of licenses are included on this line. The taxes deductible on this line include:

- State and local sales taxes imposed on the taxpayer as the seller of goods or services. If the taxpayer collected this tax from the buyer, the taxpayer must also include the amount collected in gross receipts or sales on line 1.
- Real estate and personal property taxes on business assets.
- Licenses and regulatory fees for the taxpayer's trade or business paid each year to state or local governments.
- Social security and Medicare taxes paid to match required withholding from the employees' wages.
- Federal unemployment tax paid.
- Federal highway use tax.
- Contributions to state unemployment insurance fund or disability benefit fund, if they are considered taxes under state law.

**Line 24:** Travel expenses that are the ordinary and necessary expenses of traveling away from home for the business are deductible on this line. If the taxpayer has to temporarily travel away from their tax home to meet job requirements, those expenses may be deductible. The taxpayer is traveling away from home if:

- The taxpayer's duties require the taxpayer to be away from the general area of the tax home substantially longer than an ordinary day's work.
- The taxpayer needs to sleep or rest to meet the demands of work while away from home.

To meet the travel requirements, the taxpayer must be away from their "tax home". The taxpayer's tax home is the regular place of business or post of duty, regardless of where the home is maintained. If the taxpayer has more than one regular place of business, the tax home is determined by time, the level of business activity, and the income. If the taxpayer has no regular or main place of business because of the nature of work, the tax home is wherever the taxpayer regularly lives.

Some travel expenses are easy to ascertain; for example, business meetings, seminars, and research. However, sometimes it's not so easy to determine. If the taxpayer has a temporary assignment, the tax home remains at the location of the regular place of business. A temporary assignment is one that is realistically

expected to last (and does last) for one year or less. If the assignment is indefinite, the location of the job or assignment becomes the new tax home, and the travel expenses are not deductible. An assignment or job becomes indefinite if it is expected to last for more than one year (whether or not it actually lasts that long).

Sometimes, the taxpayer will travel to an assignment or job that is expected to last one year or less, but ends up taking longer than one year. The travel expenses for the time the job is expected to be temporary are deductible. Once the taxpayer realizes the job is going to last for longer than one year, the expenses stop being deductible.

## Deductible Expenses

While traveling away from home on business, any ordinary and necessary expenses incurred will be deductible. The types of expenses that are deductible are shown in Illustration 6.

If the taxpayer's spouse or dependent travels along with the taxpayer on a business trip, the taxpayer cannot deduct the expenses of the spouse or dependent. If the taxpayer's employee or business associate travels with the taxpayer, those expenses are deductible if the employee or business associate:

- Has a bona fide business purpose for the travel and
- Would otherwise be allowed to deduct the travel expenses.

Bona fide business purpose – A bona fide business purpose exists if the taxpayer can prove a real business purpose for the individual's presence.

The cost of meals is deductible if:

- It is necessary for the taxpayer to stop for substantial sleep or rest to properly perform the duties while traveling away from home on business.
- The meal is business-related entertainment.

The meals cannot be lavish or extravagant to be deductible. The expense is not lavish or extravagant if it is reasonable, based on the facts and circumstances. Only 50% of the total meal expense is deductible.

## Actual Cost

The taxpayer may use the actual cost of meals to calculate the deduction. The taxpayer must keep records of the actual cost to deduct this amount.

## Standard Meal Allowance

Rather than use the actual cost method, the taxpayer may use the standard meal allowance. It allows the taxpayer to use a set amount for the daily meals and incidental expenses (M&IE). The incidental expenses are:

- Fees and tips given to porters, baggage carriers, bellhops, hotel maids, stewards, or stewardesses and others on ships, and hotel servants in foreign countries,
- Transportation between places of lodging or business, and places where meals are taken, if suitable meals can be obtained at the temporary duty site, and
- Mailing costs associated with filing travel vouchers and payment of employer-sponsored charge card billings.

If the taxpayer did not incur any meal expenses, but did incur some of these incidental expenses, the standard amount for the incidental expense is $3 a day.

The standard meal allowance can either be an amount determined by where the taxpayer is traveling or the federal rate. The rates determined by the location can be found in IRS Pub. 1542. In this text, we will be using the federal M&IE rate which is $46 per day for travel within the United States for 2011.

**Special rate for transportation workers**

A transportation worker is someone who's work:

- Directly involves moving people or goods by airplane, barge, bus, ship, train, or truck, and
- Regularly requires the taxpayer to travel away from home, and during any single trip, usually involves travel to areas eligible for different standard meal allowance rates.

The special rate for a transportation worker is $59 per day for travel within the United States for 2011.

# Limit

The deduction for meals is limited to 50% of the cost or standard meal allowance. If the taxpayer is subject to the Department of Transportation's "hours of service" limits, the deduction is limited to 80%. The individuals subject to the Department of Transportation's "hours of service" limit include:

- Certain air transportation workers (such as pilots, crew, dispatchers, mechanics, and control tower operators) who are under Federal Aviation Administration regulations.
- Interstate truck operators and bus drivers who are under Department of Transportation regulations.
- Certain railroad employees (such as engineers, conductors, train crews, dispatchers, and control operations personnel) who are under Federal Railroad Administration regulations.
- Merchant mariners who are under Coast Guard regulations and are off ship, in port awaiting sail.

Illustration 6

# Travel Expenses

| If you have expenses for: | THEN you can deduct the cost of: |
|---|---|
| Transportation | Travel by airplane, train, bus, or car between your home and your business destination. If you were provided with a ticket or you are riding free as a result of frequent traveler or similar program, your cost is zero. |
| Taxi, commuter bus, and airport limousine | Fares for these and other types of transportation that take you between:<br>• The airport or station and your hotel, and<br>• The hotel and the work location of your customers or clients, your business meeting place, or your temporary work location. |
| Baggage and shipping | Sending baggage and sample or display material between your regular and temporary work locations. |
| Car | Operating and maintaining your car when traveling away from home on business. You can deduct actual expenses or the standard mileage rate, as well as business-related tolls and parking. If you rent a car while away from home on business, you can deduct only the business-use portion of the expense. |
| Lodging and meals | Your lodging and meals, if your business trip is overnight or long enough that you need to stop for sleep or rest to properly perform your duties. Meals include the amounts you spend for food, beverages, taxes, and related tips. See *Meals* for additional rules and limits. |
| Cleaning | Dry cleaning and laundry. |
| Telephone | Business calls while on your business trip. This includes business communication by fax machine or other communication devices. |
| Tips | Tips you pay for any expenses in this chart. |
| Other | Other similar ordinary and necessary expenses related to your business travel. These expenses might include transportation to or from a business meal, public stenographer's fees, computer rental fees, and operating and maintaining a house trailer. |

# Entertainment

For the taxpayer to be able to claim an entertainment expense, the expense must be ordinary and necessary and meet **one** of the following tests:

- Directly-related test
- Associated test

Only 50% of the total entertainment expense is deductible.

## Directly Related

To be considered directly related the taxpayer must show that:

- The main purpose of the combined business and entertainment was the active conduct of business.
- The taxpayer did engage in business with the person during the entertainment period, and
- The taxpayer had more than a general expectation of getting income or some other specific business benefit at some future time.

Entertainment expenses in a situation where there is a substantial distraction are not considered directly related. Examples of situations where there are substantial distractions:

- A meeting or discussion at a nightclub, theater, or sporting event.
- A meeting or discussion during what is essentially a social gathering, such as a cocktail party.
- A meeting with a group that includes persons who are not business associates, at places such as cocktail lounges, country clubs, golf clubs, athletic clubs, or vacation resorts.

## Associated

To meet the associated test, the entertainment must be:

- Associated with the active conduct of the trade or business of the taxpayer and
- Directly before or after a substantial business discussion.

The entertainment expense may be to get new business or to encourage the continuation of an existing business relationship. For the discussion to be a substantial business discussion, the taxpayer must be able to show that they engaged in the discussion, meeting, negotiation, or other business transaction to get income or some other specific business benefit. If the entertainment and business discussion are held during the same day, the entertainment is considered held directly before or after the business discussion. Keep in mind that the entertainment expense does not have to meet both the associated and directly related tests. It only needs to meet one of the tests to be deductible.

## Deductible Expenses

Illustration 7 shows what entertainment expenses are deductible. Entertainment expenses include any activity generally considered to provide entertainment, amusement, or recreation. These expenses include, but are not limited to, entertaining guests at the theater, at sporting events, at nightclubs, or at a sporting club.

Expenses that are **not deductible:**

- Membership in any club organized for:
  - Business,
  - Pleasure,
  - Recreation, or
  - Other social purpose.

- Dues paid to:
  - Country clubs,
  - Golf and athletic clubs,
  - Airline clubs,
  - Hotel clubs, and
  - Clubs operated to provide meals under circumstances generally considered to be conducive to business discussions.

**Line 26:** Enter the total salaries and wages paid to employees on this line. Do not include amounts claimed for the Work Opportunity Credit, Empowerment Zone and Renewal Community Employment Credit, Indian Employment Credit, and Credit for Employer Differential Wage Payments.

**Line 27a:** This line is for the total other expenses, as listed on page 2, part V. These expenses are ordinary and necessary expenses for operating the business that are not included on any of the other lines on Schedule C.

**Line 30:** Expenses for the business use of home are entered on this line. These expenses will be carried from Form 8829 (Illustration 8). If the taxpayer uses part of their home for business, they may be able to deduct otherwise nondeductible expenses in relation to the business use of home. To qualify to deduct expenses for the business use of home, the taxpayer must use part of the home _exclusively_ and _regularly_ as the principal place of business. To satisfy the _exclusive_ use test, the taxpayer must use a specific area of the home only for the trade or business. The area the taxpayer uses for the trade or business cannot be used for any other reason. If the taxpayer does not meet the exclusive use test, they may not take a deduction for the business use of home.

**Example:** You have an extra room that you set up as a home office with a computer and desk. The computer is the only one in the house, and your daughter uses it to surf the internet and do her homework. The office does not satisfy the exclusive use test.

**Exceptions:** The storage of inventory or product samples, and a daycare facility. These topics will be discussed in the chapter on Sole Proprietors.

To satisfy the _regular_ use test, the taxpayer must use a specific area of the home for business on a regular basis. If the taxpayer only uses it every now and then, or on an infrequent basis, they do not meet the regular use test and may not deduct expenses for the business use of home.

**Example:** You set up a home office and use it exclusively for business, but you only use it when you cannot complete your work at your regular workplace. In the last 3 months, you've used it 4 times. You do not meet the regular use test.

Illustration 7

# Entertainment Expenses

| General rule | You can deduct ordinary and necessary expenses to entertain a client, customer, or employee if the expenses meet the directly-related test or the associated test. |
|---|---|
| Definitions | • Entertainment includes any activity generally considered to provide entertainment, amusement, or recreation, and includes meals provided to a customer or client.<br>• An ordinary expense is one that is common and accepted in your field of business, trade, or profession.<br>• A necessary expense is one that is helpful and appropriate. |
| Tests to be met | Directly-related test<br>• The entertainment took place in a clear business setting, or<br>• Main purpose of entertainment was the active conduct of business, and<br>   o you did engage in business with the person during the entertainment period, and<br>   o you had more than a general expectation of getting income or some other specified business benefit. |
| | Associated test<br>• Entertainment is associated with your trade or business, and<br>• Entertainment directly precedes or follows a substantial business discussion. |
| Other rules | • You cannot deduct the cost of your meal as an entertainment expense if you are claiming the meal as a travel expense.<br>• You cannot deduct expenses that are lavish or extravagant under the circumstances.<br>• You generally can deduct only 50% of your unreimbursed entertainment expenses. |

To qualify as the principal place of business, the home must be the principal place of business for the taxpayer. The taxpayer may have more than one business location, but the home must be the principal place. To qualify as the principal place, the taxpayer must consider:

- The relative importance of the activities performed at each place where the business is conducted, and
- The amount of time spent at each place where the business is conducted.

If the taxpayer uses the home office exclusively and regularly for administrative or management activities of the trade or business, and the taxpayer has no other fixed location for substantial administrative or management activities of the trade or business, the home office will qualify as the principle place of business. Administrative activities include billing customers, keeping books, ordering supplies, setting up appointments, and forwarding orders or writing reports.

If the taxpayer has a separate structure, such as a garage or barn, they may deduct business use of home expenses, if the area is used regularly and exclusively. It does not need to be the principal place of business to qualify.

# *Form 8829*

Generally, the business use of home expense is determined by what area of the house is used regularly and exclusively for business. However, if the home is used as a daycare facility, business use of home expenses can be deducted, even though the area of the house that is used for daycare is also used for personal purposes. If the house is used as a daycare facility, instead of using the square footage of the house, the hours it is used as such are divided by the total hours in a year to arrive at the business percentage. This calculation is made on Part I of the Form 8829 (Illustration 8).

**Part 1 – Part of the home used for business**

In this section, the area of the office is divided by the area of the entire home to calculate the percentage of the home used for business.

**Part 2 – Figure your allowable deduction**

**Line 8 – Gross income from business**

Enter the total business income that is related to the business use of the home. The deduction for business use of home is limited to this amount.

**Column a – Direct Expenses**

Direct expenses are expenses only for the business part of the home. These expenses include painting and repairs only to the home office.

**Column b – Indirect Expenses**

Indirect expenses are expenses that relate to the entire home. These expenses include utilities, insurance, and rent. The indirect expenses will be multiplied by the percentage on line 3. The mortgage interest and real estate taxes will fall into this category. The taxpayer may not deduct the expense for the phone unless there is

Illustration 8

# Form **8829**

Department of the Treasury
Internal Revenue Service (99)

## Expenses for Business Use of Your Home

▶ File only with Schedule C (Form 1040). Use a separate Form 8829 for each
home you used for business during the year.
▶ See separate instructions.

OMB No. 1545-0074

**2011**

Attachment
Sequence No. **176**

Name(s) of proprietor(s)

Your social security number

### Part I — Part of Your Home Used for Business

| | | | |
|---|---|---|---|
| 1 | Area used regularly and exclusively for business, regularly for daycare, or for storage of inventory or product samples (see instructions) . . . . . . . . . . . . . | **1** | |
| 2 | Total area of home . . . . . . . . . . . . . . . . . . | **2** | |
| 3 | Divide line 1 by line 2. Enter the result as a percentage . . . . . . . . . | **3** | % |

**For daycare facilities not used exclusively for business, go to line 4. All others go to line 7.**

| | | | | | |
|---|---|---|---|---|---|
| 4 | Multiply days used for daycare during year by hours used per day | **4** | | hr. | |
| 5 | Total hours available for use during the year (365 days x 24 hours) (see instructions) | **5** | 8,760 hr. | | |
| 6 | Divide line 4 by line 5. Enter the result as a decimal amount . . . | **6** | . | | |
| 7 | Business percentage. For daycare facilities not used exclusively for business, multiply line 6 by line 3 (enter the result as a percentage). All others, enter the amount from line 3 . . . . . ▶ | **7** | | | % |

### Part II — Figure Your Allowable Deduction

8 Enter the amount from Schedule C, line 29, **plus** any gain derived from the business use of your home and shown on Schedule D or Form 4797, minus any loss from the trade or business not derived from the business use of your home and shown on Schedule D or Form 4797. See instructions . . — **8**

See instructions for columns (a) and (b) before completing lines 9–21.

| | | | (a) Direct expenses | (b) Indirect expenses | | |
|---|---|---|---|---|---|---|
| 9 | Casualty losses (see instructions). . . . . | **9** | | | | |
| 10 | Deductible mortgage interest (see instructions) | **10** | | | | |
| 11 | Real estate taxes (see instructions) . . . . | **11** | | | | |
| 12 | Add lines 9, 10, and 11 . . . . . . . . | **12** | | | | |
| 13 | Multiply line 12, column (b) by line 7 . . . . | | | **13** | | |
| 14 | Add line 12, column (a) and line 13 . . . . | | | | **14** | |
| 15 | Subtract line 14 from line 8. If zero or less, enter -0- | | | | **15** | |
| 16 | Excess mortgage interest (see instructions) . | **16** | | | | |
| 17 | Insurance . . . . . . . . . . . | **17** | | | | |
| 18 | Rent . . . . . . . . . . . . . | **18** | | | | |
| 19 | Repairs and maintenance . . . . . . . | **19** | | | | |
| 20 | Utilities . . . . . . . . . . . . | **20** | | | | |
| 21 | Other expenses (see instructions). . . . . | **21** | | | | |
| 22 | Add lines 16 through 21 . . . . . . . . | **22** | | | | |
| 23 | Multiply line 22, column (b) by line 7 . . . . . . . . . . . | | | **23** | | |
| 24 | Carryover of operating expenses from 2010 Form 8829, line 42 . . | | | **24** | | |
| 25 | Add line 22 column (a), line 23, and line 24. . . . . . . . . . . | | | | **25** | |
| 26 | Allowable operating expenses. Enter the **smaller** of line 15 or line 25 . . . . . . | | | | **26** | |
| 27 | Limit on excess casualty losses and depreciation. Subtract line 26 from line 15 . . . . | | | | **27** | |
| 28 | Excess casualty losses (see instructions) . . . . . . . . | | | **28** | | |
| 29 | Depreciation of your home from line 41 below . . . . . . . | | | **29** | | |
| 30 | Carryover of excess casualty losses and depreciation from 2010 Form 8829, line 43 | | | **30** | | |
| 31 | Add lines 28 through 30 . . . . . . . . . . . . . . . . | | | | **31** | |
| 32 | Allowable excess casualty losses and depreciation. Enter the **smaller** of line 27 or line 31 . . | | | | **32** | |
| 33 | Add lines 14, 26, and 32. . . . . . . . . . . . . . . . | | | | **33** | |
| 34 | Casualty loss portion, if any, from lines 14 and 32. Carry amount to **Form 4684** (see instructions) | | | | **34** | |
| 35 | **Allowable expenses for business use of your home.** Subtract line 34 from line 33. Enter here and on Schedule C, line 30. If your home was used for more than one business, see instructions ▶ | | | | **35** | |

### Part III — Depreciation of Your Home

| | | | |
|---|---|---|---|
| 36 | Enter the **smaller** of your home's adjusted basis or its fair market value (see instructions) . . | **36** | |
| 37 | Value of land included on line 36 . . . . . . . . . . . . . . . | **37** | |
| 38 | Basis of building. Subtract line 37 from line 36 . . . . . . . . . . | **38** | |
| 39 | Business basis of building. Multiply line 38 by line 7. . . . . . . . . . | **39** | |
| 40 | Depreciation percentage (see instructions). . . . . . . . . . . . . | **40** | % |
| 41 | Depreciation allowable (see instructions). Multiply line 39 by line 40. Enter here and on line 29 above | **41** | |

### Part IV — Carryover of Unallowed Expenses to 2012

| | | | |
|---|---|---|---|
| 42 | Operating expenses. Subtract line 26 from line 25. If less than zero, enter -0- . . . . . . | **42** | |
| 43 | Excess casualty losses and depreciation. Subtract line 32 from line 31. If less than zero, enter -0- | **43** | |

For Paperwork Reduction Act Notice, see your tax return instructions.      Cat. No. 13232M      Form **8829** (2011)

a second line used exclusively for business. Otherwise, the taxpayer will only be able to deduct any long distance calls made for the business as a direct expense.

**Part 3 – Depreciation**

This will be covered in the next chapter.

**Part 4 – Carryover of unallowed expenses to next year**

If the taxpayer's business use of home expenses are limited due to their income, the expenses may be deductible in the next tax year.

**Line 31:** This is the result of the gross income minus all of the expenses. If it is a positive amount, the business has a profit. If the result has a negative amount, the business has a loss. Any profit is carried to Form 1040, line 12, and the Schedule SE (Illustration 9). If the result is a loss, it is subject to the at-risk rules. The loss is only deductible up to the amount the taxpayer has at risk. The at-risk amount is the actual cash, and the adjusted basis of other property, the taxpayer has invested in the business. The allowable loss is carried to the Form 1040, line 12.

# *Schedule SE*

As stated earlier, self employment taxes are the social security and Medicare taxes the self employed taxpayer must pay on their business income. A Schedule SE (Illustration 7) must be filed if the taxpayer has net earnings of $400 or more, or if the taxpayer has church employee income and that income is $108.28 or more. There are two pages to the Schedule SE. The first page is the Short Schedule SE. Page 2 is the Long Schedule SE. The Long Schedule SE must be used if any of the following apply:

- The taxpayer received wages and other income subject to Social Security tax, and the net earnings that are subject to Social Security tax is more than $106,800,
- The taxpayer received tips subject to Social Security and Medicare tax that they did not report to their employer,
- The taxpayer reported any wages on Form 8919 (Uncollected Social Security and Medicare tax on Wages),
- The taxpayer is a minister, member of a religious order, or Christian Science practitioner who received IRS approval not to be taxed on earnings from these sources, but the taxpayer owes self-employment tax on other earnings,
- The taxpayer is using an optional method to figure their net earnings (see page SE-4 of the 1040 Instructions), or
- The taxpayer received church employee income reported on Form W-2 of $108.28 or more.

illustratiion 9

# Self-Employment Tax

▶ **Attach to Form 1040 or Form 1040NR.**    ▶ **See separate instructions.**

OMB No. 1545-0074

20**11**

Attachment
Sequence No. **17**

| Name of person with **self-employment** income (as shown on Form 1040) | Social security number of person with **self-employment** income ▶ | |
|---|---|---|

**Before you begin:** To determine if you must file Schedule SE, see the instructions.

## May I Use Short Schedule SE or Must I Use Long Schedule SE?

**Note.** Use this flowchart **only if** you must file Schedule SE. If unsure, see *Who Must File Schedule SE* in the instructions.

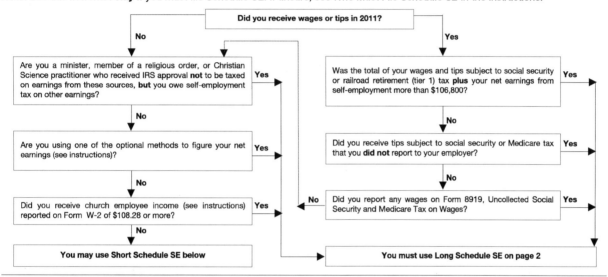

---

**Section A—Short Schedule SE.   Caution.** Read above to see if you can use Short Schedule SE.

| | | | |
|---|---|---|---|
| **1a** | Net farm profit or (loss) from Schedule F, line 34, and farm partnerships, Schedule K-1 (Form 1065), box 14, code A . . . . . . . . . . . . . . . . . . | **1a** | |
| **b** | If you received social security retirement or disability benefits, enter the amount of Conservation Reserve Program payments included on Schedule F, line 4b, or listed on Schedule K-1 (Form 1065), box 20, code Y | **1b** | ( ) |
| **2** | Net profit or (loss) from Schedule C, line 31; Schedule C-EZ, line 3; Schedule K-1 (Form 1065), box 14, code A (other than farming); and Schedule K-1 (Form 1065-B), box 9, code J1. Ministers and members of religious orders, see instructions for types of income to report on this line. See instructions for other income to report . . . . . . . . . . | **2** | |
| **3** | Combine lines 1a, 1b, and 2   . . . . . . . . . . . . . . . . . | **3** | |
| **4** | Multiply line 3 by 92.35% (.9235). If less than $400, you do not owe self-employment tax; **do not** file this schedule unless you have an amount on line 1b . . . . . . . . . . . ▶ | **4** | |
| | **Note.** If line 4 is less than $400 due to Conservation Reserve Program payments on line 1b, see instructions. | | |
| **5** | **Self-employment tax.** If the amount on line 4 is: • $106,800 or less, multiply line 4 by 13.3% (.133). Enter the result here and on **Form 1040, line 56,** or **Form 1040NR, line 54** • More than $106,800, multiply line 4 by 2.9% (.029). Then, add $11,107.20 to the result. Enter the total here and on **Form 1040, line 56,** or **Form 1040NR, line 54** . . . . . . . | **5** | |
| **6** | **Deduction for employer-equivalent portion of self-employment tax.** If the amount on line 5 is: • $14,204.40 or less, multiply line 5 by 57.51% (.5751) • More than $14,204.40, multiply line 5 by 50% (.50) and add $1,067 to the result. Enter the result here and on **Form 1040, line 27,** or **Form 1040NR, line 27**   . . . . . . . . . . . . . . . . . . | **6** | |

# Illustration 9 continued

| Name of person with **self-employment** income (as shown on Form 1040) | Social security number of person with **self-employment** income ▶ |
|---|---|

## Section B—Long Schedule SE

### Part I   Self-Employment Tax

**Note.** If your only income subject to self-employment tax is **church employee income,** see instructions. Also see instructions for the definition of church employee income.

| | | | | | |
|---|---|---|---|---|---|
| **A** | If you are a minister, member of a religious order, or Christian Science practitioner **and** you filed Form 4361, but you had $400 or more of **other** net earnings from self-employment, check here and continue with Part I . . . . . . . ▶ ☐ | | | | |
| **1a** | Net farm profit or (loss) from Schedule F, line 34, and farm partnerships, Schedule K-1 (Form 1065), box 14, code A. **Note.** Skip lines 1a and 1b if you use the farm optional method (see instructions) | **1a** | | | |
| **b** | If you received social security retirement or disability benefits, enter the amount of Conservation Reserve Program payments included on Schedule F, line 4b, or listed on Schedule K-1 (Form 1065), box 20, code Y | **1b** | ( | | ) |
| **2** | Net profit or (loss) from Schedule C, line 31; Schedule C-EZ, line 3; Schedule K-1 (Form 1065), box 14, code A (other than farming); and Schedule K-1 (Form 1065-B), box 9, code J1. Ministers and members of religious orders, see instructions for types of income to report on this line. See instructions for other income to report. **Note.** Skip this line if you use the nonfarm optional method (see instructions) . . . . . . . . . . . . . . | **2** | | | |
| **3** | Combine lines 1a, 1b, and 2 . . . . . . . . . . . . . | **3** | | | |
| **4a** | If line 3 is more than zero, multiply line 3 by 92.35% (.9235). Otherwise, enter amount from line 3 | **4a** | | | |
| | **Note.** If line 4a is less than $400 due to Conservation Reserve Program payments on line 1b, see instructions. | | | | |
| **b** | If you elect one or both of the optional methods, enter the total of lines 15 and 17 here . . | **4b** | | | |
| **c** | Combine lines 4a and 4b. If less than $400, **stop;** you do not owe self-employment tax. **Exception.** If less than $400 and you had **church employee income,** enter -0- and continue ▶ | **4c** | | | |
| **5a** | Enter your **church employee income** from Form W-2. See instructions for definition of church employee income . . .   **5a** | **5b** | | | |
| **b** | Multiply line 5a by 92.35% (.9235). If less than $100, enter -0- . . . . . . . . . | **5b** | | | |
| **6** | Add lines 4c and 5b . . . . . . . . . . . . . . | **6** | | | |
| **7** | Maximum amount of combined wages and self-employment earnings subject to social security tax or the 4.2% portion of the 5.65% railroad retirement (tier 1) tax for 2011 . . . . . . | **7** | | 106,800 | 00 |
| **8a** | Total social security wages and tips (total of boxes 3 and 7 on Form(s) W-2) and railroad retirement (tier 1) compensation. If $106,800 or more, skip lines 8b through 10, and go to line 11   **8a** | | | | |
| **b** | Unreported tips subject to social security tax (from Form 4137, line 10)   **8b** | | | | |
| **c** | Wages subject to social security tax (from Form 8919, line 10)   **8c** | | | | |
| **d** | Add lines 8a, 8b, and 8c . . . . . . . . . . . . . | **8d** | | | |
| **9** | Subtract line 8d from line 7. If zero or less, enter -0- here and on line 10 and go to line 11 . ▶ | **9** | | | |
| **10** | Multiply the **smaller** of line 6 or line 9 by 10.4% (.104) . . . . . . . . . . | **10** | | | |
| **11** | Multiply line 6 by 2.9% (.029) . . . . . . . . . . . . . . | **11** | | | |
| **12** | **Self-employment tax.** Add lines 10 and 11. Enter here and on **Form 1040, line 56,** or **Form 1040NR, line 54** | **12** | | | |
| **13** | **Deduction for employer-equivalent portion of self-employment tax.** Add the two following amounts. • 59.6% (.596) of line 10. • One-half of line 11. Enter the result here and on **Form 1040, line 27,** or **Form 1040NR, line 27** . . . . . . . . . . . . . .   **13** | | | | |

### Part II   Optional Methods To Figure Net Earnings (see instructions)

**Farm Optional Method.** You may use this method **only** if **(a)** your gross farm income[1] was not more than $6,720, **or (b)** your net farm profits[2] were less than $4,851.

| | | | | |
|---|---|---|---|---|
| **14** | Maximum income for optional methods . . . . . . . . . . . . . | **14** | 4,480 | 00 |
| **15** | Enter the **smaller** of: two-thirds (²/₃) of gross farm income[1] (not less than zero) **or** $4,480. Also include this amount on line 4b above . . . . . . . . . . . . . . | **15** | | |

**Nonfarm Optional Method.** You may use this method **only** if **(a)** your net nonfarm profits[3] were less than $4,851 and also less than 72.189% of your gross nonfarm income,[4] **and (b)** you had net earnings from self-employment of at least $400 in 2 of the prior 3 years. **Caution.** You may use this method no more than five times.

| | | | |
|---|---|---|
| **16** | Subtract line 15 from line 14 . . . . . . . . . . . . . | **16** | |
| **17** | Enter the **smaller** of: two-thirds (²/₃) of gross nonfarm income[4] (not less than zero) **or** the amount on line 16. Also include this amount on line 4b above . . . . . . . . . . | **17** | |

[1] From Sch. F, line 9, and Sch. K-1 (Form 1065), box 14, code B.

[2] From Sch. F, line 34, and Sch. K-1 (Form 1065), box 14, code A—minus the amount you would have entered on line 1b had you not used the optional method.

[3] From Sch. C, line 31; Sch. C-EZ, line 3; Sch. K-1 (Form 1065), box 14, code A; and Sch. K-1 (Form 1065-B), box 9, code J1.

[4] From Sch. C, line 7; Sch. C-EZ, line 1d; Sch. K-1 (Form 1065), box 14, code C; and Sch. K-1 (Form 1065-B), box 9, code J2.

# Net operating loss (NOL)

If the taxpayer's deductions for the year are more than their income for the year, the taxpayer may have a net operating loss (NOL). The taxpayer can use an NOL by deducting it from their income in a year or years other than the current tax year. To have an NOL, the loss must generally be caused by deductions from their:

- Trade or business,
- Work as an employee,
- Casualty and theft losses,
- Moving expenses,
- Rental property.

In this case, we are discussing an NOL caused by a trade or business. If an NOL occurs, additional research is required.

# Estimated Tax

If the taxpayer does not have enough or any taxes withheld from their income, they may pay estimated taxes to keep from owing an underpayment penalty. This is especially true of sole proprietors. Remember, they will not only have to pay income tax, but will also be required to pay self-employment tax with their tax return. Paying estimated tax is a way to pay the tax owed, over four quarterly installments, during the tax year. Generally, the taxpayer must make estimated tax payments if both of the following apply:

- The taxpayer expects to owe at least $1,000 in tax for 2012, after subtracting the withholding and credits.
- The taxpayer expects the withholding and credits to be less than the smaller of:
  - 90% of the tax liability shown on your 2012 tax return, or
  - 100% of the tax liability shown on the taxpayer's 2011 tax return. The 2011 tax return must cover all 12 months.

Even if the taxpayer is not required to make estimated payments, they may if they are going to owe tax when they file their tax return.

Estimated tax payments are due on the 15th of the month following the close of each quarter:

- Jan 1 – March 31...........April 15
- April 1 – May 31.............June 15
- June 1 – August 31........September 15
- Sept 1 – Dec 31............January 15 of the next year.

If the due date falls on a Saturday, Sunday, or legal holiday, the due date is the next business day. The IRS has a worksheet (Illustration 9) to help calculate the amount of estimated tax the taxpayer should pay. The taxpayer will be required to mail in a voucher with the payment as shown in Illustration 10.

Illustration 10

## 2012 Estimated Tax Worksheet

*Keep for Your Records*

| | | | | |
|---|---|---|---|---|
| **1** | Adjusted gross income you expect in 2012 (see instructions) . . . . . . . . . . . | **1** | | |
| **2** | • If you plan to itemize deductions, enter the estimated total of your itemized deductions. | | | |
| | • If you do not plan to itemize deductions, enter your standard deduction. } | **2** | | |
| **3** | Subtract line 2 from line 1. . . . . . . . . . . . . . . . | **3** | | |
| **4** | Exemptions. Multiply $3,800 by the number of personal exemptions . . . . . . . . | **4** | | |
| **5** | Subtract line 4 from line 3. . . . . . . . . . . . . . . . | **5** | | |
| **6** | **Tax.** Figure your tax on the amount on line 5 by using the **2012 Tax Rate Schedules.** **Caution:** *If you will have qualified dividends or a net capital gain, or expect to exclude or deduct foreign earned income or housing, see chapter 2 of Pub. 505 to figure the tax* . . . . . . . | **6** | | |
| **7** | Alternative minimum tax from **Form 6251** . . . . . . . . . . . . | **7** | | |
| **8** | Add lines 6 and 7. Add to this amount any other taxes you expect to include in the total on Form 1040, line 44 . . . . . . . . . . . . . . . . . | **8** | | |
| **9** | Credits (see instructions). **Do not** include any income tax withholding on this line . . . . . . | **9** | | |
| **10** | Subtract line 9 from line 8. If zero or less, enter -0- . . . . . . . . . . | **10** | | |
| **11** | Self-employment tax (see instructions) . . . . . . . . . . . . . . | **11** | | |
| **12** | Other taxes (see instructions) . . . . . . . . . . . . . . . | **12** | | |
| **13a** | Add lines 10 through 12 . . . . . . . . . . . . . . . . | **13a** | | |
| **b** | Earned income credit, additional child tax credit, fuel tax credit, refundable American opportunity credit, and refundable credits from **Forms 8801** and **8885.** . . . . . . . . | **13b** | | |
| **c** | **Total 2012 estimated tax.** Subtract line 13b from line 13a. If zero or less, enter -0- . . . ▶ | **13c** | | |

| | | | | | | |
|---|---|---|---|---|---|---|
| **14a** | Multiply line 13c by 90% (66²/₃% for farmers and fishermen) . . . . | **14a** | | | | |
| **b** | Required annual payment based on prior year's tax (see instructions) . | **14b** | | | | |
| **c** | **Required annual payment to avoid a penalty.** Enter the **smaller** of line 14a or 14b . . . ▶ | | | **14c** | | |

**Caution:** *Generally, if you do not prepay (through income tax withholding and estimated tax payments) at least the amount on line 14c, you may owe a penalty for not paying enough estimated tax. To avoid a penalty, make sure your estimate on line 13c is as accurate as possible. Even if you pay the required annual payment, you may still owe tax when you file your return. If you prefer, you can pay the amount shown on line 13c. For details, see chapter 2 of Pub. 505.*

| | | | | | | |
|---|---|---|---|---|---|---|
| **15** | Income tax withheld and estimated to be withheld during 2012 (including income tax withholding on pensions, annuities, certain deferred income, etc.) . . . . . . . . . . | | | **15** | | |

| | | | | | | |
|---|---|---|---|---|---|---|
| **16a** | Subtract line 15 from line 14c . . . . . . . . . . . | **16a** | | | | |
| | Is the result zero or less? | | | | | |
| | ☐ **Yes.** Stop here. You are not required to make estimated tax payments. | | | | | |
| | ☐ **No.** Go to line 16b. | | | | | |
| **b** | Subtract line 15 from line 13c . . . . . . . . . . . | **16b** | | | | |
| | Is the result less than $1,000? | | | | | |
| | ☐ **Yes.** Stop here. You are not required to make estimated tax payments. | | | | | |
| | ☐ **No.** Go to line 17 to figure your required payment. | | | | | |
| **17** | If the first payment you are required to make is due April 17, 2012, enter ¼ of line 16a (minus any 2011 overpayment that you are applying to this installment) here, and on your estimated tax payment voucher(s) if you are paying by check or money order. . . . . . . . . . . | | | **17** | | |

Illustration 10

Form **1040-ES**
Department of the Treasury
Internal Revenue Service

## 20**12 Estimated Tax**

**Payment** **3**
**Voucher**

OMB No. 1545-0074

| **Calendar year—Due Sept. 17, 2012** | | |
|---|---|---|

File only if you are making a payment of estimated tax by check or money order. Mail this voucher with your check or money order payable to **"United States Treasury."** Write your social security number and "2012 Form 1040-ES" on your check or money order. Do not send cash. Enclose, but do not staple or attach, your payment with this voucher.

Amount of estimated tax you are paying by check or money order.

| | Dollars | Cents |
|---|---|---|

Print or type

| Your first name and initial | Your last name | Your social security number |
|---|---|---|
| If joint payment, complete for spouse | | |
| Spouse's first name and initial | Spouse's last name | Spouse's social security number |
| Address (number, street, and apt. no.) | | |
| City, state, and ZIP code. (If a foreign address, enter city, province or state, postal code, and country.) | | |

**For Privacy Act and Paperwork Reduction Act Notice, see instructions.**

Tear off here

Form **1040-ES**
Department of the Treasury
Internal Revenue Service

## 20**12 Estimated Tax**

**Payment** **2**
**Voucher**

OMB No. 1545-0074

| **Calendar year—Due June 15, 2012** | | |
|---|---|---|

File only if you are making a payment of estimated tax by check or money order. Mail this voucher with your check or money order payable to **"United States Treasury."** Write your social security number and "2012 Form 1040-ES" on your check or money order. Do not send cash. Enclose, but do not staple or attach, your payment with this voucher.

Amount of estimated tax you are paying by check or money order.

| | Dollars | Cents |
|---|---|---|

Print or type

| Your first name and initial | Your last name | Your social security number |
|---|---|---|
| If joint payment, complete for spouse | | |
| Spouse's first name and initial | Spouse's last name | Spouse's social security number |
| Address (number, street, and apt. no.) | | |
| City, state, and ZIP code. (If a foreign address, enter city, province or state, postal code, and country.) | | |

**For Privacy Act and Paperwork Reduction Act Notice, see instructions.**

Tear off here

Form **1040-ES**
Department of the Treasury
Internal Revenue Service

## 20**12 Estimated Tax**

**Payment** **1**
**Voucher**

OMB No. 1545-0074

| **Calendar year—Due April 17, 2012** | | |
|---|---|---|

File only if you are making a payment of estimated tax by check or money order. Mail this voucher with your check or money order payable to **"United States Treasury."** Write your social security number and "2012 Form 1040-ES" on your check or money order. Do not send cash. Enclose, but do not staple or attach, your payment with this voucher.

Amount of estimated tax you are paying by check or money order.

| | Dollars | Cents |
|---|---|---|

Print or type

| Your first name and initial | Your last name | Your social security number |
|---|---|---|
| If joint payment, complete for spouse | | |
| Spouse's first name and initial | Spouse's last name | Spouse's social security number |
| Address (number, street, and apt. no.) | | |
| City, state, and ZIP code. (If a foreign address, enter city, province or state, postal code, and country.) | | |

**For Privacy Act and Paperwork Reduction Act Notice, see instructions.**

Form 1040-ES (2012)                    -11-

# *Chapter Review*

1) The hybrid method of accounting is a combination of what two methods?

2) The taxpayer has to keep what to have a cost of goods sold?

3) What are the two methods of inventory valuation?

4) Define FIFO.

5) Define LIFO.

6) What is the standard mileage rate for 2011?

7) If the taxpayer pays a contractor $600 or more, what must they do?

8) What is the federal MI&E rate for 2011?

9) What are indirect expenses on a Form 8829?

10) What two taxes make up SE tax?

# *Exercise*

Timothy Thompson is a self employed taxpayer. Prepare his tax return. His SSN is 567-87-4321and his date of birth is May 29, 1979. He is divorced and his daughter, Lena, lived with him all year. Her date of birth is December 1, 2006 and her SSN is 439-51-5882. His business is Plumbers R Us and he has operated since January 1, 2008. His business address is the same as his house address. He has an office set up in his home. His accounting method is cash. His income and expenses are as follows:

| | |
|---|---:|
| Gross receipts | $87,890 |
| Business cards | 250 |
| Signs | 1,344 |
| Business license | 856 |
| Office Supplies | 2,655 |
| Bookkeeping | 3,500 |
| Equipment Rental | 12,000 |
| Liability Insurance | 2,433 |
| Supplies | 5,688 |
| Repairs | 2,313 |

He uses his truck for his business. He has used it ever since he started the business. His total mileage for the year was 25,666. His business mileage was 8,695 before July 1$^{st}$, and 10,282 after June 30$^{th}$. He keeps written records of his mileage. He has another vehicle available for personal use. His business truck is available to him during off-duty hours.

His office is 165 square feet and the total area of his home is 1,825 square feet. He bought the house in May of 2007 for $63,400. The land portion of the purchase price was 12,500. He began using the office space when he moved into the house. His expenses for his home are as follows:

| | |
|---|---|
| Electricity | $  144 per month |
| Gas | 32 per month |
| Phone | 82 per month |
| Business phone | 26 per month |
| Insurance | 2,566 per year |
| Repainting the office | 450 |

**Note:** Since we have not covered depreciation yet, the depreciation deduction will not be included in the solution to this exercise.

He had some gambling winnings of $550. He paid personal property tax of $133 and tithed to his church in the amount of $1,250. Lena attended the We Love Kids Daycare during the year while he was at work. Timothy paid them $1,398 during the year. Their EIN is 39-5392431 and their address is 222 Toddler Lane, Your City, Your State, Your Zip Code.

Timothy paid $8,000 in Federal estimated taxes during 2011 (the last payment was made before December 31st). (This amount is entered on line 63 of the Form 1040). He also paid $1,500 of State estimated taxes in 2011. He would like you to figure out how much he needs to pay this year. He projects that he will make about $10,000 more in business income this year. He wants to come as close to breaking even as possible.

☐ CORRECTED (if checked)

**Form 1099-INT — Interest Income**

| PAYER'S name, street address, city, state, ZIP code, and telephone no. | Payer's RTN (optional) | OMB No. 1545-0112 |
|---|---|---|
| Second National Bank<br>300 Gold Court<br>Your City, Your State, Your Zip Code | **1** Interest income<br>$ 532.11 | 2011 **Interest Income** |
| | **2** Early withdrawal penalty<br>$ | Form **1099-INT** |

| PAYER'S federal identification number | RECIPIENT'S identification number | **3** Interest on U.S. Savings Bonds and Treas. obligations | | Copy B |
|---|---|---|---|---|
| 45-1343242 | 567-87-4321 | $ | | **For Recipient** |

| RECIPIENT'S name | **4** Federal income tax withheld | **5** Investment expenses |
|---|---|---|
| Timothy Thompson | $ | $ |

| Street address (including apt. no.) | **6** Foreign tax paid | **7** Foreign country or U.S. possession |
|---|---|---|
| 453 Robin St. | $ | |

| City, state, and ZIP code | **8** Tax-exempt interest | **9** Specified private activity bond interest |
|---|---|---|
| Your City, Your State, Your Zip Code | $ | $ |

| Account number (see instructions) | **10** Tax-exempt bond CUSIP no. (see instructions) |
|---|---|

Form **1099-INT**          (keep for your records)          Department of the Treasury - Internal Revenue Service

---

☐ CORRECTED (if checked)

**Form 1098 — Mortgage Interest Statement**

| RECIPIENT'S/LENDER'S name, address, and telephone number | * Caution: The amount shown may not be fully deductible by you. Limits based on the loan amount and the cost and value of the secured property may apply. Also, you may only deduct interest to the extent it was incurred by you, actually paid by you, and not reimbursed by another person. | OMB No. 1545-0901 |
|---|---|---|
| First Home Mortgages<br>200 Helpful Circle<br>Your City, Your State, Your Zip Code | | 2011<br><br>**Mortgage Interest Statement** |
| | | Form **1098** |

| RECIPIENT'S federal identification no. | PAYER'S social security number | **1** Mortgage interest received from payer(s)/borrower(s)* | Copy B |
|---|---|---|---|
| 62-9876752 | 567-87-4321 | $ 3,229.12 | **For Payer/Borrower** |

| PAYER'S/BORROWER'S name | **2** Points paid on purchase of principal residence |
|---|---|
| Timothy Thompson | $ |

| Street address (including apt. no.) | **3** Refund of overpaid interest |
|---|---|
| 453 Robin St. | $ |

| City, state, and ZIP code | **4** Mortgage insurance premiums |
|---|---|
| Your City, Your State, Your Zip Code | $ |

| Account number (see instructions) | **5** Real Estate Taxes          $288.55 |
|---|---|

Form **1098**          (keep for your records)          Department of the Treasury - Internal Revenue Service

# Chapter 3 - Depreciation

Depreciation is an annual deduction that allows a taxpayer to recover the cost or other basis of certain property over the life of the property. Different types of property require different methods of depreciation. This chapter will explain how to calculate the depreciable basis of the property, determine the class of the property, determine the method of depreciation, and calculate the depreciation.

## Terms

**Accelerated Cost Recovery System (ACRS)** – A depreciation system generally used for property placed in service during the years 1981 – 1986.

**Alternative Depreciation System (ADS)** – An alternate form of depreciation which allows for a longer recovery period than does the General Depreciation System (GDS).

**Alternative Minimum Tax (AMT)** – A tax that applies to taxpayers who have certain types of income that receive favorable treatment, or who qualify for certain deductions, under the tax law.

**Business/Investment use** – Usually, a percentage showing how much an item or property, such as an automobile, is used for business and investment purposes.

**Cost Recovery** – The deducting of the cost of qualified assets over a certain time period.

**Convention** – A method established under the Modified Accelerated Cost Recovery System (MACRS) to determine the portion of the year to depreciate property, both in the year the property is placed in service and in the year of disposition.

**Declining Balance Method** – An accelerated method to depreciate property. The General Depreciation System (GDS) of MACRS uses the 150% and 200% declining balance methods for certain types of property. A depreciation rate (percentage) is determined by dividing the declining balance percentage by the recovery period for the property.

**Depreciate** – To recover the cost of property or assets placed in service.

**Disposition** – The permanent withdrawal from use in a trade or business or from the production of income by sale or nonuse.

**General Depreciation System (GDS)** – The most commonly used Modified Accelerated Cost Recovery System for calculating depreciation.

**Half-Year Convention** – The convention under which all property placed in service or disposed of during a tax year is treated as placed in service or disposed of at the midpoint of the year.

**Listed Property** – Passenger automobiles; any other property used for transportation; property of a type generally used for entertainment, recreation or amusement; computers; and their peripheral equipment (unless used only at a regular business establishment and owned or leased by the person operating the establishment); and cellular telephones or similar telecommunications equipment.

**Mid-month Convention** – The convention used for nonresidential real property, residential rental property, and any railroad grading or tunnel bore. Under this convention, all property placed in service or disposed of during a month is treated as placed in service or disposed of at the midpoint of the month.

**Mid-quarter Convention** – Under this convention, all property placed in service or disposed of during any quarter of the tax year is treated as placed in service or disposed of at the midpoint of that quarter.

**Modified Accelerated Cost Recovery System (MACRS)** – A depreciation system used to recover the basis of most business and investment property placed in service after 1986.

**Personal Type Property** – In general, all property other than real property.

**Placed in Service** – Property is placed in service when it is ready and available for a specific use, whether in a business activity, an income-producing activity, a tax-exempt activity, or a personal activity.

**Property Class** – A category for property under MACRS. It generally determines the depreciation method, recovery period, and convention.

**Real Property** – Lands, buildings, and structural components of building.

**Recapture** – To include as income, on the taxpayer's return, an amount allowed or allowable as a deduction in a prior year.

**Recovery Period** – The number of years over which the basis of an item of property is recovered.

**Section 179 Deduction** – An election to recover all or part of the cost of certain qualifying property, up to a limit by deducting it in the year the taxpayer placed the property in service.

**Straight-Line Method** – A way to figure depreciation for property that ratably deducts the same amount for each year in the recovery period.

**Tangible Property** – Property that can be seen or touched, such as buildings, machinery, vehicles, furniture, and equipment.

# *Depreciable Property*

To be depreciable property, the property must meet the following 4 requirements:
- It must be property the taxpayer owns.
- It must be used in the taxpayer's business or income-producing activity.
- It must have a determinable useful life.
- It must be expected to last more than one year.

## It must be property the taxpayer owns.

The taxpayer must be the owner of the property. The taxpayer is considered the owner even if the property is subject to a debt. For example, the taxpayer purchased a house, but had to take a mortgage on it to be able to buy it. The taxpayer owns the house and can depreciate it if it meets the other requirements.

## It must be used in the taxpayer's business or income-producing activity.

To be able to depreciate property, the taxpayer must use it in their business or in their income-producing activity. If the property is used to produce income, the income must be taxable. If the property is only partly used for the business or income-producing activity, depreciation can be taken only on that part of the property. Inventory cannot be depreciated because it is held for the sale to customers.

## It must have a determinable useful life.

The property must have a determinable useful life to be depreciable. This means that the property must wear out, decay, get used up, become obsolete, or lose its value from natural causes.

## It must be expected to last more than one year.

The property must have a useful life of more than one year. If the property's useful life is one year or less, the taxpayer may deduct the entire cost of the property as a business expense.

# *Types of Property*

Property falls into two categories: real and personal. Real property is also called real estate. It includes land, buildings, and their structural components. Land is never depreciable. If the taxpayer purchased real property which consisted of a building and land, the portion of the purchase price attributable to the land must be deducted from the total price before the property is depreciated.

Personal property is all other property. Personal property can be personal-use or business-use property. In this course, we are concentrating on personal business-use property. Personal property falls into two categories: tangible and intangible. Tangible property has physical substance and its value is intrinsic. Intrinsic means the property has value in and of itself. Tangible property includes furniture, tools, and vehicles. Intangible property has no intrinsic value. The best example of intangible property is money in the form of bills. The bill itself is not worth anything because it is just made of paper. However, the bill gives the owner the right to purchase property and services, therefore it has value. Other intangible properties include insurance policies, stocks, and bonds.

# *Basis (a recap)*

The basis of purchased property is usually its cost plus any amounts paid for items, such as sales tax, freight charges, and installation and testing fees. If the property has been held for personal use, but it's changed to use for a business or an income producing activity, the basis is the lesser of the following:

- The fair market value (FMV) of the property on the date of the change in use.
- The original cost or other basis adjusted as follows:
    - Increased by the cost of any permanent improvements or additions and other costs that must be added to the basis.
    - Decreased by any deductions the taxpayer claimed for casualty and theft losses and other items that reduced the basis.

To find the depreciable basis of the property, some adjustments may have to be made. Any changes that incurred between the time the taxpayer acquired the property and placed it into service must

be taken into account. Add in any amounts that are paid out to assist in the purchase of the property or retaining the property, such as installing utility lines, paying legal fees for perfecting the title, or settling zoning issues. If improvements are made to the property prior to placing the property in service, add these amounts to the basis. If improvements are made to the property after the property has been placed in service, treat the improvement as a separate depreciable property.

As stated earlier, if the taxpayer purchased depreciable real property but the purchase price included the land the building was on, the amount attributable to the land must be subtracted to determine the depreciable basis. The taxpayer can do this by deducting the fair market value of the land at the time the real property was purchased from the purchase price. If the taxpayer does not know what the fair market value was, he or she may obtain an assessment.

**Example:** Sharon purchased an office building which included the ½ acre the building was on. She paid $150,000 for all of it. The purchase price included $100,000 for the building and $50,000 for the land. The depreciable basis of the building is $100,000 because land is never depreciable.

# *Which Depreciation to Use*

Modified Accelerated Cost Recovery System (MACRS) must be used to depreciate most property. First, we will discuss the other types of depreciation, and then we will delve into MACRS.

## Property Placed in Service Before 1987
If the property was place in service before 1987, Accelerated Cost Recovery System must be used to depreciate it (except property placed in service after July 31, 1986 if MACRS was elected). If personal property was placed in service after 1986, but any of the following situations apply, ACRS must be used:

- The taxpayer or someone related to the taxpayer owned or used the property in 1986.
- The taxpayer acquired the property from a person who owned it in 1986, and as part of the transaction the user of the property did not change.
- The taxpayer leases the property to a person who owned or used the property in 1986.
- The taxpayer acquired the property in a transaction in which:
  - o The user of the property did not change, and
  - o The property was not MACRS property in the hands of the person from whom the taxpayer acquired it because of the prior 2 situations.

If the property falls into any of these categories and ACRS must be used, additional research will be required. Begin with IRS Pub. 534.

## MACRS
MACRS consists of two depreciation systems. The General Depreciation System (GDS) is the one that will generally be used. Alternative Depreciation System (ADS) will be used if specifically required or elected. ADS will allow for a longer recovery period than GDS and is depreciated using the SL method. ADS is required for the following property:

- Listed property used 50% or less in a qualified business use. (We will discuss this later.)

- Any tangible property used predominantly outside the United States during the year.
- Any tax-exempt use property.
- Any tax-exempt bond-financed property.
- All property used predominantly in a farming business and placed in service in any tax year during which an election not to apply the uniform capitalization rules to certain farming costs is in effect.
- Any property imported from a foreign country for which an Executive Order is in effect because the country maintains trade restrictions or engages in other discriminatory acts.

Even if the property qualifies for GDS, the taxpayer may use ADS. If the taxpayer makes this election for a personal type asset in any given year, then generally all the property in the same class, that was placed into service that year, must be depreciated using ADS. The election for 27.5, 31.5, or 39 year property is made on a property by property basis. This generally provides for a longer recovery period, and while allowing a smaller deduction, the taxpayer may take the deduction for more years than is allowed under GDS.

# *Learning to Depreciate Step-By-Step*

There are many more intricacies to depreciation, but we will postpone them until we learn the basics of depreciation.

## The First Step

The first step to depreciation is to determine the recovery period of the property. To find out the recovery period of personal property, we will use the table of MACRS recovery periods for common assets (Illustration 1) of personal property that appears in Pub. 946. (These tables are of the more commonly depreciated property. For a more detailed list see the tables in Appendix A and IRS Pub. 946.) The first thing we will do is find the property we are going to depreciate. What is the recovery period for an office desk? Notice it is under office furniture. The GDS Recovery Period is 7 years and the ADS Recovery Period is 10 years. Now, let's find the recovery period for a copy machine. We will find that under data handling equipment. The GDS Recovery Period is 5 years and the ADS Recovery Period is 6 years. Let's try one more. What is the recovery period for a car used for business purposes? This, we will find under transportation, and the GDS and the ADS Recovery Periods are 5 years.

Real property is easier to classify because it can fall into only two categories if placed in service in 1987 or later: nonresidential real property and residential rental property.

**Nonresidential real property** includes offices, stores, and other business structures. These properties have a GDS recovery period of 39 years if placed into service after May 12, 1993. The GDS recovery period for nonresidential real property placed into service before May 13, 1993 is 31.5 years.

**Residential rental property** includes buildings that are set up as residences that someone rents. Residential rental property has a GDS recovery period of 27.5 years.

Illustration 1

# MACRS Recovery Periods for Common Assets

| Property Type | Recovery Period | |
|---|---|---|
| **Office Related** | **GDS** | **ADS** |
| • Office Furniture: Includes furniture and fixtures that are not a structural component of the building. Also, includes such assets as desks, files, safes, and communications equipment. Does not include communications equipment that is included in other classes. | 7yrs | 10yrs |
| • Data Handling Equipment; except computers Includes only typewriters, calculators, adding and accounting machines, copiers, and duplicating equipment. | 5yrs | 6yrs |
| • Information systems Includes computers and their peripheral equipment used in administering normal business transactions and the maintenance of business records, and their retrieval, and analysis. | 5yrs | 5yrs |
| **Transportation** | | |
| • Airplanes (noncommercial) and Helicopters | 5yrs | 6yrs |
| • Automobiles, Taxis | 5yrs | 5yrs |
| • Buses | 5yrs | 9yrs |
| • Light General Purpose Trucks (less and 13,000 pounds) | 5yrs | 5yrs |
| • Heavy General Purpose Trucks (13,000 pounds or more) | 5yrs | 6yrs |
| • Tractor units for use over the road | 3yrs | 4yrs |
| • Trailers and Trailer mounted containers | 5yrs | 6yrs |
| **Agricultural** | | |
| • Agricultural machinery and equipment Includes grain bins and fences, but no other land improvements, that are used in production of crops or plants, vines, and trees; livestock; the operation of farm dairies, nurseries, greenhouses, sod farms, mushroom cellars, cranberry bogs, apiaries and fur farms; the performance of agriculture, animal husbandry, and horticultural services. | 7yrs | 10 yrs |
| • Breeding or dairy cattle | 5yrs | 7yrs |
| • Breeding or work horses (12 yrs old or less at the time placed in service) | 7yrs | 10yrs |
| • Breeding or work horses (more than 12 yrs old at the time placed in service) | 3yrs | 10yrs |
| • Breeding hogs | 3yrs | 3yrs |
| • Breeding sheep and goats | 5yrs | 5yrs |
| • Single purpose agricultural or horticultural structures | 10yrs | 15yrs |
| **Real Property** | | |
| • Residential rental property | 27.5yrs | 40yrs |
| • Nonresidential real property placed in service on or after May 13, 1993. | 39yrs | 40yrs |
| • Nonresidential real property placed in service before May 13, 1993. | 31.5yrs | 40yrs |
| **Other** | | |
| • Appliances, carpets, and furniture used in rental property | 5yrs | 9yrs |
| • Personal property with no class life | 7yrs | 12yrs |

# The Second Step

The second step to calculating depreciation is to find the correct MACRS table to use. To find the correct table, we must determine the method and convention of depreciation.

## Convention

There are three different conventions: half- year, mid-quarter, and mid-month. Personal property falls into either half-year or mid-quarter. Generally, the half-year convention (HY) will be used. This means that for the first year the property is placed into service, it is depreciated for half of the year. Mid-quarter (MQ) convention is treated as having been placed in service in the middle of the quarter it's actually placed into service. Mid-quarter convention must be used if over 40% of the depreciable basis of all of the depreciable property placed into service during that year was placed into service during the last 3 months.

**Example:** Dianne purchased a desk, two chairs, and a filing cabinet to use for her business this year. She purchased the desk on January 5$^{th}$ for $250. She purchased the two chairs and the filing cabinet on November 1$^{st}$. The chairs were $85 each and the filing cabinet was $150. The total depreciable basis of the property is $570 (250 + 85 + 85 + 150). The percentage of the basis that was placed into service during the last quarter is 56% (85 + 85 + 150 = 320;  320 ÷ 570 = 0.56). Dianne must use the mid-quarter convention to depreciate her property.

Real property requires the use of mid-month convention (MM). The property is treated as having been placed into service in the middle of the month it is actually placed into service.

## Method

The different methods of depreciation are illustrated in Illustration 2. The methods are 150% declining balance, 200% declining balance, and straight line. The Straight Line method is the easiest to understand. When you find out what the recovery period of the property is, you can divide 100% by the number of years in the recovery period to get the yearly depreciation rates. Remember, under the half year convention, you only take half of the depreciation in the first year. The straight line method table is shown in Illustration 3.

**Example:** The property you are depreciating is 5 year property. 100% ÷ 5 years = 20%. The depreciation deduction is 20% per year. The first year you will compute the depreciation deduction for only half of the year (20% ÷ 2) which is 10%. You will take the deduction of the other 10% in the final year.

The 150% declining balance method gives a greater deduction in the earlier years than does the straight line method. This method changes to the straight line method when the straight line method will give an equal or greater deduction (Don't worry, the table does this for us). The table is shown in Illustration 3.

**Example:** For five year property, the straight line method gives a deduction for 10% in the first year. Take 150% of the 10% deduction to arrive at the depreciation deduction for 150% declining balance. 10% x 150% = 15%. Note that the first year's deduction under the 150% declining balance method is 15%. In year two, 85% of the basis remains
(100% of the basis – 15%). The depreciation deduction for year two is 85% x 20% (year 2 SL method depreciation rate) x 150% = 25.50%
Year three:
85% - 25.50% = 59.50%
59.50% x 20% x 150% = 17.85%

The 200% declining balance method works the same as the 150% declining balance method, but the taxpayer receives an even greater deduction at the beginning. This method also switches to the straight line method when the deduction is equal to or greater. This is the method most widely used because it gives a greater deduction in the earlier years. The table is shown in Illustration 3.

**Example:** For five year property, the depreciation rate using the SL method is 10% the first year. 10% x 200% = 20% depreciation rate for year one using the 200% DB method. Year two:
100% - 20% = 80%
80% x 20% x 200% = 32 % depreciation rate for year two.
Year three:
80% - 32% = 48%
48% x 20% x 200% = 19.20% depreciation rate.

For most personal property, the 200%DB (200% Declining Balance) will be used. Depreciating real property requires the SL (Straight Line) method. A comparison of the three methods is shown in Illustration 2.

# Depreciation Methods

| | | |
|---|---|---|
| **Note:** The declining balance method is abbreviated as DB and the straight line method is abbreviated as SL. | | |
| **Method** | **Type of property** | **Benefit** |
| GDS using 200% DB | • Nonfarm 3-, 5- ,7-, and 10-year property | • Provides a greater deduction during the earlier recovery years.<br>• Changes to SL when that method provides an equal to or greater deduction. |
| GDS using 150% DB | • All farm property (except real property).<br>• All 15- and 20-year property (except qualified leasehold improvement property and qualified restaurant property placed in service before (January 1, 2010)<br>• Nonfarm 3-, 5-, 7-, and 10-year property | • Provides a greater deduction during the earlier recovery years<br>• Changes to SL when that method provides an equal to or greater deduction. |
| GDS using SL | • Nonresidential real property<br>• Qualified leasehold improvement property placed in service before January 1, 2010.<br>• Qualified restaurant property placed in service before January 1, 2010.<br>• Residential rental property<br>• Trees or vines bearing fruits or nuts<br>• Water Utility property<br>• All 3-, 5-, 7-, 10-, 15-, 20-year property | • Provides for equal yearly deductions (except for the first and last years) |
| ADS using SL | • Listed Property used 50% or less for business.<br>• Property used predominately outside the U.S.<br>• Qualified leasehold improvement property placed in service before January 1st, 2010.<br>• Tax exempt property.<br>• Tax exempt bond-financed property.<br>• Farm property used when an election not to apply the uniform capitalization rules is in effect.<br>• Imported property.<br>• Any property for which the taxpayer elects to use this method. | • Provides for equal yearly deductions. |

# Find the Correct Table

Some of the more commonly used tables are illustrated (Illustration 3) in the next few pages as well as in the appendix. Notice Table A is used for personal property that has a recovery period of 3, 5, or 7 years, and is depreciated using the half-year convention and the 200%DB method. Table B is for personal property with a recovery period of 3, 5, or 7 years, and is depreciated using the half-year convention and the 150%DB method. Table C is for personal property with a recovery period of 3, 5, or 7 years, and is depreciated using the half-year convention and the SL method. Tables D through G are for properties with the same recovery periods, but property that must be depreciated using the mid-quarter convention. You will use whichever table is for the quarter the property you're looking up was placed in service.

Table H is for residential property. Table J is for nonresidential property placed in service before May 13, 1993. Table I is for nonresidential property that was placed in service on or after May 13, 1993.

Notice the headings at the top of the table are for the recovery period the property you are depreciating has. The headings down the left side have to do with what year you are calculating the depreciation for.

**Example:** Edward has a business and has been depreciating a desk he placed in service on March 13, 2009. We can look up the recovery period and find that the desk is 7 year property. Using Table A, we look in the column for 7 year property. On the side, we find the number 3 because this is the $3^{rd}$ year the property is being depreciated with 2009 being the $1^{st}$ and 2010 being the $2^{nd}$. The percentage we will use to calculate the depreciation is 17.49%.

**Table A**

**MACRS 3-year, 5-year, and 7-year property**
**Half – Year Convention          200%DB**

| Year | Depreciation rate for recovery period | | |
|---|---|---|---|
| | 3-year | 5-year | 7-year |
| 1 | 33.33% | 20.00% | 14.29% |
| 2 | 44.45% | 32.00% | 24.49% |
| 3 | 14.81% | 19.20% | 17.49% |
| 4 | 7.41% | 11.52% | 12.49% |
| 5 | | 11.52% | 8.93% |
| 6 | | 5.76% | 8.92% |
| 7 | | | 8.93% |
| 8 | | | 4.46% |

**Table B**

**MACRS 3-year, 5-year, and 7-year property**
**Half – Year Convention          150%DB**

| Year | Depreciation rate for recovery period | | |
|---|---|---|---|
| | 3-year | 5-year | 7-year |
| 1 | 25.00% | 15.00% | 10.71% |
| 2 | 37.50% | 25.50% | 19.13% |
| 3 | 25.00% | 17.85% | 15.03% |
| 4 | 12.50% | 16.66% | 12.25% |
| 5 | | 16.66% | 12.25% |
| 6 | | 8.33% | 12.25% |
| 7 | | | 12.25% |
| 8 | | | 6.13% |

**Table C**

**MACRS 3-year, 5-year, and 7-year property**
**Half – Year Convention          Straight Line**

| Year | Depreciation rate for recovery period | | |
|---|---|---|---|
| | 3-year | 5-year | 7-year |
| 1 | 16.67% | 10.00% | 7.14% |
| 2 | 33.33% | 20.00% | 14.29% |
| 3 | 33.33% | 20.00% | 14.29% |
| 4 | 16.67% | 20.00% | 14.28% |
| 5 | | 20.00% | 14.29% |
| 6 | | 10.00% | 14.28% |
| 7 | | | 14.29% |
| 8 | | | 7.14% |

*Table D*    MACRS 3-year, 5-year, and 7-year property    200DB%
Mid-Quarter Convention placed in Service in First

| Year | Depreciation rate for recovery period | | |
|------|--------|--------|--------|
|      | 3-year | 5-year | 7-year |
| 1    | 58.33% | 35.00% | 25.00% |
| 2    | 27.78% | 26.00% | 21.43% |
| 3    | 12.35% | 15.60% | 15.31% |
| 4    | 1.54%  | 11.01% | 10.93% |
| 5    |        | 11.01% | 8.75%  |
| 6    |        | 1.38%  | 8.74%  |
| 7    |        |        | 8.75%  |
| 8    |        |        | 1.09%  |

*Table E*    MACRS 3-year, 5-year, and 7-year property    200DB%
Mid-Quarter Convention placed in Service in Second

| Year | Depreciation rate for recovery period | | |
|------|--------|--------|--------|
|      | 3-year | 5-year | 7-year |
| 1    | 41.67% | 25.00% | 17.85% |
| 2    | 38.89% | 30.00% | 23.47% |
| 3    | 14.14% | 18.00% | 16.76% |
| 4    | 5.30%  | 11.37% | 11.97% |
| 5    |        | 11.37% | 8.87%  |
| 6    |        | 4.26%  | 8.87%  |
| 7    |        |        | 8.87%  |
| 8    |        |        | 3.34%  |

*Table F*    MACRS 3-year, 5-year, and 7-year property    200DB%
Mid-Quarter Convention placed in Service in Third

| Year | Depreciation rate for recovery period | | |
|------|--------|--------|--------|
|      | 3-year | 5-year | 7-year |
| 1    | 58.33% | 35.00% | 25.00% |
| 2    | 27.78% | 26.00% | 21.43% |
| 3    | 12.35% | 15.60% | 15.31% |
| 4    | 1.54%  | 11.01% | 10.93% |
| 5    |        | 11.01% | 8.75%  |
| 6    |        | 1.38%  | 8.74%  |
| 7    |        |        | 8.75%  |
| 8    |        |        | 1.09%  |

*Table G*

### MACRS 3-year, 5-year, and 7-year property    200DB%
### Mid-Quarter Convention placed in Service in Fourth

| Year | Depreciation rate for recovery period | | |
|------|--------|--------|--------|
|      | 3-year | 5-year | 7-year |
| 1 | 8.33% | 5.00% | 3.57% |
| 2 | 61.11% | 38.00% | 27.55% |
| 3 | 20.37% | 22.80% | 19.68% |
| 4 | 10.19% | 13.68% | 14.06% |
| 5 |  | 10.94% | 10.04% |
| 6 |  | 9.58% | 8.73% |
| 7 |  |  | 8.73% |
| 8 |  |  | 7.64% |

*Table H*      **MACRS Residential Rental Property**      **Straight Line**
### Mid-Month Convention      27.5years

| Year | Month Property was placed in service | | | | | | | | | | | |
|------|---|---|---|---|---|---|---|---|---|---|---|---|
|   | 1 | 2 | 3 | 4 | 5 | 6 | 7 | 8 | 9 | 10 | 11 | 12 |
| 1 | 3.485% | 3.182% | 2.879% | 2.576% | 2.273% | 1.970% | 1.667% | 1.364% | 1.061% | 0.758% | 0.455% | 0.152% |
| 2-9 | 3.636% | 3.636% | 3.636% | 3.636% | 3.636% | 3.636% | 3.636% | 3.636% | 3.636% | 3.636% | 3.636% | 3.636% |
| 10 | 3.637% | 3.637% | 3.637% | 3.637% | 3.637% | 3.637% | 3.636% | 3.636% | 3.636% | 3.636% | 3.636% | 3.636% |
| 11 | 3.636% | 3.636% | 3.636% | 3.636% | 3.636% | 3.636% | 3.637% | 3.637% | 3.637% | 3.637% | 3.637% | 3.637% |
| 12 | 3.637% | 3.637% | 3.637% | 3.637% | 3.637% | 3.637% | 3.636% | 3.636% | 3.636% | 3.636% | 3.636% | 3.636% |
| 13 | 3.636% | 3.636% | 3.636% | 3.636% | 3.636% | 3.636% | 3.637% | 3.637% | 3.637% | 3.637% | 3.637% | 3.637% |
| 14 | 3.637% | 3.637% | 3.637% | 3.637% | 3.637% | 3.637% | 3.636% | 3.636% | 3.636% | 3.636% | 3.636% | 3.636% |
| 15 | 3.636% | 3.636% | 3.636% | 3.636% | 3.636% | 3.636% | 3.637% | 3.637% | 3.637% | 3.637% | 3.637% | 3.637% |
| 16 | 3.637% | 3.637% | 3.637% | 3.637% | 3.637% | 3.637% | 3.636% | 3.636% | 3.636% | 3.636% | 3.636% | 3.636% |
| 17 | 3.636% | 3.636% | 3.636% | 3.636% | 3.636% | 3.636% | 3.637% | 3.637% | 3.637% | 3.637% | 3.637% | 3.637% |
| 18 | 3.637% | 3.637% | 3.637% | 3.637% | 3.637% | 3.637% | 3.636% | 3.636% | 3.636% | 3.636% | 3.636% | 3.636% |
| 19 | 3.636% | 3.636% | 3.636% | 3.636% | 3.636% | 3.636% | 3.637% | 3.637% | 3.637% | 3.637% | 3.637% | 3.637% |
| 20 | 3.637% | 3.637% | 3.637% | 3.637% | 3.637% | 3.637% | 3.636% | 3.636% | 3.636% | 3.636% | 3.636% | 3.636% |
| 21 | 3.636% | 3.636% | 3.636% | 3.636% | 3.636% | 3.636% | 3.637% | 3.637% | 3.637% | 3.637% | 3.637% | 3.637% |
| 22 | 3.637% | 3.637% | 3.637% | 3.637% | 3.637% | 3.637% | 3.636% | 3.636% | 3.636% | 3.636% | 3.636% | 3.636% |
| 23 | 3.636% | 3.636% | 3.636% | 3.636% | 3.636% | 3.636% | 3.637% | 3.637% | 3.637% | 3.637% | 3.637% | 3.637% |
| 24 | 3.637% | 3.637% | 3.637% | 3.637% | 3.637% | 3.637% | 3.636% | 3.636% | 3.636% | 3.636% | 3.636% | 3.636% |
| 25 | 3.636% | 3.636% | 3.636% | 3.636% | 3.636% | 3.636% | 3.637% | 3.637% | 3.637% | 3.637% | 3.637% | 3.637% |
| 26 | 3.637% | 3.637% | 3.637% | 3.637% | 3.637% | 3.637% | 3.636% | 3.636% | 3.636% | 3.636% | 3.636% | 3.636% |
| 27 | 3.636% | 3.636% | 3.636% | 3.636% | 3.636% | 3.636% | 3.637% | 3.637% | 3.637% | 3.637% | 3.637% | 3.637% |
| 28 | 1.97% | 2.273% | 2.576% | 2.879% | 3.182% | 3.485% | 3.636% | 3.636% | 3.636% | 3.636% | 3.636% | 3.636% |
| 29 |  |  |  |  |  |  | 0.152% | 0.455% | 0.758% | 1.061% | 1.364% | 1.667% |

*Table I*

## MACRS Nonresidential Real Property  Straight Line  39 years
## Placed in service on or after May 13<sup>th</sup>, 1993  Mid-Month Convention

| Year | Month Property was placed in service | | | | | | | | | | | |
|---|---|---|---|---|---|---|---|---|---|---|---|---|
| | 1 | 2 | 3 | 4 | 5 | 6 | 7 | 8 | 9 | 10 | 11 | 12 |
| 1 | 2.461% | 2.247% | 2.033% | 1.819% | 1.605% | 1.391% | 1.177% | 0.963% | 0.749% | 0.535% | 0.321% | 0.107% |
| 2-39 | 2.564% | 2.564% | 2.564% | 2.564% | 2.564% | 2.564% | 2.564% | 2.564% | 2.564% | 2.564% | 2.564% | 2.564% |
| 40 | 0.107% | 0.321% | 0.535% | 0.749% | 0.963% | 1.177% | 1.391% | 1.605% | 1.819% | 2.033% | 2.247% | 2.461% |

*Table J*

## MACRS Nonresidential Real Property  Straight Line  31.5 years
## Placed in service before  May 13<sup>th</sup>, 1993  Mid-Month Convention

| Year | Month Property was placed in service | | | | | | | | | | | | |
|---|---|---|---|---|---|---|---|---|---|---|---|---|---|
| | 1 | 2 | 3 | 4 | 5 | 6 | 7 | 8 | 9 | 10 | 11 | 12 | |
| 1 | 3.042% | 2.778% | 2.513% | 2.249% | 1.984% | 1.720% | 1.455% | 1.190% | 0.926% | 0.661% | 0.397% | 0.132% | |
| 2-7 | 3.175% | 3.175% | 3.175% | 3.175% | 3.175% | 3.175% | 3.175% | 3.175% | 3.175% | 3.175% | 3.175% | 3.175% | |
| 8 | 3.175% | 3.174% | 3.175% | 3.174% | 3.175% | 3.174% | 3.175% | 3.175% | 3.175% | 3.175% | 3.175% | 3.175% | |
| 9 | 3.174% | 3.175% | 3.174% | 3.175% | 3.174% | 3.175% | 3.174% | 3.175% | 3.174% | 3.175% | 3.174% | 3.175% | |
| 10 | 3.175% | 3.174% | 3.175% | 3.174% | 3.175% | 3.174% | 3.175% | 3.174% | 3.175% | 3.174% | 3.175% | 3.174% | |
| 11 | 3.174% | 3.175% | 3.174% | 3.175% | 3.174% | 3.175% | 3.174% | 3.175% | 3.174% | 3.175% | 3.174% | 3.175% | |
| 12 | 3.175% | 3.174% | 3.175% | 3.174% | 3.175% | 3.174% | 3.175% | 3.174% | 3.175% | 3.174% | 3.175% | 3.174% | |
| 13 | 3.174% | 3.175% | 3.174% | 3.175% | 3.174% | 3.175% | 3.174% | 3.175% | 3.174% | 3.175% | 3.174% | 3.175% | |
| 14 | 3.175% | 3.174% | 3.175% | 3.174% | 3.175% | 3.174% | 3.175% | 3.174% | 3.175% | 3.174% | 3.175% | 3.174% | |
| 15 | 3.174% | 3.175% | 3.174% | 3.175% | 3.174% | 3.175% | 3.174% | 3.175% | 3.174% | 3.175% | 3.174% | 3.175% | |
| 16 | 3.175% | 3.174% | 3.175% | 3.174% | 3.175% | 3.174% | 3.175% | 3.174% | 3.175% | 3.174% | 3.175% | 3.174% | |
| 17 | 3.174% | 3.175% | 3.174% | 3.175% | 3.174% | 3.175% | 3.174% | 3.175% | 3.174% | 3.175% | 3.174% | 3.175% | |
| 18 | 3.175% | 3.174% | 3.175% | 3.174% | 3.175% | 3.174% | 3.175% | 3.174% | 3.175% | 3.174% | 3.175% | 3.174% | |
| 19 | 3.174% | 3.175% | 3.174% | 3.175% | 3.174% | 3.175% | 3.174% | 3.175% | 3.174% | 3.175% | 3.174% | 3.175% | |
| 20 | 3.175% | 3.174% | 3.175% | 3.174% | 3.175% | 3.174% | 3.175% | 3.174% | 3.175% | 3.174% | 3.175% | 3.174% | |
| 21 | 3.174% | 3.175% | 3.174% | 3.175% | 3.174% | 3.175% | 3.174% | 3.175% | 3.174% | 3.175% | 3.174% | 3.175% | |
| 22 | 3.175% | 3.174% | 3.175% | 3.174% | 3.175% | 3.174% | 3.175% | 3.174% | 3.175% | 3.174% | 3.175% | 3.174% | |
| 23 | 3.174% | 3.175% | 3.174% | 3.175% | 3.174% | 3.175% | 3.174% | 3.175% | 3.174% | 3.175% | 3.174% | 3.175% | |
| 24 | 3.175% | 3.174% | 3.175% | 3.174% | 3.175% | 3.174% | 3.175% | 3.174% | 3.175% | 3.174% | 3.175% | 3.174% | |
| 25 | 3.174% | 3.175% | 3.174% | 3.175% | 3.174% | 3.175% | 3.174% | 3.175% | 3.174% | 3.175% | 3.174% | 3.175% | |
| 26 | 3.175% | 3.174% | 3.175% | 3.174% | 3.175% | 3.174% | 3.175% | 3.174% | 3.175% | 3.174% | 3.175% | 3.174% | |
| 27 | 3.174% | 3.175% | 3.174% | 3.175% | 3.174% | 3.175% | 3.174% | 3.175% | 3.174% | 3.175% | 3.174% | 3.175% | |
| 28 | 3.175% | 3.174% | 3.175% | 3.174% | 3.175% | 3.174% | 3.175% | 3.174% | 3.175% | 3.174% | 3.175% | 3.174% | |
| 29 | 3.174% | 3.175% | 3.174% | 3.175% | 3.174% | 3.175% | 3.174% | 3.175% | 3.174% | 3.175% | 3.174% | 3.175% | |
| 30 | 3.175% | 3.174% | 3.175% | 3.174% | 3.175% | 3.174% | 3.175% | 3.174% | 3.175% | 3.174% | 3.175% | 3.174% | |
| 31 | 3.174% | 3.175% | 3.174% | 3.175% | 3.174% | 3.175% | 3.174% | 3.175% | 3.174% | 3.175% | 3.174% | 3.175% | |
| 32 | 1.720% | 1.984% | 2.249% | 2.513% | 2.778% | 3.042% | 3.175% | 3.174% | 3.175% | 3.174% | 3.175% | 3.174% | |
| 33 | | | | | | | 0.132% | 0.397% | 0.661% | 0.926% | 1.190% | 1.455% | |

## Table K

### Straight Line Method         Half-Year Convention

| Year | Recovery Periods in years | | | | | | | | | | | | |
|---|---|---|---|---|---|---|---|---|---|---|---|---|---|
| | 2.5 | 3 | 3.5 | 4 | 5 | 6 | 6.5 | 7 | 7.5 | 8 | 8.5 | 9 | 9.5 |
| 1 | 20.0% | 16.67% | 14.29% | 12.5% | 10.0% | 8.33% | 7.69% | 7.14% | 6.67% | 6.25% | 5.88% | 5.56% | 5.26% |
| 2 | 40.0 | 33.33 | 28.57 | 25.0 | 20.0 | 16.67 | 15.39 | 14.29 | 13.33 | 12.50 | 11.77 | 11.11 | 10.53 |
| 3 | 40.0 | 33.33 | 28.57 | 25.0 | 20.0 | 16.67 | 15.38 | 14.29 | 13.33 | 12.50 | 11.76 | 11.11 | 10.53 |
| 4 | | 16.67 | 28.57 | 25.0 | 20.0 | 16.67 | 15.39 | 14.28 | 13.33 | 12.50 | 11.77 | 11.11 | 10.53 |
| 5 | | | | 12.5 | 20.0 | 16.66 | 15.38 | 14.29 | 13.34 | 12.50 | 11.76 | 11.11 | 10.52 |
| 6 | | | | | 10.0 | 16.67 | 15.39 | 14.28 | 13.33 | 12.50 | 11.77 | 11.11 | 10.53 |
| 7 | | | | | | 8.33 | 15.38 | 14.29 | 13.34 | 12.50 | 11.76 | 11.11 | 10.52 |
| 8 | | | | | | | | 7.14 | 13.33 | 12.50 | 11.77 | 11.11 | 10.53 |
| 9 | | | | | | | | | | 6.25 | 11.76 | 11.11 | 10.52 |
| 10 | | | | | | | | | | | | 5.56 | 10.53 |

## Table K continued

### Straight Line Method         Half-Year Convention

| Year | Recovery Periods in Years | | | | | | | | | | | | |
|---|---|---|---|---|---|---|---|---|---|---|---|---|---|
| | 10 | 10.5 | 11 | 11.5 | 12 | 12.5 | 13 | 13.5 | 14 | 15 | 16 | 16.5 | 17 |
| 1 | 5.0% | 4.76% | 4.55% | 4.35 | 4.17% | 4.0% | 3.85% | 3.70% | 3.57% | 3.33% | 3.13% | 3.03% | 2.94% |
| 2 | 10.0 | 9.52 | 9.09 | 8.70 | 8.33 | 8.0 | 7.69 | 7.41 | 7.14 | 6.67 | 6.25 | 6.06 | 5.88 |
| 3 | 10.0 | 9.52 | 9.09 | 8.70 | 8.33 | 8.0 | 7.69 | 7.41 | 7.14 | 6.67 | 6.25 | 6.06 | 5.88 |
| 4 | 10.0 | 9.53 | 9.09 | 8.69 | 8.33 | 8.0 | 7.69 | 7.41 | 7.14 | 6.67 | 6.25 | 6.06 | 5.88 |
| 5 | 10.0 | 9.52 | 9.09 | 8.70 | 8.33 | 8.0 | 7.69 | 7.41 | 7.14 | 6.67 | 6.25 | 6.06 | 5.88 |
| 6 | 10.0 | 9.53 | 9.09 | 8.69 | 8.33 | 8.0 | 7.69 | 7.41 | 7.14 | 6.67 | 6.25 | 6.06 | 5.88 |
| 7 | 10.0 | 9.52 | 9.09 | 8.70 | 8.34 | 8.0 | 7.69 | 7.41 | 7.14 | 6.67 | 6.25 | 6.06 | 5.88 |
| 8 | 10.0 | 9.53 | 9.09 | 8.69 | 8.33 | 8.0 | 7.69 | 7.41 | 7.15 | 6.66 | 6.25 | 6.06 | 5.88 |
| 9 | 10.0 | 9.52 | 9.09 | 8.70 | 8.34 | 8.0 | 7.69 | 7.41 | 7.14 | 6.67 | 6.25 | 6.06 | 5.88 |
| 10 | 10.0 | 9.53 | 9.09 | 8.69 | 8.33 | 8.0 | 7.70 | 7.40 | 7.15 | 6.66 | 6.25 | 6.06 | 5.88 |
| 11 | 5.0 | 9.52 | 9.09 | 8.70 | 8.34 | 8.0 | 7.69 | 7.41 | 7.14 | 6.67 | 6.25 | 6.06 | 5.89 |
| 12 | | | 4.55 | 8.69 | 8.33 | 8.0 | 7.70 | 7.40 | 7.15 | 6.66 | 6.25 | 6.06 | 5.88 |
| 13 | | | | | 4.17 | 8.0 | 7.69 | 7.41 | 7.14 | 6.67 | 6.25 | 6.06 | 5.89 |
| 14 | | | | | | | 3.85 | 7.40 | 7.15 | 6.66 | 6.25 | 6.06 | 5.88 |
| 15 | | | | | | | | 3.57 | 6.67 | 6.25 | 6.06 | 5.89 |
| 16 | | | | | | | | | | 3.33 | 6.25 | 6.06 | 5.88 |
| 17 | | | | | | | | | | | 3.12 | 6.07 | 5.89 |
| 18 | | | | | | | | | | | | | 2.94 |

# The Third Step

The third step is the actual calculation of the depreciation. Let's do this while we are filling out a depreciation worksheet (Illustration 4). Let's start with something fairly easy. How about a desk chair purchased on April 2, 2011 for $125? The first thing we'll do is enter the description of the property, the date placed in service, and the basis (Illustration 5).

Next, we will enter the business use. The desk chair is used in the office; therefore it is used 100% for business. We are going to ignore the Section 179 column for now.

The next column is basis for depreciation. Because we are using the property 100% and have no Section 179 deduction or Special allowance, the basis for depreciation is the same as the cost. The method for depreciation is 200%DB because it is personal property, and the convention is half-year.

Now, we will look for the recovery period for the desk chair. It is listed under the asset class of office furniture and the recovery period for that class is 7 years.

Finally, we will find the Rate % and calculate the depreciation. Table A is for 7 year property depreciation using the half-year convention. The percentage for the 1$^{st}$ year under 7 year property is 14.29%. Now, we multiply the basis for depreciation by the percentage and end up with the depreciation deduction. ($125 x 14.29% = $18). The Depreciation for prior years will be 0 because it was just placed into service this year.

**Note:** Property can never be depreciated for an amount over its depreciable basis. Because of the rounding, there may be a case in which the last year of depreciation causes the total depreciation to be over the basis. In this case, an adjustment should be made to the last year's depreciation deduction.

Now, if we depreciated the same desk chair using ADS, the recovery period would be 10 years. The method is SL (SL is always the method for ADS), and the convention will still be half year. If we look at table K we will see that the depreciation percentage this year is 5%, giving a depreciation deduction of $6.

# *Prior Depreciation*

If the taxpayer has depreciable property that was not placed in service during the current tax year, they will have prior depreciation. As the note above states, property cannot be depreciated for an amount over its basis. In order to make sure that doesn't happen, we have to keep track of the prior depreciation. Sometimes it is easy because we have the prior year's return to go by, but many times the prior depreciation is not clearly stated on the taxpayer's prior return, or the taxpayer does not have their prior return. In this case, we will have to calculate the prior depreciation. Following is an example of depreciating property, and calculating the prior depreciation.

Illustration 4

| Description of Property | Date Placed in Service | Cost or other Basis | Business/ Investment Use % | Business Basis (C x D) | Salvage/ Land Value | Section 179 Deduction or Bonus Depreciation | Depreciation Basis [E − (F + G)] | Method/ Convention | Recovery Period | Prior Depreciation | Depreciation Percentage | Depreciation Deduction (H x L) |
|---|---|---|---|---|---|---|---|---|---|---|---|---|
| A | B | C | D | E | F | G | H | I | J | K | L | M |
| | | | | | | | | | | | | |
| | | | | | | | | | | | | |
| | | | | | | | | | | | | |
| | | | | | | | | | | | | |
| | | | | | | | | | | | | |
| | | | | | | | | | | | | |
| | | | | | | | | | | | | |
| | | | | | | | | | | | | |
| | | | | | | | | | | | | |
| | | | | | | | | | | | | |
| | | | | | | | | | | | | |

Illustration 5

| Description of Property | Date Placed in Service | Cost or other Basis | Business/ Investment Use % | Business Basis (C x D) | Salvage/ Land Value | Section 179 Deduction or Bonus Depreciation | Depreciation Basis [E – (F + G)] | Method/ Convention | Recovery Period | Prior Depreciation | Depreciation Percentage | Depreciation Deduction (H x L) |
|---|---|---|---|---|---|---|---|---|---|---|---|---|
| A | B | C | D | E | F | G | H | I | J | K | L | M |
| Desk Chair | 04/02/11 | $125 | 100% | $125 | | | $125 | 200%DB/ HY | 7yrs | | 14.29% | $18 |
| | | | | | | | | | | | | |
| | | | | | | | | | | | | |
| | | | | | | | | | | | | |
| | | | | | | | | | | | | |
| | | | | | | | | | | | | |
| | | | | | | | | | | | | |
| | | | | | | | | | | | | |
| | | | | | | | | | | | | |
| | | | | | | | | | | | | |
| | | | | | | | | | | | | |
| | | | | | | | | | | | | |
| | | | | | | | | | | | | |

**Example:** Bob needs us to depreciate 4 different properties. His tax records were lost in a move from one house to another. All he can provide us with is the dates placed in service and the basis of the properties. Illustration 6 shows a depreciation worksheet.

Rental house – placed in service on June 6, 2005. He paid $56,000 for the entire property. The land was worth $10,000 when purchased.

Copy machine – placed in service on May 5, 2009. He purchased it for $363.

Computer – placed in service on October 16, 2008. He purchased it for $969.

Filing cabinet – placed in service on January 30, 2004. He purchased it for $313.

To calculate the prior depreciation, we have to figure out what the depreciation would have been for each year the property was eligible for depreciation.

| Rental house: | Year | Percentage | Depreciation |
|---|---|---|---|
| | 2005 | 1.970% | $ 906 |
| | 2006 | 3.636% | 1,673 |
| | 2007 | 3.636% | 1,673 |
| | 2008 | 3.636% | 1,673 |
| | 2009 | 3.636% | 1,673 |
| | 2010 | 3.636% | 1,673 |
| | | | |
| Copy machine | 2009 | 20% | 73 |
| | 2010 | 32% | 116 |
| | | | |
| Computer | 2008 | 20% | 194 |
| | 2009 | 32% | 310 |
| | 2010 | 19.20% | 186 |
| | | | |
| Filing Cabinet | 2004 | 14.29% | 45 |
| | 2005 | 24.49% | 77 |
| | 2006 | 17.49% | 55 |
| | 2007 | 12.49% | 39 |
| | 2008 | 8.93% | 28 |
| | 2009 | 8.92% | 28 |
| | 2010 | 8.93% | 28 |

Notice that this is the last year the filing cabinet is going to be depreciated. The prior depreciation for it is $300. 2010's depreciation would be $13.95 which would be rounded up to $14. However, the basis of the filing cabinet is $313 and the total depreciation would total $314 (300 prior depreciation + 14 for this year's depreciation). Therefore an adjustment would be made for this year's depreciation and he would claim $13.

Illustration 6

| A | B | C | D | E | F | G | H | I | J | K | L | M |
|---|---|---|---|---|---|---|---|---|---|---|---|---|
| Description of Property | Date Placed in Service | Cost or other Basis | Business/ Investment Use % | Business Basis (C x D) | Salvage/ Land Value | Section 179 Deduction or Bonus Depreciation | Depreciation Basis [E − (F + G)] | Method/ Convention | Recovery Period | Prior Depreciation | Depreciation Percentage | Depreciation Deduction (H x L) |
| Rental House | 06/06/05 | $56,000 | 100% | $56,000 | $10,000 | | $46,000 | SL/ MM | 27.5 yrs | $9,271 | 3.636% | $1,673 |
| Copy Machine | 05/05/09 | $363 | 100% | $363 | | | $363 | 200%DB/HY | 5yrs | $189 | 19.20% | $70 |
| Computer | 10/16/08 | $969 | 100% | $969 | | | $969 | 200%DB/HY | 5yrs | $690 | 11.52% | $112 |
| Filing Cabinet | 01/30/04 | $313 | 100% | $313 | | | $313 | 200%DB/HY | 7yrs | $300 | 4.46% | $13 |

# Alternative minimum tax (AMT) and depreciation

AMT applies to taxpayers who have certain types of income that receive favorable treatment, or who qualify for certain deductions, under the tax law. These benefits can significantly reduce the regular tax of some taxpayers with higher economic income. To calculate AMT, certain adjustments must be made. Depreciation is one of these adjustments.

The following property must be refigured for AMT:

- Property placed in service after 1998 that is depreciated for the regular tax using the 200% DB (generally 3, 5, 7, and 10 year property under MACRS), except for qualified property eligible for the special depreciation allowance.
- Section 1250 property placed in service after 1998 that is not depreciated for the regular tax using the straight line method; and
- Tangible property placed in service after 1986 and before 1999. (If the transitional election was made under Section 203(a)(1)(B) of the Tax Reform Act of 1986, this rule applies to property after July 31, 1986).

For property placed in service after 1998, the same convention and recovery period that was used to calculate the depreciation for regular tax will be used to calculate the depreciation for AMT. For property other than Section 1250 property, use the 150% declining balance method, switching to straight line the first tax year it gives a larger deduction. For Section 1250 property, use the straight line method.

**Note:** Section 1250 property will be discussed in the next chapter.

# Depreciation in the year of disposition

If the taxpayer sells or otherwise disposes of his or her property before the recovery period ends, the depreciation deduction for the year of disposition will be only part of the depreciation amount for the full year. The property has been disposed of if it has been permanently withdrawn from use in the taxpayer's business or income-producing activity because of its sale, exchange, retirement, abandonment, involuntary conversion, or destruction.

*Half-year convention*
If the half-year convention was used, the depreciation deduction for the year of the disposition is half the depreciation determined for the full year.

*Mid-quarter convention*
If the mid-quarter convention was used, the depreciation deduction for the year of disposition is figured by multiplying a full year of depreciation by the percentage listed below for the quarter in which the property was disposed of:

| Quarter | Percentage |
|---------|------------|
| First | 12.5% |
| Second | 37.5% |
| Third | 62.5% |
| Fourth | 87.5% |

*Mid-month convention*

If the taxpayer disposed of residential rental or nonresidential real property, figure the deprecation deduction for the year of disposition by multiplying a full year of depreciation by a fraction. The numerator is the number of months (including partial months) in the year that the property is considered in service. Treat the month of disposition as one-half month of use. The denominator is 12. For example, if the property is disposed of in May, the total depreciation would be multiplied by $\frac{4.5}{12}$ to figure the depreciation deduction.

# *Form 4562*

A Form 4562 (Illustration 7) must be filed if any of the following are being claimed by the taxpayer:

- A section 179 deduction for the current year or a section 179 carryover from a prior year.
- Depreciation for property placed in service during the current year.
- Depreciation on any vehicle or other listed property, regardless of when it was placed in service.
- A deduction for any vehicle if the deduction is reported on a form other than Schedule C or Schedule C-EZ.
- Amortization of costs if the current year is the first year of the amortization period.
- Depreciation or amortization on any asset on a corporate income tax return (other than Form 1120S, U.S. Income Tax Return for an S Corporation) regardless of when it was placed in service.

If the taxpayer has more than one activity in which a Form 4562 is required, a separate Form 4562 must be used for each activity.

## Part I – Election to Expense Certain Property Under Section 179

The taxpayer can elect to recover all or part of the cost of certain qualifying property, up to a limit, by deducting it in the year they place the property in service. This is the election to take a section 179 deduction. To qualify for the deduction the property must meet the following requirements:

- It must be eligible property,
- It must be acquired for business use,
- It must have been acquired by purchase, and
- It must not be property that does not qualify (defined later).

### Eligible Property

To be eligible property it must be one of the following types of property:

- Tangible personal property.
- Other tangible property (except buildings and their structural components) used as:
  - An integral part of manufacturing, production, or extraction or of furnishing transportation, communications, electricity, gas, water, or sewage disposal services,

- A research facility used in connection with any of the activities in the above point, or
- A facility used in connection with any of the same activities for the bulk storage of fungible commodities.
- Single purpose agricultural (livestock) or horticultural structures.
- Storage facilities (except buildings and their structural components) used in connection with distributing petroleum or any primary product of petroleum.
- Off-the-shelf computer software.
- Qualified real property.

**Qualified real property:** The following real property qualifies for the Section 179 deduction.

- Qualified leasehold improvement property,
- Qualified restaurant property, or
- Qualified retail improvement property.

# Property Acquired for Business Use

To be eligible for the section 179 deduction, the property must have been purchased for business use. If the property was acquired only for the production of income, such as rental property or investment property, it does not qualify for the section 179 deduction.

# Property Acquired by Purchase

The property must have been purchased by the person seeking the deduction to be eligible for the section 179 deduction. The property does not qualify if it was acquired by inheritance or gift.

# Property That does not Qualify

If the property meets the previous requirements and is not listed in this section, it qualifies for the section 179 deduction. Property listed in this section does not qualify for the section 179 deduction:

- Certain leased property (see Pub. 946 for more information).
- Certain property used predominantly to furnish lodging or in connection with the furnishing of lodging (see Pub. 946 for more information).
- Air conditioning or heating units.
- Property used predominantly outside the United States.
- Property used by certain tax-exempt organizations, except property used in connection with the production of income subject to the tax on unrelated trade or business income.
- Property used by governmental units or foreign persons or entities, except property used under a lease with a term of less than 6 months.

# Section 179 Limitations

## General Limit

The section 179 deduction is limited to $500,000. This is the most section 179 deduction that a taxpayer is allowed to use on their return. If the taxpayer has more than one property they would like to elect the section 179 deduction for, they may allocate the deduction to each property. The taxpayer does not have to claim a section 179 deduction for the entire cost of the property; they may only take the deduction for a portion of it and depreciate the remainder.

## Cost of Property Exceeding $2,000,000.

If the cost of most qualifying section 179 deduction property placed into service during the tax year is more than $2,000,000, the general limit will be reduced. This includes the property that would be eligible for the section 179 deduction, whether the election is made for that particular property or not. Once the cost of the property exceeds $2,000,000, the $500,000 limitation is reduced dollar for dollar, of the excess. For example, if the taxpayer placed $2,075,000 worth of qualifying section 179 deduction properties into service during the tax year, the limit would be $425,000. If the cost of the qualifying property reaches or exceeds $2,500,000 a section 179 deduction is not allowed.

**Note:** Qualified real property that the taxpayer elects to treat as Section 179 real property is limited to $250,000 of the maximum deduction of $500,000 for 2011.

## Business Income Limit

The section 179 deduction is further limited to the amount of taxable income from the active conduct of any trade or business by the taxpayer. For this purpose, taxable income is the total net income and losses from all trades and businesses, including the interest from working capital of the taxpayer's trade or business and wages, salaries, tips, or other pay earned as an employee. When figuring the taxable income, do not take into account any section 179 deduction.

# Electing the Section 179 Deduction

To make the election to claim a section 179 deduction, the taxpayer must complete part I of Form 4562.

**Example:** Jonah Jacobs has total taxable income of $75,000. He placed a small trailer into service this year. He purchased the trailer in June for $2,500 and a desk in March for $350. He would like to take a section 179 deduction for the trailer, but he would like to depreciate the desk. See Illustration 8.

Illustration 7

<table>
<tr><td colspan="2">Form **4562**</td><td colspan="2" align="center">**Depreciation and Amortization**<br>**(Including Information on Listed Property)**</td><td>OMB No. 1545-0172</td></tr>
<tr><td colspan="2">Department of the Treasury<br>Internal Revenue Service (99)</td><td colspan="2" align="center">▶ See separate instructions.  ▶ Attach to your tax return.</td><td>2011<br>Attachment<br>Sequence No. **179**</td></tr>
</table>

| Name(s) shown on return | Business or activity to which this form relates | Identifying number |
|---|---|---|

**Part I**  **Election To Expense Certain Property Under Section 179**
**Note:** *If you have any listed property, complete Part V before you complete Part I.*

| | | |
|---|---|---|
| **1** | Maximum amount (see instructions) . . . . . . . . . . . . . . . . . . . | **1** |
| **2** | Total cost of section 179 property placed in service (see instructions) . . . . . . . | **2** |
| **3** | Threshold cost of section 179 property before reduction in limitation (see instructions) . . . . . | **3** |
| **4** | Reduction in limitation. Subtract line 3 from line 2. If zero or less, enter -0- . . . . . . . . | **4** |
| **5** | Dollar limitation for tax year. Subtract line 4 from line 1. If zero or less, enter -0-. If married filing separately, see instructions . . . . . . . . . . . . . . . . . . . . . | **5** |

| **6** | (a) Description of property | (b) Cost (business use only) | (c) Elected cost |
|---|---|---|---|
| | | | |
| | | | |

| | | |
|---|---|---|
| **7** | Listed property. Enter the amount from line 29 . . . . . . . . . | **7** |
| **8** | Total elected cost of section 179 property. Add amounts in column (c), lines 6 and 7 . . . . . . | **8** |
| **9** | Tentative deduction. Enter the **smaller** of line 5 or line 8 . . . . . . . . | **9** |
| **10** | Carryover of disallowed deduction from line 13 of your 2010 Form 4562 . . . . . . . . . . | **10** |
| **11** | Business income limitation. Enter the smaller of business income (not less than zero) or line 5 (see instructions) | **11** |
| **12** | Section 179 expense deduction. Add lines 9 and 10, but do not enter more than line 11 . . . . . | **12** |
| **13** | Carryover of disallowed deduction to 2012. Add lines 9 and 10, less line 12 ▶ | **13** |

**Note:** *Do not use Part II or Part III below for listed property. Instead, use Part V.*

**Part II**  **Special Depreciation Allowance and Other Depreciation (Do not** include listed property.) (See instructions.)

| | | |
|---|---|---|
| **14** | Special depreciation allowance for qualified property (other than listed property) placed in service during the tax year (see instructions) . . . . . . . . . . . . . . . | **14** |
| **15** | Property subject to section 168(f)(1) election . . . . . . . . . . . . . . . | **15** |
| **16** | Other depreciation (including ACRS) . . . . . . . . . . . . . . . . . . | **16** |

**Part III**  **MACRS Depreciation (Do not** include listed property.) (See instructions.)

**Section A**

| | | |
|---|---|---|
| **17** | MACRS deductions for assets placed in service in tax years beginning before 2011 . . . . . . . | **17** |
| **18** | If you are electing to group any assets placed in service during the tax year into one or more general asset accounts, check here . . . . . . . . . . . . . . . . ▶ ☐ | |

**Section B—Assets Placed in Service During 2011 Tax Year Using the General Depreciation System**

| (a) Classification of property | (b) Month and year placed in service | (c) Basis for depreciation (business/investment use only—see instructions) | (d) Recovery period | (e) Convention | (f) Method | (g) Depreciation deduction |
|---|---|---|---|---|---|---|
| **19a** 3-year property | | | | | | |
| **b** 5-year property | | | | | | |
| **c** 7-year property | | | | | | |
| **d** 10-year property | | | | | | |
| **e** 15-year property | | | | | | |
| **f** 20-year property | | | | | | |
| **g** 25-year property | | | 25 yrs. | | S/L | |
| **h** Residential rental property | | | 27.5 yrs. | MM | S/L | |
| | | | 27.5 yrs. | MM | S/L | |
| **i** Nonresidential real property | | | 39 yrs. | MM | S/L | |
| | | | | MM | S/L | |

**Section C—Assets Placed in Service During 2011 Tax Year Using the Alternative Depreciation System**

| | | | | | | |
|---|---|---|---|---|---|---|
| **20a** Class life | | | | | S/L | |
| **b** 12-year | | | 12 yrs. | | S/L | |
| **c** 40-year | | | 40 yrs. | MM | S/L | |

**Part IV**  **Summary** (See instructions.)

| | | |
|---|---|---|
| **21** | Listed property. Enter amount from line 28 . . . . . . . . . . . . . . . | **21** |
| **22** | **Total.** Add amounts from line 12, lines 14 through 17, lines 19 and 20 in column (g), and line 21. Enter here and on the appropriate lines of your return. Partnerships and S corporations—see instructions . . . . . | **22** |
| **23** | For assets shown above and placed in service during the current year, enter the portion of the basis attributable to section 263A costs . . . . . . . | **23** |

For Paperwork Reduction Act Notice, see separate instructions.    Cat. No. 12906N    Form **4562** (2011)

## Illustration 7 continued

**Part V** **Listed Property** (Include automobiles, certain other vehicles, certain computers, and property used for entertainment, recreation, or amusement.)

**Note:** *For any vehicle for which you are using the standard mileage rate or deducting lease expense, complete only 24a, 24b, columns (a) through (c) of Section A, all of Section B, and Section C if applicable.*

### Section A—Depreciation and Other Information (Caution: *See the instructions for limits for passenger automobiles.*)

**24a** Do you have evidence to support the business/investment use claimed? ☐ **Yes** ☐ **No**   **24b** If "Yes," is the evidence written? ☐ **Yes** ☐ **No**

| (a) Type of property (list vehicles first) | (b) Date placed in service | (c) Business/ investment use percentage | (d) Cost or other basis | (e) Basis for depreciation (business/investment use only) | (f) Recovery period | (g) Method/ Convention | (h) Depreciation deduction | (i) Elected section 179 cost |
|---|---|---|---|---|---|---|---|---|
| **25** Special depreciation allowance for qualified listed property placed in service during the tax year and used more than 50% in a qualified business use (see instructions) . **25** | | | | | | | | |
| **26** Property used more than 50% in a qualified business use: | | | | | | | | |
| | | % | | | | | | |
| | | % | | | | | | |
| | | % | | | | | | |
| **27** Property used 50% or less in a qualified business use: | | | | | | | | |
| | | % | | | | S/L – | | |
| | | % | | | | S/L – | | |
| | | % | | | | S/L – | | |
| **28** Add amounts in column (h), lines 25 through 27. Enter here and on line 21, page 1 . **28** | | | | | | | | |
| **29** Add amounts in column (i), line 26. Enter here and on line 7, page 1 . . . . . . . . . . . . **29** | | | | | | | | |

### Section B—Information on Use of Vehicles

Complete this section for vehicles used by a sole proprietor, partner, or other "more than 5% owner," or related person. If you provided vehicles to your employees, first answer the questions in Section C to see if you meet an exception to completing this section for those vehicles.

| | (a) Vehicle 1 | | (b) Vehicle 2 | | (c) Vehicle 3 | | (d) Vehicle 4 | | (e) Vehicle 5 | | (f) Vehicle 6 | |
|---|---|---|---|---|---|---|---|---|---|---|---|---|
| **30** Total business/investment miles driven during the year (**do not** include commuting miles) . | | | | | | | | | | | | |
| **31** Total commuting miles driven during the year | | | | | | | | | | | | |
| **32** Total other personal (noncommuting) miles driven . . . . . . . . . . | | | | | | | | | | | | |
| **33** Total miles driven during the year. Add lines 30 through 32 . . . . . . . . . | | | | | | | | | | | | |
| **34** Was the vehicle available for personal use during off-duty hours? . . . . . . . | Yes | No | Yes | No | Yes | No | Yes | No | Yes | No | Yes | No |
| **35** Was the vehicle used primarily by a more than 5% owner or related person? . . . | | | | | | | | | | | | |
| **36** Is another vehicle available for personal use? | | | | | | | | | | | | |

### Section C—Questions for Employers Who Provide Vehicles for Use by Their Employees

Answer these questions to determine if you meet an exception to completing Section B for vehicles used by employees who **are not** more than 5% owners or related persons (see instructions).

| | Yes | No |
|---|---|---|
| **37** Do you maintain a written policy statement that prohibits all personal use of vehicles, including commuting, by your employees? . . . . . . . . . . . . . . . . . . . . . . . | | |
| **38** Do you maintain a written policy statement that prohibits personal use of vehicles, except commuting, by your employees? See the instructions for vehicles used by corporate officers, directors, or 1% or more owners . . . . | | |
| **39** Do you treat all use of vehicles by employees as personal use? . . . . . . . . . . . . . | | |
| **40** Do you provide more than five vehicles to your employees, obtain information from your employees about the use of the vehicles, and retain the information received? . . . . . . . . . . . . . . . | | |
| **41** Do you meet the requirements concerning qualified automobile demonstration use? (See instructions.) . . . . | | |

**Note:** *If your answer to 37, 38, 39, 40, or 41 is "Yes," do not complete Section B for the covered vehicles.*

**Part VI** **Amortization**

| (a) Description of costs | (b) Date amortization begins | (c) Amortizable amount | (d) Code section | (e) Amortization period or percentage | (f) Amortization for this year |
|---|---|---|---|---|---|
| **42** Amortization of costs that begins during your 2011 tax year (see instructions): | | | | | |
| | | | | | |
| | | | | | |
| **43** Amortization of costs that began before your 2011 tax year . . . . . . . . . . **43** | | | | | |
| **44** **Total.** Add amounts in column (f). See the instructions for where to report . . . . . . . . **44** | | | | | |

Form **4562** (2011)

Illustration 8

# Form **4562**

**Depreciation and Amortization**
**(Including Information on Listed Property)**

Department of the Treasury
Internal Revenue Service   (99)

▶ See separate instructions.          ▶ Attach to your tax return.

20**11**

Attachment
Sequence No. **179**

| Name(s) shown on return | Business or activity to which this form relates | Identifying number |
|---|---|---|
| John Jacobs | Lawn Care | 111-11-1111 |

## Part I   Election To Expense Certain Property Under Section 179

**Note:** *If you have any listed property, complete Part V before you complete Part I.*

| | | | |
|---|---|---|---:|
| 1 | Maximum amount (see instructions) . . . . . . . . . . . . . . . . . . . . . | **1** | 500,000 |
| 2 | Total cost of section 179 property placed in service (see instructions) . . . . . . | **2** | 2,850 |
| 3 | Threshold cost of section 179 property before reduction in limitation (see instructions) . . . . . | **3** | 2,000,000 |
| 4 | Reduction in limitation. Subtract line 3 from line 2. If zero or less, enter -0- . . . . . . . | **4** | 0 |
| 5 | Dollar limitation for tax year. Subtract line 4 from line 1. If zero or less, enter -0-. If married filing separately, see instructions . . . . . . . . . . . . . . . . . . . . | **5** | 500,000 |

| 6 | **(a)** Description of property | **(b)** Cost (business use only) | **(c)** Elected cost | |
|---|---|---|---|---|
| | Trailer | 2,500 | 2,500 | |
| | | | | |

| | | | |
|---|---|---|---:|
| 7 | Listed property. Enter the amount from line 29 . . . . . . . . | **7** | |
| 8 | Total elected cost of section 179 property. Add amounts in column (c), lines 6 and 7 . . . . . | **8** | 2,500 |
| 9 | Tentative deduction. Enter the **smaller** of line 5 or line 8 . . . . . . | **9** | 2,500 |
| 10 | Carryover of disallowed deduction from line 13 of your 2010 Form 4562 . . . . | **10** | |
| 11 | Business income limitation. Enter the smaller of business income (not less than zero) or line 5 (see instructions) | **11** | 75,000 |
| 12 | Section 179 expense deduction. Add lines 9 and 10, but do not enter more than line 11 . . . . | **12** | 2,500 |
| 13 | Carryover of disallowed deduction to 2012. Add lines 9 and 10, less line 12 ▶ | **13** | |

**Note:** *Do not use Part II or Part III below for listed property. Instead, use Part V.*

## Part II   Special Depreciation Allowance and Other Depreciation (Do not include listed property.) (See instructions.)

| | | | |
|---|---|---|---|
| 14 | Special depreciation allowance for qualified property (other than listed property) placed in service during the tax year (see instructions) . . . . . . . . . . . . . . . | **14** | |
| 15 | Property subject to section 168(f)(1) election . . . . . . . . . . . . . . . | **15** | |
| 16 | Other depreciation (including ACRS) . . . . . . . . . . . . . . . . . | **16** | |

## Part III   MACRS Depreciation (Do not include listed property.) (See instructions.)

### Section A

| | | | |
|---|---|---|---|
| 17 | MACRS deductions for assets placed in service in tax years beginning before 2011 . . . . . . . | **17** | |
| 18 | If you are electing to group any assets placed in service during the tax year into one or more general asset accounts, check here . . . . . . . . . . . . . . . . . ▶ ☐ | | |

### Section B—Assets Placed in Service During 2011 Tax Year Using the General Depreciation System

| **(a)** Classification of property | **(b)** Month and year placed in service | **(c)** Basis for depreciation (business/investment use only—see instructions) | **(d)** Recovery period | **(e)** Convention | **(f)** Method | **(g)** Depreciation deduction |
|---|---|---|---|---|---|---|
| 19a   3-year property | | | | | | |
| b   5-year property | | | | | | |
| c   7-year property | | 350 | 7yrs | HY | 200%DB | 50 |
| d   10-year property | | | | | | |
| e   15-year property | | | | | | |
| f   20-year property | | | | | | |
| g   25-year property | | | 25 yrs. | | S/L | |
| h   Residential rental property | | | 27.5 yrs. | MM | S/L | |
| | | | 27.5 yrs. | MM | S/L | |
| i   Nonresidential real property | | | 39 yrs. | MM | S/L | |
| | | | | MM | S/L | |

### Section C—Assets Placed in Service During 2011 Tax Year Using the Alternative Depreciation System

| | | | | | | |
|---|---|---|---|---|---|---|
| 20a   Class life | | | | | S/L | |
| b   12-year | | | 12 yrs. | | S/L | |
| c   40-year | | | 40 yrs. | MM | S/L | |

## Part IV   Summary (See instructions.)

| | | | |
|---|---|---|---:|
| 21 | Listed property. Enter amount from line 28 . . . . . . . . . . . . . . . . | **21** | |
| 22 | **Total.** Add amounts from line 12, lines 14 through 17, lines 19 and 20 in column (g), and line 21. Enter here and on the appropriate lines of your return. Partnerships and S corporations—see instructions . . . . . | **22** | 2,550 |
| 23 | For assets shown above and placed in service during the current year, enter the portion of the basis attributable to section 263A costs . . . . . . . | **23** | |

**For Paperwork Reduction Act Notice, see separate instructions.**          Cat. No. 12906N          Form **4562** (2011)

# Part II – Special Depreciation Allowance...

For tax years 2010 and 2011, the taxpayer may receive an additional 50% or 100% special depreciation allowance. This allowance is taken after any Section 179 deduction, and before the regular depreciation is calculated. The property that qualifies for the special depreciation allowance is:

- Qualified Gulf Opportunity Zone extension property
- Qualified reuse and recycling property
- Qualified cellulosic biofuel plant property
- Qualified disaster assistance property
- Certain qualified property placed in service after December 31, 2007, and before January 1, 2013.

If you encounter any of the first four items, additional research will be required.

## Certain Qualified Property Acquired After September 8, 2010, and Before January 1, 2012

The taxpayer can take a special depreciation deduction allowance of 100%, if applicable, for property that meets the following requirements:

- It is one of the following types of property:
  - Tangible property depreciated under MACRS with a recovery period of 20 years or less.
  - Water utility property
  - Computer software that is readily available for purchase by the general public, is subject to a nonexclusive license, and has not been substantially modified. (The cost of some computer software is treated as part of the cost of hardware and is depreciated under MACRS.)
  - Qualified leasehold improvement property
- The property must have been acquired by purchase after September 8, 2010, with no binding written contract for the acquisition of the property, in effect before September 9, 2010.
- The original use of the property must begin with the taxpayer after September 8, 2010.
- The property must be placed in service for use in the trade or business or, for the production of income before January 1, 2012.
- It is not excepted property.

Qualified property does not include any of the following (excepted property):

- Property placed in service and disposed of in the same tax year.
- Property converted from business use to personal use in the same tax year acquired. Property converted from personal use to business use in the same or later tax year may be qualified property.
- Property required to be depreciated under the Alternative Depreciation System. This includes listed property used 50% or less in a qualified business (explained later in the chapter).
- Qualified restaurant property placed in service after December 31, 2008.
- Qualified retail improvement property placed in service after December 31, 2008.
- Property for which the taxpayer elected not to claim any special depreciation allowance.

## Electing Not to Claim an Allowance

The taxpayer can elect, for any classes of property, not to deduct any special allowances for all property in such class placed in service during the tax year. To make that election, attach a statement to the return indicating what election the taxpayer is making, and the class of property for which they are making the election.

**Example:** Bobby Schultz (122-45-9832) operates his own business as an insurance agent, with net business income of $63,251. On February 2, 2011, he bought and placed in service a new desk. He purchased the desk for $1,819. He wants to take a Section 179 deduction for $500 of the cost. He does not want to take the special depreciation allowance. See Illustration 9.

**Note:** If the taxpayer took the special depreciation deduction allowance last year, remember to adjust the depreciable basis accordingly. Filling out the depreciation worksheet will help you remember.

The next item that appears in part II is property that is subject to section 168(f)(1) election. This is property that the taxpayer elects to depreciate under the unit-of-production method. This is beyond the scope of this course and will require additional research if encountered.

The next item that appears in part II is property that is subject to section 168(f)(1) election. This is property that the taxpayer elects to depreciation under the unit-of-production method. This is beyond the scope of this course and will require additional research if encountered.

The last item in this section is any other depreciation. This line is for property that is not eligible for MACRS. If this is encountered, additional research will be required.

Illustration 9

| Form **4562** | **Depreciation and Amortization**<br>**(Including Information on Listed Property)** | OMB No. 1545-0172 |
|---|---|---|
| Department of the Treasury<br>Internal Revenue Service   (99) | ▶ See separate instructions.          ▶ Attach to your tax return. | 20**11**<br>Attachment<br>Sequence No. **179** |

| Name(s) shown on return<br>Bobby Schultz | Business or activity to which this form relates<br>Insurance Agent | Identifying number<br>122-45-9832 |
|---|---|---|

### Part I   Election To Expense Certain Property Under Section 179

**Note:** *If you have any listed property, complete Part V before you complete Part I.*

| | | | |
|---|---|---|---|
| 1 | Maximum amount (see instructions) . . . . . . . . . . . . . . . . . . . | **1** | 500,000 |
| 2 | Total cost of section 179 property placed in service (see instructions)   . . . . . . . . . | **2** | 1,819 |
| 3 | Threshold cost of section 179 property before reduction in limitation (see instructions) . . . . . | **3** | 2,000,000 |
| 4 | Reduction in limitation. Subtract line 3 from line 2. If zero or less, enter -0- . . . . . . . . | **4** | 0 |
| 5 | Dollar limitation for tax year. Subtract line 4 from line 1. If zero or less, enter -0-. If married filing separately, see instructions   . . . . . . . . . . . . . . . . . . | **5** | 500,000 |

| 6 | (a) Description of property | (b) Cost (business use only) | (c) Elected cost | |
|---|---|---|---|---|
| | Desk | 1,819 | 500 | |
| | | | | |

| | | | |
|---|---|---|---|
| 7 | Listed property. Enter the amount from line 29   . . . . . . . . . | **7** | |
| 8 | Total elected cost of section 179 property. Add amounts in column (c), lines 6 and 7   . . . . . . | **8** | 500 |
| 9 | Tentative deduction. Enter the **smaller** of line 5 or line 8  . . . . . . . . . . . . | **9** | 500 |
| 10 | Carryover of disallowed deduction from line 13 of your 2010 Form 4562 . . . . . | **10** | |
| 11 | Business income limitation. Enter the smaller of business income (not less than zero) or line 5 (see instructions) | **11** | 63,251 |
| 12 | Section 179 expense deduction. Add lines 9 and 10, but do not enter more than line 11   . . . . . | **12** | 500 |
| 13 | Carryover of disallowed deduction to 2012. Add lines 9 and 10, less line 12  ▶ | **13** | |

**Note:** *Do not use Part II or Part III below for listed property. Instead, use Part V.*

### Part II   Special Depreciation Allowance and Other Depreciation (Do not include listed property.) (See instructions.)

| | | | |
|---|---|---|---|
| 14 | Special depreciation allowance for qualified property (other than listed property) placed in service during the tax year (see instructions)   . . . . . . . . . . . . . . . . | **14** | |
| 15 | Property subject to section 168(f)(1) election . . . . . . . . . . . . . . . . | **15** | |
| 16 | Other depreciation (including ACRS)   . . . . . . . . . . . . . . . . . . | **16** | |

### Part III   MACRS Depreciation (Do not include listed property.) (See instructions.)

**Section A**

| | | | |
|---|---|---|---|
| 17 | MACRS deductions for assets placed in service in tax years beginning before 2011 . . . . . . . . | **17** | |
| 18 | If you are electing to group any assets placed in service during the tax year into one or more general asset accounts, check here   . . . . . . . . . . . . . . . . . . . ▶  ☐ | | |

**Section B—Assets Placed in Service During 2011 Tax Year Using the General Depreciation System**

| (a) Classification of property | (b) Month and year placed in service | (c) Basis for depreciation (business/investment use only—see instructions) | (d) Recovery period | (e) Convention | (f) Method | (g) Depreciation deduction |
|---|---|---|---|---|---|---|
| 19a  3-year property | | | | | | |
| b   5-year property | | | | | | |
| c   7-year property | | 1,319 | 7yrs | HY | 200%DB | 188 |
| d   10-year property | | | | | | |
| e   15-year property | | | | | | |
| f   20-year property | | | | | | |
| g   25-year property | | | 25 yrs. | | S/L | |
| h   Residential rental property | | | 27.5 yrs. | MM | S/L | |
| | | | 27.5 yrs. | MM | S/L | |
| i   Nonresidential real property | | | 39 yrs. | MM | S/L | |
| | | | | MM | S/L | |

**Section C—Assets Placed in Service During 2011 Tax Year Using the Alternative Depreciation System**

| | | | | | | |
|---|---|---|---|---|---|---|
| 20a  Class life | | | | | S/L | |
| b   12-year | | | 12 yrs. | | S/L | |
| c   40-year | | | 40 yrs. | MM | S/L | |

### Part IV   Summary (See instructions.)

| | | | |
|---|---|---|---|
| 21 | Listed property. Enter amount from line 28   . . . . . . . . . . . . . . . . . | **21** | |
| 22 | **Total.** Add amounts from line 12, lines 14 through 17, lines 19 and 20 in column (g), and line 21. Enter here and on the appropriate lines of your return. Partnerships and S corporations—see instructions   . . . . . | **22** | 688 |
| 23 | For assets shown above and placed in service during the current year, enter the portion of the basis attributable to section 263A costs   . . . . . . . . | **23** | |

**For Paperwork Reduction Act Notice, see separate instructions.**          Cat. No. 12906N          Form **4562** (2011)

Illustration 9 continued

| Description of Property | Date Placed in Service | Cost or other Basis | Business/ Investment Use % | Business Basis (C x D) | Salvage/ Land Value | Section 179 Deduction or Bonus Depreciation | Depreciation Basis [E – (F + G)] | Method/ Convention | Recovery Period | Prior Depreciation | Depreciation Percentage | Depreciation Deduction (H x L) |
|---|---|---|---|---|---|---|---|---|---|---|---|---|
| A | B | C | D | E | F | G | H | I | J | K | L | M |
| Desk | 02/02/11 | $1,819 | 100% | $1,819 | | $500 | $1,319 | 200%DB/HY | 7yrs | | 14.29% | $188 |
| | | | | | | | | | | | | |
| | | | | | | | | | | | | |
| | | | | | | | | | | | | |
| | | | | | | | | | | | | |
| | | | | | | | | | | | | |
| | | | | | | | | | | | | |
| | | | | | | | | | | | | |
| | | | | | | | | | | | | |
| | | | | | | | | | | | | |
| | | | | | | | | | | | | |

# Part III – MACRS Depreciation

Remember, if all the taxpayer has is property that was placed into service in a prior year, and they are still depreciating it, a Form 4562 is not required. However, if the taxpayer placed depreciable property in service during the current tax year, a Form 4562 is required. In this case, the current year depreciation deduction for all of the property placed into service in a prior year is entered on line 17. Then, the depreciation for any property that was placed in service during the current tax year will be entered on line 19, beside the correct classification listed in column b. If there is more than one property for a classification that was placed in service during the current tax year, they will be added together and entered on the correct line.

**Example:** John Jacob (from the previous example) has a desk he has been depreciating for 2 years and the depreciation deduction on it this year is $87. He also placed another desk in service in March that he purchased for $350. He does not want to take the special depreciation allowance. See Illustration 9 for the completed Form 4562, including the section 179 deduction from the previous example.

# Part V – Listed Property

Listed property is property that is subject to additional limits on depreciation. Listed property is any of the following:

- Passenger automobiles weighing 6,000 pounds or less.
- Any other property used for transportation, unless it is an excepted vehicle.
- Property generally used for entertainment, recreation, or amusement (including photographic, communication, and video-recording equipment).
- Computers and related peripheral equipment, unless used only at a regular business establishment and owned or leased by the person operating the establishment. A regular business establishment includes a portion of a dwelling unit that is used both regularly and exclusively for business.
- Cellular telephones (or similar telecommunication equipment).

Deductions for these properties are subject to the following special rules and limits:

- Deductions for employees: If the taxpayer's use of the property is not for the employer's convenience or is not required as a condition of their employment, the taxpayer cannot deduct depreciation or rent expenses for the use of the property as an employee.
- Business use requirement: If the property is not used predominantly (more than 50%) for qualified business use, the taxpayer cannot claim the section 179 deduction or a special depreciation allowance. In addition, the taxpayer must figure the depreciation deduction under the Modified Accelerated Cost Recovery System (MACRS) using the straight line method over the ADS recovery period. The taxpayer may also have to recapture any excess depreciation claimed in previous years.
- Passenger automobile limits and rules: Annual limits apply to depreciation deductions (including section 179 deductions) for certain passenger automobiles. The taxpayer can continue to deduct depreciation for the unrecovered basis resulting from these limits after the end of the recovery period.

In summary, if the taxpayer is depreciating listed property and the business use of the property is 50% or less, no section 179 deduction is allowed and the property must be depreciated using MACRS alternative depreciation system. Any listed property that is depreciated must be reported on Form 4562, part V. If the property was used over 50%, depreciation or section 179 deduction was claimed, and the business use of the property falls to 50% or less, the taxpayer must recapture any excess depreciation claimed.

## Automobile limitations

Now, let's discuss the actual auto expense. Included in the deductible auto expenses under this method, will be depreciation, if the car belongs to the taxpayer. The taxpayer cannot deduct depreciation if they are deducting transportation expenses using the standard mileage rate. To take a depreciation deduction, the taxpayer must first calculate what percent of use of the vehicle was for business. The depreciation is then calculated but is subject to further limitations (shown below). These limits are first multiplied by the percent of business use of the vehicle, and then applied to the depreciation deduction. If the taxpayer is taking a depreciation deduction for his or her vehicle, Form 4562, page 2, Section B should be completed.

Illustration 10

## Maximum
## Depreciation Deduction
## for Cars

| Date Placed In Service | 1st Year | 2nd Year | 3rd Year | 4th & Later Years |
|---|---|---|---|---|
| 2010–2011 | $11,060[1] | $4,900 | $2,950 | $1,775 |
| 2008–2009 | 10,960[2] | 4,800 | 2,850 | 1,775 |
| 2007 | 3,060 | 4,900 | 2,850 | 1,775 |
| 2006 | 2,960 | 4,800 | 2,850 | 1,775 |
| 2005 | 2,960 | 4,700 | 2,850 | 1,675 |
| 2004 | 10,610[2] | 4,800 | 2,850 | 1,675 |
| 5/06/2003– 12/31/2003 | 10,710[3] | 4,900 | 2,950 | 1,775 |
| 1/01/2003– 5/05/2003 | 7,660[4] | 4,900 | 2,950 | 1,775 |
| 2001–2002 | 7,660[4] | 4,900 | 2,950 | 1,775 |
| 2000 | 3,060 | 4,900 | 2,950 | 1,775 |

[1]$3,060 if the car is not qualified property or if you elect not to claim the special depreciation allowance.

[2]$2,960 if the car is not qualified property or if you elect not to claim the special depreciation allowance.

[3]$7,660 if you acquired the car before 5/6/2003. $3,060 if the car is not qualified property or if you elect not to claim any special depreciation allowance.

[4]$3,060 if you acquired the car before 9/11/2001, the car is not qualified property, or you elect not to claim the special depreciation allowance.

## Maximum
## Depreciation Deduction
## for Trucks and Vans

| Date Placed In Service | 1st Year | 2nd Year | 3rd Year | 4th & Later Years |
|---|---|---|---|---|
| 2011 | $11,260[1] | $5,200 | $3,150 | $1,875 |
| 2010 | 11,160[1] | 5,100 | 3,050 | 1,875 |
| 2009 | 11,060[1] | 4,900 | 2,950 | 1,775 |
| 2008 | 11,160[1] | 5,100 | 3,050 | 1,875 |
| 2007 | 3,260 | 5,200 | 3,050 | 1,875 |
| 2005–2006 | 3,260 | 5,200 | 3,150 | 1,875 |
| 2004 | 10,910[1] | 5,300 | 3,150 | 1,875 |
| 2003 | 11,010[2] | 5,400 | 3,250 | 1,975 |

[1]If the special depreciation allowance does not apply or you make the election not to claim the special depreciation allowance, the first-year limit is $3,260 for 2011, $3,160 for 2010, $3,060 for 2009, $3,160 for 2008, $3,260 for 2004, and $3,360 for 2003.

[2]If the truck or van was acquired before 5/06/03, the truck or van is qualified property, and you claim the special depreciation allowance for the truck or van, the maximum deduction is $7,960.

# *Chapter Review*

1) What four requirements must property meet to be considered depreciable property?

2) List three types of tangible property.

3) List three types of intangible property.

4) What method is used to depreciate most personal property? What about real property?

5) What information do you need to calculate prior depreciation?

6) What requirements must property meet to qualify for the section 179 deduction?

7) What is the special depreciation allowance for 2011 and when can it be taken?

8) What is listed property and when is it depreciated using the MACRS alternative depreciation system?

# *Exercises*

(1) Find this year's depreciation deduction for the following properties. Use the HY convention for personal property unless specifically stated otherwise. Also determine the prior year depreciation.

Rental house: Purchased for $27,500 ($10,000 for the land); placed in service in October of 2002.

Computer: Purchased for $1,309; placed in service on July 5, 2009.

Copy machine: Purchased for $599; placed in service on August 7, 2011.

Heavy General Purpose Truck: Purchased for $17,289; placed in service on August 19, 2010.

Sofa purchased for $921 for use in the rental house; placed in service on June 23, 2007.

Refrigerator purchased for $1,126 for use in the rental house; placed in service February 3, 2010.

(2) James has an insurance sales business. Calculate his depreciation deduction for 2011 as well as his prior depreciation.

| Desk | $565 | placed in service June 3, 2008 |
|---|---|---|
| Bookshelf | 123 | placed in service May 7, 2006 |
| Filing Cabinet | 234 | placed in service May 5, 2010 |
| Shelves | 156 | placed in service May 7, 2006 |
| Desk | 723 | placed in service August 21, 2007 |

He, also, purchased an office building that he place in service May 7, 2006. He paid $89,633. The land was appraised at $13,500 at the time of the sale. He elected not to take any Bonus Depreciation deductions last year.

# Chapter 4 – Sale of Business Assets and Depreciation Recapture

## Terms

**Assets** – useful or valuable property.

**Business assets** – Property used in a trade or business, such as business machinery and office furniture.

**Capital assets** – Property held by the taxpayer, except cash, inventory, receivables, and certain intangibles.

**Capital gain** – A gain from the sale or exchange of capital assets.

**Capital loss** – Loss from the sale or exchange of capital assets.

**Condemnation** – The process by which private property is legally taken for public use without the owner's consent.

**Cost recovery** – The deducting of the cost of qualified assets over a certain time period.

**Depreciation allowed or allowable** – The amount of depreciation claimed on an asset. If no depreciation was claimed, then the amount of straight-line depreciation that should have been claimed will still be deducted from the basis.

**Excess section 179 deduction** – The amount arrived at when the depreciation allowable on the amount taken as a section 179 expense deduction is deducted from the section 179 expense deduction.

**Goodwill** – The value of a trade or business based on expected continued customer patronage due to name, reputation, or any other factor.

**Intangible property** – Property that cannot be perceived by the senses, for example: goodwill, patents, copyrights, etc.

**Involuntary conversions** – When property is destroyed, stolen, condemned, or disposed of under the threat of condemnation, and the taxpayer receives other property or money in payment.

**Nonrecaptured section 1231 losses** – Net section 1231 losses for the previous 5 years that have not been applied against a net section 1231 gain.

**Ordinary income or loss** – Income or loss resulting from a sale or trade of a noncapital loss and is not subject to the capital gain or loss provisions.

**Realized gain or loss** – The gain or loss computed by taking the amount received from the sale of property and subtracting the property's adjusted basis.

**Recapture** – To include as income on the taxpayer's return an amount allowed or allowable as a deduction in a prior year.

**Recognized gain or loss** – The portion of the realized gain or loss that is subject to taxation.

**Section (followed by a number)** – Refers to the section of the tax code in which the applicable law is written.

**Section 1231** – Real or depreciable property that is 1) held for more than one year and 2) used in a trade or business. Certain property, such as inventory, U.S. government publications, copyrights, literary, musical, or artistic compositions and letters, are excluded from this definition.

**Section 1245** – Property that is or has been subject to an allowance for depreciation and amortization. Section 1245 property includes personal property, single purpose agricultural and horticulture structures, storage facilities used in connection with the distribution of petroleum or primary products of petroleum, and railroad grading or tunnel bores.

**Section 1250** – Real property (other than section 1245 property) which is or has been subject to a depreciation allowance.

**Section 179** – The code section that allows the taxpayer to recover all or part of the cost of certain qualifying property, up to a limit, by deducting it in the year the property is placed in service.

**Section 280F** – The code section that contains a list of property that inherently lends itself to personal use (listed property).

**Unrecaptured section 1250 gains** – The part of any long-term capital gain on section 1250 property that is due to depreciation.

## Realized and Recognized Gains and Losses

The amount realized from a sale or other disposition of property is the sum of any money received, the FMV of all other property received, and any debt assumed by the buyer. The realized gain or loss is the amount realized from the sale or exchange of property compared with the adjusted basis of that property. A gain is realized when the amount realized is greater than the basis, and a loss is realized when the amount realized is less than the basis of the property.

The recognized gain or loss is the amount of gain or loss that is actually reported on the tax return. For example, if the taxpayer sold personal-use property for $1,000 and they had a basis in it of $2,000; they would realize a $1,000 loss. They would have no recognized loss because losses from the disposition of personal-use property are not deductible.

## *Types of Property*

Let's review the discussion from the previous chapter about types of property:

Property falls into two categories: real and personal. Real property is also called real estate. It includes land, buildings, and their structural components. Land is never depreciable. If the taxpayer purchased real property which consisted of a building and land, the portion of the purchase price attributable to the land must be deducted from the total price before the property is depreciated.

Personal property is all other property. Personal property can be personal-use, investment use, business-use property, or inventory. In this course, we are concentrating on personal business-use property. All Personal property falls into two categories: tangible and intangible. Tangible property has physical substance and its value is intrinsic. Intrinsic means the property has value in and of itself. Tangible property includes furniture, tools, and vehicles. Intangible property has no intrinsic value. The best example of intangible property is money in the form of bills. The bill itself is not worth anything because it is just made of paper.

However, the bill gives the owner the right to purchase property and services, therefore it has value. Other intangible properties include insurance policies, stocks, and bonds.

Now that we've reviewed the different types of property, let's discuss the uses of the property. The different uses of property are personal-use, investment-use, business-use, and inventory.

**Personal-use property** is a type of property that an individual does not use for business purposes or hold as an investment. In other words, personal-use property is property an individual owns for personal enjoyment.

**Investment-use property** is a property that is not occupied by the owner, usually purchased specifically to generate profit through rental income and/or capital gains.

**Business-use property** is an asset used in the generation of income, such as factory, machinery, or an office building.

**Inventory** is property held mainly for the sale to customers or property that will physically become a part of the merchandise that is for sale to customers.

Of the four types of property, only business-use and investment properties are eligible for depreciation. When business-use property, investment-use property, and inventory are sold at a loss, the losses are deductible (often subject to limits); while a loss from personal-use property is not deductible. However, gains from the sale of any types of property are always taxable.

# Section 1231 Property

When you dispose of business property, the taxable gain or loss is usually a section 1231 gain or loss. The following transactions are subject to section 1231 treatment:

- Sales or exchanges of real property or depreciable personal property used in a trade or business and held for longer than one year. Generally, property held for the production of rents or royalties is considered to be used in a trade or business.
- Sales or exchanges of leaseholds used in a trade or business and held longer than one year.
- Sales or exchanges of cattle and horses held for draft, breeding, dairy, or sporting purposes held for two years or longer.
- Sales or exchanges of other livestock (not including poultry) held for draft, breeding, dairy, or sporting purposes and held for one year or longer.
- Sales or exchanges of unharvested crops. The crop and land must be sold, exchanged, or involuntarily converted at the same time and to the same person, and the land must be held longer than one year.
- Cutting of timber or disposal of timber, coal, or iron ore treated as a sale.
- Condemnations of a business property or a capital asset held in connection with a trade or business or a transaction entered into for profit held longer than one year.
- Casualties and thefts that affected business property, property held for the production of rents and royalties, or investment property held longer than one year.

To determine the treatment of section 1231 gains and losses, combine all of the taxpayer's section 1231 gains and losses for the year. If the taxpayer has a net section 1231 loss, all the gains and losses are treated as ordinary losses. If the taxpayer has a net section 1231 gain, it is ordinary income up to the amount of the nonrecaptured section 1231 losses reported from the previous 5 years. This is known as the Five-Year Lookback Rule. This rule basically takes any section 1231 losses that were deducted as ordinary losses during the last five years, and the section 1231 gain for this year to the extent of any of those losses is treated as

ordinary income. The rest, if any, is treated as a long-term capital gain. Any depreciation allowed on section 1231 property is treated differently and will be discussed a little later in this chapter.

**Example:** Ashley, Inc., a graphic arts company, is a calendar year corporation. In 2009, it had a net section 1231 loss of $8,000. For tax years 2010 and 2011, the company has net section 1231 gains of $5,250 and $4,600, respectively. In figuring taxable income for 2010, Ashley treated its net section 1231 gain of $5,250 as ordinary income by recapturing $5,250 of its $8,000 net section 1231 loss from 2009. This leaves $2,750 of nonrecaptured section 1231 losses. In 2011, she applies its remaining net section 1231 loss, $2,750 ($8,000-$5,250) against its net section 1231 gain, $4,600. For 2011, the company reports $2,750 as ordinary income and $1,850 ($4,600-$2,750) as long-term capital gain.

# Section 1245 Property

Section 1245 property includes any property that is or has been subject to an allowance for depreciation or amortization and that is any of the following types of property:

1. Personal property (business use, either tangible or intangible).
2. Other tangible property (except buildings and their structural components) used as any of the following:
    a) An integral part of manufacturing, production, or extraction, or of furnishing transportation, communications, electricity, gas, water, or sewage disposal services.
    b) A research facility in any of the activities in (a).
    c) A facility in any of the activities in (a) for the bulk storage of fungible commodities.
3. That part of real property (not included in (2)) with an adjusted basis reduced by (but not limited to) the following.
    a) Amortization of certified pollution control facilities.
    b) The section 179 expense deduction.
    c) Deduction for clean-fuel vehicles and certain refueling property placed in service before 2006.
    d) Deduction for capital costs incurred in complying with Environmental Protection Agency sulfur regulations.
    e) Deduction for certain qualified refinery property placed in service after August 8, 2005.
    f) Deduction for energy efficient commercial building property placed in service after December 31, 2005.
    g) Deduction for election to expense qualified advanced mine safety equipment property.
    h) Expenditures to remove architectural and transportation barriers to the handicapped and elderly.
    i) Deduction for qualified tertiary injectant expenses.
    j) Certain reforestation expenditures.
4. Single purpose agricultural (livestock) or horticultural structures.
5. Storage facilities (except buildings and their structural components) used in distributing petroleum or any primary product of petroleum.
6. Any railroad grading or tunnel bore.

Section 1245 gain is treated as ordinary income. The gain treated as ordinary income on the sale, exchange, or involuntary conversion of section 1245 property is the lesser of the following amounts:

- The depreciation and amortization allowed or allowable on the property.
- The gain realized on the disposition (the amount realized from the disposition minus the adjusted basis of the property).

Any gain realized that is more than the part that is ordinary income from depreciation is a section 1231 gain.

**Example:** Collinder Corporation purchased some equipment in 2009 for $56,000. They took a Section 179 deduction for $16,000 and depreciated the rest. The equipment is 5 year property and they were allowed $6,000 MACRS depreciation in 2009 and $4,800 MACRS depreciation in 2010. In 2011, Collinder Corporation sold the equipment for $60,500. The adjusted basis of the equipment is now $29,200 ($56,000 - $16,000 - $6,000 - $4,800). The realized gain on the equipment is $31,300 ($60,500 – 29,200). $26,800 ($16,000 + $6,000 + $4,800) of the gain is section 1245 gain and treated as ordinary income. The remaining $4,500 gain is section 1231 gain.

## Section 1250 Property

Section 1250 property is any depreciable real property other than Sec. 1245 property. As mentioned earlier, nonresidential real estate placed in service after 1980 and before 1987 is Section 1245 property, unless the straight-line cost recovery is elected. Section 1250 property includes all real property that is subject to an allowance for depreciation and that is not and never has been section 1245 property. Gain on the disposition of section 1250 property is treated as ordinary income to the extent of additional depreciation allowed or allowable. If the section 1250 property is held for longer than one year, the additional depreciation is the actual depreciation adjustments that are more than the depreciation figured using the straight line method. If the property was placed in service after 1986, it is required to be depreciated using the straight line method and is, therefore, not subject to depreciation recapture.

Now is where it gets a little confusing. If real property is sold and it was placed in service after 1986, then there is no additional depreciation to be recaptured, therefore, no gain to be taxed as ordinary income. However, this creates what is called "unrecaptured section 1250 gain". Unrecaptured section 1250 gain is the amount of the gain that would have been subject to recapture if all of the depreciation was subject to recapture. The unrecaptured section 1250 gain is a section 1231 long term capital gain taxed at 25%. In summary, for the sale of real property that was placed in service before 1987, the portion of the gain that is section 1250 gain (additional depreciation) is treated as ordinary income. The unrecaptured section 1250 gain (the rest of the depreciation allowed) is treated as a section 1231 gain taxed at 25%. The remainder of the gain is a section 1231 gain treated solely as a long term capital gain. If the property was placed in service after 1986, it will only be subject to taxation as an unrecaptured section 1250 gain and a section 1231 gain.

**Example:** Jonathon sells an office building purchased and placed in service in 1982. He paid $700,000 not including the cost of land. $500,000 has been allowed as depreciation deductions using an accelerated method. If Jonathon used the straight-line method, he would have been allowed a depreciation deduction of only $420,000. The office building was sold for $950,000. The adjusted basis of the property is $200,000 ($700,000 - $500,000). The sale resulted in a gain of $750,000 ($950,000 – 200,000). $80,000 ($500,000 - $420,000) is a section 1250 gain and is treated as ordinary income. The remaining gain of $670,000 is section 1231 gain. $500,000 is taxed as a long term capital gain at the rate of 25% as unrecaptured 1250 gain and $70,000 is taxed at the regular long term capital gain tax rate of 15%.

## *Form 4797*

Now that we've discussed the different gains and losses and the tax treatment of them, we will talk about how they are reported on the tax return. Form 4797 (Illustration 1) is used to report the sale of business assets. Notice, Form 4797 has four parts.

## PART I – SALES OR EXCHANGES OF PROPERTY USED IN A TRADE OR BUSINESS AND INVOLUNTARY CONVERSIONS FROM OTHER THAN CASUALTY OR THEFT – MOST PROPERTY HELD MORE THAN 1 YEAR

Part I is used to report section 1231 gains and losses.

## PART II – ORDINARY GAINS AND LOSSES

Part II is used to report the sale of short term business-use property. Also, Part II will be used to report section 1245, section 1250, and section 1231 transactions that are treated as ordinary income or losses.

## PART III – GAIN FROM DISPOSITION OF PROPERTY UNDER SECTIONS 1245, 1250, 1252, 1254, AND 1255

Part III is used to calculate the part of the gain subject to recapture provisions. We've already discussed sections 1245 and 1250 property. Now, we will briefly discuss the other properties listed in this section.

**Section 1252 property** – If the taxpayer disposed of farmland held more than 1 year and less than 10 years at a gain, and he or she was allowed deductions for soil and water conservation expenses for land, part of the gain must be treated as ordinary income.

**Section 1254 property** – If the taxpayer had a gain on the disposition of oil, gas, geothermal, or other mineral properties placed in service after 1986, all expenses that were deducted as intangible drilling costs, depletion, mine exploration costs, and development costs must be recaptured.

**Section 1255 property** – If the taxpayer receives certain cost-sharing payments on property and they exclude those payments from income, they may have to treat part of any gain as ordinary income and treat the balance as a section 1231 gain.

The hardest part of filling out the Form 4797 is to understand the flow of the form. It is generally not completed sequentially. Illustration 2 is a flow chart to help you know where to start.

Illustration 1

<table>
<tr><td>Form 4797</td><td colspan="2">Sales of Business Property<br>(Also Involuntary Conversions and Recapture Amounts<br>Under Sections 179 and 280F(b)(2))<br>▶ Attach to your tax return.    ▶ See separate instructions.</td><td>OMB No. 1545-0184<br>2011</td></tr>
<tr><td>Department of the Treasury<br>Internal Revenue Service   (99)</td><td colspan="2"></td><td>Attachment<br>Sequence No. 27</td></tr>
<tr><td colspan="3">Name(s) shown on return</td><td>Identifying number</td></tr>
</table>

| | |
|---|---|
| **1** Enter the gross proceeds from sales or exchanges reported to you for 2011 on Form(s) 1099-B or 1099-S (or substitute statement) that you are including on line 2, 10, or 20 (see instructions) . . . . . . . . | **1** |

**Part I**   **Sales or Exchanges of Property Used in a Trade or Business and Involuntary Conversions From Other Than Casualty or Theft—Most Property Held More Than 1 Year** (see instructions)

| **2** | **(a)** Description of property | **(b)** Date acquired (mo., day, yr.) | **(c)** Date sold (mo., day, yr.) | **(d)** Gross sales price | **(e)** Depreciation allowed or allowable since acquisition | **(f)** Cost or other basis, plus improvements and expense of sale | **(g) Gain or (loss)** Subtract (f) from the sum of (d) and (e) |
|---|---|---|---|---|---|---|---|
| | | | | | | | |
| | | | | | | | |
| | | | | | | | |
| | | | | | | | |

| | | |
|---|---|---|
| **3** Gain, if any, from Form 4684, line 39 . . . . . . . . . . . . . . . . . | **3** | |
| **4** Section 1231 gain from installment sales from Form 6252, line 26 or 37 . . . . . . . . . | **4** | |
| **5** Section 1231 gain or (loss) from like-kind exchanges from Form 8824 . . . . . . . . . | **5** | |
| **6** Gain, if any, from line 32, from other than casualty or theft. . . . . . . . . . . | **6** | |
| **7** Combine lines 2 through 6. Enter the gain or (loss) here and on the appropriate line as follows: . . . . . . . | **7** | |

**Partnerships (except electing large partnerships) and S corporations.** Report the gain or (loss) following the instructions for Form 1065, Schedule K, line 10, or Form 1120S, Schedule K, line 9. Skip lines 8, 9, 11, and 12 below.

**Individuals, partners, S corporation shareholders, and all others.** If line 7 is zero or a loss, enter the amount from line 7 on line 11 below and skip lines 8 and 9. If line 7 is a gain and you did not have any prior year section 1231 losses, or they were recaptured in an earlier year, enter the gain from line 7 as a long-term capital gain on the Schedule D filed with your return and skip lines 8, 9, 11, and 12 below.

| | | |
|---|---|---|
| **8** Nonrecaptured net section 1231 losses from prior years (see instructions) . . . . . . . . . | **8** | |
| **9** Subtract line 8 from line 7. If zero or less, enter -0-. If line 9 is zero, enter the gain from line 7 on line 12 below. If line 9 is more than zero, enter the amount from line 8 on line 12 below and enter the gain from line 9 as a long-term capital gain on the Schedule D filed with your return (see instructions) . . . . . . . . . . . | **9** | |

**Part II**   **Ordinary Gains and Losses** (see instructions)

**10** Ordinary gains and losses not included on lines 11 through 16 (include property held 1 year or less):

| | | | | | | |
|---|---|---|---|---|---|---|
| | | | | | | |
| | | | | | | |
| | | | | | | |

| | | |
|---|---|---|
| **11** Loss, if any, from line 7 . . . . . . . . . . . . . . . . . . . . | **11** | (      ) |
| **12** Gain, if any, from line 7 or amount from line 8, if applicable . . . . . . . . . . | **12** | |
| **13** Gain, if any, from line 31 . . . . . . . . . . . . . . . . . . . | **13** | |
| **14** Net gain or (loss) from Form 4684, lines 31 and 38a . . . . . . . . . . . | **14** | |
| **15** Ordinary gain from installment sales from Form 6252, line 25 or 36 . . . . . . . . | **15** | |
| **16** Ordinary gain or (loss) from like-kind exchanges from Form 8824. . . . . . . . . | **16** | |
| **17** Combine lines 10 through 16 . . . . . . . . . . . . . . . . . | **17** | |

**18** For all except individual returns, enter the amount from line 17 on the appropriate line of your return and skip lines a and b below. For individual returns, complete lines a and b below:

| | | |
|---|---|---|
| **a** If the loss on line 11 includes a loss from Form 4684, line 35, column (b)(ii), enter that part of the loss here. Enter the part of the loss from income-producing property on Schedule A (Form 1040), line 28, and the part of the loss from property used as an employee on Schedule A (Form 1040), line 23. Identify as from "Form 4797, line 18a." See instructions . . | **18a** | |
| **b** Redetermine the gain or (loss) on line 17 excluding the loss, if any, on line 18a. Enter here and on Form 1040, line 14 | **18b** | |

**For Paperwork Reduction Act Notice, see separate instructions.**     Cat. No. 13086I     Form **4797** (2011)

Illustration 1 continued

**Part III** **Gain From Disposition of Property Under Sections 1245, 1250, 1252, 1254, and 1255** (see instructions)

| 19 | (a) Description of section 1245, 1250, 1252, 1254, or 1255 property: | | (b) Date acquired (mo., day, yr.) | (c) Date sold (mo., day, yr.) |
|---|---|---|---|---|
| A | | | | |
| B | | | | |
| C | | | | |
| D | | | | |

| | These columns relate to the properties on lines 19A through 19D. ▶ | | Property A | Property B | Property C | Property D |
|---|---|---|---|---|---|---|
| 20 | Gross sales price (**Note:** See line 1 before completing.) | 20 | | | | |
| 21 | Cost or other basis plus expense of sale | 21 | | | | |
| 22 | Depreciation (or depletion) allowed or allowable | 22 | | | | |
| 23 | Adjusted basis. Subtract line 22 from line 21 | 23 | | | | |
| 24 | Total gain. Subtract line 23 from line 20 | 24 | | | | |
| 25 | **If section 1245 property:** | | | | | |
| a | Depreciation allowed or allowable from line 22 | 25a | | | | |
| b | Enter the **smaller** of line 24 or 25a | 25b | | | | |
| 26 | **If section 1250 property:** If straight line depreciation was used, enter -0- on line 26g, except for a corporation subject to section 291. | | | | | |
| a | Additional depreciation after 1975 (see instructions) | 26a | | | | |
| b | Applicable percentage multiplied by the **smaller** of line 24 or line 26a (see instructions) | 26b | | | | |
| c | Subtract line 26a from line 24. If residential rental property or line 24 is not more than line 26a, skip lines 26d and 26e | 26c | | | | |
| d | Additional depreciation after 1969 and before 1976 | 26d | | | | |
| e | Enter the **smaller** of line 26c or 26d | 26e | | | | |
| f | Section 291 amount (corporations only) | 26f | | | | |
| g | Add lines 26b, 26e, and 26f | 26g | | | | |
| 27 | **If section 1252 property:** Skip this section if you did not dispose of farmland or if this form is being completed for a partnership (other than an electing large partnership). | | | | | |
| a | Soil, water, and land clearing expenses | 27a | | | | |
| b | Line 27a multiplied by applicable percentage (see instructions) | 27b | | | | |
| c | Enter the **smaller** of line 24 or 27b | 27c | | | | |
| 28 | **If section 1254 property:** | | | | | |
| a | Intangible drilling and development costs, expenditures for development of mines and other natural deposits, mining exploration costs, and depletion (see instructions) | 28a | | | | |
| b | Enter the **smaller** of line 24 or 28a | 28b | | | | |
| 29 | **If section 1255 property:** | | | | | |
| a | Applicable percentage of payments excluded from income under section 126 (see instructions) | 29a | | | | |
| b | Enter the **smaller** of line 24 or 29a (see instructions) | 29b | | | | |

**Summary of Part III Gains.** Complete property columns A through D through line 29b before going to line 30.

| | | | |
|---|---|---|---|
| 30 | Total gains for all properties. Add property columns A through D, line 24 | 30 | |
| 31 | Add property columns A through D, lines 25b, 26g, 27c, 28b, and 29b. Enter here and on line 13 | 31 | |
| 32 | Subtract line 31 from line 30. Enter the portion from casualty or theft on Form 4684, line 33. Enter the portion from other than casualty or theft on Form 4797, line 6 | 32 | |

**Part IV** **Recapture Amounts Under Sections 179 and 280F(b)(2) When Business Use Drops to 50% or Less** (see instructions)

| | | | (a) Section 179 | (b) Section 280F(b)(2) |
|---|---|---|---|---|
| 33 | Section 179 expense deduction or depreciation allowable in prior years | 33 | | |
| 34 | Recomputed depreciation (see instructions) | 34 | | |
| 35 | Recapture amount. Subtract line 34 from line 33. See the instructions for where to report | 35 | | |

Form **4797** (2011)

Illustration 2

# Completing Form 4797

**Example:** Megan Sharp (221-53-9232) owns and operates her own business. In 2011, she sold an office building and two pieces of equipment. The details of those properties follow:

Megan purchased the office building and placed it in service on May 15, 2007. She paid $83,000, including $11,500 for the land. She claimed MACRS depreciation of $1,148 for 2007, $1,833 for 2008, $1,833 for 2009, and $1,833 for 2010. In 2011, the depreciation deduction is $382 (the full year deduction of $1,833 multiplied by $2.5/_{12}$). She sold the office building and land for $125,300. She paid $2,850 in sales expenses.

Equipment 1 was purchased and placed in service on January 12, 2009 for $23,600. She claimed a section 179 deduction of $8,600. The equipment is 5 year property. Her depreciation deductions were $3,000 for 2009, $4,800 for 2010, and $1,440 for 2011 (half the year's deduction). She sold it on April 23, 2011 for $43,000. Her expense of sale was $200.

Equipment 2 was purchased on August 9, 2007 for $32,500. Her depreciation deductions were $6,500 for 2007, $10,400 for 2008, $6,240 for 2009, $3,744 for 2010, and $1,872 for 2011. She sold the equipment on February 19, 2011 for $14,500. Her expense of sale was $350.

The information needed to complete the rest of the return is that she made net business income of $83,986. Her SE tax is $10,316, giving her an adjustment of $5,933. She, also, claimed a section 1231 loss of $5,230 on her 2010 tax return. She is single and claiming the standard deduction. She paid estimated taxes of $41,000. Forms to complete this example are included in the back of the book. Because it is so complex, it is recommended you complete the return with the example to help you understand the forms.

> **Notes:** The land and the office building must be treated as separate properties. Remember to prorate the sales price and expense.

When doing the Form 4797, use the flow chart. You will begin with listing the properties on Parts I, II, or III, whichever is applicable. Then, calculate the sections 1245 and 1250 recaptures by completing Part III, and carry them to Part II. The gain after recapture will be carried to Part I. Complete Part I next, and carry the gains or losses to the correct forms. Finally, complete Part II, and carry the gains or losses to the Form 1040. Illustration 3 shows all of the completed forms.

Illustration 3

<table>
<tr><td colspan="3">Form 1040</td><td>Department of the Treasury—Internal Revenue Service (99)</td><td colspan="2">2011</td><td colspan="2">OMB No. 1545-0074</td><td>IRS Use Only—Do not write or staple in this space.</td></tr>
<tr><td colspan="3"></td><td colspan="5">U.S. Individual Income Tax Return</td><td></td></tr>
</table>

| For the year Jan. 1–Dec. 31, 2011, or other tax year beginning | , 2011, ending | , 20 | See separate instructions. |
|---|---|---|---|

| Your first name and initial | Last name | Your social security number |
|---|---|---|
| Megan | Sharp | 2 2 1 5 3 9 2 3 2 |

| If a joint return, spouse's first name and initial | Last name | Spouse's social security number |
|---|---|---|
| | | |

Home address (number and street). If you have a P.O. box, see instructions. | Apt. no.

100 Pine St

▲ Make sure the SSN(s) above and on line 6c are correct.

City, town or post office, state, and ZIP code. If you have a foreign address, also complete spaces below (see instructions).

Your City, Your State, Your Zip Code

**Presidential Election Campaign**
Check here if you, or your spouse if filing jointly, want $3 to go to this fund. Checking a box below will not change your tax or refund. ☐ You ☐ Spouse

| Foreign country name | Foreign province/county | Foreign postal code |
|---|---|---|
| | | |

**Filing Status**

Check only one box.

1. ☑ Single
2. ☐ Married filing jointly (even if only one had income)
3. ☐ Married filing separately. Enter spouse's SSN above and full name here. ▶
4. ☐ Head of household (with qualifying person). (See instructions.) If the qualifying person is a child but not your dependent, enter this child's name here. ▶
5. ☐ Qualifying widow(er) with dependent child

**Exemptions**

6a ☐ **Yourself.** If someone can claim you as a dependent, **do not** check box 6a . . . . .
b ☐ **Spouse** . . . . . . . . . . . . . . . .

| c **Dependents:** | | (2) Dependent's social security number | (3) Dependent's relationship to you | (4) ✓ if child under age 17 qualifying for child tax credit (see instructions) |
|---|---|---|---|---|
| (1) First name | Last name | | | ☐ |
| | | | | ☐ |
| | | | | ☐ |
| | | | | ☐ |

If more than four dependents, see instructions and check here ▶ ☐

d Total number of exemptions claimed . . . . . . . . . . . . . . .

Boxes checked on 6a and 6b **1**
No. of children on 6c who:
• lived with you
• did not live with you due to divorce or separation (see instructions)
Dependents on 6c not entered above
Add numbers on lines above ▶ **1**

**Income**

Attach Form(s) W-2 here. Also attach Forms W-2G and 1099-R if tax was withheld.

If you did not get a W-2, see instructions.

Enclose, but do not attach, any payment. Also, please use Form 1040-V.

| 7 | Wages, salaries, tips, etc. Attach Form(s) W-2 . . . . . . . . | 7 | | |
|---|---|---|---|---|
| 8a | **Taxable** interest. Attach Schedule B if required . . . . . . | 8a | | |
| b | **Tax-exempt** interest. **Do not** include on line 8a . . | 8b | | | |
| 9a | Ordinary dividends. Attach Schedule B if required . . . . . | 9a | | |
| b | Qualified dividends . . . . . . | 9b | | | |
| 10 | Taxable refunds, credits, or offsets of state and local income taxes . . . . . | 10 | | |
| 11 | Alimony received . . . . . . . . . . . . . . | 11 | | |
| 12 | Business income or (loss). Attach Schedule C or C-EZ . . . . . . | 12 | 83,986 | 00 |
| 13 | Capital gain or (loss). Attach Schedule D if required. If not required, check here ▶ ☐ | 13 | 60,449 | 00 |
| 14 | Other gains or (losses). Attach Form 4797 . . . . . . . | 14 | 33,476 | 00 |
| 15a | IRA distributions . | 15a | | b Taxable amount . . . | 15b | | |
| 16a | Pensions and annuities | 16a | | b Taxable amount . . . | 16b | | |
| 17 | Rental real estate, royalties, partnerships, S corporations, trusts, etc. Attach Schedule E | 17 | | |
| 18 | Farm income or (loss). Attach Schedule F . . . . . . . . | 18 | | |
| 19 | Unemployment compensation . . . . . . . . . . | 19 | | |
| 20a | Social security benefits | 20a | | b Taxable amount . . . | 20b | | |
| 21 | Other income. List type and amount | 21 | | |
| 22 | Combine the amounts in the far right column for lines 7 through 21. This is your **total income** ▶ | 22 | 177,911 | 00 |

**Adjusted Gross Income**

| 23 | Educator expenses . . . . . . . . . . | 23 | | |
|---|---|---|---|---|
| 24 | Certain business expenses of reservists, performing artists, and fee-basis government officials. Attach Form 2106 or 2106-EZ | 24 | | |
| 25 | Health savings account deduction. Attach Form 8889 | 25 | | |
| 26 | Moving expenses. Attach Form 3903 . . . . . . | 26 | | |
| 27 | Deductible part of self-employment tax. Attach Schedule SE | 27 | 5,933 | 00 |
| 28 | Self-employed SEP, SIMPLE, and qualified plans . . | 28 | | |
| 29 | Self-employed health insurance deduction . . . . | 29 | | |
| 30 | Penalty on early withdrawal of savings . . . . . | 30 | | |
| 31a | Alimony paid **b** Recipient's SSN ▶ | 31a | | |
| 32 | IRA deduction . . . . . . . . . . | 32 | | |
| 33 | Student loan interest deduction . . . . . . . | 33 | | |
| 34 | Tuition and fees. Attach Form 8917 . . . . . . | 34 | | |
| 35 | Domestic production activities deduction. Attach Form 8903 | 35 | | |
| 36 | Add lines 23 through 35 . . . . . . . . . . | 36 | 5,933 | 00 |
| 37 | Subtract line 36 from line 22. This is your **adjusted gross income** . . . . . ▶ | 37 | 171,978 | 00 |

**For Disclosure, Privacy Act, and Paperwork Reduction Act Notice, see separate instructions.**    Cat. No. 11320B    Form **1040** (2011)

## Illustration 3

| | | | | | |
|---|---|---|---|---|---|
| **Tax and Credits** | 38 | Amount from line 37 (adjusted gross income) . . . . . . . . . . . | 38 | 171,978 | 00 |

| | | |
|---|---|---|
| 39a | Check if: ☐ **You** were born before January 2, 1947, ☐ Blind. ☐ **Spouse** was born before January 2, 1947, ☐ Blind. } Total boxes checked ▶ 39a | |

b  If your spouse itemizes on a separate return or you were a dual-status alien, check here▶ 39b ☐

**Standard Deduction for—**

- People who check any box on line 39a or 39b **or** who can be claimed as a dependent, see instructions.
- All others:

Single or Married filing separately, $5,800

Married filing jointly or Qualifying widow(er), $11,600

Head of household, $8,500

| # | Description | Line | Amount | |
|---|---|---|---|---|
| 40 | **Itemized deductions** (from Schedule A) **or** your **standard deduction** (see left margin) . . | 40 | 5,800 | 00 |
| 41 | Subtract line 40 from line 38 . . . . . . . . . . . . . . . | 41 | 166,178 | 00 |
| 42 | **Exemptions.** Multiply $3,700 by the number on line 6d . . . . . . . . | 42 | 3,700 | 00 |
| 43 | **Taxable income.** Subtract line 42 from line 41. If line 42 is more than line 41, enter -0- . . | 43 | 162,478 | 00 |
| 44 | **Tax** (see instructions). Check if any from: **a** ☐ Form(s) 8814 **b** ☐ Form 4972 **c** ☐ 962 election | 44 | 31,428 | 00 |
| 45 | **Alternative minimum tax** (see instructions). Attach Form 6251 . . . . . . . . | 45 | | |
| 46 | Add lines 44 and 45 . . . . . . . . . . . . . . . . ▶ | 46 | 31,428 | 00 |

| # | Description | Line | Value | | |
|---|---|---|---|---|---|
| 47 | Foreign tax credit. Attach Form 1116 if required . . . . | 47 | | | |
| 48 | Credit for child and dependent care expenses. Attach Form 2441 | 48 | | | |
| 49 | Education credits from Form 8863, line 23 . . . . . . | 49 | | | |
| 50 | Retirement savings contributions credit. Attach Form 8880 | 50 | | | |
| 51 | Child tax credit (see instructions) . . . . . . . . | 51 | | | |
| 52 | Residential energy credits. Attach Form 5695 . . . . | 52 | | | |
| 53 | Other credits from Form: **a** ☐ 3800 **b** ☐ 8801 **c** ☐ | 53 | | | |
| 54 | Add lines 47 through 53. These are your **total credits** . . . . . . . . | 54 | | | |
| 55 | Subtract line 54 from line 46. If line 54 is more than line 46, enter -0- . . . . . ▶ | 55 | 31,428 | 00 |

| | | | | | |
|---|---|---|---|---|---|
| **Other Taxes** | 56 | Self-employment tax. Attach Schedule SE . . . . . . . . | 56 | 10,316 | 00 |
| | 57 | Unreported social security and Medicare tax from Form: **a** ☐ 4137 **b** ☐ 8919 . . | 57 | | |
| | 58 | Additional tax on IRAs, other qualified retirement plans, etc. Attach Form 5329 if required . . | 58 | | |
| | 59a | Household employment taxes from Schedule H . . . . . . . . . | 59a | | |
| | b | First-time homebuyer credit repayment. Attach Form 5405 if required . . . . . . | 59b | | |
| | 60 | Other taxes. Enter code(s) from instructions | 60 | | |
| | 61 | Add lines 55 through 60. This is your **total tax** . . . . . . . . . . ▶ | 61 | 41,744 | 00 |

**Payments**

If you have a qualifying child, attach Schedule EIC.

| # | Description | Line | Value | | |
|---|---|---|---|---|---|
| 62 | Federal income tax withheld from Forms W-2 and 1099 . . | 62 | | | |
| 63 | 2011 estimated tax payments and amount applied from 2010 return | 63 | 41,000 | 00 | |
| 64a | **Earned income credit (EIC)** . . . . . . . . | 64a | | | |
| b | Nontaxable combat pay election    64b | | | | |
| 65 | Additional child tax credit. Attach Form 8812 . . . . . | 65 | | | |
| 66 | American opportunity credit from Form 8863, line 14 . . . | 66 | | | |
| 67 | First-time homebuyer credit from Form 5405, line 10 . . . | 67 | | | |
| 68 | Amount paid with request for extension to file . . . . . | 68 | | | |
| 69 | Excess social security and tier 1 RRTA tax withheld . . . . | 69 | | | |
| 70 | Credit for federal tax on fuels. Attach Form 4136 . . . . | 70 | | | |
| 71 | Credits from Form: **a** ☐ 2439 **b** ☐ 8839 **c** ☐ 8801 **d** ☐ 8885 | 71 | | | |
| 72 | Add lines 62, 63, 64a, and 65 through 71. These are your **total payments** . . . . . ▶ | 72 | 41,000 | 00 |

| | | | | | |
|---|---|---|---|---|---|
| **Refund** | 73 | If line 72 is more than line 61, subtract line 61 from line 72. This is the amount you **overpaid** | 73 | | |
| | 74a | Amount of line 73 you want **refunded to you.** If Form 8888 is attached, check here . . ▶ ☐ | 74a | | |

Direct deposit? See instructions.

| | | |
|---|---|---|
| ▶ b | Routing number | ▶ c Type: ☐ Checking ☐ Savings |
| ▶ d | Account number | |
| 75 | Amount of line 73 you want **applied to your 2012 estimated tax** ▶ 75 | |

| | | | | | |
|---|---|---|---|---|---|
| **Amount You Owe** | 76 | **Amount you owe.** Subtract line 72 from line 61. For details on how to pay, see instructions ▶ | 76 | 744 | 00 |
| | 77 | Estimated tax penalty (see instructions) . . . . . . . . 77 | | | |

**Third Party Designee**

Do you want to allow another person to discuss this return with the IRS (see instructions)?  ☐ **Yes.** Complete below.  ☐ **No**

| Designee's name ▶ | Phone no. ▶ | Personal identification number (PIN) ▶ |
|---|---|---|

**Sign Here**

Under penalties of perjury, I declare that I have examined this return and accompanying schedules and statements, and to the best of my knowledge and belief, they are true, correct, and complete. Declaration of preparer (other than taxpayer) is based on all information of which preparer has any knowledge.

Joint return? See instructions. Keep a copy for your records.

| Your signature | Date | Your occupation  Sole Proprietor | Daytime phone number |
|---|---|---|---|
| Spouse's signature. If a joint return, **both** must sign. | Date | Spouse's occupation | If the IRS sent you an Identity Protection PIN, enter it here (see inst.) |

**Paid Preparer Use Only**

| Print/Type preparer's name  Jane Doe | Preparer's signature | Date | Check ☐ if self-employed | PTIN  P00000000 |
|---|---|---|---|---|
| Firm's name ▶ My Tax Service | | | Firm's EIN ▶ | 63-5555555 |
| Firm's address ▶ 100 Main St., Your City, Your State, Your Zip Code | | | Phone no. | (555)555-5555 |

Form **1040** (2011)

Illustration 3 continued

| SCHEDULE D<br>(Form 1040) | Capital Gains and Losses | OMB No. 1545-0074 |
|---|---|---|
| Department of the Treasury<br>Internal Revenue Service (99) | ▶ Attach to Form 1040 or Form 1040NR. ▶ See Instructions for Schedule D (Form 1040).<br>▶ Use Form 8949 to list your transactions for lines 1, 2, 3, 8, 9, and 10. | 2011<br>Attachment<br>Sequence No. 12 |

| Name(s) shown on return | Your social security number |
|---|---|
| Megan Sharp | 221-53-9232 |

## Part I — Short-Term Capital Gains and Losses—Assets Held One Year or Less

| Complete Form 8949 before completing line 1, 2, or 3.<br>This form may be easier to complete if you round off cents to whole dollars. | (e) Sales price from Form(s) 8949, line 2, column (e) | (f) Cost or other basis from Form(s) 8949, line 2, column (f) | (g) Adjustments to gain or loss from Form(s) 8949, line 2, column (g) | (h) Gain or (loss) Combine columns (e), (f), and (g) |
|---|---|---|---|---|
| 1 Short-term totals from all Forms 8949 with **box A** checked in **Part I** . . . . . . . . . . . . . . . . | | ( ) | | |
| 2 Short-term totals from all Forms 8949 with **box B** checked in **Part I** . . . . . . . . . . . . . . . . | | ( ) | | |
| 3 Short-term totals from all Forms 8949 with **box C** checked in **Part I** . . . . . . . . . . . . . . . . | | ( ) | | |

| | | |
|---|---|---|
| 4 Short-term gain from Form 6252 and short-term gain or (loss) from Forms 4684, 6781, and 8824 . | **4** | |
| 5 Net short-term gain or (loss) from partnerships, S corporations, estates, and trusts from Schedule(s) K-1 . . . . . . . . . . . . . . . . . . . . . . . | **5** | |
| 6 Short-term capital loss carryover. Enter the amount, if any, from line 8 of your **Capital Loss Carryover Worksheet** in the instructions . . . . . . . . . . . . . . . | **6** | ( ) |
| 7 **Net short-term capital gain or (loss).** Combine lines 1 through 6 in column (h). If you have any long-term capital gains or losses, go to Part II below. Otherwise, go to Part III on the back . . . | **7** | |

## Part II — Long-Term Capital Gains and Losses—Assets Held More Than One Year

| Complete Form 8949 before completing line 8, 9, or 10.<br>This form may be easier to complete if you round off cents to whole dollars. | (e) Sales price from Form(s) 8949, line 4, column (e) | (f) Cost or other basis from Form(s) 8949, line 4, column (f) | (g) Adjustments to gain or loss from Form(s) 8949, line 4, column (g) | (h) Gain or (loss) Combine columns (e), (f), and (g) |
|---|---|---|---|---|
| 8 Long-term totals from all Forms 8949 with **box A** checked in **Part II** . . . . . . . . . . . . . . . | | ( ) | | |
| 9 Long-term totals from all Forms 8949 with **box B** checked in **Part II** . . . . . . . . . . . . . . . | | ( ) | | |
| 10 Long-term totals from all Forms 8949 with **box C** checked in **Part II** . . . . . . . . . . . . . . . | | ( ) | | |

| | | |
|---|---|---|
| 11 Gain from Form 4797, Part I; long-term gain from Forms 2439 and 6252; and long-term gain or (loss) from Forms 4684, 6781, and 8824 . . . . . . . . . . . . . . . . | **11** | 60,449 |
| 12 Net long-term gain or (loss) from partnerships, S corporations, estates, and trusts from Schedule(s) K-1 | **12** | |
| 13 Capital gain distributions. See the instructions . . . . . . . . . . . . . . . | **13** | |
| 14 Long-term capital loss carryover. Enter the amount, if any, from line 13 of your **Capital Loss Carryover Worksheet** in the instructions . . . . . . . . . . . . . . . | **14** | ( ) |
| 15 **Net long-term capital gain or (loss).** Combine lines 8 through 14 in column (h). Then go to Part III on the back . . . . . . . . . . . . . . . . . . . . . . . | **15** | 60,449 |

For Paperwork Reduction Act Notice, see your tax return instructions.　　Cat. No. 11338H　　**Schedule D (Form 1040) 2011**

91

## Illustration 3 continued

| **Part III** | **Summary** |

| | | | |
|---|---|---|---|
| **16** | Combine lines 7 and 15 and enter the result . . . . . . . . . . . . . . . . . . . | **16** | 60,449 |

      • If line 16 is a **gain**, enter the amount from line 16 on Form 1040, line 13, or Form 1040NR, line 14. Then go to line 17 below.

      • If line 16 is a **loss**, skip lines 17 through 20 below. Then go to line 21. Also be sure to complete line 22.

      • If line 16 is **zero**, skip lines 17 through 21 below and enter -0- on Form 1040, line 13, or Form 1040NR, line 14. Then go to line 22.

**17**   Are lines 15 and 16 **both** gains?

    ☑ **Yes.** Go to line 18.

    ☐ **No.** Skip lines 18 through 21, and go to line 22.

| | | | |
|---|---|---|---|
| **18** | Enter the amount, if any, from line 7 of the **28% Rate Gain Worksheet** in the instructions . . ▶ | **18** | |
| **19** | Enter the amount, if any, from line 18 of the **Unrecaptured Section 1250 Gain Worksheet** in the instructions . . . . . . . . . . . . . . . . . . . . . . . . ▶ | **19** | 1,799 |

**20**   Are lines 18 and 19 **both** zero or blank?

    ☐ **Yes.** Complete Form 1040 through line 43, or Form 1040NR through line 41. Then complete the **Qualified Dividends and Capital Gain Tax Worksheet** in the instructions for Form 1040, line 44 (or in the instructions for Form 1040NR, line 42). **Do not** complete lines 21 and 22 below.

    ☑ **No.** Complete Form 1040 through line 43, or Form 1040NR through line 41. Then complete the **Schedule D Tax Worksheet** in the instructions. **Do not** complete lines 21 and 22 below.

| | | | |
|---|---|---|---|
| **21** | If line 16 is a loss, enter here and on Form 1040, line 13, or Form 1040NR, line 14, the **smaller** of: | | |
| | • The loss on line 16 or    } . . . . . . . . . . . . . . . . . | **21** | ( ) |
| | • ($3,000), or if married filing separately, ($1,500) } | | |

    **Note.** When figuring which amount is smaller, treat both amounts as positive numbers.

**22**   Do you have qualified dividends on Form 1040, line 9b, or Form 1040NR, line 10b?

    ☐ **Yes.** Complete Form 1040 through line 43, or Form 1040NR through line 41. Then complete the **Qualified Dividends and Capital Gain Tax Worksheet** in the instructions for Form 1040, line 44 (or in the instructions for Form 1040NR, line 42).

    ☐ **No.** Complete the rest of Form 1040 or Form 1040NR.

Illustration 3 continued

| Form **4797** | **Sales of Business Property** | OMB No. 1545-0184 |
|---|---|---|
| Department of the Treasury<br>Internal Revenue Service (99) | (Also Involuntary Conversions and Recapture Amounts<br>Under Sections 179 and 280F(b)(2))<br>▶ Attach to your tax return. ▶ See separate instructions. | **20**11<br>Attachment<br>Sequence No. **27** |

| Name(s) shown on return | Identifying number |
|---|---|
| Megan Sharp | 221-53-9232 |

**1** Enter the gross proceeds from sales or exchanges reported to you for 2011 on Form(s) 1099-B or 1099-S (or substitute statement) that you are including on line 2, 10, or 20 (see instructions) . . . . . . . . | **1** |

**Part I** **Sales or Exchanges of Property Used in a Trade or Business and Involuntary Conversions From Other Than Casualty or Theft—Most Property Held More Than 1 Year** (see instructions)

| 2 | **(a)** Description of property | **(b)** Date acquired (mo., day, yr.) | **(c)** Date sold (mo., day, yr.) | **(d)** Gross sales price | **(e)** Depreciation allowed or allowable since acquisition | **(f)** Cost or other basis, plus improvements and expense of sale | **(g)** Gain or (loss) Subtract (f) from the sum of (d) and (e) |
|---|---|---|---|---|---|---|---|
| | Land | 05-15-07 | 03-06-11 | 17,367 | | 11,895 | 5,472 |
| | | | | | | | |
| | | | | | | | |
| | | | | | | | |

| | | |
|---|---|---|
| **3** Gain, if any, from Form 4684, line 39 . . . . . . . . . . . . . . . . . . . . . | **3** | |
| **4** Section 1231 gain from installment sales from Form 6252, line 26 or 37 . . . . . . . . . | **4** | |
| **5** Section 1231 gain or (loss) from like-kind exchanges from Form 8824 . . . . . . . . . | **5** | |
| **6** Gain, if any, from line 32, from other than casualty or theft. . . . . . . . . . . . . | **6** | 60,207 |
| **7** Combine lines 2 through 6. Enter the gain or (loss) here and on the appropriate line as follows: . . . . . . . | **7** | 65,679 |

**Partnerships (except electing large partnerships) and S corporations.** Report the gain or (loss) following the instructions for Form 1065, Schedule K, line 10, or Form 1120S, Schedule K, line 9. Skip lines 8, 9, 11, and 12 below.

**Individuals, partners, S corporation shareholders, and all others.** If line 7 is zero or a loss, enter the amount from line 7 on line 11 below and skip lines 8 and 9. If line 7 is a gain and you did not have any prior year section 1231 losses, or they were recaptured in an earlier year, enter the gain from line 7 as a long-term capital gain on the Schedule D filed with your return and skip lines 8, 9, 11, and 12 below.

| | | |
|---|---|---|
| **8** Nonrecaptured net section 1231 losses from prior years (see instructions) . . . . . . . . . . | **8** | 5,230 |
| **9** Subtract line 8 from line 7. If zero or less, enter -0-. If line 9 is zero, enter the gain from line 7 on line 12 below. If line 9 is more than zero, enter the amount from line 8 on line 12 below and enter the gain from line 9 as a long-term capital gain on the Schedule D filed with your return (see instructions) . . . . . . . . . . . . . . . . . . | **9** | 60,449 |

**Part II** **Ordinary Gains and Losses** (see instructions)

**10** Ordinary gains and losses not included on lines 11 through 16 (include property held 1 year or less):

| | | | | | | |
|---|---|---|---|---|---|---|
| | | | | | | |
| | | | | | | |
| | | | | | | |
| | | | | | | |

| | | |
|---|---|---|
| **11** Loss, if any, from line 7 . . . . . . . . . . . . . . . . . . . . . . . . . . | **11** ( | ) |
| **12** Gain, if any, from line 7 or amount from line 8, if applicable . . . . . . . . . . . . . . | **12** | 5,230 |
| **13** Gain, if any, from line 31 . . . . . . . . . . . . . . . . . . . . . . . . . | **13** | 28,246 |
| **14** Net gain or (loss) from Form 4684, lines 31 and 38a . . . . . . . . . . . . . . . | **14** | |
| **15** Ordinary gain from installment sales from Form 6252, line 25 or 36 . . . . . . . . . . . | **15** | |
| **16** Ordinary gain or (loss) from like-kind exchanges from Form 8824. . . . . . . . . . . . | **16** | |
| **17** Combine lines 10 through 16 . . . . . . . . . . . . . . . . . . . . . . . . | **17** | 33,476 |

**18** For all except individual returns, enter the amount from line 17 on the appropriate line of your return and skip lines a and b below. For individual returns, complete lines a and b below:

**a** If the loss on line 11 includes a loss from Form 4684, line 35, column (b)(ii), enter that part of the loss here. Enter the part of the loss from income-producing property on Schedule A (Form 1040), line 28, and the part of the loss from property used as an employee on Schedule A (Form 1040), line 23. Identify as from "Form 4797, line 18a." See instructions . . | **18a** |

**b** Redetermine the gain or (loss) on line 17 excluding the loss, if any, on line 18a. Enter here and on Form 1040, line 14 | **18b** | 33,476 |

| For Paperwork Reduction Act Notice, see separate instructions. | Cat. No. 13086I | Form **4797** (2011) |
|---|---|---|

## Illustration 3 continued

**Part III**   Gain From Disposition of Property Under Sections 1245, 1250, 1252, 1254, and 1255 (see instructions)

| 19 | (a) Description of section 1245, 1250, 1252, 1254, or 1255 property: | (b) Date acquired (mo., day, yr.) | (c) Date sold (mo., day, yr.) |
|---|---|---|---|
| A | Office Building | 05-17-07 | 03-06-11 |
| B | Equipment 1 | 01-12-09 | 04-23-11 |
| C | Equipment 2 | 08-09-07 | 02-19-11 |
| D | | | |

| | These columns relate to the properties on lines 19A through 19D. ▶ | | Property A | Property B | Property C | Property D |
|---|---|---|---|---|---|---|
| 20 | Gross sales price (**Note:** *See line 1 before completing.*) | 20 | 107,933 | 43,000 | 14,500 | |
| 21 | Cost or other basis plus expense of sale | 21 | 73,955 | 23,800 | 32,850 | |
| 22 | Depreciation (or depletion) allowed or allowable | 22 | 7,029 | 17,840 | 28,756 | |
| 23 | Adjusted basis. Subtract line 22 from line 21 | 23 | 66,926 | 5,960 | 4,094 | |
| 24 | Total gain. Subtract line 23 from line 20 | 24 | 41,007 | 37,040 | 10,406 | |
| 25 | **If section 1245 property:** | | | | | |
| a | Depreciation allowed or allowable from line 22 | 25a | | 17,840 | 28,756 | |
| b | Enter the **smaller** of line 24 or 25a | 25b | | 17,840 | 10,406 | |
| 26 | **If section 1250 property:** If straight line depreciation was used, enter -0- on line 26g, except for a corporation subject to section 291. | | | | | |
| a | Additional depreciation after 1975 (see instructions) | 26a | | | | |
| b | Applicable percentage multiplied by the **smaller** of line 24 or line 26a (see instructions) | 26b | | | | |
| c | Subtract line 26a from line 24. If residential rental property **or** line 24 is not more than line 26a, skip lines 26d and 26e | 26c | | | | |
| d | Additional depreciation after 1969 and before 1976 | 26d | | | | |
| e | Enter the **smaller** of line 26c or 26d | 26e | | | | |
| f | Section 291 amount (corporations only) | 26f | | | | |
| g | Add lines 26b, 26e, and 26f | 26g | | | | |
| 27 | **If section 1252 property:** Skip this section if you did not dispose of farmland or if this form is being completed for a partnership (other than an electing large partnership). | | | | | |
| a | Soil, water, and land clearing expenses | 27a | | | | |
| b | Line 27a multiplied by applicable percentage (see instructions) | 27b | | | | |
| c | Enter the **smaller** of line 24 or 27b | 27c | | | | |
| 28 | **If section 1254 property:** | | | | | |
| a | Intangible drilling and development costs, expenditures for development of mines and other natural deposits, mining exploration costs, and depletion (see instructions) | 28a | | | | |
| b | Enter the **smaller** of line 24 or 28a | 28b | | | | |
| 29 | **If section 1255 property:** | | | | | |
| a | Applicable percentage of payments excluded from income under section 126 (see instructions) | 29a | | | | |
| b | Enter the **smaller** of line 24 or 29a (see instructions) | 29b | | | | |

**Summary of Part III Gains.** Complete property columns A through D through line 29b before going to line 30.

| 30 | Total gains for all properties. Add property columns A through D, line 24 | 30 | 88,453 |
|---|---|---|---|
| 31 | Add property columns A through D, lines 25b, 26g, 27c, 28b, and 29b. Enter here and on line 13 | 31 | 28,246 |
| 32 | Subtract line 31 from line 30. Enter the portion from casualty or theft on Form 4684, line 33. Enter the portion from other than casualty or theft on Form 4797, line 6 | 32 | 60,207 |

**Part IV**   Recapture Amounts Under Sections 179 and 280F(b)(2) When Business Use Drops to 50% or Less (see instructions)

| | | | (a) Section 179 | (b) Section 280F(b)(2) |
|---|---|---|---|---|
| 33 | Section 179 expense deduction or depreciation allowable in prior years | 33 | | |
| 34 | Recomputed depreciation (see instructions) | 34 | | |
| 35 | Recapture amount. Subtract line 34 from line 33. See the instructions for where to report | 35 | | |

Form **4797** (2011)

Illustration 3 continued

## Unrecaptured Section 1250 Gain Worksheet—Line 19

*Keep for Your Records*

**If you are not reporting a gain on Form 4797, line 7, skip lines 1 through 9 and go to line 10.**

| | | |
|---|---|---|
| 1. If you have a section 1250 property in Part III of Form 4797 for which you made an entry in Part I of Form 4797 (but not on Form 6252), enter the **smaller** of line 22 or line 24 of Form 4797 for that property. If you did not have any such property, go to line 4. If you had more than one such property, see instructions . . . . . . . . . | **1.** | 7,029 |
| 2. Enter the amount from Form 4797, line 26g, for the property for which you made an entry on line 1 . . . . . . . | **2.** | |
| 3. Subtract line 2 from line 1 . . . . . . . . . . . . . . . . . . . . . . . . . . . . . . . . . . . . . . . . . . | **3.** | 7,029 |
| 4. Enter the total unrecaptured section 1250 gain included on line 26 or line 37 of Form(s) 6252 from installment sales of trade or business property held more than 1 year (see instructions) . . . . . . . . . . . . . . . . . . . . | **4.** | |
| 5. Enter the total of any amounts reported to you on a Schedule K-1 from a partnership or an S corporation as "unrecaptured section 1250 gain" . . . . . . . . . . . . . . . . . . . . . . . . . . . . . . . . . . . . . | **5.** | |
| 6. Add lines 3 through 5 . . . . . . . . . . . . . . . . . . . . . . . . . . . . . . . . . . . . . . . . . . . | **6.** | 7,029 |
| 7. Enter the **smaller** of line 6 or the gain from Form 4797, line 7 . . . . . . . . . . . . . . . . . . . **7.** 7,029 | | |
| 8. Enter the amount, if any, from Form 4797, line 8 . . . . . . . . . . . . . . . . . . . . . . . . . . **8.** 5,230 | | |
| 9. Subtract line 8 from line 7. If zero or less, enter -0- . . . . . . . . . . . . . . . . . . . . . . . . . . | **9.** | 1,799 |
| 10. Enter the amount of any gain from the sale or exchange of an interest in a partnership attributable to unrecaptured section 1250 gain (see instructions) . . . . . . . . . . . . . . . . . . . . . . . . . . . . . . . | **10.** | |
| 11. Enter the total of any amounts reported to you as "unrecaptured section 1250 gain" on a Schedule K-1, Form 1099-DIV, or Form 2439 from an estate, trust, real estate investment trust, or mutual fund (or other regulated investment company) or in connection with a Form 1099-R . . . . . . . . . . . . . . . . . . . . . . . . . . | **11.** | |
| 12. Enter the total of any unrecaptured section 1250 gain from sales (including installment sales) or other dispositions of section 1250 property held more than 1 year for which you did not make an entry in Part I of Form 4797 for the year of sale (see instructions) . . . . . . . . . . . . . . . . . . . . . . . . . . . . . . . | **12.** | |
| 13. Add lines 9 through 12 . . . . . . . . . . . . . . . . . . . . . . . . . . . . . . . . . . . . . . . . . | **13.** | 1,799 |
| 14. If you had any section 1202 gain or collectibles gain or (loss), enter the total of lines 1 through 4 of the **28% Rate Gain Worksheet**. Otherwise, enter -0- . . . . . . . . . . . . . . . **14.** | | |
| 15. Enter the (loss), if any, from Schedule D, line 7. If Schedule D, line 7, is zero or a gain, enter -0- . . . . . . . . . . . . . . . . . . . . . . . . . . . . . . . . . . . . . . . . . . . . . . **15.** ( ) | | |
| 16. Enter your long-term capital loss carryovers from Schedule D, line 14, and Schedule K-1 (Form 1041), box 11, code C* . . . . . . . . . . . . . . . . . . . . . . . . . . . . . **16.** ( ) | | |
| 17. Combine lines 14 through 16. If the result is a (loss), enter it as a positive amount. If the result is zero or a gain, enter -0- . . . . . . . . . . . . . . . . . . . . . . . . . . . . . . . . . . . . . . . . . . . . . . . . | **17.** | |
| 18. **Unrecaptured section 1250 gain.** Subtract line 17 from line 13. If zero or less, enter -0-. If more than zero, enter the result here and on Schedule D, line 19 . . . . . . . . . . . . . . . . . . . . . . . . . . . . . . . | **18.** | 1,799 |

*If you are filing Form 2555 or 2555-EZ (relating to foreign earned income), see the footnote in the Foreign Earned Income Tax Worksheet in the Form 1040 instructions before completing this line.

Illustration 3 continued

## Schedule D Tax Worksheet

*Keep for Your Records*

Complete this worksheet only if line 18 or line 19 of Schedule D is more than zero. Otherwise, complete the Qualified Dividends and Capital Gain Tax Worksheet in the Instructions for Form 1040, line 44 (or in the Instructions for Form 1040NR, line 42) to figure your tax.

**Exception: Do not** use the Qualified Dividends and Capital Gain Tax Worksheet **or** this worksheet to figure your tax if:
- Line 15 or line 16 of Schedule D is zero or less **and** you have no qualified dividends on Form 1040, line 9b (or Form 1040NR, line 10b); **or**
- Form 1040, line 43 (or Form 1040NR, line 41) is zero or less.

Instead, see the instructions for Form 1040, line 44 (or Form 1040NR, line 42).

| | | | |
|---|---|---|---|
| 1. | Enter your taxable income from Form 1040, line 43 (or Form 1040NR, line 41). (However, if you are filing Form 2555 or 2555-EZ (relating to foreign earned income), enter instead the amount from line 3 of the Foreign Earned Income Tax Worksheet in the Instructions for Form 1040, line 44) | 1. | 162,478 |
| 2. | Enter your qualified dividends from Form 1040, line 9b (or Form 1040NR, line 10b) ........ 2. **0** | | |
| 3. | Enter the amount from Form 4952 (used to figure investment interest expense deduction), line 4g ........ 3. **0** | | |
| 4. | Enter the amount from Form 4952, line 4e* 4. **0** | | |
| 5. | Subtract line 4 from line 3. If zero or less, enter -0- ........ 5. **0** | | |
| 6. | Subtract line 5 from line 2. If zero or less, enter -0-** ... 6. **0** | | |
| 7. | Enter the **smaller** of line 15 or line 16 of Schedule D ........ 7. **60,449** | | |
| 8. | Enter the **smaller** of line 3 or line 4 ........ 8. **0** | | |
| 9. | Subtract line 8 from line 7. If zero or less, enter -0-** ........ 9. **60,449** | | |
| 10. | Add lines 6 and 9 ........ 10. **60,449** | | |
| 11. | Add lines 18 and 19 of Schedule D** ........ 11. **1,799** | | |
| 12. | Enter the **smaller** of line 9 or line 11 ........ 12. **1,799** | | |
| 13. | Subtract line 12 from line 10 ........ | 13. | 58,650 |
| 14. | Subtract line 13 from line 1. If zero or less, enter -0- ........ | 14. | 103,828 |
| 15. | Enter: <br> • $34,500 if single or married filing separately; <br> • $69,000 if married filing jointly or qualifying widow(er); or <br> • $46,250 if head of household ........ 15. **34,500** | | |
| 16. | Enter the **smaller** of line 1 or line 15 ........ 16. **34,500** | | |
| 17. | Enter the **smaller** of line 14 or line 16 ........ 17. **34,500** | | |
| 18. | Subtract line 10 from line 1. If zero or less, enter -0- ........ 18. **102,029** | | |
| 19. | Enter the **larger** of line 17 or line 18 ........ ▶ 19. **102,029** | | |
| 20. | Subtract line 17 from line 16. This amount is taxed at 0%. ........ ▶ 20. **0** | | |
| | If lines 1 and 16 are the same, skip lines 21 through 33 and go to line 34. Otherwise, go to line 21. | | |
| 21. | Enter the **smaller** of line 1 or line 13 ........ 21. **58,650** | | |
| 22. | Enter the amount from line 20 (if line 20 is blank, enter -0-) ........ 22. **0** | | |
| 23. | Subtract line 22 from line 21. If zero or less, enter -0- ........ ▶ 23. **58,650** | | |
| 24. | Multiply line 23 by 15% (.15) ........ | 24. | 8,793 |
| | If Schedule D, line 19, is zero or blank, skip lines 25 through 30 and go to line 31. Otherwise, go to line 25. | | |
| 25. | Enter the **smaller** of line 9 above or Schedule D, line 19 ........ 25. **1,799** | | |
| 26. | Add lines 10 and 19 ........ 26. **162,478** | | |
| 27. | Enter the amount from line 1 above ........ 27. **162,478** | | |
| 28. | Subtract line 27 from line 26. If zero or less, enter -0- ........ 28. **0** | | |
| 29. | Subtract line 28 from line 25. If zero or less, enter -0- ........ ▶ 29. **1,799** | | |
| 30. | Multiply line 29 by 25% (.25) ........ | 30. | 450 |
| | If Schedule D, line 18, is zero or blank, skip lines 31 through 33 and go to line 34. Otherwise, go to line 31. | | |
| 31. | Add lines 19, 20, 23, and 29 ........ 31. | | |
| 32. | Subtract line 31 from line 1 ........ 32. | | |
| 33. | Multiply line 32 by 28% (.28) ........ | 33. | 22,185 |
| 34. | Figure the tax on the amount on **line 19**. If the amount on line 19 is less than $100,000, use the Tax Table to figure the tax. If the amount on line 19 is $100,000 or more, use the Tax Computation Worksheet ........ | 34. | |
| 35. | Add lines 24, 30, 33, and 34 ........ | 35. | 31,428 |
| 36. | Figure the tax on the amount on **line 1**. If the amount on line 1 is less than $100,000, use the Tax Table to figure the tax. If the amount on line 1 is $100,000 or more, use the Tax Computation Worksheet ........ | 36. | 39,111 |
| 37. | **Tax on all taxable income (including capital gains and qualified dividends).** Enter the **smaller** of line 35 or line 36. Also include this amount on Form 1040, line 44 (or Form 1040NR, line 42). (If you are filing Form 2555 or 2555-EZ, do not enter this amount on Form 1040, line 44. Instead, enter it on line 4 of the Foreign Earned Income Tax Worksheet in the Form 1040 instructions) ... | 37. | 31,428 |

*If applicable, enter instead the smaller amount you entered on the dotted line next to line 4e of Form 4952.

**If you are filing Form 2555 or 2555-EZ, see the footnote in the Foreign Earned Income Tax Worksheet in the Instructions for Form 1040, line 44, before completing this line.

# The Recapture of Section 179 Property

Remember, one of the qualifications for claiming the section 179 expense deduction is the business use requirement. The business use requirement states that if the property is not used predominantly (more than 50%) for qualified business use, the taxpayer cannot claim the section 179 deduction. In addition, if the business use falls to 50% or below, the taxpayer must recapture the excess section 179 deduction. Keep in mind; this only applies to nonlisted property. We will discuss the recapture of listed property later in this chapter.

To determine the amount of excess section 179 deduction that must be recaptured, calculate what the allowable depreciation deduction would have been on the section 179 amount, including the current year, and deduct it from the section 179 deduction. For the following years, add the section 179 deduction back to the depreciable basis to calculate the depreciation deduction for the property.

**Example:** Mable placed a piece of 7 year equipment in service on May 5, 2008. The cost of the equipment is $2,345. She took a section 179 deduction for $1,000 in the year she placed it into service. The equipment was used 100% for business in 2008, 2009, and 2010. However, in 2011, it was used only 38% for business purposes. The allowable depreciation deduction on the section 179 deduction amount is:

| | |
|---|---|
| 2008 | $1,000 x 14.29% = $143 |
| 2009 | $1,000 x 24.49% = $245 |
| 2010 | $1,000 x 17.49% = $175 |
| 2011 | $1,000 x 38% x 12.49% = $47 |

$143 + $245 + $175 + $47 = $610

Mable's excess section 179 deduction is $390($1,000 - $610).

## Reporting the Recapture

Form 4797, Part IV, is used to report the section 179 recapture. The section 179 deduction is entered in column a, line 33. The allowable depreciation deduction on that amount is then entered in column a, line 34. Column a, line 35 shows the recapture amount. This amount is then carried to the same form on which the taxpayer originally took the deduction. Part IV of the Form 4797 is shown in Illustration 4, with the information taken from the previous example.

# The Recapture of Section 280F Property

Section 280F of the IRS code is the section that contains a list of property that inherently lends itself to personal use. The property listed in this code is called listed property. It includes items such as automobiles, computers, cellular telephones, and property generally used for purposes of entertainment and amusement.

As stated in Chapter 3, if the taxpayer is depreciating listed property and the business use of the property is 50% or less, no section 179 deduction is allowed, and the property must be depreciated using the MACRS alternative depreciation system. If the property was used over 50% for business and regular

Illustration 4

Form 4797 (2011)

Page **2**

**Part III** Gain From Disposition of Property Under Sections 1245, 1250, 1252, 1254, and 1255 (see instructions)

| 19 | (a) Description of section 1245, 1250, 1252, 1254, or 1255 property: | | (b) Date acquired (mo., day, yr.) | (c) Date sold (mo., day, yr.) |
|---|---|---|---|---|
| A | | | | |
| B | | | | |
| C | | | | |
| D | | | | |

| | These columns relate to the properties on lines 19A through 19D. ▶ | | Property A | Property B | Property C | Property D |
|---|---|---|---|---|---|---|
| 20 | Gross sales price (**Note:** *See line 1 before completing.*) | 20 | | | | |
| 21 | Cost or other basis plus expense of sale | 21 | | | | |
| 22 | Depreciation (or depletion) allowed or allowable | 22 | | | | |
| 23 | Adjusted basis. Subtract line 22 from line 21 | 23 | | | | |
| 24 | Total gain. Subtract line 23 from line 20 | 24 | | | | |
| 25 | **If section 1245 property:** | | | | | |
| a | Depreciation allowed or allowable from line 22 | 25a | | | | |
| b | Enter the **smaller** of line 24 or 25a | 25b | | | | |
| 26 | **If section 1250 property:** If straight line depreciation was used, enter -0- on line 26g, except for a corporation subject to section 291. | | | | | |
| a | Additional depreciation after 1975 (see instructions) | 26a | | | | |
| b | Applicable percentage multiplied by the **smaller** of line 24 or line 26a (see instructions) | 26b | | | | |
| c | Subtract line 26a from line 24. If residential rental property **or** line 24 is not more than line 26a, skip lines 26d and 26e | 26c | | | | |
| d | Additional depreciation after 1969 and before 1976 | 26d | | | | |
| e | Enter the **smaller** of line 26c or 26d | 26e | | | | |
| f | Section 291 amount (corporations only) | 26f | | | | |
| g | Add lines 26b, 26e, and 26f | 26g | | | | |
| 27 | **If section 1252 property:** Skip this section if you did not dispose of farmland or if this form is being completed for a partnership (other than an electing large partnership). | | | | | |
| a | Soil, water, and land clearing expenses | 27a | | | | |
| b | Line 27a multiplied by applicable percentage (see instructions) | 27b | | | | |
| c | Enter the **smaller** of line 24 or 27b | 27c | | | | |
| 28 | **If section 1254 property:** | | | | | |
| a | Intangible drilling and development costs, expenditures for development of mines and other natural deposits, mining exploration costs, and depletion (see instructions) | 28a | | | | |
| b | Enter the **smaller** of line 24 or 28a | 28b | | | | |
| 29 | **If section 1255 property:** | | | | | |
| a | Applicable percentage of payments excluded from income under section 126 (see instructions) | 29a | | | | |
| b | Enter the **smaller** of line 24 or 29a (see instructions) | 29b | | | | |

**Summary of Part III Gains.** Complete property columns A through D through line 29b before going to line 30.

| 30 | Total gains for all properties. Add property columns A through D, line 24 | 30 | |
|---|---|---|---|
| 31 | Add property columns A through D, lines 25b, 26g, 27c, 28b, and 29b. Enter here and on line 13 | 31 | |
| 32 | Subtract line 31 from line 30. Enter the portion from casualty or theft on Form 4684, line 33. Enter the portion from other than casualty or theft on Form 4797, line 6 | 32 | |

**Part IV** Recapture Amounts Under Sections 179 and 280F(b)(2) When Business Use Drops to 50% or Less (see instructions)

| | | | (a) Section 179 | (b) Section 280F(b)(2) |
|---|---|---|---|---|
| 33 | Section 179 expense deduction or depreciation allowable in prior years | 33 | 1,000 | |
| 34 | Recomputed depreciation (see instructions) | 34 | 610 | |
| 35 | Recapture amount. Subtract line 34 from line 33. See the instructions for where to report | 35 | 390 | |

Form **4797** (2011)

98

depreciation or a section 179 deduction was claimed in previous years, and the business use falls to below 50%, the taxpayer must recapture any excess depreciation and section 179 deductions reported.

For listed property placed in service after 1986, if regular MACRS, straight line MACRS, or 150% DB MACRS has been claimed and the business use falls to 50% or less during the ADS recovery period, the section 280F recapture may apply. To calculate the recapture amount, first, add any section 179 deduction claimed back to the basis. Then, recompute the depreciation for the years the property has been in service, using the ADS recovery period and MACRS straight line depreciation. Deduct this amount from the allowable depreciation deduction for the prior years, including any section 179 deduction reported. This is the recapture amount. The current and future depreciation deductions will be computed using the ADS recovery period and MACRS straight line, even if the business use goes back to above 50%.

**Example:** Miranda purchased a computer she uses at home for business, on March 23, 2008 for $2,399. She took a $500 section 179 deduction and used regular MACRS to depreciate in 2008, 2009, and 2010. The computer was used 100% for business in 2008 and 2009. In 2010, it was used 78% for business. In 2011, it was used 43% for business. The following were the allowable depreciation deductions:

The $500 section 179 deduction leaves us with a depreciable basis of $1,899 for 2008 and 2009. For 2010, we'll multiply the basis of $2,399 by 78% and then subtract the $500 section 179 deduction. That will give us a depreciable basis of $1,371 for 2010.

> 2008: $380

> 2009: $608

> 2010: $263

Total: $1,751 including the $500 section 179 deduction.

Using the ADS recovery period of 10 years and MACRS straight line, the depreciation deductions would have been:

> 2008: $120

> 2009: $240

> 2010: $187

Total: $547. The $500 section 179 deduction was added back into the basis before the depreciation was calculated.

> The recapture amount is $1,204: $1751 - $547.

## Reporting the Recapture

Form 4797, Part IV, is used to report the section 280F recapture. The depreciation deduction, including any section 179 deduction, is entered in column b, line 33. The allowable depreciation deduction on that amount is then entered in column b, line 34. Column b, line 35 shows the recapture amount. This amount is

then carried to the same form on which the taxpayer originally took the deduction. Part IV of the Form 4797 is shown in Illustration 5, with the information taken from the previous example.

**Note**: If recapture is needed for an automobile, the limits still apply when calculating the allowable straight line depreciation.

# *Basis Adjustments*

If property that was subject to recapture was then sold, basis adjustments will be needed. To determine the basis of the property, first deduct all of the depreciation deductions allowed or allowable, then deduct any section 179 deductions claimed. Add any section 179 or section 280F recapture amounts to arrive at the adjusted basis. This is done to ensure the basis is reduced only by the deductions from which the taxpayer benefitted.

**Example:** The adjusted basis of the computer from the previous example is computed as follows:

> The cost basis of $2,399 minus the allowable depreciation deductions of $1,251 and the section 179 deduction of $500. 2,399 – (1,251 + 500) = 648.

> Next, add the amount that was recaptured of $1,204. $1,204 + $648 = $1,852

Miranda's adjusted basis of the computer is $1,852.

**Part III** Gain From Disposition of Property Under Sections 1245, 1250, 1252, 1254, and 1255 (see instructions)

| 19 | (a) Description of section 1245, 1250, 1252, 1254, or 1255 property: | | (b) Date acquired (mo., day, yr.) | (c) Date sold (mo., day, yr.) |
|---|---|---|---|---|
| A | | | | |
| B | | | | |
| C | | | | |
| D | | | | |

| | These columns relate to the properties on lines 19A through 19D. ▶ | | Property A | Property B | Property C | Property D |
|---|---|---|---|---|---|---|
| 20 | Gross sales price (**Note:** *See line 1 before completing.*) . | 20 | | | | |
| 21 | Cost or other basis plus expense of sale . . . . . | 21 | | | | |
| 22 | Depreciation (or depletion) allowed or allowable. . . | 22 | | | | |
| 23 | Adjusted basis. Subtract line 22 from line 21. . . . | 23 | | | | |
| 24 | Total gain. Subtract line 23 from line 20 . . . . . | 24 | | | | |
| 25 | **If section 1245 property:** | | | | | |
| a | Depreciation allowed or allowable from line 22 . . . | 25a | | | | |
| b | Enter the **smaller** of line 24 or 25a . . . . . . | 25b | | | | |
| 26 | **If section 1250 property:** If straight line depreciation was used, enter -0- on line 26g, except for a corporation subject to section 291. | | | | | |
| a | Additional depreciation after 1975 (see instructions) . | 26a | | | | |
| b | Applicable percentage multiplied by the **smaller** of line 24 or line 26a (see instructions) . . . . . . | 26b | | | | |
| c | Subtract line 26a from line 24. If residential rental property **or** line 24 is not more than line 26a, skip lines 26d and 26e | 26c | | | | |
| d | Additional depreciation after 1969 and before 1976. . | 26d | | | | |
| e | Enter the **smaller** of line 26c or 26d . . . . . . | 26e | | | | |
| f | Section 291 amount (corporations only) . . . . . | 26f | | | | |
| g | Add lines 26b, 26e, and 26f. . . . . . . . . | 26g | | | | |
| 27 | **If section 1252 property:** Skip this section if you did not dispose of farmland or if this form is being completed for a partnership (other than an electing large partnership). | | | | | |
| a | Soil, water, and land clearing expenses . . . . . | 27a | | | | |
| b | Line 27a multiplied by applicable percentage (see instructions) | 27b | | | | |
| c | Enter the **smaller** of line 24 or 27b . . . . . . | 27c | | | | |
| 28 | **If section 1254 property:** | | | | | |
| a | Intangible drilling and development costs, expenditures for development of mines and other natural deposits, mining exploration costs, and depletion (see instructions) . . . . . . . . . . . . . . | 28a | | | | |
| b | Enter the **smaller** of line 24 or 28a . . . . . . | 28b | | | | |
| 29 | **If section 1255 property:** | | | | | |
| a | Applicable percentage of payments excluded from income under section 126 (see instructions) . . . . | 29a | | | | |
| b | Enter the **smaller** of line 24 or 29a (see instructions) . | 29b | | | | |

**Summary of Part III Gains.** Complete property columns A through D through line 29b before going to line 30.

| 30 | Total gains for all properties. Add property columns A through D, line 24 . . . . . . . . . . | 30 | |
|---|---|---|---|
| 31 | Add property columns A through D, lines 25b, 26g, 27c, 28b, and 29b. Enter here and on line 13 . . . . . . | 31 | |
| 32 | Subtract line 31 from line 30. Enter the portion from casualty or theft on Form 4684, line 33. Enter the portion from other than casualty or theft on Form 4797, line 6 . . . . . . . . . . . . . . . . . . . . | 32 | |

**Part IV** Recapture Amounts Under Sections 179 and 280F(b)(2) When Business Use Drops to 50% or Less (see instructions)

| | | | (a) Section 179 | (b) Section 280F(b)(2) |
|---|---|---|---|---|
| 33 | Section 179 expense deduction or depreciation allowable in prior years. . . . . . . . . | 33 | | 1751 |
| 34 | Recomputed depreciation (see instructions) . . . . . . . . . . . . . . . . . . . | 34 | | 547 |
| 35 | Recapture amount. Subtract line 34 from line 33. See the instructions for where to report . . | 35 | | 1204 |

Form **4797** (2011)

# Chapter Review

1) What is the difference between realized gains and losses, and recognized gains and losses?

2) List two examples of transactions that are subject to section 1231 treatment?

3) What is all real property subject to an allowance for depreciation that is not, and never has been section 1245 property?

4) What is reported on Form 4797? How many parts are there on the form?

5) How do you determine the amount of excess section 179 deduction that must be recaptured?

6) Give three examples of section 280F property?

7) What do you do if property that was subject to recapture is sold?

# *Exercise*

Prepare a return for George Gaslow. His birthdate is July 5th, 1972 and his social security number is 564-55-9856. He lives at 455 Oak Dr., Your City, Your State, Your Zip Code. George's automotive repair business is George's Automotive. It is located at 453 Magnolia Drive, Your City, Your State, Your Zip Code. He started his business on February 5, 2001. He uses the cash method of accounting.

His gross receipts are $96,234. His expenses are as follows:

| | |
|---|---|
| Supplies | $23,499 |
| Advertising | 856 |
| Insurance | 3,522 |
| Legal & Professional | 899 |
| Office expense | 433 |
| Taxes & Licenses | 1,135 |

He bought a new automotive shop and moved his business to it. He sold his old shop in 2011. His new automotive shop was purchased and place in service on June 30, 2011. He paid $112,500 which included $13,200 for the land. His old shop, at 233 Warren Ave., was placed in service on February 5, 2001. He paid $98,200 the week before to purchase it. The purchase price included $9,300 for the land. He sold it on July 5, 2011 for $125,933. He paid $3,290 for sales expenses. His prior depreciation is $22,509.

He sold two machines in 2011. Machine 1 was purchased and placed in service on February 16, 2006. He paid $26,459 for it. His prior depreciation deductions are $20,557. He sold it for $32,899 on July 5, 2011, and paid $435 in sales expenses. Machine 2 was purchased and placed in service on March 19, 2006. The cost was $33,959. His prior depreciation is $26,383. He sold it for $28,950 on July 5, 2011, and paid $59 in sales expenses.

He has a computer he placed in service on July 16, 2009 with a basis of $1,895. His prior depreciation is $985. He placed shelves in service on September 26, 2008 with a basis of $2,325. His prior depreciation is $1,308.

He has a fax machine at home that he uses for business as well as personal reasons. He placed it in service on July 13, 2008, with a basis of $2,931. He took a section 179 deduction of $700. In 2008, he used it 93% for business. In 2009, he used it 85% for business. In 2010, he used it 67% for business. In 2011, he used it 43% for business. His prior depreciation allowed was $950. He used MACRS, 200% declining balance method.

George paid $40,000 in estimated taxes. He made his last payment in December of 2011.

# Appendix A – Tax Tables

# 2011 Tax Table

**CAUTION**

*See the instructions for line 44 to see if you must use the Tax Table below to figure your tax.*

**Example.** Mr. and Mrs. Brown are filing a joint return. Their taxable income on Form 1040, line 43, is $25,300. First, they find the $25,300 – 25,350 taxable income line. Next, they find the column for married filing jointly and read down the column. The amount shown where the taxable income line and filing status column meet is $2,949. This is the tax amount they should enter on Form 1040, line 44.

## Sample Table

| At Least | But Less Than | Single | Married filing jointly * | Married filing separately | Head of a household |
|---|---|---|---|---|---|
| | | | **Your tax is—** | | |
| 25,200 | 25,250 | 3,359 | 2,934 | 3,359 | 3,176 |
| 25,250 | 25,300 | 3,366 | 2,941 | 3,366 | 3,184 |
| 25,300 | 25,350 | 3,374 | (2,949) | 3,374 | 3,191 |
| 25,350 | 25,400 | 3,381 | 2,956 | 3,381 | 3,199 |

| If line 43 (taxable income) is— | | And you are— | | | |
|---|---|---|---|---|---|
| At least | But less than | Single | Married filing jointly * | Married filing separately | Head of a household |
| | | | **Your tax is—** | | |
| 0 | 5 | 0 | 0 | 0 | 0 |
| 5 | 15 | 1 | 1 | 1 | 1 |
| 15 | 25 | 2 | 2 | 2 | 2 |
| 25 | 50 | 4 | 4 | 4 | 4 |
| 50 | 75 | 6 | 6 | 6 | 6 |
| 75 | 100 | 9 | 9 | 9 | 9 |
| 100 | 125 | 11 | 11 | 11 | 11 |
| 125 | 150 | 14 | 14 | 14 | 14 |
| 150 | 175 | 16 | 16 | 16 | 16 |
| 175 | 200 | 19 | 19 | 19 | 19 |
| 200 | 225 | 21 | 21 | 21 | 21 |
| 225 | 250 | 24 | 24 | 24 | 24 |
| 250 | 275 | 26 | 26 | 26 | 26 |
| 275 | 300 | 29 | 29 | 29 | 29 |
| 300 | 325 | 31 | 31 | 31 | 31 |
| 325 | 350 | 34 | 34 | 34 | 34 |
| 350 | 375 | 36 | 36 | 36 | 36 |
| 375 | 400 | 39 | 39 | 39 | 39 |
| 400 | 425 | 41 | 41 | 41 | 41 |
| 425 | 450 | 44 | 44 | 44 | 44 |
| 450 | 475 | 46 | 46 | 46 | 46 |
| 475 | 500 | 49 | 49 | 49 | 49 |
| 500 | 525 | 51 | 51 | 51 | 51 |
| 525 | 550 | 54 | 54 | 54 | 54 |
| 550 | 575 | 56 | 56 | 56 | 56 |
| 575 | 600 | 59 | 59 | 59 | 59 |
| 600 | 625 | 61 | 61 | 61 | 61 |
| 625 | 650 | 64 | 64 | 64 | 64 |
| 650 | 675 | 66 | 66 | 66 | 66 |
| 675 | 700 | 69 | 69 | 69 | 69 |
| 700 | 725 | 71 | 71 | 71 | 71 |
| 725 | 750 | 74 | 74 | 74 | 74 |
| 750 | 775 | 76 | 76 | 76 | 76 |
| 775 | 800 | 79 | 79 | 79 | 79 |
| 800 | 825 | 81 | 81 | 81 | 81 |
| 825 | 850 | 84 | 84 | 84 | 84 |
| 850 | 875 | 86 | 86 | 86 | 86 |
| 875 | 900 | 89 | 89 | 89 | 89 |
| 900 | 925 | 91 | 91 | 91 | 91 |
| 925 | 950 | 94 | 94 | 94 | 94 |
| 950 | 975 | 96 | 96 | 96 | 96 |
| 975 | 1,000 | 99 | 99 | 99 | 99 |

### 1,000

| At least | But less than | Single | Married filing jointly * | Married filing separately | Head of a household |
|---|---|---|---|---|---|
| 1,000 | 1,025 | 101 | 101 | 101 | 101 |
| 1,025 | 1,050 | 104 | 104 | 104 | 104 |
| 1,050 | 1,075 | 106 | 106 | 106 | 106 |
| 1,075 | 1,100 | 109 | 109 | 109 | 109 |
| 1,100 | 1,125 | 111 | 111 | 111 | 111 |
| 1,125 | 1,150 | 114 | 114 | 114 | 114 |
| 1,150 | 1,175 | 116 | 116 | 116 | 116 |
| 1,175 | 1,200 | 119 | 119 | 119 | 119 |
| 1,200 | 1,225 | 121 | 121 | 121 | 121 |
| 1,225 | 1,250 | 124 | 124 | 124 | 124 |
| 1,250 | 1,275 | 126 | 126 | 126 | 126 |
| 1,275 | 1,300 | 129 | 129 | 129 | 129 |

| At least | But less than | Single | Married filing jointly * | Married filing separately | Head of a household |
|---|---|---|---|---|---|
| 1,300 | 1,325 | 131 | 131 | 131 | 131 |
| 1,325 | 1,350 | 134 | 134 | 134 | 134 |
| 1,350 | 1,375 | 136 | 136 | 136 | 136 |
| 1,375 | 1,400 | 139 | 139 | 139 | 139 |
| 1,400 | 1,425 | 141 | 141 | 141 | 141 |
| 1,425 | 1,450 | 144 | 144 | 144 | 144 |
| 1,450 | 1,475 | 146 | 146 | 146 | 146 |
| 1,475 | 1,500 | 149 | 149 | 149 | 149 |
| 1,500 | 1,525 | 151 | 151 | 151 | 151 |
| 1,525 | 1,550 | 154 | 154 | 154 | 154 |
| 1,550 | 1,575 | 156 | 156 | 156 | 156 |
| 1,575 | 1,600 | 159 | 159 | 159 | 159 |
| 1,600 | 1,625 | 161 | 161 | 161 | 161 |
| 1,625 | 1,650 | 164 | 164 | 164 | 164 |
| 1,650 | 1,675 | 166 | 166 | 166 | 166 |
| 1,675 | 1,700 | 169 | 169 | 169 | 169 |
| 1,700 | 1,725 | 171 | 171 | 171 | 171 |
| 1,725 | 1,750 | 174 | 174 | 174 | 174 |
| 1,750 | 1,775 | 176 | 176 | 176 | 176 |
| 1,775 | 1,800 | 179 | 179 | 179 | 179 |
| 1,800 | 1,825 | 181 | 181 | 181 | 181 |
| 1,825 | 1,850 | 184 | 184 | 184 | 184 |
| 1,850 | 1,875 | 186 | 186 | 186 | 186 |
| 1,875 | 1,900 | 189 | 189 | 189 | 189 |
| 1,900 | 1,925 | 191 | 191 | 191 | 191 |
| 1,925 | 1,950 | 194 | 194 | 194 | 194 |
| 1,950 | 1,975 | 196 | 196 | 196 | 196 |
| 1,975 | 2,000 | 199 | 199 | 199 | 199 |

### 2,000

| At least | But less than | Single | Married filing jointly * | Married filing separately | Head of a household |
|---|---|---|---|---|---|
| 2,000 | 2,025 | 201 | 201 | 201 | 201 |
| 2,025 | 2,050 | 204 | 204 | 204 | 204 |
| 2,050 | 2,075 | 206 | 206 | 206 | 206 |
| 2,075 | 2,100 | 209 | 209 | 209 | 209 |
| 2,100 | 2,125 | 211 | 211 | 211 | 211 |
| 2,125 | 2,150 | 214 | 214 | 214 | 214 |
| 2,150 | 2,175 | 216 | 216 | 216 | 216 |
| 2,175 | 2,200 | 219 | 219 | 219 | 219 |
| 2,200 | 2,225 | 221 | 221 | 221 | 221 |
| 2,225 | 2,250 | 224 | 224 | 224 | 224 |
| 2,250 | 2,275 | 226 | 226 | 226 | 226 |
| 2,275 | 2,300 | 229 | 229 | 229 | 229 |
| 2,300 | 2,325 | 231 | 231 | 231 | 231 |
| 2,325 | 2,350 | 234 | 234 | 234 | 234 |
| 2,350 | 2,375 | 236 | 236 | 236 | 236 |
| 2,375 | 2,400 | 239 | 239 | 239 | 239 |
| 2,400 | 2,425 | 241 | 241 | 241 | 241 |
| 2,425 | 2,450 | 244 | 244 | 244 | 244 |
| 2,450 | 2,475 | 246 | 246 | 246 | 246 |
| 2,475 | 2,500 | 249 | 249 | 249 | 249 |
| 2,500 | 2,525 | 251 | 251 | 251 | 251 |
| 2,525 | 2,550 | 254 | 254 | 254 | 254 |
| 2,550 | 2,575 | 256 | 256 | 256 | 256 |
| 2,575 | 2,600 | 259 | 259 | 259 | 259 |
| 2,600 | 2,625 | 261 | 261 | 261 | 261 |
| 2,625 | 2,650 | 264 | 264 | 264 | 264 |
| 2,650 | 2,675 | 266 | 266 | 266 | 266 |
| 2,675 | 2,700 | 269 | 269 | 269 | 269 |

| At least | But less than | Single | Married filing jointly * | Married filing separately | Head of a household |
|---|---|---|---|---|---|
| 2,700 | 2,725 | 271 | 271 | 271 | 271 |
| 2,725 | 2,750 | 274 | 274 | 274 | 274 |
| 2,750 | 2,775 | 276 | 276 | 276 | 276 |
| 2,775 | 2,800 | 279 | 279 | 279 | 279 |
| 2,800 | 2,825 | 281 | 281 | 281 | 281 |
| 2,825 | 2,850 | 284 | 284 | 284 | 284 |
| 2,850 | 2,875 | 286 | 286 | 286 | 286 |
| 2,875 | 2,900 | 289 | 289 | 289 | 289 |
| 2,900 | 2,925 | 291 | 291 | 291 | 291 |
| 2,925 | 2,950 | 294 | 294 | 294 | 294 |
| 2,950 | 2,975 | 296 | 296 | 296 | 296 |
| 2,975 | 3,000 | 299 | 299 | 299 | 299 |

### 3,000

| At least | But less than | Single | Married filing jointly * | Married filing separately | Head of a household |
|---|---|---|---|---|---|
| 3,000 | 3,050 | 303 | 303 | 303 | 303 |
| 3,050 | 3,100 | 308 | 308 | 308 | 308 |
| 3,100 | 3,150 | 313 | 313 | 313 | 313 |
| 3,150 | 3,200 | 318 | 318 | 318 | 318 |
| 3,200 | 3,250 | 323 | 323 | 323 | 323 |
| 3,250 | 3,300 | 328 | 328 | 328 | 328 |
| 3,300 | 3,350 | 333 | 333 | 333 | 333 |
| 3,350 | 3,400 | 338 | 338 | 338 | 338 |
| 3,400 | 3,450 | 343 | 343 | 343 | 343 |
| 3,450 | 3,500 | 348 | 348 | 348 | 348 |
| 3,500 | 3,550 | 353 | 353 | 353 | 353 |
| 3,550 | 3,600 | 358 | 358 | 358 | 358 |
| 3,600 | 3,650 | 363 | 363 | 363 | 363 |
| 3,650 | 3,700 | 368 | 368 | 368 | 368 |
| 3,700 | 3,750 | 373 | 373 | 373 | 373 |
| 3,750 | 3,800 | 378 | 378 | 378 | 378 |
| 3,800 | 3,850 | 383 | 383 | 383 | 383 |
| 3,850 | 3,900 | 388 | 388 | 388 | 388 |
| 3,900 | 3,950 | 393 | 393 | 393 | 393 |
| 3,950 | 4,000 | 398 | 398 | 398 | 398 |

### 4,000

| At least | But less than | Single | Married filing jointly * | Married filing separately | Head of a household |
|---|---|---|---|---|---|
| 4,000 | 4,050 | 403 | 403 | 403 | 403 |
| 4,050 | 4,100 | 408 | 408 | 408 | 408 |
| 4,100 | 4,150 | 413 | 413 | 413 | 413 |
| 4,150 | 4,200 | 418 | 418 | 418 | 418 |
| 4,200 | 4,250 | 423 | 423 | 423 | 423 |
| 4,250 | 4,300 | 428 | 428 | 428 | 428 |
| 4,300 | 4,350 | 433 | 433 | 433 | 433 |
| 4,350 | 4,400 | 438 | 438 | 438 | 438 |
| 4,400 | 4,450 | 443 | 443 | 443 | 443 |
| 4,450 | 4,500 | 448 | 448 | 448 | 448 |
| 4,500 | 4,550 | 453 | 453 | 453 | 453 |
| 4,550 | 4,600 | 458 | 458 | 458 | 458 |
| 4,600 | 4,650 | 463 | 463 | 463 | 463 |
| 4,650 | 4,700 | 468 | 468 | 468 | 468 |
| 4,700 | 4,750 | 473 | 473 | 473 | 473 |
| 4,750 | 4,800 | 478 | 478 | 478 | 478 |
| 4,800 | 4,850 | 483 | 483 | 483 | 483 |
| 4,850 | 4,900 | 488 | 488 | 488 | 488 |
| 4,900 | 4,950 | 493 | 493 | 493 | 493 |
| 4,950 | 5,000 | 498 | 498 | 498 | 498 |

* This column must also be used by a qualifying widow(er).

*(Continued)*

## 5,000

| At least | But less than | Single | Married filing jointly * | Married filing separately | Head of a household |
|---|---|---|---|---|---|
| 5,000 | 5,050 | 503 | 503 | 503 | 503 |
| 5,050 | 5,100 | 508 | 508 | 508 | 508 |
| 5,100 | 5,150 | 513 | 513 | 513 | 513 |
| 5,150 | 5,200 | 518 | 518 | 518 | 518 |
| 5,200 | 5,250 | 523 | 523 | 523 | 523 |
| 5,250 | 5,300 | 528 | 528 | 528 | 528 |
| 5,300 | 5,350 | 533 | 533 | 533 | 533 |
| 5,350 | 5,400 | 538 | 538 | 538 | 538 |
| 5,400 | 5,450 | 543 | 543 | 543 | 543 |
| 5,450 | 5,500 | 548 | 548 | 548 | 548 |
| 5,500 | 5,550 | 553 | 553 | 553 | 553 |
| 5,550 | 5,600 | 558 | 558 | 558 | 558 |
| 5,600 | 5,650 | 563 | 563 | 563 | 563 |
| 5,650 | 5,700 | 568 | 568 | 568 | 568 |
| 5,700 | 5,750 | 573 | 573 | 573 | 573 |
| 5,750 | 5,800 | 578 | 578 | 578 | 578 |
| 5,800 | 5,850 | 583 | 583 | 583 | 583 |
| 5,850 | 5,900 | 588 | 588 | 588 | 588 |
| 5,900 | 5,950 | 593 | 593 | 593 | 593 |
| 5,950 | 6,000 | 598 | 598 | 598 | 598 |

## 6,000

| At least | But less than | Single | Married filing jointly * | Married filing separately | Head of a household |
|---|---|---|---|---|---|
| 6,000 | 6,050 | 603 | 603 | 603 | 603 |
| 6,050 | 6,100 | 608 | 608 | 608 | 608 |
| 6,100 | 6,150 | 613 | 613 | 613 | 613 |
| 6,150 | 6,200 | 618 | 618 | 618 | 618 |
| 6,200 | 6,250 | 623 | 623 | 623 | 623 |
| 6,250 | 6,300 | 628 | 628 | 628 | 628 |
| 6,300 | 6,350 | 633 | 633 | 633 | 633 |
| 6,350 | 6,400 | 638 | 638 | 638 | 638 |
| 6,400 | 6,450 | 643 | 643 | 643 | 643 |
| 6,450 | 6,500 | 648 | 648 | 648 | 648 |
| 6,500 | 6,550 | 653 | 653 | 653 | 653 |
| 6,550 | 6,600 | 658 | 658 | 658 | 658 |
| 6,600 | 6,650 | 663 | 663 | 663 | 663 |
| 6,650 | 6,700 | 668 | 668 | 668 | 668 |
| 6,700 | 6,750 | 673 | 673 | 673 | 673 |
| 6,750 | 6,800 | 678 | 678 | 678 | 678 |
| 6,800 | 6,850 | 683 | 683 | 683 | 683 |
| 6,850 | 6,900 | 688 | 688 | 688 | 688 |
| 6,900 | 6,950 | 693 | 693 | 693 | 693 |
| 6,950 | 7,000 | 698 | 698 | 698 | 698 |

## 7,000

| At least | But less than | Single | Married filing jointly * | Married filing separately | Head of a household |
|---|---|---|---|---|---|
| 7,000 | 7,050 | 703 | 703 | 703 | 703 |
| 7,050 | 7,100 | 708 | 708 | 708 | 708 |
| 7,100 | 7,150 | 713 | 713 | 713 | 713 |
| 7,150 | 7,200 | 718 | 718 | 718 | 718 |
| 7,200 | 7,250 | 723 | 723 | 723 | 723 |
| 7,250 | 7,300 | 728 | 728 | 728 | 728 |
| 7,300 | 7,350 | 733 | 733 | 733 | 733 |
| 7,350 | 7,400 | 738 | 738 | 738 | 738 |
| 7,400 | 7,450 | 743 | 743 | 743 | 743 |
| 7,450 | 7,500 | 748 | 748 | 748 | 748 |
| 7,500 | 7,550 | 753 | 753 | 753 | 753 |
| 7,550 | 7,600 | 758 | 758 | 758 | 758 |
| 7,600 | 7,650 | 763 | 763 | 763 | 763 |
| 7,650 | 7,700 | 768 | 768 | 768 | 768 |
| 7,700 | 7,750 | 773 | 773 | 773 | 773 |
| 7,750 | 7,800 | 778 | 778 | 778 | 778 |
| 7,800 | 7,850 | 783 | 783 | 783 | 783 |
| 7,850 | 7,900 | 788 | 788 | 788 | 788 |
| 7,900 | 7,950 | 793 | 793 | 793 | 793 |
| 7,950 | 8,000 | 798 | 798 | 798 | 798 |

## 8,000

| At least | But less than | Single | Married filing jointly * | Married filing separately | Head of a household |
|---|---|---|---|---|---|
| 8,000 | 8,050 | 803 | 803 | 803 | 803 |
| 8,050 | 8,100 | 808 | 808 | 808 | 808 |
| 8,100 | 8,150 | 813 | 813 | 813 | 813 |
| 8,150 | 8,200 | 818 | 818 | 818 | 818 |
| 8,200 | 8,250 | 823 | 823 | 823 | 823 |
| 8,250 | 8,300 | 828 | 828 | 828 | 828 |
| 8,300 | 8,350 | 833 | 833 | 833 | 833 |
| 8,350 | 8,400 | 838 | 838 | 838 | 838 |
| 8,400 | 8,450 | 843 | 843 | 843 | 843 |
| 8,450 | 8,500 | 848 | 848 | 848 | 848 |
| 8,500 | 8,550 | 854 | 853 | 854 | 853 |
| 8,550 | 8,600 | 861 | 858 | 861 | 858 |
| 8,600 | 8,650 | 869 | 863 | 869 | 863 |
| 8,650 | 8,700 | 876 | 868 | 876 | 868 |
| 8,700 | 8,750 | 884 | 873 | 884 | 873 |
| 8,750 | 8,800 | 891 | 878 | 891 | 878 |
| 8,800 | 8,850 | 899 | 883 | 899 | 883 |
| 8,850 | 8,900 | 906 | 888 | 906 | 888 |
| 8,900 | 8,950 | 914 | 893 | 914 | 893 |
| 8,950 | 9,000 | 921 | 898 | 921 | 898 |

## 9,000

| At least | But less than | Single | Married filing jointly * | Married filing separately | Head of a household |
|---|---|---|---|---|---|
| 9,000 | 9,050 | 929 | 903 | 929 | 903 |
| 9,050 | 9,100 | 936 | 908 | 936 | 908 |
| 9,100 | 9,150 | 944 | 913 | 944 | 913 |
| 9,150 | 9,200 | 951 | 918 | 951 | 918 |
| 9,200 | 9,250 | 959 | 923 | 959 | 923 |
| 9,250 | 9,300 | 966 | 928 | 966 | 928 |
| 9,300 | 9,350 | 974 | 933 | 974 | 933 |
| 9,350 | 9,400 | 981 | 938 | 981 | 938 |
| 9,400 | 9,450 | 989 | 943 | 989 | 943 |
| 9,450 | 9,500 | 996 | 948 | 996 | 948 |
| 9,500 | 9,550 | 1,004 | 953 | 1,004 | 953 |
| 9,550 | 9,600 | 1,011 | 958 | 1,011 | 958 |
| 9,600 | 9,650 | 1,019 | 963 | 1,019 | 963 |
| 9,650 | 9,700 | 1,026 | 968 | 1,026 | 968 |
| 9,700 | 9,750 | 1,034 | 973 | 1,034 | 973 |
| 9,750 | 9,800 | 1,041 | 978 | 1,041 | 978 |
| 9,800 | 9,850 | 1,049 | 983 | 1,049 | 983 |
| 9,850 | 9,900 | 1,056 | 988 | 1,056 | 988 |
| 9,900 | 9,950 | 1,064 | 993 | 1,064 | 993 |
| 9,950 | 10,000 | 1,071 | 998 | 1,071 | 998 |

## 10,000

| At least | But less than | Single | Married filing jointly * | Married filing separately | Head of a household |
|---|---|---|---|---|---|
| 10,000 | 10,050 | 1,079 | 1,003 | 1,079 | 1,003 |
| 10,050 | 10,100 | 1,086 | 1,008 | 1,086 | 1,008 |
| 10,100 | 10,150 | 1,094 | 1,013 | 1,094 | 1,013 |
| 10,150 | 10,200 | 1,101 | 1,018 | 1,101 | 1,018 |
| 10,200 | 10,250 | 1,109 | 1,023 | 1,109 | 1,023 |
| 10,250 | 10,300 | 1,116 | 1,028 | 1,116 | 1,028 |
| 10,300 | 10,350 | 1,124 | 1,033 | 1,124 | 1,033 |
| 10,350 | 10,400 | 1,131 | 1,038 | 1,131 | 1,038 |
| 10,400 | 10,450 | 1,139 | 1,043 | 1,139 | 1,043 |
| 10,450 | 10,500 | 1,146 | 1,048 | 1,146 | 1,048 |
| 10,500 | 10,550 | 1,154 | 1,053 | 1,154 | 1,053 |
| 10,550 | 10,600 | 1,161 | 1,058 | 1,161 | 1,058 |
| 10,600 | 10,650 | 1,169 | 1,063 | 1,169 | 1,063 |
| 10,650 | 10,700 | 1,176 | 1,068 | 1,176 | 1,068 |
| 10,700 | 10,750 | 1,184 | 1,073 | 1,184 | 1,073 |
| 10,750 | 10,800 | 1,191 | 1,078 | 1,191 | 1,078 |
| 10,800 | 10,850 | 1,199 | 1,083 | 1,199 | 1,083 |
| 10,850 | 10,900 | 1,206 | 1,088 | 1,206 | 1,088 |
| 10,900 | 10,950 | 1,214 | 1,093 | 1,214 | 1,093 |
| 10,950 | 11,000 | 1,221 | 1,098 | 1,221 | 1,098 |

## 11,000

| At least | But less than | Single | Married filing jointly * | Married filing separately | Head of a household |
|---|---|---|---|---|---|
| 11,000 | 11,050 | 1,229 | 1,103 | 1,229 | 1,103 |
| 11,050 | 11,100 | 1,236 | 1,108 | 1,236 | 1,108 |
| 11,100 | 11,150 | 1,244 | 1,113 | 1,244 | 1,113 |
| 11,150 | 11,200 | 1,251 | 1,118 | 1,251 | 1,118 |
| 11,200 | 11,250 | 1,259 | 1,123 | 1,259 | 1,123 |
| 11,250 | 11,300 | 1,266 | 1,128 | 1,266 | 1,128 |
| 11,300 | 11,350 | 1,274 | 1,133 | 1,274 | 1,133 |
| 11,350 | 11,400 | 1,281 | 1,138 | 1,281 | 1,138 |
| 11,400 | 11,450 | 1,289 | 1,143 | 1,289 | 1,143 |
| 11,450 | 11,500 | 1,296 | 1,148 | 1,296 | 1,148 |
| 11,500 | 11,550 | 1,304 | 1,153 | 1,304 | 1,153 |
| 11,550 | 11,600 | 1,311 | 1,158 | 1,311 | 1,158 |
| 11,600 | 11,650 | 1,319 | 1,163 | 1,319 | 1,163 |
| 11,650 | 11,700 | 1,326 | 1,168 | 1,326 | 1,168 |
| 11,700 | 11,750 | 1,334 | 1,173 | 1,334 | 1,173 |
| 11,750 | 11,800 | 1,341 | 1,178 | 1,341 | 1,178 |
| 11,800 | 11,850 | 1,349 | 1,183 | 1,349 | 1,183 |
| 11,850 | 11,900 | 1,356 | 1,188 | 1,356 | 1,188 |
| 11,900 | 11,950 | 1,364 | 1,193 | 1,364 | 1,193 |
| 11,950 | 12,000 | 1,371 | 1,198 | 1,371 | 1,198 |

## 12,000

| At least | But less than | Single | Married filing jointly * | Married filing separately | Head of a household |
|---|---|---|---|---|---|
| 12,000 | 12,050 | 1,379 | 1,203 | 1,379 | 1,203 |
| 12,050 | 12,100 | 1,386 | 1,208 | 1,386 | 1,208 |
| 12,100 | 12,150 | 1,394 | 1,213 | 1,394 | 1,213 |
| 12,150 | 12,200 | 1,401 | 1,218 | 1,401 | 1,219 |
| 12,200 | 12,250 | 1,409 | 1,223 | 1,409 | 1,226 |
| 12,250 | 12,300 | 1,416 | 1,228 | 1,416 | 1,234 |
| 12,300 | 12,350 | 1,424 | 1,233 | 1,424 | 1,241 |
| 12,350 | 12,400 | 1,431 | 1,238 | 1,431 | 1,249 |
| 12,400 | 12,450 | 1,439 | 1,243 | 1,439 | 1,256 |
| 12,450 | 12,500 | 1,446 | 1,248 | 1,446 | 1,264 |
| 12,500 | 12,550 | 1,454 | 1,253 | 1,454 | 1,271 |
| 12,550 | 12,600 | 1,461 | 1,258 | 1,461 | 1,279 |
| 12,600 | 12,650 | 1,469 | 1,263 | 1,469 | 1,286 |
| 12,650 | 12,700 | 1,476 | 1,268 | 1,476 | 1,294 |
| 12,700 | 12,750 | 1,484 | 1,273 | 1,484 | 1,301 |
| 12,750 | 12,800 | 1,491 | 1,278 | 1,491 | 1,309 |
| 12,800 | 12,850 | 1,499 | 1,283 | 1,499 | 1,316 |
| 12,850 | 12,900 | 1,506 | 1,288 | 1,506 | 1,324 |
| 12,900 | 12,950 | 1,514 | 1,293 | 1,514 | 1,331 |
| 12,950 | 13,000 | 1,521 | 1,298 | 1,521 | 1,339 |

## 13,000

| At least | But less than | Single | Married filing jointly * | Married filing separately | Head of a household |
|---|---|---|---|---|---|
| 13,000 | 13,050 | 1,529 | 1,303 | 1,529 | 1,346 |
| 13,050 | 13,100 | 1,536 | 1,308 | 1,536 | 1,354 |
| 13,100 | 13,150 | 1,544 | 1,313 | 1,544 | 1,361 |
| 13,150 | 13,200 | 1,551 | 1,318 | 1,551 | 1,369 |
| 13,200 | 13,250 | 1,559 | 1,323 | 1,559 | 1,376 |
| 13,250 | 13,300 | 1,566 | 1,328 | 1,566 | 1,384 |
| 13,300 | 13,350 | 1,574 | 1,333 | 1,574 | 1,391 |
| 13,350 | 13,400 | 1,581 | 1,338 | 1,581 | 1,399 |
| 13,400 | 13,450 | 1,589 | 1,343 | 1,589 | 1,406 |
| 13,450 | 13,500 | 1,596 | 1,348 | 1,596 | 1,414 |
| 13,500 | 13,550 | 1,604 | 1,353 | 1,604 | 1,421 |
| 13,550 | 13,600 | 1,611 | 1,358 | 1,611 | 1,429 |
| 13,600 | 13,650 | 1,619 | 1,363 | 1,619 | 1,436 |
| 13,650 | 13,700 | 1,626 | 1,368 | 1,626 | 1,444 |
| 13,700 | 13,750 | 1,634 | 1,373 | 1,634 | 1,451 |
| 13,750 | 13,800 | 1,641 | 1,378 | 1,641 | 1,459 |
| 13,800 | 13,850 | 1,649 | 1,383 | 1,649 | 1,466 |
| 13,850 | 13,900 | 1,656 | 1,388 | 1,656 | 1,474 |
| 13,900 | 13,950 | 1,664 | 1,393 | 1,664 | 1,481 |
| 13,950 | 14,000 | 1,671 | 1,398 | 1,671 | 1,489 |

* This column must also be used by a qualifying widow(er).

(*Continued*)

## 2011 Tax Table—*Continued*

| At least | But less than | Single | Married filing jointly * | Married filing separately | Head of a household |
|---|---|---|---|---|---|
| **14,000** | | | | | |
| 14,000 | 14,050 | 1,679 | 1,403 | 1,679 | 1,496 |
| 14,050 | 14,100 | 1,686 | 1,408 | 1,686 | 1,504 |
| 14,100 | 14,150 | 1,694 | 1,413 | 1,694 | 1,511 |
| 14,150 | 14,200 | 1,701 | 1,418 | 1,701 | 1,519 |
| 14,200 | 14,250 | 1,709 | 1,423 | 1,709 | 1,526 |
| 14,250 | 14,300 | 1,716 | 1,428 | 1,716 | 1,534 |
| 14,300 | 14,350 | 1,724 | 1,433 | 1,724 | 1,541 |
| 14,350 | 14,400 | 1,731 | 1,438 | 1,731 | 1,549 |
| 14,400 | 14,450 | 1,739 | 1,443 | 1,739 | 1,556 |
| 14,450 | 14,500 | 1,746 | 1,448 | 1,746 | 1,564 |
| 14,500 | 14,550 | 1,754 | 1,453 | 1,754 | 1,571 |
| 14,550 | 14,600 | 1,761 | 1,458 | 1,761 | 1,579 |
| 14,600 | 14,650 | 1,769 | 1,463 | 1,769 | 1,586 |
| 14,650 | 14,700 | 1,776 | 1,468 | 1,776 | 1,594 |
| 14,700 | 14,750 | 1,784 | 1,473 | 1,784 | 1,601 |
| 14,750 | 14,800 | 1,791 | 1,478 | 1,791 | 1,609 |
| 14,800 | 14,850 | 1,799 | 1,483 | 1,799 | 1,616 |
| 14,850 | 14,900 | 1,806 | 1,488 | 1,806 | 1,624 |
| 14,900 | 14,950 | 1,814 | 1,493 | 1,814 | 1,631 |
| 14,950 | 15,000 | 1,821 | 1,498 | 1,821 | 1,639 |
| **15,000** | | | | | |
| 15,000 | 15,050 | 1,829 | 1,503 | 1,829 | 1,646 |
| 15,050 | 15,100 | 1,836 | 1,508 | 1,836 | 1,654 |
| 15,100 | 15,150 | 1,844 | 1,513 | 1,844 | 1,661 |
| 15,150 | 15,200 | 1,851 | 1,518 | 1,851 | 1,669 |
| 15,200 | 15,250 | 1,859 | 1,523 | 1,859 | 1,676 |
| 15,250 | 15,300 | 1,866 | 1,528 | 1,866 | 1,684 |
| 15,300 | 15,350 | 1,874 | 1,533 | 1,874 | 1,691 |
| 15,350 | 15,400 | 1,881 | 1,538 | 1,881 | 1,699 |
| 15,400 | 15,450 | 1,889 | 1,543 | 1,889 | 1,706 |
| 15,450 | 15,500 | 1,896 | 1,548 | 1,896 | 1,714 |
| 15,500 | 15,550 | 1,904 | 1,553 | 1,904 | 1,721 |
| 15,550 | 15,600 | 1,911 | 1,558 | 1,911 | 1,729 |
| 15,600 | 15,650 | 1,919 | 1,563 | 1,919 | 1,736 |
| 15,650 | 15,700 | 1,926 | 1,568 | 1,926 | 1,744 |
| 15,700 | 15,750 | 1,934 | 1,573 | 1,934 | 1,751 |
| 15,750 | 15,800 | 1,941 | 1,578 | 1,941 | 1,759 |
| 15,800 | 15,850 | 1,949 | 1,583 | 1,949 | 1,766 |
| 15,850 | 15,900 | 1,956 | 1,588 | 1,956 | 1,774 |
| 15,900 | 15,950 | 1,964 | 1,593 | 1,964 | 1,781 |
| 15,950 | 16,000 | 1,971 | 1,598 | 1,971 | 1,789 |
| **16,000** | | | | | |
| 16,000 | 16,050 | 1,979 | 1,603 | 1,979 | 1,796 |
| 16,050 | 16,100 | 1,986 | 1,608 | 1,986 | 1,804 |
| 16,100 | 16,150 | 1,994 | 1,613 | 1,994 | 1,811 |
| 16,150 | 16,200 | 2,001 | 1,618 | 2,001 | 1,819 |
| 16,200 | 16,250 | 2,009 | 1,623 | 2,009 | 1,826 |
| 16,250 | 16,300 | 2,016 | 1,628 | 2,016 | 1,834 |
| 16,300 | 16,350 | 2,024 | 1,633 | 2,024 | 1,841 |
| 16,350 | 16,400 | 2,031 | 1,638 | 2,031 | 1,849 |
| 16,400 | 16,450 | 2,039 | 1,643 | 2,039 | 1,856 |
| 16,450 | 16,500 | 2,046 | 1,648 | 2,046 | 1,864 |
| 16,500 | 16,550 | 2,054 | 1,653 | 2,054 | 1,871 |
| 16,550 | 16,600 | 2,061 | 1,658 | 2,061 | 1,879 |
| 16,600 | 16,650 | 2,069 | 1,663 | 2,069 | 1,886 |
| 16,650 | 16,700 | 2,076 | 1,668 | 2,076 | 1,894 |
| 16,700 | 16,750 | 2,084 | 1,673 | 2,084 | 1,901 |
| 16,750 | 16,800 | 2,091 | 1,678 | 2,091 | 1,909 |
| 16,800 | 16,850 | 2,099 | 1,683 | 2,099 | 1,916 |
| 16,850 | 16,900 | 2,106 | 1,688 | 2,106 | 1,924 |
| 16,900 | 16,950 | 2,114 | 1,693 | 2,114 | 1,931 |
| 16,950 | 17,000 | 2,121 | 1,698 | 2,121 | 1,939 |
| **17,000** | | | | | |
| 17,000 | 17,050 | 2,129 | 1,704 | 2,129 | 1,946 |
| 17,050 | 17,100 | 2,136 | 1,711 | 2,136 | 1,954 |
| 17,100 | 17,150 | 2,144 | 1,719 | 2,144 | 1,961 |
| 17,150 | 17,200 | 2,151 | 1,726 | 2,151 | 1,969 |
| 17,200 | 17,250 | 2,159 | 1,734 | 2,159 | 1,976 |
| 17,250 | 17,300 | 2,166 | 1,741 | 2,166 | 1,984 |
| 17,300 | 17,350 | 2,174 | 1,749 | 2,174 | 1,991 |
| 17,350 | 17,400 | 2,181 | 1,756 | 2,181 | 1,999 |
| 17,400 | 17,450 | 2,189 | 1,764 | 2,189 | 2,006 |
| 17,450 | 17,500 | 2,196 | 1,771 | 2,196 | 2,014 |
| 17,500 | 17,550 | 2,204 | 1,779 | 2,204 | 2,021 |
| 17,550 | 17,600 | 2,211 | 1,786 | 2,211 | 2,029 |
| 17,600 | 17,650 | 2,219 | 1,794 | 2,219 | 2,036 |
| 17,650 | 17,700 | 2,226 | 1,801 | 2,226 | 2,044 |
| 17,700 | 17,750 | 2,234 | 1,809 | 2,234 | 2,051 |
| 17,750 | 17,800 | 2,241 | 1,816 | 2,241 | 2,059 |
| 17,800 | 17,850 | 2,249 | 1,824 | 2,249 | 2,066 |
| 17,850 | 17,900 | 2,256 | 1,831 | 2,256 | 2,074 |
| 17,900 | 17,950 | 2,264 | 1,839 | 2,264 | 2,081 |
| 17,950 | 18,000 | 2,271 | 1,846 | 2,271 | 2,089 |
| **18,000** | | | | | |
| 18,000 | 18,050 | 2,279 | 1,854 | 2,279 | 2,096 |
| 18,050 | 18,100 | 2,286 | 1,861 | 2,286 | 2,104 |
| 18,100 | 18,150 | 2,294 | 1,869 | 2,294 | 2,111 |
| 18,150 | 18,200 | 2,301 | 1,876 | 2,301 | 2,119 |
| 18,200 | 18,250 | 2,309 | 1,884 | 2,309 | 2,126 |
| 18,250 | 18,300 | 2,316 | 1,891 | 2,316 | 2,134 |
| 18,300 | 18,350 | 2,324 | 1,899 | 2,324 | 2,141 |
| 18,350 | 18,400 | 2,331 | 1,906 | 2,331 | 2,149 |
| 18,400 | 18,450 | 2,339 | 1,914 | 2,339 | 2,156 |
| 18,450 | 18,500 | 2,346 | 1,921 | 2,346 | 2,164 |
| 18,500 | 18,550 | 2,354 | 1,929 | 2,354 | 2,171 |
| 18,550 | 18,600 | 2,361 | 1,936 | 2,361 | 2,179 |
| 18,600 | 18,650 | 2,369 | 1,944 | 2,369 | 2,186 |
| 18,650 | 18,700 | 2,376 | 1,951 | 2,376 | 2,194 |
| 18,700 | 18,750 | 2,384 | 1,959 | 2,384 | 2,201 |
| 18,750 | 18,800 | 2,391 | 1,966 | 2,391 | 2,209 |
| 18,800 | 18,850 | 2,399 | 1,974 | 2,399 | 2,216 |
| 18,850 | 18,900 | 2,406 | 1,981 | 2,406 | 2,224 |
| 18,900 | 18,950 | 2,414 | 1,989 | 2,414 | 2,231 |
| 18,950 | 19,000 | 2,421 | 1,996 | 2,421 | 2,239 |
| **19,000** | | | | | |
| 19,000 | 19,050 | 2,429 | 2,004 | 2,429 | 2,246 |
| 19,050 | 19,100 | 2,436 | 2,011 | 2,436 | 2,254 |
| 19,100 | 19,150 | 2,444 | 2,019 | 2,444 | 2,261 |
| 19,150 | 19,200 | 2,451 | 2,026 | 2,451 | 2,269 |
| 19,200 | 19,250 | 2,459 | 2,034 | 2,459 | 2,276 |
| 19,250 | 19,300 | 2,466 | 2,041 | 2,466 | 2,284 |
| 19,300 | 19,350 | 2,474 | 2,049 | 2,474 | 2,291 |
| 19,350 | 19,400 | 2,481 | 2,056 | 2,481 | 2,299 |
| 19,400 | 19,450 | 2,489 | 2,064 | 2,489 | 2,306 |
| 19,450 | 19,500 | 2,496 | 2,071 | 2,496 | 2,314 |
| 19,500 | 19,550 | 2,504 | 2,079 | 2,504 | 2,321 |
| 19,550 | 19,600 | 2,511 | 2,086 | 2,511 | 2,329 |
| 19,600 | 19,650 | 2,519 | 2,094 | 2,519 | 2,336 |
| 19,650 | 19,700 | 2,526 | 2,101 | 2,526 | 2,344 |
| 19,700 | 19,750 | 2,534 | 2,109 | 2,534 | 2,351 |
| 19,750 | 19,800 | 2,541 | 2,116 | 2,541 | 2,359 |
| 19,800 | 19,850 | 2,549 | 2,124 | 2,549 | 2,366 |
| 19,850 | 19,900 | 2,556 | 2,131 | 2,556 | 2,374 |
| 19,900 | 19,950 | 2,564 | 2,139 | 2,564 | 2,381 |
| 19,950 | 20,000 | 2,571 | 2,146 | 2,571 | 2,389 |
| **20,000** | | | | | |
| 20,000 | 20,050 | 2,579 | 2,154 | 2,579 | 2,396 |
| 20,050 | 20,100 | 2,586 | 2,161 | 2,586 | 2,404 |
| 20,100 | 20,150 | 2,594 | 2,169 | 2,594 | 2,411 |
| 20,150 | 20,200 | 2,601 | 2,176 | 2,601 | 2,419 |
| 20,200 | 20,250 | 2,609 | 2,184 | 2,609 | 2,426 |
| 20,250 | 20,300 | 2,616 | 2,191 | 2,616 | 2,434 |
| 20,300 | 20,350 | 2,624 | 2,199 | 2,624 | 2,441 |
| 20,350 | 20,400 | 2,631 | 2,206 | 2,631 | 2,449 |
| 20,400 | 20,450 | 2,639 | 2,214 | 2,639 | 2,456 |
| 20,450 | 20,500 | 2,646 | 2,221 | 2,646 | 2,464 |
| 20,500 | 20,550 | 2,654 | 2,229 | 2,654 | 2,471 |
| 20,550 | 20,600 | 2,661 | 2,236 | 2,661 | 2,479 |
| 20,600 | 20,650 | 2,669 | 2,244 | 2,669 | 2,486 |
| 20,650 | 20,700 | 2,676 | 2,251 | 2,676 | 2,494 |
| 20,700 | 20,750 | 2,684 | 2,259 | 2,684 | 2,501 |
| 20,750 | 20,800 | 2,691 | 2,266 | 2,691 | 2,509 |
| 20,800 | 20,850 | 2,699 | 2,274 | 2,699 | 2,516 |
| 20,850 | 20,900 | 2,706 | 2,281 | 2,706 | 2,524 |
| 20,900 | 20,950 | 2,714 | 2,289 | 2,714 | 2,531 |
| 20,950 | 21,000 | 2,721 | 2,296 | 2,721 | 2,539 |
| **21,000** | | | | | |
| 21,000 | 21,050 | 2,729 | 2,304 | 2,729 | 2,546 |
| 21,050 | 21,100 | 2,736 | 2,311 | 2,736 | 2,554 |
| 21,100 | 21,150 | 2,744 | 2,319 | 2,744 | 2,561 |
| 21,150 | 21,200 | 2,751 | 2,326 | 2,751 | 2,569 |
| 21,200 | 21,250 | 2,759 | 2,334 | 2,759 | 2,576 |
| 21,250 | 21,300 | 2,766 | 2,341 | 2,766 | 2,584 |
| 21,300 | 21,350 | 2,774 | 2,349 | 2,774 | 2,591 |
| 21,350 | 21,400 | 2,781 | 2,356 | 2,781 | 2,599 |
| 21,400 | 21,450 | 2,789 | 2,364 | 2,789 | 2,606 |
| 21,450 | 21,500 | 2,796 | 2,371 | 2,796 | 2,614 |
| 21,500 | 21,550 | 2,804 | 2,379 | 2,804 | 2,621 |
| 21,550 | 21,600 | 2,811 | 2,386 | 2,811 | 2,629 |
| 21,600 | 21,650 | 2,819 | 2,394 | 2,819 | 2,636 |
| 21,650 | 21,700 | 2,826 | 2,401 | 2,826 | 2,644 |
| 21,700 | 21,750 | 2,834 | 2,409 | 2,834 | 2,651 |
| 21,750 | 21,800 | 2,841 | 2,416 | 2,841 | 2,659 |
| 21,800 | 21,850 | 2,849 | 2,424 | 2,849 | 2,666 |
| 21,850 | 21,900 | 2,856 | 2,431 | 2,856 | 2,674 |
| 21,900 | 21,950 | 2,864 | 2,439 | 2,864 | 2,681 |
| 21,950 | 22,000 | 2,871 | 2,446 | 2,871 | 2,689 |
| **22,000** | | | | | |
| 22,000 | 22,050 | 2,879 | 2,454 | 2,879 | 2,696 |
| 22,050 | 22,100 | 2,886 | 2,461 | 2,886 | 2,704 |
| 22,100 | 22,150 | 2,894 | 2,469 | 2,894 | 2,711 |
| 22,150 | 22,200 | 2,901 | 2,476 | 2,901 | 2,719 |
| 22,200 | 22,250 | 2,909 | 2,484 | 2,909 | 2,726 |
| 22,250 | 22,300 | 2,916 | 2,491 | 2,916 | 2,734 |
| 22,300 | 22,350 | 2,924 | 2,499 | 2,924 | 2,741 |
| 22,350 | 22,400 | 2,931 | 2,506 | 2,931 | 2,749 |
| 22,400 | 22,450 | 2,939 | 2,514 | 2,939 | 2,756 |
| 22,450 | 22,500 | 2,946 | 2,521 | 2,946 | 2,764 |
| 22,500 | 22,550 | 2,954 | 2,529 | 2,954 | 2,771 |
| 22,550 | 22,600 | 2,961 | 2,536 | 2,961 | 2,779 |
| 22,600 | 22,650 | 2,969 | 2,544 | 2,969 | 2,786 |
| 22,650 | 22,700 | 2,976 | 2,551 | 2,976 | 2,794 |
| 22,700 | 22,750 | 2,984 | 2,559 | 2,984 | 2,801 |
| 22,750 | 22,800 | 2,991 | 2,566 | 2,991 | 2,809 |
| 22,800 | 22,850 | 2,999 | 2,574 | 2,999 | 2,816 |
| 22,850 | 22,900 | 3,006 | 2,581 | 3,006 | 2,824 |
| 22,900 | 22,950 | 3,014 | 2,589 | 3,014 | 2,831 |
| 22,950 | 23,000 | 3,021 | 2,596 | 3,021 | 2,839 |

* This column must also be used by a qualifying widow(er).

*(Continued)*

| If line 43 (taxable income) is— | | And you are— | | | |
|---|---|---|---|---|---|
| At least | But less than | Single | Married filing jointly * | Married filing separately | Head of a house-hold |
| | | Your tax is— | | | |

## 23,000

| At least | But less than | Single | MFJ | MFS | HoH |
|---|---|---|---|---|---|
| 23,000 | 23,050 | 3,029 | 2,604 | 3,029 | 2,846 |
| 23,050 | 23,100 | 3,036 | 2,611 | 3,036 | 2,854 |
| 23,100 | 23,150 | 3,044 | 2,619 | 3,044 | 2,861 |
| 23,150 | 23,200 | 3,051 | 2,626 | 3,051 | 2,869 |
| 23,200 | 23,250 | 3,059 | 2,634 | 3,059 | 2,876 |
| 23,250 | 23,300 | 3,066 | 2,641 | 3,066 | 2,884 |
| 23,300 | 23,350 | 3,074 | 2,649 | 3,074 | 2,891 |
| 23,350 | 23,400 | 3,081 | 2,656 | 3,081 | 2,899 |
| 23,400 | 23,450 | 3,089 | 2,664 | 3,089 | 2,906 |
| 23,450 | 23,500 | 3,096 | 2,671 | 3,096 | 2,914 |
| 23,500 | 23,550 | 3,104 | 2,679 | 3,104 | 2,921 |
| 23,550 | 23,600 | 3,111 | 2,686 | 3,111 | 2,929 |
| 23,600 | 23,650 | 3,119 | 2,694 | 3,119 | 2,936 |
| 23,650 | 23,700 | 3,126 | 2,701 | 3,126 | 2,944 |
| 23,700 | 23,750 | 3,134 | 2,709 | 3,134 | 2,951 |
| 23,750 | 23,800 | 3,141 | 2,716 | 3,141 | 2,959 |
| 23,800 | 23,850 | 3,149 | 2,724 | 3,149 | 2,966 |
| 23,850 | 23,900 | 3,156 | 2,731 | 3,156 | 2,974 |
| 23,900 | 23,950 | 3,164 | 2,739 | 3,164 | 2,981 |
| 23,950 | 24,000 | 3,171 | 2,746 | 3,171 | 2,989 |

## 24,000

| At least | But less than | Single | MFJ | MFS | HoH |
|---|---|---|---|---|---|
| 24,000 | 24,050 | 3,179 | 2,754 | 3,179 | 2,996 |
| 24,050 | 24,100 | 3,186 | 2,761 | 3,186 | 3,004 |
| 24,100 | 24,150 | 3,194 | 2,769 | 3,194 | 3,011 |
| 24,150 | 24,200 | 3,201 | 2,776 | 3,201 | 3,019 |
| 24,200 | 24,250 | 3,209 | 2,784 | 3,209 | 3,026 |
| 24,250 | 24,300 | 3,216 | 2,791 | 3,216 | 3,034 |
| 24,300 | 24,350 | 3,224 | 2,799 | 3,224 | 3,041 |
| 24,350 | 24,400 | 3,231 | 2,806 | 3,231 | 3,049 |
| 24,400 | 24,450 | 3,239 | 2,814 | 3,239 | 3,056 |
| 24,450 | 24,500 | 3,246 | 2,821 | 3,246 | 3,064 |
| 24,500 | 24,550 | 3,254 | 2,829 | 3,254 | 3,071 |
| 24,550 | 24,600 | 3,261 | 2,836 | 3,261 | 3,079 |
| 24,600 | 24,650 | 3,269 | 2,844 | 3,269 | 3,086 |
| 24,650 | 24,700 | 3,276 | 2,851 | 3,276 | 3,094 |
| 24,700 | 24,750 | 3,284 | 2,859 | 3,284 | 3,101 |
| 24,750 | 24,800 | 3,291 | 2,866 | 3,291 | 3,109 |
| 24,800 | 24,850 | 3,299 | 2,874 | 3,299 | 3,116 |
| 24,850 | 24,900 | 3,306 | 2,881 | 3,306 | 3,124 |
| 24,900 | 24,950 | 3,314 | 2,889 | 3,314 | 3,131 |
| 24,950 | 25,000 | 3,321 | 2,896 | 3,321 | 3,139 |

## 25,000

| At least | But less than | Single | MFJ | MFS | HoH |
|---|---|---|---|---|---|
| 25,000 | 25,050 | 3,329 | 2,904 | 3,329 | 3,146 |
| 25,050 | 25,100 | 3,336 | 2,911 | 3,336 | 3,154 |
| 25,100 | 25,150 | 3,344 | 2,919 | 3,344 | 3,161 |
| 25,150 | 25,200 | 3,351 | 2,926 | 3,351 | 3,169 |
| 25,200 | 25,250 | 3,359 | 2,934 | 3,359 | 3,176 |
| 25,250 | 25,300 | 3,366 | 2,941 | 3,366 | 3,184 |
| 25,300 | 25,350 | 3,374 | 2,949 | 3,374 | 3,191 |
| 25,350 | 25,400 | 3,381 | 2,956 | 3,381 | 3,199 |
| 25,400 | 25,450 | 3,389 | 2,964 | 3,389 | 3,206 |
| 25,450 | 25,500 | 3,396 | 2,971 | 3,396 | 3,214 |
| 25,500 | 25,550 | 3,404 | 2,979 | 3,404 | 3,221 |
| 25,550 | 25,600 | 3,411 | 2,986 | 3,411 | 3,229 |
| 25,600 | 25,650 | 3,419 | 2,994 | 3,419 | 3,236 |
| 25,650 | 25,700 | 3,426 | 3,001 | 3,426 | 3,244 |
| 25,700 | 25,750 | 3,434 | 3,009 | 3,434 | 3,251 |
| 25,750 | 25,800 | 3,441 | 3,016 | 3,441 | 3,259 |
| 25,800 | 25,850 | 3,449 | 3,024 | 3,449 | 3,266 |
| 25,850 | 25,900 | 3,456 | 3,031 | 3,456 | 3,274 |
| 25,900 | 25,950 | 3,464 | 3,039 | 3,464 | 3,281 |
| 25,950 | 26,000 | 3,471 | 3,046 | 3,471 | 3,289 |

## 26,000

| At least | But less than | Single | MFJ | MFS | HoH |
|---|---|---|---|---|---|
| 26,000 | 26,050 | 3,479 | 3,054 | 3,479 | 3,296 |
| 26,050 | 26,100 | 3,486 | 3,061 | 3,486 | 3,304 |
| 26,100 | 26,150 | 3,494 | 3,069 | 3,494 | 3,311 |
| 26,150 | 26,200 | 3,501 | 3,076 | 3,501 | 3,319 |
| 26,200 | 26,250 | 3,509 | 3,084 | 3,509 | 3,326 |
| 26,250 | 26,300 | 3,516 | 3,091 | 3,516 | 3,334 |
| 26,300 | 26,350 | 3,524 | 3,099 | 3,524 | 3,341 |
| 26,350 | 26,400 | 3,531 | 3,106 | 3,531 | 3,349 |
| 26,400 | 26,450 | 3,539 | 3,114 | 3,539 | 3,356 |
| 26,450 | 26,500 | 3,546 | 3,121 | 3,546 | 3,364 |
| 26,500 | 26,550 | 3,554 | 3,129 | 3,554 | 3,371 |
| 26,550 | 26,600 | 3,561 | 3,136 | 3,561 | 3,379 |
| 26,600 | 26,650 | 3,569 | 3,144 | 3,569 | 3,386 |
| 26,650 | 26,700 | 3,576 | 3,151 | 3,576 | 3,394 |
| 26,700 | 26,750 | 3,584 | 3,159 | 3,584 | 3,401 |
| 26,750 | 26,800 | 3,591 | 3,166 | 3,591 | 3,409 |
| 26,800 | 26,850 | 3,599 | 3,174 | 3,599 | 3,416 |
| 26,850 | 26,900 | 3,606 | 3,181 | 3,606 | 3,424 |
| 26,900 | 26,950 | 3,614 | 3,189 | 3,614 | 3,431 |
| 26,950 | 27,000 | 3,621 | 3,196 | 3,621 | 3,439 |

## 27,000

| At least | But less than | Single | MFJ | MFS | HoH |
|---|---|---|---|---|---|
| 27,000 | 27,050 | 3,629 | 3,204 | 3,629 | 3,446 |
| 27,050 | 27,100 | 3,636 | 3,211 | 3,636 | 3,454 |
| 27,100 | 27,150 | 3,644 | 3,219 | 3,644 | 3,461 |
| 27,150 | 27,200 | 3,651 | 3,226 | 3,651 | 3,469 |
| 27,200 | 27,250 | 3,659 | 3,234 | 3,659 | 3,476 |
| 27,250 | 27,300 | 3,666 | 3,241 | 3,666 | 3,484 |
| 27,300 | 27,350 | 3,674 | 3,249 | 3,674 | 3,491 |
| 27,350 | 27,400 | 3,681 | 3,256 | 3,681 | 3,499 |
| 27,400 | 27,450 | 3,689 | 3,264 | 3,689 | 3,506 |
| 27,450 | 27,500 | 3,696 | 3,271 | 3,696 | 3,514 |
| 27,500 | 27,550 | 3,704 | 3,279 | 3,704 | 3,521 |
| 27,550 | 27,600 | 3,711 | 3,286 | 3,711 | 3,529 |
| 27,600 | 27,650 | 3,719 | 3,294 | 3,719 | 3,536 |
| 27,650 | 27,700 | 3,726 | 3,301 | 3,726 | 3,544 |
| 27,700 | 27,750 | 3,734 | 3,309 | 3,734 | 3,551 |
| 27,750 | 27,800 | 3,741 | 3,316 | 3,741 | 3,559 |
| 27,800 | 27,850 | 3,749 | 3,324 | 3,749 | 3,566 |
| 27,850 | 27,900 | 3,756 | 3,331 | 3,756 | 3,574 |
| 27,900 | 27,950 | 3,764 | 3,339 | 3,764 | 3,581 |
| 27,950 | 28,000 | 3,771 | 3,346 | 3,771 | 3,589 |

## 28,000

| At least | But less than | Single | MFJ | MFS | HoH |
|---|---|---|---|---|---|
| 28,000 | 28,050 | 3,779 | 3,354 | 3,779 | 3,596 |
| 28,050 | 28,100 | 3,786 | 3,361 | 3,786 | 3,604 |
| 28,100 | 28,150 | 3,794 | 3,369 | 3,794 | 3,611 |
| 28,150 | 28,200 | 3,801 | 3,376 | 3,801 | 3,619 |
| 28,200 | 28,250 | 3,809 | 3,384 | 3,809 | 3,626 |
| 28,250 | 28,300 | 3,816 | 3,391 | 3,816 | 3,634 |
| 28,300 | 28,350 | 3,824 | 3,399 | 3,824 | 3,641 |
| 28,350 | 28,400 | 3,831 | 3,406 | 3,831 | 3,649 |
| 28,400 | 28,450 | 3,839 | 3,414 | 3,839 | 3,656 |
| 28,450 | 28,500 | 3,846 | 3,421 | 3,846 | 3,664 |
| 28,500 | 28,550 | 3,854 | 3,429 | 3,854 | 3,671 |
| 28,550 | 28,600 | 3,861 | 3,436 | 3,861 | 3,679 |
| 28,600 | 28,650 | 3,869 | 3,444 | 3,869 | 3,686 |
| 28,650 | 28,700 | 3,876 | 3,451 | 3,876 | 3,694 |
| 28,700 | 28,750 | 3,884 | 3,459 | 3,884 | 3,701 |
| 28,750 | 28,800 | 3,891 | 3,466 | 3,891 | 3,709 |
| 28,800 | 28,850 | 3,899 | 3,474 | 3,899 | 3,716 |
| 28,850 | 28,900 | 3,906 | 3,481 | 3,906 | 3,724 |
| 28,900 | 28,950 | 3,914 | 3,489 | 3,914 | 3,731 |
| 28,950 | 29,000 | 3,921 | 3,496 | 3,921 | 3,739 |

## 29,000

| At least | But less than | Single | MFJ | MFS | HoH |
|---|---|---|---|---|---|
| 29,000 | 29,050 | 3,929 | 3,504 | 3,929 | 3,746 |
| 29,050 | 29,100 | 3,936 | 3,511 | 3,936 | 3,754 |
| 29,100 | 29,150 | 3,944 | 3,519 | 3,944 | 3,761 |
| 29,150 | 29,200 | 3,951 | 3,526 | 3,951 | 3,769 |
| 29,200 | 29,250 | 3,959 | 3,534 | 3,959 | 3,776 |
| 29,250 | 29,300 | 3,966 | 3,541 | 3,966 | 3,784 |
| 29,300 | 29,350 | 3,974 | 3,549 | 3,974 | 3,791 |
| 29,350 | 29,400 | 3,981 | 3,556 | 3,981 | 3,799 |
| 29,400 | 29,450 | 3,989 | 3,564 | 3,989 | 3,806 |
| 29,450 | 29,500 | 3,996 | 3,571 | 3,996 | 3,814 |
| 29,500 | 29,550 | 4,004 | 3,579 | 4,004 | 3,821 |
| 29,550 | 29,600 | 4,011 | 3,586 | 4,011 | 3,829 |
| 29,600 | 29,650 | 4,019 | 3,594 | 4,019 | 3,836 |
| 29,650 | 29,700 | 4,026 | 3,601 | 4,026 | 3,844 |
| 29,700 | 29,750 | 4,034 | 3,609 | 4,034 | 3,851 |
| 29,750 | 29,800 | 4,041 | 3,616 | 4,041 | 3,859 |
| 29,800 | 29,850 | 4,049 | 3,624 | 4,049 | 3,866 |
| 29,850 | 29,900 | 4,056 | 3,631 | 4,056 | 3,874 |
| 29,900 | 29,950 | 4,064 | 3,639 | 4,064 | 3,881 |
| 29,950 | 30,000 | 4,071 | 3,646 | 4,071 | 3,889 |

## 30,000

| At least | But less than | Single | MFJ | MFS | HoH |
|---|---|---|---|---|---|
| 30,000 | 30,050 | 4,079 | 3,654 | 4,079 | 3,896 |
| 30,050 | 30,100 | 4,086 | 3,661 | 4,086 | 3,904 |
| 30,100 | 30,150 | 4,094 | 3,669 | 4,094 | 3,911 |
| 30,150 | 30,200 | 4,101 | 3,676 | 4,101 | 3,919 |
| 30,200 | 30,250 | 4,109 | 3,684 | 4,109 | 3,926 |
| 30,250 | 30,300 | 4,116 | 3,691 | 4,116 | 3,934 |
| 30,300 | 30,350 | 4,124 | 3,699 | 4,124 | 3,941 |
| 30,350 | 30,400 | 4,131 | 3,706 | 4,131 | 3,949 |
| 30,400 | 30,450 | 4,139 | 3,714 | 4,139 | 3,956 |
| 30,450 | 30,500 | 4,146 | 3,721 | 4,146 | 3,964 |
| 30,500 | 30,550 | 4,154 | 3,729 | 4,154 | 3,971 |
| 30,550 | 30,600 | 4,161 | 3,736 | 4,161 | 3,979 |
| 30,600 | 30,650 | 4,169 | 3,744 | 4,169 | 3,986 |
| 30,650 | 30,700 | 4,176 | 3,751 | 4,176 | 3,994 |
| 30,700 | 30,750 | 4,184 | 3,759 | 4,184 | 4,001 |
| 30,750 | 30,800 | 4,191 | 3,766 | 4,191 | 4,009 |
| 30,800 | 30,850 | 4,199 | 3,774 | 4,199 | 4,016 |
| 30,850 | 30,900 | 4,206 | 3,781 | 4,206 | 4,024 |
| 30,900 | 30,950 | 4,214 | 3,789 | 4,214 | 4,031 |
| 30,950 | 31,000 | 4,221 | 3,796 | 4,221 | 4,039 |

## 31,000

| At least | But less than | Single | MFJ | MFS | HoH |
|---|---|---|---|---|---|
| 31,000 | 31,050 | 4,229 | 3,804 | 4,229 | 4,046 |
| 31,050 | 31,100 | 4,236 | 3,811 | 4,236 | 4,054 |
| 31,100 | 31,150 | 4,244 | 3,819 | 4,244 | 4,061 |
| 31,150 | 31,200 | 4,251 | 3,826 | 4,251 | 4,069 |
| 31,200 | 31,250 | 4,259 | 3,834 | 4,259 | 4,076 |
| 31,250 | 31,300 | 4,266 | 3,841 | 4,266 | 4,084 |
| 31,300 | 31,350 | 4,274 | 3,849 | 4,274 | 4,091 |
| 31,350 | 31,400 | 4,281 | 3,856 | 4,281 | 4,099 |
| 31,400 | 31,450 | 4,289 | 3,864 | 4,289 | 4,106 |
| 31,450 | 31,500 | 4,296 | 3,871 | 4,296 | 4,114 |
| 31,500 | 31,550 | 4,304 | 3,879 | 4,304 | 4,121 |
| 31,550 | 31,600 | 4,311 | 3,886 | 4,311 | 4,129 |
| 31,600 | 31,650 | 4,319 | 3,894 | 4,319 | 4,136 |
| 31,650 | 31,700 | 4,326 | 3,901 | 4,326 | 4,144 |
| 31,700 | 31,750 | 4,334 | 3,909 | 4,334 | 4,151 |
| 31,750 | 31,800 | 4,341 | 3,916 | 4,341 | 4,159 |
| 31,800 | 31,850 | 4,349 | 3,924 | 4,349 | 4,166 |
| 31,850 | 31,900 | 4,356 | 3,931 | 4,356 | 4,174 |
| 31,900 | 31,950 | 4,364 | 3,939 | 4,364 | 4,181 |
| 31,950 | 32,000 | 4,371 | 3,946 | 4,371 | 4,189 |

* This column must also be used by a qualifying widow(er).

(Continued)

## 32,000

| If line 43 (taxable income) is— | | And you are— | | | |
|---|---|---|---|---|---|
| At least | But less than | Single | Married filing jointly * | Married filing separately | Head of a household |
| | | Your tax is— | | | |
| 32,000 | 32,050 | 4,379 | 3,954 | 4,379 | 4,196 |
| 32,050 | 32,100 | 4,386 | 3,961 | 4,386 | 4,204 |
| 32,100 | 32,150 | 4,394 | 3,969 | 4,394 | 4,211 |
| 32,150 | 32,200 | 4,401 | 3,976 | 4,401 | 4,219 |
| 32,200 | 32,250 | 4,409 | 3,984 | 4,409 | 4,226 |
| 32,250 | 32,300 | 4,416 | 3,991 | 4,416 | 4,234 |
| 32,300 | 32,350 | 4,424 | 3,999 | 4,424 | 4,241 |
| 32,350 | 32,400 | 4,431 | 4,006 | 4,431 | 4,249 |
| 32,400 | 32,450 | 4,439 | 4,014 | 4,439 | 4,256 |
| 32,450 | 32,500 | 4,446 | 4,021 | 4,446 | 4,264 |
| 32,500 | 32,550 | 4,454 | 4,029 | 4,454 | 4,271 |
| 32,550 | 32,600 | 4,461 | 4,036 | 4,461 | 4,279 |
| 32,600 | 32,650 | 4,469 | 4,044 | 4,469 | 4,286 |
| 32,650 | 32,700 | 4,476 | 4,051 | 4,476 | 4,294 |
| 32,700 | 32,750 | 4,484 | 4,059 | 4,484 | 4,301 |
| 32,750 | 32,800 | 4,491 | 4,066 | 4,491 | 4,309 |
| 32,800 | 32,850 | 4,499 | 4,074 | 4,499 | 4,316 |
| 32,850 | 32,900 | 4,506 | 4,081 | 4,506 | 4,324 |
| 32,900 | 32,950 | 4,514 | 4,089 | 4,514 | 4,331 |
| 32,950 | 33,000 | 4,521 | 4,096 | 4,521 | 4,339 |

## 33,000

| At least | But less than | Single | Married filing jointly * | Married filing separately | Head of a household |
|---|---|---|---|---|---|
| 33,000 | 33,050 | 4,529 | 4,104 | 4,529 | 4,346 |
| 33,050 | 33,100 | 4,536 | 4,111 | 4,536 | 4,354 |
| 33,100 | 33,150 | 4,544 | 4,119 | 4,544 | 4,361 |
| 33,150 | 33,200 | 4,551 | 4,126 | 4,551 | 4,369 |
| 33,200 | 33,250 | 4,559 | 4,134 | 4,559 | 4,376 |
| 33,250 | 33,300 | 4,566 | 4,141 | 4,566 | 4,384 |
| 33,300 | 33,350 | 4,574 | 4,149 | 4,574 | 4,391 |
| 33,350 | 33,400 | 4,581 | 4,156 | 4,581 | 4,399 |
| 33,400 | 33,450 | 4,589 | 4,164 | 4,589 | 4,406 |
| 33,450 | 33,500 | 4,596 | 4,171 | 4,596 | 4,414 |
| 33,500 | 33,550 | 4,604 | 4,179 | 4,604 | 4,421 |
| 33,550 | 33,600 | 4,611 | 4,186 | 4,611 | 4,429 |
| 33,600 | 33,650 | 4,619 | 4,194 | 4,619 | 4,436 |
| 33,650 | 33,700 | 4,626 | 4,201 | 4,626 | 4,444 |
| 33,700 | 33,750 | 4,634 | 4,209 | 4,634 | 4,451 |
| 33,750 | 33,800 | 4,641 | 4,216 | 4,641 | 4,459 |
| 33,800 | 33,850 | 4,649 | 4,224 | 4,649 | 4,466 |
| 33,850 | 33,900 | 4,656 | 4,231 | 4,656 | 4,474 |
| 33,900 | 33,950 | 4,664 | 4,239 | 4,664 | 4,481 |
| 33,950 | 34,000 | 4,671 | 4,246 | 4,671 | 4,489 |

## 34,000

| At least | But less than | Single | Married filing jointly * | Married filing separately | Head of a household |
|---|---|---|---|---|---|
| 34,000 | 34,050 | 4,679 | 4,254 | 4,679 | 4,496 |
| 34,050 | 34,100 | 4,686 | 4,261 | 4,686 | 4,504 |
| 34,100 | 34,150 | 4,694 | 4,269 | 4,694 | 4,511 |
| 34,150 | 34,200 | 4,701 | 4,276 | 4,701 | 4,519 |
| 34,200 | 34,250 | 4,709 | 4,284 | 4,709 | 4,526 |
| 34,250 | 34,300 | 4,716 | 4,291 | 4,716 | 4,534 |
| 34,300 | 34,350 | 4,724 | 4,299 | 4,724 | 4,541 |
| 34,350 | 34,400 | 4,731 | 4,306 | 4,731 | 4,549 |
| 34,400 | 34,450 | 4,739 | 4,314 | 4,739 | 4,556 |
| 34,450 | 34,500 | 4,746 | 4,321 | 4,746 | 4,564 |
| 34,500 | 34,550 | 4,756 | 4,329 | 4,756 | 4,571 |
| 34,550 | 34,600 | 4,769 | 4,336 | 4,769 | 4,579 |
| 34,600 | 34,650 | 4,781 | 4,344 | 4,781 | 4,586 |
| 34,650 | 34,700 | 4,794 | 4,351 | 4,794 | 4,594 |
| 34,700 | 34,750 | 4,806 | 4,359 | 4,806 | 4,601 |
| 34,750 | 34,800 | 4,819 | 4,366 | 4,819 | 4,609 |
| 34,800 | 34,850 | 4,831 | 4,374 | 4,831 | 4,616 |
| 34,850 | 34,900 | 4,844 | 4,381 | 4,844 | 4,624 |
| 34,900 | 34,950 | 4,856 | 4,389 | 4,856 | 4,631 |
| 34,950 | 35,000 | 4,869 | 4,396 | 4,869 | 4,639 |

## 35,000

| At least | But less than | Single | Married filing jointly * | Married filing separately | Head of a household |
|---|---|---|---|---|---|
| 35,000 | 35,050 | 4,881 | 4,404 | 4,881 | 4,646 |
| 35,050 | 35,100 | 4,894 | 4,411 | 4,894 | 4,654 |
| 35,100 | 35,150 | 4,906 | 4,419 | 4,906 | 4,661 |
| 35,150 | 35,200 | 4,919 | 4,426 | 4,919 | 4,669 |
| 35,200 | 35,250 | 4,931 | 4,434 | 4,931 | 4,676 |
| 35,250 | 35,300 | 4,944 | 4,441 | 4,944 | 4,684 |
| 35,300 | 35,350 | 4,956 | 4,449 | 4,956 | 4,691 |
| 35,350 | 35,400 | 4,969 | 4,456 | 4,969 | 4,699 |
| 35,400 | 35,450 | 4,981 | 4,464 | 4,981 | 4,706 |
| 35,450 | 35,500 | 4,994 | 4,471 | 4,994 | 4,714 |
| 35,500 | 35,550 | 5,006 | 4,479 | 5,006 | 4,721 |
| 35,550 | 35,600 | 5,019 | 4,486 | 5,019 | 4,729 |
| 35,600 | 35,650 | 5,031 | 4,494 | 5,031 | 4,736 |
| 35,650 | 35,700 | 5,044 | 4,501 | 5,044 | 4,744 |
| 35,700 | 35,750 | 5,056 | 4,509 | 5,056 | 4,751 |
| 35,750 | 35,800 | 5,069 | 4,516 | 5,069 | 4,759 |
| 35,800 | 35,850 | 5,081 | 4,524 | 5,081 | 4,766 |
| 35,850 | 35,900 | 5,094 | 4,531 | 5,094 | 4,774 |
| 35,900 | 35,950 | 5,106 | 4,539 | 5,106 | 4,781 |
| 35,950 | 36,000 | 5,119 | 4,546 | 5,119 | 4,789 |

## 36,000

| At least | But less than | Single | Married filing jointly * | Married filing separately | Head of a household |
|---|---|---|---|---|---|
| 36,000 | 36,050 | 5,131 | 4,554 | 5,131 | 4,796 |
| 36,050 | 36,100 | 5,144 | 4,561 | 5,144 | 4,804 |
| 36,100 | 36,150 | 5,156 | 4,569 | 5,156 | 4,811 |
| 36,150 | 36,200 | 5,169 | 4,576 | 5,169 | 4,819 |
| 36,200 | 36,250 | 5,181 | 4,584 | 5,181 | 4,826 |
| 36,250 | 36,300 | 5,194 | 4,591 | 5,194 | 4,834 |
| 36,300 | 36,350 | 5,206 | 4,599 | 5,206 | 4,841 |
| 36,350 | 36,400 | 5,219 | 4,606 | 5,219 | 4,849 |
| 36,400 | 36,450 | 5,231 | 4,614 | 5,231 | 4,856 |
| 36,450 | 36,500 | 5,244 | 4,621 | 5,244 | 4,864 |
| 36,500 | 36,550 | 5,256 | 4,629 | 5,256 | 4,871 |
| 36,550 | 36,600 | 5,269 | 4,636 | 5,269 | 4,879 |
| 36,600 | 36,650 | 5,281 | 4,644 | 5,281 | 4,886 |
| 36,650 | 36,700 | 5,294 | 4,651 | 5,294 | 4,894 |
| 36,700 | 36,750 | 5,306 | 4,659 | 5,306 | 4,901 |
| 36,750 | 36,800 | 5,319 | 4,666 | 5,319 | 4,909 |
| 36,800 | 36,850 | 5,331 | 4,674 | 5,331 | 4,916 |
| 36,850 | 36,900 | 5,344 | 4,681 | 5,344 | 4,924 |
| 36,900 | 36,950 | 5,356 | 4,689 | 5,356 | 4,931 |
| 36,950 | 37,000 | 5,369 | 4,696 | 5,369 | 4,939 |

## 37,000

| At least | But less than | Single | Married filing jointly * | Married filing separately | Head of a household |
|---|---|---|---|---|---|
| 37,000 | 37,050 | 5,381 | 4,704 | 5,381 | 4,946 |
| 37,050 | 37,100 | 5,394 | 4,711 | 5,394 | 4,954 |
| 37,100 | 37,150 | 5,406 | 4,719 | 5,406 | 4,961 |
| 37,150 | 37,200 | 5,419 | 4,726 | 5,419 | 4,969 |
| 37,200 | 37,250 | 5,431 | 4,734 | 5,431 | 4,976 |
| 37,250 | 37,300 | 5,444 | 4,741 | 5,444 | 4,984 |
| 37,300 | 37,350 | 5,456 | 4,749 | 5,456 | 4,991 |
| 37,350 | 37,400 | 5,469 | 4,756 | 5,469 | 4,999 |
| 37,400 | 37,450 | 5,481 | 4,764 | 5,481 | 5,006 |
| 37,450 | 37,500 | 5,494 | 4,771 | 5,494 | 5,014 |
| 37,500 | 37,550 | 5,506 | 4,779 | 5,506 | 5,021 |
| 37,550 | 37,600 | 5,519 | 4,786 | 5,519 | 5,029 |
| 37,600 | 37,650 | 5,531 | 4,794 | 5,531 | 5,036 |
| 37,650 | 37,700 | 5,544 | 4,801 | 5,544 | 5,044 |
| 37,700 | 37,750 | 5,556 | 4,809 | 5,556 | 5,051 |
| 37,750 | 37,800 | 5,569 | 4,816 | 5,569 | 5,059 |
| 37,800 | 37,850 | 5,581 | 4,824 | 5,581 | 5,066 |
| 37,850 | 37,900 | 5,594 | 4,831 | 5,594 | 5,074 |
| 37,900 | 37,950 | 5,606 | 4,839 | 5,606 | 5,081 |
| 37,950 | 38,000 | 5,619 | 4,846 | 5,619 | 5,089 |

## 38,000

| At least | But less than | Single | Married filing jointly * | Married filing separately | Head of a household |
|---|---|---|---|---|---|
| 38,000 | 38,050 | 5,631 | 4,854 | 5,631 | 5,096 |
| 38,050 | 38,100 | 5,644 | 4,861 | 5,644 | 5,104 |
| 38,100 | 38,150 | 5,656 | 4,869 | 5,656 | 5,111 |
| 38,150 | 38,200 | 5,669 | 4,876 | 5,669 | 5,119 |
| 38,200 | 38,250 | 5,681 | 4,884 | 5,681 | 5,126 |
| 38,250 | 38,300 | 5,694 | 4,891 | 5,694 | 5,134 |
| 38,300 | 38,350 | 5,706 | 4,899 | 5,706 | 5,141 |
| 38,350 | 38,400 | 5,719 | 4,906 | 5,719 | 5,149 |
| 38,400 | 38,450 | 5,731 | 4,914 | 5,731 | 5,156 |
| 38,450 | 38,500 | 5,744 | 4,921 | 5,744 | 5,164 |
| 38,500 | 38,550 | 5,756 | 4,929 | 5,756 | 5,171 |
| 38,550 | 38,600 | 5,769 | 4,936 | 5,769 | 5,179 |
| 38,600 | 38,650 | 5,781 | 4,944 | 5,781 | 5,186 |
| 38,650 | 38,700 | 5,794 | 4,951 | 5,794 | 5,194 |
| 38,700 | 38,750 | 5,806 | 4,959 | 5,806 | 5,201 |
| 38,750 | 38,800 | 5,819 | 4,966 | 5,819 | 5,209 |
| 38,800 | 38,850 | 5,831 | 4,974 | 5,831 | 5,216 |
| 38,850 | 38,900 | 5,844 | 4,981 | 5,844 | 5,224 |
| 38,900 | 38,950 | 5,856 | 4,989 | 5,856 | 5,231 |
| 38,950 | 39,000 | 5,869 | 4,996 | 5,869 | 5,239 |

## 39,000

| At least | But less than | Single | Married filing jointly * | Married filing separately | Head of a household |
|---|---|---|---|---|---|
| 39,000 | 39,050 | 5,881 | 5,004 | 5,881 | 5,246 |
| 39,050 | 39,100 | 5,894 | 5,011 | 5,894 | 5,254 |
| 39,100 | 39,150 | 5,906 | 5,019 | 5,906 | 5,261 |
| 39,150 | 39,200 | 5,919 | 5,026 | 5,919 | 5,269 |
| 39,200 | 39,250 | 5,931 | 5,034 | 5,931 | 5,276 |
| 39,250 | 39,300 | 5,944 | 5,041 | 5,944 | 5,284 |
| 39,300 | 39,350 | 5,956 | 5,049 | 5,956 | 5,291 |
| 39,350 | 39,400 | 5,969 | 5,056 | 5,969 | 5,299 |
| 39,400 | 39,450 | 5,981 | 5,064 | 5,981 | 5,306 |
| 39,450 | 39,500 | 5,994 | 5,071 | 5,994 | 5,314 |
| 39,500 | 39,550 | 6,006 | 5,079 | 6,006 | 5,321 |
| 39,550 | 39,600 | 6,019 | 5,086 | 6,019 | 5,329 |
| 39,600 | 39,650 | 6,031 | 5,094 | 6,031 | 5,336 |
| 39,650 | 39,700 | 6,044 | 5,101 | 6,044 | 5,344 |
| 39,700 | 39,750 | 6,056 | 5,109 | 6,056 | 5,351 |
| 39,750 | 39,800 | 6,069 | 5,116 | 6,069 | 5,359 |
| 39,800 | 39,850 | 6,081 | 5,124 | 6,081 | 5,366 |
| 39,850 | 39,900 | 6,094 | 5,131 | 6,094 | 5,374 |
| 39,900 | 39,950 | 6,106 | 5,139 | 6,106 | 5,381 |
| 39,950 | 40,000 | 6,119 | 5,146 | 6,119 | 5,389 |

## 40,000

| At least | But less than | Single | Married filing jointly * | Married filing separately | Head of a household |
|---|---|---|---|---|---|
| 40,000 | 40,050 | 6,131 | 5,154 | 6,131 | 5,396 |
| 40,050 | 40,100 | 6,144 | 5,161 | 6,144 | 5,404 |
| 40,100 | 40,150 | 6,156 | 5,169 | 6,156 | 5,411 |
| 40,150 | 40,200 | 6,169 | 5,176 | 6,169 | 5,419 |
| 40,200 | 40,250 | 6,181 | 5,184 | 6,181 | 5,426 |
| 40,250 | 40,300 | 6,194 | 5,191 | 6,194 | 5,434 |
| 40,300 | 40,350 | 6,206 | 5,199 | 6,206 | 5,441 |
| 40,350 | 40,400 | 6,219 | 5,206 | 6,219 | 5,449 |
| 40,400 | 40,450 | 6,231 | 5,214 | 6,231 | 5,456 |
| 40,450 | 40,500 | 6,244 | 5,221 | 6,244 | 5,464 |
| 40,500 | 40,550 | 6,256 | 5,229 | 6,256 | 5,471 |
| 40,550 | 40,600 | 6,269 | 5,236 | 6,269 | 5,479 |
| 40,600 | 40,650 | 6,281 | 5,244 | 6,281 | 5,486 |
| 40,650 | 40,700 | 6,294 | 5,251 | 6,294 | 5,494 |
| 40,700 | 40,750 | 6,306 | 5,259 | 6,306 | 5,501 |
| 40,750 | 40,800 | 6,319 | 5,266 | 6,319 | 5,509 |
| 40,800 | 40,850 | 6,331 | 5,274 | 6,331 | 5,516 |
| 40,850 | 40,900 | 6,344 | 5,281 | 6,344 | 5,524 |
| 40,900 | 40,950 | 6,356 | 5,289 | 6,356 | 5,531 |
| 40,950 | 41,000 | 6,369 | 5,296 | 6,369 | 5,539 |

* This column must also be used by a qualifying widow(er).

(Continued)

## 41,000

| At least | But less than | Single | Married filing jointly * | Married filing separately | Head of a household |
|---|---|---|---|---|---|
| 41,000 | 41,050 | 6,381 | 5,304 | 6,381 | 5,546 |
| 41,050 | 41,100 | 6,394 | 5,311 | 6,394 | 5,554 |
| 41,100 | 41,150 | 6,406 | 5,319 | 6,406 | 5,561 |
| 41,150 | 41,200 | 6,419 | 5,326 | 6,419 | 5,569 |
| 41,200 | 41,250 | 6,431 | 5,334 | 6,431 | 5,576 |
| 41,250 | 41,300 | 6,444 | 5,341 | 6,444 | 5,584 |
| 41,300 | 41,350 | 6,456 | 5,349 | 6,456 | 5,591 |
| 41,350 | 41,400 | 6,469 | 5,356 | 6,469 | 5,599 |
| 41,400 | 41,450 | 6,481 | 5,364 | 6,481 | 5,606 |
| 41,450 | 41,500 | 6,494 | 5,371 | 6,494 | 5,614 |
| 41,500 | 41,550 | 6,506 | 5,379 | 6,506 | 5,621 |
| 41,550 | 41,600 | 6,519 | 5,386 | 6,519 | 5,629 |
| 41,600 | 41,650 | 6,531 | 5,394 | 6,531 | 5,636 |
| 41,650 | 41,700 | 6,544 | 5,401 | 6,544 | 5,644 |
| 41,700 | 41,750 | 6,556 | 5,409 | 6,556 | 5,651 |
| 41,750 | 41,800 | 6,569 | 5,416 | 6,569 | 5,659 |
| 41,800 | 41,850 | 6,581 | 5,424 | 6,581 | 5,666 |
| 41,850 | 41,900 | 6,594 | 5,431 | 6,594 | 5,674 |
| 41,900 | 41,950 | 6,606 | 5,439 | 6,606 | 5,681 |
| 41,950 | 42,000 | 6,619 | 5,446 | 6,619 | 5,689 |

## 42,000

| At least | But less than | Single | Married filing jointly * | Married filing separately | Head of a household |
|---|---|---|---|---|---|
| 42,000 | 42,050 | 6,631 | 5,454 | 6,631 | 5,696 |
| 42,050 | 42,100 | 6,644 | 5,461 | 6,644 | 5,704 |
| 42,100 | 42,150 | 6,656 | 5,469 | 6,656 | 5,711 |
| 42,150 | 42,200 | 6,669 | 5,476 | 6,669 | 5,719 |
| 42,200 | 42,250 | 6,681 | 5,484 | 6,681 | 5,726 |
| 42,250 | 42,300 | 6,694 | 5,491 | 6,694 | 5,734 |
| 42,300 | 42,350 | 6,706 | 5,499 | 6,706 | 5,741 |
| 42,350 | 42,400 | 6,719 | 5,506 | 6,719 | 5,749 |
| 42,400 | 42,450 | 6,731 | 5,514 | 6,731 | 5,756 |
| 42,450 | 42,500 | 6,744 | 5,521 | 6,744 | 5,764 |
| 42,500 | 42,550 | 6,756 | 5,529 | 6,756 | 5,771 |
| 42,550 | 42,600 | 6,769 | 5,536 | 6,769 | 5,779 |
| 42,600 | 42,650 | 6,781 | 5,544 | 6,781 | 5,786 |
| 42,650 | 42,700 | 6,794 | 5,551 | 6,794 | 5,794 |
| 42,700 | 42,750 | 6,806 | 5,559 | 6,806 | 5,801 |
| 42,750 | 42,800 | 6,819 | 5,566 | 6,819 | 5,809 |
| 42,800 | 42,850 | 6,831 | 5,574 | 6,831 | 5,816 |
| 42,850 | 42,900 | 6,844 | 5,581 | 6,844 | 5,824 |
| 42,900 | 42,950 | 6,856 | 5,589 | 6,856 | 5,831 |
| 42,950 | 43,000 | 6,869 | 5,596 | 6,869 | 5,839 |

## 43,000

| At least | But less than | Single | Married filing jointly * | Married filing separately | Head of a household |
|---|---|---|---|---|---|
| 43,000 | 43,050 | 6,881 | 5,604 | 6,881 | 5,846 |
| 43,050 | 43,100 | 6,894 | 5,611 | 6,894 | 5,854 |
| 43,100 | 43,150 | 6,906 | 5,619 | 6,906 | 5,861 |
| 43,150 | 43,200 | 6,919 | 5,626 | 6,919 | 5,869 |
| 43,200 | 43,250 | 6,931 | 5,634 | 6,931 | 5,876 |
| 43,250 | 43,300 | 6,944 | 5,641 | 6,944 | 5,884 |
| 43,300 | 43,350 | 6,956 | 5,649 | 6,956 | 5,891 |
| 43,350 | 43,400 | 6,969 | 5,656 | 6,969 | 5,899 |
| 43,400 | 43,450 | 6,981 | 5,664 | 6,981 | 5,906 |
| 43,450 | 43,500 | 6,994 | 5,671 | 6,994 | 5,914 |
| 43,500 | 43,550 | 7,006 | 5,679 | 7,006 | 5,921 |
| 43,550 | 43,600 | 7,019 | 5,686 | 7,019 | 5,929 |
| 43,600 | 43,650 | 7,031 | 5,694 | 7,031 | 5,936 |
| 43,650 | 43,700 | 7,044 | 5,701 | 7,044 | 5,944 |
| 43,700 | 43,750 | 7,056 | 5,709 | 7,056 | 5,951 |
| 43,750 | 43,800 | 7,069 | 5,716 | 7,069 | 5,959 |
| 43,800 | 43,850 | 7,081 | 5,724 | 7,081 | 5,966 |
| 43,850 | 43,900 | 7,094 | 5,731 | 7,094 | 5,974 |
| 43,900 | 43,950 | 7,106 | 5,739 | 7,106 | 5,981 |
| 43,950 | 44,000 | 7,119 | 5,746 | 7,119 | 5,989 |

## 44,000

| At least | But less than | Single | Married filing jointly * | Married filing separately | Head of a household |
|---|---|---|---|---|---|
| 44,000 | 44,050 | 7,131 | 5,754 | 7,131 | 5,996 |
| 44,050 | 44,100 | 7,144 | 5,761 | 7,144 | 6,004 |
| 44,100 | 44,150 | 7,156 | 5,769 | 7,156 | 6,011 |
| 44,150 | 44,200 | 7,169 | 5,776 | 7,169 | 6,019 |
| 44,200 | 44,250 | 7,181 | 5,784 | 7,181 | 6,026 |
| 44,250 | 44,300 | 7,194 | 5,791 | 7,194 | 6,034 |
| 44,300 | 44,350 | 7,206 | 5,799 | 7,206 | 6,041 |
| 44,350 | 44,400 | 7,219 | 5,806 | 7,219 | 6,049 |
| 44,400 | 44,450 | 7,231 | 5,814 | 7,231 | 6,056 |
| 44,450 | 44,500 | 7,244 | 5,821 | 7,244 | 6,064 |
| 44,500 | 44,550 | 7,256 | 5,829 | 7,256 | 6,071 |
| 44,550 | 44,600 | 7,269 | 5,836 | 7,269 | 6,079 |
| 44,600 | 44,650 | 7,281 | 5,844 | 7,281 | 6,086 |
| 44,650 | 44,700 | 7,294 | 5,851 | 7,294 | 6,094 |
| 44,700 | 44,750 | 7,306 | 5,859 | 7,306 | 6,101 |
| 44,750 | 44,800 | 7,319 | 5,866 | 7,319 | 6,109 |
| 44,800 | 44,850 | 7,331 | 5,874 | 7,331 | 6,116 |
| 44,850 | 44,900 | 7,344 | 5,881 | 7,344 | 6,124 |
| 44,900 | 44,950 | 7,356 | 5,889 | 7,356 | 6,131 |
| 44,950 | 45,000 | 7,369 | 5,896 | 7,369 | 6,139 |

## 45,000

| At least | But less than | Single | Married filing jointly * | Married filing separately | Head of a household |
|---|---|---|---|---|---|
| 45,000 | 45,050 | 7,381 | 5,904 | 7,381 | 6,146 |
| 45,050 | 45,100 | 7,394 | 5,911 | 7,394 | 6,154 |
| 45,100 | 45,150 | 7,406 | 5,919 | 7,406 | 6,161 |
| 45,150 | 45,200 | 7,419 | 5,926 | 7,419 | 6,169 |
| 45,200 | 45,250 | 7,431 | 5,934 | 7,431 | 6,176 |
| 45,250 | 45,300 | 7,444 | 5,941 | 7,444 | 6,184 |
| 45,300 | 45,350 | 7,456 | 5,949 | 7,456 | 6,191 |
| 45,350 | 45,400 | 7,469 | 5,956 | 7,469 | 6,199 |
| 45,400 | 45,450 | 7,481 | 5,964 | 7,481 | 6,206 |
| 45,450 | 45,500 | 7,494 | 5,971 | 7,494 | 6,214 |
| 45,500 | 45,550 | 7,506 | 5,979 | 7,506 | 6,221 |
| 45,550 | 45,600 | 7,519 | 5,986 | 7,519 | 6,229 |
| 45,600 | 45,650 | 7,531 | 5,994 | 7,531 | 6,236 |
| 45,650 | 45,700 | 7,544 | 6,001 | 7,544 | 6,244 |
| 45,700 | 45,750 | 7,556 | 6,009 | 7,556 | 6,251 |
| 45,750 | 45,800 | 7,569 | 6,016 | 7,569 | 6,259 |
| 45,800 | 45,850 | 7,581 | 6,024 | 7,581 | 6,266 |
| 45,850 | 45,900 | 7,594 | 6,031 | 7,594 | 6,274 |
| 45,900 | 45,950 | 7,606 | 6,039 | 7,606 | 6,281 |
| 45,950 | 46,000 | 7,619 | 6,046 | 7,619 | 6,289 |

## 46,000

| At least | But less than | Single | Married filing jointly * | Married filing separately | Head of a household |
|---|---|---|---|---|---|
| 46,000 | 46,050 | 7,631 | 6,054 | 7,631 | 6,296 |
| 46,050 | 46,100 | 7,644 | 6,061 | 7,644 | 6,304 |
| 46,100 | 46,150 | 7,656 | 6,069 | 7,656 | 6,311 |
| 46,150 | 46,200 | 7,669 | 6,076 | 7,669 | 6,319 |
| 46,200 | 46,250 | 7,681 | 6,084 | 7,681 | 6,326 |
| 46,250 | 46,300 | 7,694 | 6,091 | 7,694 | 6,336 |
| 46,300 | 46,350 | 7,706 | 6,099 | 7,706 | 6,349 |
| 46,350 | 46,400 | 7,719 | 6,106 | 7,719 | 6,361 |
| 46,400 | 46,450 | 7,731 | 6,114 | 7,731 | 6,374 |
| 46,450 | 46,500 | 7,744 | 6,121 | 7,744 | 6,386 |
| 46,500 | 46,550 | 7,756 | 6,129 | 7,756 | 6,399 |
| 46,550 | 46,600 | 7,769 | 6,136 | 7,769 | 6,411 |
| 46,600 | 46,650 | 7,781 | 6,144 | 7,781 | 6,424 |
| 46,650 | 46,700 | 7,794 | 6,151 | 7,794 | 6,436 |
| 46,700 | 46,750 | 7,806 | 6,159 | 7,806 | 6,449 |
| 46,750 | 46,800 | 7,819 | 6,166 | 7,819 | 6,461 |
| 46,800 | 46,850 | 7,831 | 6,174 | 7,831 | 6,474 |
| 46,850 | 46,900 | 7,844 | 6,181 | 7,844 | 6,486 |
| 46,900 | 46,950 | 7,856 | 6,189 | 7,856 | 6,499 |
| 46,950 | 47,000 | 7,869 | 6,196 | 7,869 | 6,511 |

## 47,000

| At least | But less than | Single | Married filing jointly * | Married filing separately | Head of a household |
|---|---|---|---|---|---|
| 47,000 | 47,050 | 7,881 | 6,204 | 7,881 | 6,524 |
| 47,050 | 47,100 | 7,894 | 6,211 | 7,894 | 6,536 |
| 47,100 | 47,150 | 7,906 | 6,219 | 7,906 | 6,549 |
| 47,150 | 47,200 | 7,919 | 6,226 | 7,919 | 6,561 |
| 47,200 | 47,250 | 7,931 | 6,234 | 7,931 | 6,574 |
| 47,250 | 47,300 | 7,944 | 6,241 | 7,944 | 6,586 |
| 47,300 | 47,350 | 7,956 | 6,249 | 7,956 | 6,599 |
| 47,350 | 47,400 | 7,969 | 6,256 | 7,969 | 6,611 |
| 47,400 | 47,450 | 7,981 | 6,264 | 7,981 | 6,624 |
| 47,450 | 47,500 | 7,994 | 6,271 | 7,994 | 6,636 |
| 47,500 | 47,550 | 8,006 | 6,279 | 8,006 | 6,649 |
| 47,550 | 47,600 | 8,019 | 6,286 | 8,019 | 6,661 |
| 47,600 | 47,650 | 8,031 | 6,294 | 8,031 | 6,674 |
| 47,650 | 47,700 | 8,044 | 6,301 | 8,044 | 6,686 |
| 47,700 | 47,750 | 8,056 | 6,309 | 8,056 | 6,699 |
| 47,750 | 47,800 | 8,069 | 6,316 | 8,069 | 6,711 |
| 47,800 | 47,850 | 8,081 | 6,324 | 8,081 | 6,724 |
| 47,850 | 47,900 | 8,094 | 6,331 | 8,094 | 6,736 |
| 47,900 | 47,950 | 8,106 | 6,339 | 8,106 | 6,749 |
| 47,950 | 48,000 | 8,119 | 6,346 | 8,119 | 6,761 |

## 48,000

| At least | But less than | Single | Married filing jointly * | Married filing separately | Head of a household |
|---|---|---|---|---|---|
| 48,000 | 48,050 | 8,131 | 6,354 | 8,131 | 6,774 |
| 48,050 | 48,100 | 8,144 | 6,361 | 8,144 | 6,786 |
| 48,100 | 48,150 | 8,156 | 6,369 | 8,156 | 6,799 |
| 48,150 | 48,200 | 8,169 | 6,376 | 8,169 | 6,811 |
| 48,200 | 48,250 | 8,181 | 6,384 | 8,181 | 6,824 |
| 48,250 | 48,300 | 8,194 | 6,391 | 8,194 | 6,836 |
| 48,300 | 48,350 | 8,206 | 6,399 | 8,206 | 6,849 |
| 48,350 | 48,400 | 8,219 | 6,406 | 8,219 | 6,861 |
| 48,400 | 48,450 | 8,231 | 6,414 | 8,231 | 6,874 |
| 48,450 | 48,500 | 8,244 | 6,421 | 8,244 | 6,886 |
| 48,500 | 48,550 | 8,256 | 6,429 | 8,256 | 6,899 |
| 48,550 | 48,600 | 8,269 | 6,436 | 8,269 | 6,911 |
| 48,600 | 48,650 | 8,281 | 6,444 | 8,281 | 6,924 |
| 48,650 | 48,700 | 8,294 | 6,451 | 8,294 | 6,936 |
| 48,700 | 48,750 | 8,306 | 6,459 | 8,306 | 6,949 |
| 48,750 | 48,800 | 8,319 | 6,466 | 8,319 | 6,961 |
| 48,800 | 48,850 | 8,331 | 6,474 | 8,331 | 6,974 |
| 48,850 | 48,900 | 8,344 | 6,481 | 8,344 | 6,986 |
| 48,900 | 48,950 | 8,356 | 6,489 | 8,356 | 6,999 |
| 48,950 | 49,000 | 8,369 | 6,496 | 8,369 | 7,011 |

## 49,000

| At least | But less than | Single | Married filing jointly * | Married filing separately | Head of a household |
|---|---|---|---|---|---|
| 49,000 | 49,050 | 8,381 | 6,504 | 8,381 | 7,024 |
| 49,050 | 49,100 | 8,394 | 6,511 | 8,394 | 7,036 |
| 49,100 | 49,150 | 8,406 | 6,519 | 8,406 | 7,049 |
| 49,150 | 49,200 | 8,419 | 6,526 | 8,419 | 7,061 |
| 49,200 | 49,250 | 8,431 | 6,534 | 8,431 | 7,074 |
| 49,250 | 49,300 | 8,444 | 6,541 | 8,444 | 7,086 |
| 49,300 | 49,350 | 8,456 | 6,549 | 8,456 | 7,099 |
| 49,350 | 49,400 | 8,469 | 6,556 | 8,469 | 7,111 |
| 49,400 | 49,450 | 8,481 | 6,564 | 8,481 | 7,124 |
| 49,450 | 49,500 | 8,494 | 6,571 | 8,494 | 7,136 |
| 49,500 | 49,550 | 8,506 | 6,579 | 8,506 | 7,149 |
| 49,550 | 49,600 | 8,519 | 6,586 | 8,519 | 7,161 |
| 49,600 | 49,650 | 8,531 | 6,594 | 8,531 | 7,174 |
| 49,650 | 49,700 | 8,544 | 6,601 | 8,544 | 7,186 |
| 49,700 | 49,750 | 8,556 | 6,609 | 8,556 | 7,199 |
| 49,750 | 49,800 | 8,569 | 6,616 | 8,569 | 7,211 |
| 49,800 | 49,850 | 8,581 | 6,624 | 8,581 | 7,224 |
| 49,850 | 49,900 | 8,594 | 6,631 | 8,594 | 7,236 |
| 49,900 | 49,950 | 8,606 | 6,639 | 8,606 | 7,249 |
| 49,950 | 50,000 | 8,619 | 6,646 | 8,619 | 7,261 |

* This column must also be used by a qualifying widow(er).

(Continued)

## 50,000

| If line 43 (taxable income) is— | | And you are— | | | |
|---|---|---|---|---|---|
| At least | But less than | Single | Married filing jointly * | Married filing separately | Head of a household |
| | | Your tax is— | | | |
| 50,000 | 50,050 | 8,631 | 6,654 | 8,631 | 7,274 |
| 50,050 | 50,100 | 8,644 | 6,661 | 8,644 | 7,286 |
| 50,100 | 50,150 | 8,656 | 6,669 | 8,656 | 7,299 |
| 50,150 | 50,200 | 8,669 | 6,676 | 8,669 | 7,311 |
| 50,200 | 50,250 | 8,681 | 6,684 | 8,681 | 7,324 |
| 50,250 | 50,300 | 8,694 | 6,691 | 8,694 | 7,336 |
| 50,300 | 50,350 | 8,706 | 6,699 | 8,706 | 7,349 |
| 50,350 | 50,400 | 8,719 | 6,706 | 8,719 | 7,361 |
| 50,400 | 50,450 | 8,731 | 6,714 | 8,731 | 7,374 |
| 50,450 | 50,500 | 8,744 | 6,721 | 8,744 | 7,386 |
| 50,500 | 50,550 | 8,756 | 6,729 | 8,756 | 7,399 |
| 50,550 | 50,600 | 8,769 | 6,736 | 8,769 | 7,411 |
| 50,600 | 50,650 | 8,781 | 6,744 | 8,781 | 7,424 |
| 50,650 | 50,700 | 8,794 | 6,751 | 8,794 | 7,436 |
| 50,700 | 50,750 | 8,806 | 6,759 | 8,806 | 7,449 |
| 50,750 | 50,800 | 8,819 | 6,766 | 8,819 | 7,461 |
| 50,800 | 50,850 | 8,831 | 6,774 | 8,831 | 7,474 |
| 50,850 | 50,900 | 8,844 | 6,781 | 8,844 | 7,486 |
| 50,900 | 50,950 | 8,856 | 6,789 | 8,856 | 7,499 |
| 50,950 | 51,000 | 8,869 | 6,796 | 8,869 | 7,511 |

## 51,000

| At least | But less than | Single | Married filing jointly * | Married filing separately | Head of a household |
|---|---|---|---|---|---|
| 51,000 | 51,050 | 8,881 | 6,804 | 8,881 | 7,524 |
| 51,050 | 51,100 | 8,894 | 6,811 | 8,894 | 7,536 |
| 51,100 | 51,150 | 8,906 | 6,819 | 8,906 | 7,549 |
| 51,150 | 51,200 | 8,919 | 6,826 | 8,919 | 7,561 |
| 51,200 | 51,250 | 8,931 | 6,834 | 8,931 | 7,574 |
| 51,250 | 51,300 | 8,944 | 6,841 | 8,944 | 7,586 |
| 51,300 | 51,350 | 8,956 | 6,849 | 8,956 | 7,599 |
| 51,350 | 51,400 | 8,969 | 6,856 | 8,969 | 7,611 |
| 51,400 | 51,450 | 8,981 | 6,864 | 8,981 | 7,624 |
| 51,450 | 51,500 | 8,994 | 6,871 | 8,994 | 7,636 |
| 51,500 | 51,550 | 9,006 | 6,879 | 9,006 | 7,649 |
| 51,550 | 51,600 | 9,019 | 6,886 | 9,019 | 7,661 |
| 51,600 | 51,650 | 9,031 | 6,894 | 9,031 | 7,674 |
| 51,650 | 51,700 | 9,044 | 6,901 | 9,044 | 7,686 |
| 51,700 | 51,750 | 9,056 | 6,909 | 9,056 | 7,699 |
| 51,750 | 51,800 | 9,069 | 6,916 | 9,069 | 7,711 |
| 51,800 | 51,850 | 9,081 | 6,924 | 9,081 | 7,724 |
| 51,850 | 51,900 | 9,094 | 6,931 | 9,094 | 7,736 |
| 51,900 | 51,950 | 9,106 | 6,939 | 9,106 | 7,749 |
| 51,950 | 52,000 | 9,119 | 6,946 | 9,119 | 7,761 |

## 52,000

| At least | But less than | Single | Married filing jointly * | Married filing separately | Head of a household |
|---|---|---|---|---|---|
| 52,000 | 52,050 | 9,131 | 6,954 | 9,131 | 7,774 |
| 52,050 | 52,100 | 9,144 | 6,961 | 9,144 | 7,786 |
| 52,100 | 52,150 | 9,156 | 6,969 | 9,156 | 7,799 |
| 52,150 | 52,200 | 9,169 | 6,976 | 9,169 | 7,811 |
| 52,200 | 52,250 | 9,181 | 6,984 | 9,181 | 7,824 |
| 52,250 | 52,300 | 9,194 | 6,991 | 9,194 | 7,836 |
| 52,300 | 52,350 | 9,206 | 6,999 | 9,206 | 7,849 |
| 52,350 | 52,400 | 9,219 | 7,006 | 9,219 | 7,861 |
| 52,400 | 52,450 | 9,231 | 7,014 | 9,231 | 7,874 |
| 52,450 | 52,500 | 9,244 | 7,021 | 9,244 | 7,886 |
| 52,500 | 52,550 | 9,256 | 7,029 | 9,256 | 7,899 |
| 52,550 | 52,600 | 9,269 | 7,036 | 9,269 | 7,911 |
| 52,600 | 52,650 | 9,281 | 7,044 | 9,281 | 7,924 |
| 52,650 | 52,700 | 9,294 | 7,051 | 9,294 | 7,936 |
| 52,700 | 52,750 | 9,306 | 7,059 | 9,306 | 7,949 |
| 52,750 | 52,800 | 9,319 | 7,066 | 9,319 | 7,961 |
| 52,800 | 52,850 | 9,331 | 7,074 | 9,331 | 7,974 |
| 52,850 | 52,900 | 9,344 | 7,081 | 9,344 | 7,986 |
| 52,900 | 52,950 | 9,356 | 7,089 | 9,356 | 7,999 |
| 52,950 | 53,000 | 9,369 | 7,096 | 9,369 | 8,011 |

## 53,000

| At least | But less than | Single | Married filing jointly * | Married filing separately | Head of a household |
|---|---|---|---|---|---|
| 53,000 | 53,050 | 9,381 | 7,104 | 9,381 | 8,024 |
| 53,050 | 53,100 | 9,394 | 7,111 | 9,394 | 8,036 |
| 53,100 | 53,150 | 9,406 | 7,119 | 9,406 | 8,049 |
| 53,150 | 53,200 | 9,419 | 7,126 | 9,419 | 8,061 |
| 53,200 | 53,250 | 9,431 | 7,134 | 9,431 | 8,074 |
| 53,250 | 53,300 | 9,444 | 7,141 | 9,444 | 8,086 |
| 53,300 | 53,350 | 9,456 | 7,149 | 9,456 | 8,099 |
| 53,350 | 53,400 | 9,469 | 7,156 | 9,469 | 8,111 |
| 53,400 | 53,450 | 9,481 | 7,164 | 9,481 | 8,124 |
| 53,450 | 53,500 | 9,494 | 7,171 | 9,494 | 8,136 |
| 53,500 | 53,550 | 9,506 | 7,179 | 9,506 | 8,149 |
| 53,550 | 53,600 | 9,519 | 7,186 | 9,519 | 8,161 |
| 53,600 | 53,650 | 9,531 | 7,194 | 9,531 | 8,174 |
| 53,650 | 53,700 | 9,544 | 7,201 | 9,544 | 8,186 |
| 53,700 | 53,750 | 9,556 | 7,209 | 9,556 | 8,199 |
| 53,750 | 53,800 | 9,569 | 7,216 | 9,569 | 8,211 |
| 53,800 | 53,850 | 9,581 | 7,224 | 9,581 | 8,224 |
| 53,850 | 53,900 | 9,594 | 7,231 | 9,594 | 8,236 |
| 53,900 | 53,950 | 9,606 | 7,239 | 9,606 | 8,249 |
| 53,950 | 54,000 | 9,619 | 7,246 | 9,619 | 8,261 |

## 54,000

| At least | But less than | Single | Married filing jointly * | Married filing separately | Head of a household |
|---|---|---|---|---|---|
| 54,000 | 54,050 | 9,631 | 7,254 | 9,631 | 8,274 |
| 54,050 | 54,100 | 9,644 | 7,261 | 9,644 | 8,286 |
| 54,100 | 54,150 | 9,656 | 7,269 | 9,656 | 8,299 |
| 54,150 | 54,200 | 9,669 | 7,276 | 9,669 | 8,311 |
| 54,200 | 54,250 | 9,681 | 7,284 | 9,681 | 8,324 |
| 54,250 | 54,300 | 9,694 | 7,291 | 9,694 | 8,336 |
| 54,300 | 54,350 | 9,706 | 7,299 | 9,706 | 8,349 |
| 54,350 | 54,400 | 9,719 | 7,306 | 9,719 | 8,361 |
| 54,400 | 54,450 | 9,731 | 7,314 | 9,731 | 8,374 |
| 54,450 | 54,500 | 9,744 | 7,321 | 9,744 | 8,386 |
| 54,500 | 54,550 | 9,756 | 7,329 | 9,756 | 8,399 |
| 54,550 | 54,600 | 9,769 | 7,336 | 9,769 | 8,411 |
| 54,600 | 54,650 | 9,781 | 7,344 | 9,781 | 8,424 |
| 54,650 | 54,700 | 9,794 | 7,351 | 9,794 | 8,436 |
| 54,700 | 54,750 | 9,806 | 7,359 | 9,806 | 8,449 |
| 54,750 | 54,800 | 9,819 | 7,366 | 9,819 | 8,461 |
| 54,800 | 54,850 | 9,831 | 7,374 | 9,831 | 8,474 |
| 54,850 | 54,900 | 9,844 | 7,381 | 9,844 | 8,486 |
| 54,900 | 54,950 | 9,856 | 7,389 | 9,856 | 8,499 |
| 54,950 | 55,000 | 9,869 | 7,396 | 9,869 | 8,511 |

## 55,000

| At least | But less than | Single | Married filing jointly * | Married filing separately | Head of a household |
|---|---|---|---|---|---|
| 55,000 | 55,050 | 9,881 | 7,404 | 9,881 | 8,524 |
| 55,050 | 55,100 | 9,894 | 7,411 | 9,894 | 8,536 |
| 55,100 | 55,150 | 9,906 | 7,419 | 9,906 | 8,549 |
| 55,150 | 55,200 | 9,919 | 7,426 | 9,919 | 8,561 |
| 55,200 | 55,250 | 9,931 | 7,434 | 9,931 | 8,574 |
| 55,250 | 55,300 | 9,944 | 7,441 | 9,944 | 8,586 |
| 55,300 | 55,350 | 9,956 | 7,449 | 9,956 | 8,599 |
| 55,350 | 55,400 | 9,969 | 7,456 | 9,969 | 8,611 |
| 55,400 | 55,450 | 9,981 | 7,464 | 9,981 | 8,624 |
| 55,450 | 55,500 | 9,994 | 7,471 | 9,994 | 8,636 |
| 55,500 | 55,550 | 10,006 | 7,479 | 10,006 | 8,649 |
| 55,550 | 55,600 | 10,019 | 7,486 | 10,019 | 8,661 |
| 55,600 | 55,650 | 10,031 | 7,494 | 10,031 | 8,674 |
| 55,650 | 55,700 | 10,044 | 7,501 | 10,044 | 8,686 |
| 55,700 | 55,750 | 10,056 | 7,509 | 10,056 | 8,699 |
| 55,750 | 55,800 | 10,069 | 7,516 | 10,069 | 8,711 |
| 55,800 | 55,850 | 10,081 | 7,524 | 10,081 | 8,724 |
| 55,850 | 55,900 | 10,094 | 7,531 | 10,094 | 8,736 |
| 55,900 | 55,950 | 10,106 | 7,539 | 10,106 | 8,749 |
| 55,950 | 56,000 | 10,119 | 7,546 | 10,119 | 8,761 |

## 56,000

| At least | But less than | Single | Married filing jointly * | Married filing separately | Head of a household |
|---|---|---|---|---|---|
| 56,000 | 56,050 | 10,131 | 7,554 | 10,131 | 8,774 |
| 56,050 | 56,100 | 10,144 | 7,561 | 10,144 | 8,786 |
| 56,100 | 56,150 | 10,156 | 7,569 | 10,156 | 8,799 |
| 56,150 | 56,200 | 10,169 | 7,576 | 10,169 | 8,811 |
| 56,200 | 56,250 | 10,181 | 7,584 | 10,181 | 8,824 |
| 56,250 | 56,300 | 10,194 | 7,591 | 10,194 | 8,836 |
| 56,300 | 56,350 | 10,206 | 7,599 | 10,206 | 8,849 |
| 56,350 | 56,400 | 10,219 | 7,606 | 10,219 | 8,861 |
| 56,400 | 56,450 | 10,231 | 7,614 | 10,231 | 8,874 |
| 56,450 | 56,500 | 10,244 | 7,621 | 10,244 | 8,886 |
| 56,500 | 56,550 | 10,256 | 7,629 | 10,256 | 8,899 |
| 56,550 | 56,600 | 10,269 | 7,636 | 10,269 | 8,911 |
| 56,600 | 56,650 | 10,281 | 7,644 | 10,281 | 8,924 |
| 56,650 | 56,700 | 10,294 | 7,651 | 10,294 | 8,936 |
| 56,700 | 56,750 | 10,306 | 7,659 | 10,306 | 8,949 |
| 56,750 | 56,800 | 10,319 | 7,666 | 10,319 | 8,961 |
| 56,800 | 56,850 | 10,331 | 7,674 | 10,331 | 8,974 |
| 56,850 | 56,900 | 10,344 | 7,681 | 10,344 | 8,986 |
| 56,900 | 56,950 | 10,356 | 7,689 | 10,356 | 8,999 |
| 56,950 | 57,000 | 10,369 | 7,696 | 10,369 | 9,011 |

## 57,000

| At least | But less than | Single | Married filing jointly * | Married filing separately | Head of a household |
|---|---|---|---|---|---|
| 57,000 | 57,050 | 10,381 | 7,704 | 10,381 | 9,024 |
| 57,050 | 57,100 | 10,394 | 7,711 | 10,394 | 9,036 |
| 57,100 | 57,150 | 10,406 | 7,719 | 10,406 | 9,049 |
| 57,150 | 57,200 | 10,419 | 7,726 | 10,419 | 9,061 |
| 57,200 | 57,250 | 10,431 | 7,734 | 10,431 | 9,074 |
| 57,250 | 57,300 | 10,444 | 7,741 | 10,444 | 9,086 |
| 57,300 | 57,350 | 10,456 | 7,749 | 10,456 | 9,099 |
| 57,350 | 57,400 | 10,469 | 7,756 | 10,469 | 9,111 |
| 57,400 | 57,450 | 10,481 | 7,764 | 10,481 | 9,124 |
| 57,450 | 57,500 | 10,494 | 7,771 | 10,494 | 9,136 |
| 57,500 | 57,550 | 10,506 | 7,779 | 10,506 | 9,149 |
| 57,550 | 57,600 | 10,519 | 7,786 | 10,519 | 9,161 |
| 57,600 | 57,650 | 10,531 | 7,794 | 10,531 | 9,174 |
| 57,650 | 57,700 | 10,544 | 7,801 | 10,544 | 9,186 |
| 57,700 | 57,750 | 10,556 | 7,809 | 10,556 | 9,199 |
| 57,750 | 57,800 | 10,569 | 7,816 | 10,569 | 9,211 |
| 57,800 | 57,850 | 10,581 | 7,824 | 10,581 | 9,224 |
| 57,850 | 57,900 | 10,594 | 7,831 | 10,594 | 9,236 |
| 57,900 | 57,950 | 10,606 | 7,839 | 10,606 | 9,249 |
| 57,950 | 58,000 | 10,619 | 7,846 | 10,619 | 9,261 |

## 58,000

| At least | But less than | Single | Married filing jointly * | Married filing separately | Head of a household |
|---|---|---|---|---|---|
| 58,000 | 58,050 | 10,631 | 7,854 | 10,631 | 9,274 |
| 58,050 | 58,100 | 10,644 | 7,861 | 10,644 | 9,286 |
| 58,100 | 58,150 | 10,656 | 7,869 | 10,656 | 9,299 |
| 58,150 | 58,200 | 10,669 | 7,876 | 10,669 | 9,311 |
| 58,200 | 58,250 | 10,681 | 7,884 | 10,681 | 9,324 |
| 58,250 | 58,300 | 10,694 | 7,891 | 10,694 | 9,336 |
| 58,300 | 58,350 | 10,706 | 7,899 | 10,706 | 9,349 |
| 58,350 | 58,400 | 10,719 | 7,906 | 10,719 | 9,361 |
| 58,400 | 58,450 | 10,731 | 7,914 | 10,731 | 9,374 |
| 58,450 | 58,500 | 10,744 | 7,921 | 10,744 | 9,386 |
| 58,500 | 58,550 | 10,756 | 7,929 | 10,756 | 9,399 |
| 58,550 | 58,600 | 10,769 | 7,936 | 10,769 | 9,411 |
| 58,600 | 58,650 | 10,781 | 7,944 | 10,781 | 9,424 |
| 58,650 | 58,700 | 10,794 | 7,951 | 10,794 | 9,436 |
| 58,700 | 58,750 | 10,806 | 7,959 | 10,806 | 9,449 |
| 58,750 | 58,800 | 10,819 | 7,966 | 10,819 | 9,461 |
| 58,800 | 58,850 | 10,831 | 7,974 | 10,831 | 9,474 |
| 58,850 | 58,900 | 10,844 | 7,981 | 10,844 | 9,486 |
| 58,900 | 58,950 | 10,856 | 7,989 | 10,856 | 9,499 |
| 58,950 | 59,000 | 10,869 | 7,996 | 10,869 | 9,511 |

* This column must also be used by a qualifying widow(er).

(Continued)

| If line 43 (taxable income) is— | | And you are— | | | |
|---|---|---|---|---|---|
| At least | But less than | Single | Married filing jointly * | Married filing separately | Head of a house-hold |
| | | Your tax is— | | | |

**59,000**

| At least | But less than | Single | Married filing jointly * | Married filing separately | Head of a house-hold |
|---|---|---|---|---|---|
| 59,000 | 59,050 | 10,881 | 8,004 | 10,881 | 9,524 |
| 59,050 | 59,100 | 10,894 | 8,011 | 10,894 | 9,536 |
| 59,100 | 59,150 | 10,906 | 8,019 | 10,906 | 9,549 |
| 59,150 | 59,200 | 10,919 | 8,026 | 10,919 | 9,561 |
| 59,200 | 59,250 | 10,931 | 8,034 | 10,931 | 9,574 |
| 59,250 | 59,300 | 10,944 | 8,041 | 10,944 | 9,586 |
| 59,300 | 59,350 | 10,956 | 8,049 | 10,956 | 9,599 |
| 59,350 | 59,400 | 10,969 | 8,056 | 10,969 | 9,611 |
| 59,400 | 59,450 | 10,981 | 8,064 | 10,981 | 9,624 |
| 59,450 | 59,500 | 10,994 | 8,071 | 10,994 | 9,636 |
| 59,500 | 59,550 | 11,006 | 8,079 | 11,006 | 9,649 |
| 59,550 | 59,600 | 11,019 | 8,086 | 11,019 | 9,661 |
| 59,600 | 59,650 | 11,031 | 8,094 | 11,031 | 9,674 |
| 59,650 | 59,700 | 11,044 | 8,101 | 11,044 | 9,686 |
| 59,700 | 59,750 | 11,056 | 8,109 | 11,056 | 9,699 |
| 59,750 | 59,800 | 11,069 | 8,116 | 11,069 | 9,711 |
| 59,800 | 59,850 | 11,081 | 8,124 | 11,081 | 9,724 |
| 59,850 | 59,900 | 11,094 | 8,131 | 11,094 | 9,736 |
| 59,900 | 59,950 | 11,106 | 8,139 | 11,106 | 9,749 |
| 59,950 | 60,000 | 11,119 | 8,146 | 11,119 | 9,761 |

**60,000**

| At least | But less than | Single | Married filing jointly * | Married filing separately | Head of a house-hold |
|---|---|---|---|---|---|
| 60,000 | 60,050 | 11,131 | 8,154 | 11,131 | 9,774 |
| 60,050 | 60,100 | 11,144 | 8,161 | 11,144 | 9,786 |
| 60,100 | 60,150 | 11,156 | 8,169 | 11,156 | 9,799 |
| 60,150 | 60,200 | 11,169 | 8,176 | 11,169 | 9,811 |
| 60,200 | 60,250 | 11,181 | 8,184 | 11,181 | 9,824 |
| 60,250 | 60,300 | 11,194 | 8,191 | 11,194 | 9,836 |
| 60,300 | 60,350 | 11,206 | 8,199 | 11,206 | 9,849 |
| 60,350 | 60,400 | 11,219 | 8,206 | 11,219 | 9,861 |
| 60,400 | 60,450 | 11,231 | 8,214 | 11,231 | 9,874 |
| 60,450 | 60,500 | 11,244 | 8,221 | 11,244 | 9,886 |
| 60,500 | 60,550 | 11,256 | 8,229 | 11,256 | 9,899 |
| 60,550 | 60,600 | 11,269 | 8,236 | 11,269 | 9,911 |
| 60,600 | 60,650 | 11,281 | 8,244 | 11,281 | 9,924 |
| 60,650 | 60,700 | 11,294 | 8,251 | 11,294 | 9,936 |
| 60,700 | 60,750 | 11,306 | 8,259 | 11,306 | 9,949 |
| 60,750 | 60,800 | 11,319 | 8,266 | 11,319 | 9,961 |
| 60,800 | 60,850 | 11,331 | 8,274 | 11,331 | 9,974 |
| 60,850 | 60,900 | 11,344 | 8,281 | 11,344 | 9,986 |
| 60,900 | 60,950 | 11,356 | 8,289 | 11,356 | 9,999 |
| 60,950 | 61,000 | 11,369 | 8,296 | 11,369 | 10,011 |

**61,000**

| At least | But less than | Single | Married filing jointly * | Married filing separately | Head of a house-hold |
|---|---|---|---|---|---|
| 61,000 | 61,050 | 11,381 | 8,304 | 11,381 | 10,024 |
| 61,050 | 61,100 | 11,394 | 8,311 | 11,394 | 10,036 |
| 61,100 | 61,150 | 11,406 | 8,319 | 11,406 | 10,049 |
| 61,150 | 61,200 | 11,419 | 8,326 | 11,419 | 10,061 |
| 61,200 | 61,250 | 11,431 | 8,334 | 11,431 | 10,074 |
| 61,250 | 61,300 | 11,444 | 8,341 | 11,444 | 10,086 |
| 61,300 | 61,350 | 11,456 | 8,349 | 11,456 | 10,099 |
| 61,350 | 61,400 | 11,469 | 8,356 | 11,469 | 10,111 |
| 61,400 | 61,450 | 11,481 | 8,364 | 11,481 | 10,124 |
| 61,450 | 61,500 | 11,494 | 8,371 | 11,494 | 10,136 |
| 61,500 | 61,550 | 11,506 | 8,379 | 11,506 | 10,149 |
| 61,550 | 61,600 | 11,519 | 8,386 | 11,519 | 10,161 |
| 61,600 | 61,650 | 11,531 | 8,394 | 11,531 | 10,174 |
| 61,650 | 61,700 | 11,544 | 8,401 | 11,544 | 10,186 |
| 61,700 | 61,750 | 11,556 | 8,409 | 11,556 | 10,199 |
| 61,750 | 61,800 | 11,569 | 8,416 | 11,569 | 10,211 |
| 61,800 | 61,850 | 11,581 | 8,424 | 11,581 | 10,224 |
| 61,850 | 61,900 | 11,594 | 8,431 | 11,594 | 10,236 |
| 61,900 | 61,950 | 11,606 | 8,439 | 11,606 | 10,249 |
| 61,950 | 62,000 | 11,619 | 8,446 | 11,619 | 10,261 |

**62,000**

| At least | But less than | Single | Married filing jointly * | Married filing separately | Head of a house-hold |
|---|---|---|---|---|---|
| 62,000 | 62,050 | 11,631 | 8,454 | 11,631 | 10,274 |
| 62,050 | 62,100 | 11,644 | 8,461 | 11,644 | 10,286 |
| 62,100 | 62,150 | 11,656 | 8,469 | 11,656 | 10,299 |
| 62,150 | 62,200 | 11,669 | 8,476 | 11,669 | 10,311 |
| 62,200 | 62,250 | 11,681 | 8,484 | 11,681 | 10,324 |
| 62,250 | 62,300 | 11,694 | 8,491 | 11,694 | 10,336 |
| 62,300 | 62,350 | 11,706 | 8,499 | 11,706 | 10,349 |
| 62,350 | 62,400 | 11,719 | 8,506 | 11,719 | 10,361 |
| 62,400 | 62,450 | 11,731 | 8,514 | 11,731 | 10,374 |
| 62,450 | 62,500 | 11,744 | 8,521 | 11,744 | 10,386 |
| 62,500 | 62,550 | 11,756 | 8,529 | 11,756 | 10,399 |
| 62,550 | 62,600 | 11,769 | 8,536 | 11,769 | 10,411 |
| 62,600 | 62,650 | 11,781 | 8,544 | 11,781 | 10,424 |
| 62,650 | 62,700 | 11,794 | 8,551 | 11,794 | 10,436 |
| 62,700 | 62,750 | 11,806 | 8,559 | 11,806 | 10,449 |
| 62,750 | 62,800 | 11,819 | 8,566 | 11,819 | 10,461 |
| 62,800 | 62,850 | 11,831 | 8,574 | 11,831 | 10,474 |
| 62,850 | 62,900 | 11,844 | 8,581 | 11,844 | 10,486 |
| 62,900 | 62,950 | 11,856 | 8,589 | 11,856 | 10,499 |
| 62,950 | 63,000 | 11,869 | 8,596 | 11,869 | 10,511 |

**63,000**

| At least | But less than | Single | Married filing jointly * | Married filing separately | Head of a house-hold |
|---|---|---|---|---|---|
| 63,000 | 63,050 | 11,881 | 8,604 | 11,881 | 10,524 |
| 63,050 | 63,100 | 11,894 | 8,611 | 11,894 | 10,536 |
| 63,100 | 63,150 | 11,906 | 8,619 | 11,906 | 10,549 |
| 63,150 | 63,200 | 11,919 | 8,626 | 11,919 | 10,561 |
| 63,200 | 63,250 | 11,931 | 8,634 | 11,931 | 10,574 |
| 63,250 | 63,300 | 11,944 | 8,641 | 11,944 | 10,586 |
| 63,300 | 63,350 | 11,956 | 8,649 | 11,956 | 10,599 |
| 63,350 | 63,400 | 11,969 | 8,656 | 11,969 | 10,611 |
| 63,400 | 63,450 | 11,981 | 8,664 | 11,981 | 10,624 |
| 63,450 | 63,500 | 11,994 | 8,671 | 11,994 | 10,636 |
| 63,500 | 63,550 | 12,006 | 8,679 | 12,006 | 10,649 |
| 63,550 | 63,600 | 12,019 | 8,686 | 12,019 | 10,661 |
| 63,600 | 63,650 | 12,031 | 8,694 | 12,031 | 10,674 |
| 63,650 | 63,700 | 12,044 | 8,701 | 12,044 | 10,686 |
| 63,700 | 63,750 | 12,056 | 8,709 | 12,056 | 10,699 |
| 63,750 | 63,800 | 12,069 | 8,716 | 12,069 | 10,711 |
| 63,800 | 63,850 | 12,081 | 8,724 | 12,081 | 10,724 |
| 63,850 | 63,900 | 12,094 | 8,731 | 12,094 | 10,736 |
| 63,900 | 63,950 | 12,106 | 8,739 | 12,106 | 10,749 |
| 63,950 | 64,000 | 12,119 | 8,746 | 12,119 | 10,761 |

**64,000**

| At least | But less than | Single | Married filing jointly * | Married filing separately | Head of a house-hold |
|---|---|---|---|---|---|
| 64,000 | 64,050 | 12,131 | 8,754 | 12,131 | 10,774 |
| 64,050 | 64,100 | 12,144 | 8,761 | 12,144 | 10,786 |
| 64,100 | 64,150 | 12,156 | 8,769 | 12,156 | 10,799 |
| 64,150 | 64,200 | 12,169 | 8,776 | 12,169 | 10,811 |
| 64,200 | 64,250 | 12,181 | 8,784 | 12,181 | 10,824 |
| 64,250 | 64,300 | 12,194 | 8,791 | 12,194 | 10,836 |
| 64,300 | 64,350 | 12,206 | 8,799 | 12,206 | 10,849 |
| 64,350 | 64,400 | 12,219 | 8,806 | 12,219 | 10,861 |
| 64,400 | 64,450 | 12,231 | 8,814 | 12,231 | 10,874 |
| 64,450 | 64,500 | 12,244 | 8,821 | 12,244 | 10,886 |
| 64,500 | 64,550 | 12,256 | 8,829 | 12,256 | 10,899 |
| 64,550 | 64,600 | 12,269 | 8,836 | 12,269 | 10,911 |
| 64,600 | 64,650 | 12,281 | 8,844 | 12,281 | 10,924 |
| 64,650 | 64,700 | 12,294 | 8,851 | 12,294 | 10,936 |
| 64,700 | 64,750 | 12,306 | 8,859 | 12,306 | 10,949 |
| 64,750 | 64,800 | 12,319 | 8,866 | 12,319 | 10,961 |
| 64,800 | 64,850 | 12,331 | 8,874 | 12,331 | 10,974 |
| 64,850 | 64,900 | 12,344 | 8,881 | 12,344 | 10,986 |
| 64,900 | 64,950 | 12,356 | 8,889 | 12,356 | 10,999 |
| 64,950 | 65,000 | 12,369 | 8,896 | 12,369 | 11,011 |

**65,000**

| At least | But less than | Single | Married filing jointly * | Married filing separately | Head of a house-hold |
|---|---|---|---|---|---|
| 65,000 | 65,050 | 12,381 | 8,904 | 12,381 | 11,024 |
| 65,050 | 65,100 | 12,394 | 8,911 | 12,394 | 11,036 |
| 65,100 | 65,150 | 12,406 | 8,919 | 12,406 | 11,049 |
| 65,150 | 65,200 | 12,419 | 8,926 | 12,419 | 11,061 |
| 65,200 | 65,250 | 12,431 | 8,934 | 12,431 | 11,074 |
| 65,250 | 65,300 | 12,444 | 8,941 | 12,444 | 11,086 |
| 65,300 | 65,350 | 12,456 | 8,949 | 12,456 | 11,099 |
| 65,350 | 65,400 | 12,469 | 8,956 | 12,469 | 11,111 |
| 65,400 | 65,450 | 12,481 | 8,964 | 12,481 | 11,124 |
| 65,450 | 65,500 | 12,494 | 8,971 | 12,494 | 11,136 |
| 65,500 | 65,550 | 12,506 | 8,979 | 12,506 | 11,149 |
| 65,550 | 65,600 | 12,519 | 8,986 | 12,519 | 11,161 |
| 65,600 | 65,650 | 12,531 | 8,994 | 12,531 | 11,174 |
| 65,650 | 65,700 | 12,544 | 9,001 | 12,544 | 11,186 |
| 65,700 | 65,750 | 12,556 | 9,009 | 12,556 | 11,199 |
| 65,750 | 65,800 | 12,569 | 9,016 | 12,569 | 11,211 |
| 65,800 | 65,850 | 12,581 | 9,024 | 12,581 | 11,224 |
| 65,850 | 65,900 | 12,594 | 9,031 | 12,594 | 11,236 |
| 65,900 | 65,950 | 12,606 | 9,039 | 12,606 | 11,249 |
| 65,950 | 66,000 | 12,619 | 9,046 | 12,619 | 11,261 |

**66,000**

| At least | But less than | Single | Married filing jointly * | Married filing separately | Head of a house-hold |
|---|---|---|---|---|---|
| 66,000 | 66,050 | 12,631 | 9,054 | 12,631 | 11,274 |
| 66,050 | 66,100 | 12,644 | 9,061 | 12,644 | 11,286 |
| 66,100 | 66,150 | 12,656 | 9,069 | 12,656 | 11,299 |
| 66,150 | 66,200 | 12,669 | 9,076 | 12,669 | 11,311 |
| 66,200 | 66,250 | 12,681 | 9,084 | 12,681 | 11,324 |
| 66,250 | 66,300 | 12,694 | 9,091 | 12,694 | 11,336 |
| 66,300 | 66,350 | 12,706 | 9,099 | 12,706 | 11,349 |
| 66,350 | 66,400 | 12,719 | 9,106 | 12,719 | 11,361 |
| 66,400 | 66,450 | 12,731 | 9,114 | 12,731 | 11,374 |
| 66,450 | 66,500 | 12,744 | 9,121 | 12,744 | 11,386 |
| 66,500 | 66,550 | 12,756 | 9,129 | 12,756 | 11,399 |
| 66,550 | 66,600 | 12,769 | 9,136 | 12,769 | 11,411 |
| 66,600 | 66,650 | 12,781 | 9,144 | 12,781 | 11,424 |
| 66,650 | 66,700 | 12,794 | 9,151 | 12,794 | 11,436 |
| 66,700 | 66,750 | 12,806 | 9,159 | 12,806 | 11,449 |
| 66,750 | 66,800 | 12,819 | 9,166 | 12,819 | 11,461 |
| 66,800 | 66,850 | 12,831 | 9,174 | 12,831 | 11,474 |
| 66,850 | 66,900 | 12,844 | 9,181 | 12,844 | 11,486 |
| 66,900 | 66,950 | 12,856 | 9,189 | 12,856 | 11,499 |
| 66,950 | 67,000 | 12,869 | 9,196 | 12,869 | 11,511 |

**67,000**

| At least | But less than | Single | Married filing jointly * | Married filing separately | Head of a house-hold |
|---|---|---|---|---|---|
| 67,000 | 67,050 | 12,881 | 9,204 | 12,881 | 11,524 |
| 67,050 | 67,100 | 12,894 | 9,211 | 12,894 | 11,536 |
| 67,100 | 67,150 | 12,906 | 9,219 | 12,906 | 11,549 |
| 67,150 | 67,200 | 12,919 | 9,226 | 12,919 | 11,561 |
| 67,200 | 67,250 | 12,931 | 9,234 | 12,931 | 11,574 |
| 67,250 | 67,300 | 12,944 | 9,241 | 12,944 | 11,586 |
| 67,300 | 67,350 | 12,956 | 9,249 | 12,956 | 11,599 |
| 67,350 | 67,400 | 12,969 | 9,256 | 12,969 | 11,611 |
| 67,400 | 67,450 | 12,981 | 9,264 | 12,981 | 11,624 |
| 67,450 | 67,500 | 12,994 | 9,271 | 12,994 | 11,636 |
| 67,500 | 67,550 | 13,006 | 9,279 | 13,006 | 11,649 |
| 67,550 | 67,600 | 13,019 | 9,286 | 13,019 | 11,661 |
| 67,600 | 67,650 | 13,031 | 9,294 | 13,031 | 11,674 |
| 67,650 | 67,700 | 13,044 | 9,301 | 13,044 | 11,686 |
| 67,700 | 67,750 | 13,056 | 9,309 | 13,056 | 11,699 |
| 67,750 | 67,800 | 13,069 | 9,316 | 13,069 | 11,711 |
| 67,800 | 67,850 | 13,081 | 9,324 | 13,081 | 11,724 |
| 67,850 | 67,900 | 13,094 | 9,331 | 13,094 | 11,736 |
| 67,900 | 67,950 | 13,106 | 9,339 | 13,106 | 11,749 |
| 67,950 | 68,000 | 13,119 | 9,346 | 13,119 | 11,761 |

* This column must also be used by a qualifying widow(er).

*(Continued)*

| If line 43 (taxable income) is— | | And you are— | | | |
|---|---|---|---|---|---|
| At least | But less than | Single | Married filing jointly * | Married filing sepa-rately | Head of a house-hold |
| | | Your tax is— | | | |
| **68,000** | | | | | |
| **68,000** | **68,050** | 13,131 | 9,354 | 13,131 | 11,774 |
| **68,050** | **68,100** | 13,144 | 9,361 | 13,144 | 11,786 |
| **68,100** | **68,150** | 13,156 | 9,369 | 13,156 | 11,799 |
| **68,150** | **68,200** | 13,169 | 9,376 | 13,169 | 11,811 |
| **68,200** | **68,250** | 13,181 | 9,384 | 13,181 | 11,824 |
| **68,250** | **68,300** | 13,194 | 9,391 | 13,194 | 11,836 |
| **68,300** | **68,350** | 13,206 | 9,399 | 13,206 | 11,849 |
| **68,350** | **68,400** | 13,219 | 9,406 | 13,219 | 11,861 |
| **68,400** | **68,450** | 13,231 | 9,414 | 13,231 | 11,874 |
| **68,450** | **68,500** | 13,244 | 9,421 | 13,244 | 11,886 |
| **68,500** | **68,550** | 13,256 | 9,429 | 13,256 | 11,899 |
| **68,550** | **68,600** | 13,269 | 9,436 | 13,269 | 11,911 |
| **68,600** | **68,650** | 13,281 | 9,444 | 13,281 | 11,924 |
| **68,650** | **68,700** | 13,294 | 9,451 | 13,294 | 11,936 |
| **68,700** | **68,750** | 13,306 | 9,459 | 13,306 | 11,949 |
| **68,750** | **68,800** | 13,319 | 9,466 | 13,319 | 11,961 |
| **68,800** | **68,850** | 13,331 | 9,474 | 13,331 | 11,974 |
| **68,850** | **68,900** | 13,344 | 9,481 | 13,344 | 11,986 |
| **68,900** | **68,950** | 13,356 | 9,489 | 13,356 | 11,999 |
| **68,950** | **69,000** | 13,369 | 9,496 | 13,369 | 12,011 |
| **69,000** | | | | | |
| **69,000** | **69,050** | 13,381 | 9,506 | 13,381 | 12,024 |
| **69,050** | **69,100** | 13,394 | 9,519 | 13,394 | 12,036 |
| **69,100** | **69,150** | 13,406 | 9,531 | 13,406 | 12,049 |
| **69,150** | **69,200** | 13,419 | 9,544 | 13,419 | 12,061 |
| **69,200** | **69,250** | 13,431 | 9,556 | 13,431 | 12,074 |
| **69,250** | **69,300** | 13,444 | 9,569 | 13,444 | 12,086 |
| **69,300** | **69,350** | 13,456 | 9,581 | 13,456 | 12,099 |
| **69,350** | **69,400** | 13,469 | 9,594 | 13,469 | 12,111 |
| **69,400** | **69,450** | 13,481 | 9,606 | 13,481 | 12,124 |
| **69,450** | **69,500** | 13,494 | 9,619 | 13,494 | 12,136 |
| **69,500** | **69,550** | 13,506 | 9,631 | 13,506 | 12,149 |
| **69,550** | **69,600** | 13,519 | 9,644 | 13,519 | 12,161 |
| **69,600** | **69,650** | 13,531 | 9,656 | 13,531 | 12,174 |
| **69,650** | **69,700** | 13,544 | 9,669 | 13,544 | 12,186 |
| **69,700** | **69,750** | 13,556 | 9,681 | 13,558 | 12,199 |
| **69,750** | **69,800** | 13,569 | 9,694 | 13,572 | 12,211 |
| **69,800** | **69,850** | 13,581 | 9,706 | 13,586 | 12,224 |
| **69,850** | **69,900** | 13,594 | 9,719 | 13,600 | 12,236 |
| **69,900** | **69,950** | 13,606 | 9,731 | 13,614 | 12,249 |
| **69,950** | **70,000** | 13,619 | 9,744 | 13,628 | 12,261 |
| **70,000** | | | | | |
| **70,000** | **70,050** | 13,631 | 9,756 | 13,642 | 12,274 |
| **70,050** | **70,100** | 13,644 | 9,769 | 13,656 | 12,286 |
| **70,100** | **70,150** | 13,656 | 9,781 | 13,670 | 12,299 |
| **70,150** | **70,200** | 13,669 | 9,794 | 13,684 | 12,311 |
| **70,200** | **70,250** | 13,681 | 9,806 | 13,698 | 12,324 |
| **70,250** | **70,300** | 13,694 | 9,819 | 13,712 | 12,336 |
| **70,300** | **70,350** | 13,706 | 9,831 | 13,726 | 12,349 |
| **70,350** | **70,400** | 13,719 | 9,844 | 13,740 | 12,361 |
| **70,400** | **70,450** | 13,731 | 9,856 | 13,754 | 12,374 |
| **70,450** | **70,500** | 13,744 | 9,869 | 13,768 | 12,386 |
| **70,500** | **70,550** | 13,756 | 9,881 | 13,782 | 12,399 |
| **70,550** | **70,600** | 13,769 | 9,894 | 13,796 | 12,411 |
| **70,600** | **70,650** | 13,781 | 9,906 | 13,810 | 12,424 |
| **70,650** | **70,700** | 13,794 | 9,919 | 13,824 | 12,436 |
| **70,700** | **70,750** | 13,806 | 9,931 | 13,838 | 12,449 |
| **70,750** | **70,800** | 13,819 | 9,944 | 13,852 | 12,461 |
| **70,800** | **70,850** | 13,831 | 9,956 | 13,866 | 12,474 |
| **70,850** | **70,900** | 13,844 | 9,969 | 13,880 | 12,486 |
| **70,900** | **70,950** | 13,856 | 9,981 | 13,894 | 12,499 |
| **70,950** | **71,000** | 13,869 | 9,994 | 13,908 | 12,511 |

| If line 43 (taxable income) is— | | And you are— | | | |
|---|---|---|---|---|---|
| At least | But less than | Single | Married filing jointly * | Married filing sepa-rately | Head of a house-hold |
| | | Your tax is— | | | |
| **71,000** | | | | | |
| **71,000** | **71,050** | 13,881 | 10,006 | 13,922 | 12,524 |
| **71,050** | **71,100** | 13,894 | 10,019 | 13,936 | 12,536 |
| **71,100** | **71,150** | 13,906 | 10,031 | 13,950 | 12,549 |
| **71,150** | **71,200** | 13,919 | 10,044 | 13,964 | 12,561 |
| **71,200** | **71,250** | 13,931 | 10,056 | 13,978 | 12,574 |
| **71,250** | **71,300** | 13,944 | 10,069 | 13,992 | 12,586 |
| **71,300** | **71,350** | 13,956 | 10,081 | 14,006 | 12,599 |
| **71,350** | **71,400** | 13,969 | 10,094 | 14,020 | 12,611 |
| **71,400** | **71,450** | 13,981 | 10,106 | 14,034 | 12,624 |
| **71,450** | **71,500** | 13,994 | 10,119 | 14,048 | 12,636 |
| **71,500** | **71,550** | 14,006 | 10,131 | 14,062 | 12,649 |
| **71,550** | **71,600** | 14,019 | 10,144 | 14,076 | 12,661 |
| **71,600** | **71,650** | 14,031 | 10,156 | 14,090 | 12,674 |
| **71,650** | **71,700** | 14,044 | 10,169 | 14,104 | 12,686 |
| **71,700** | **71,750** | 14,056 | 10,181 | 14,118 | 12,699 |
| **71,750** | **71,800** | 14,069 | 10,194 | 14,132 | 12,711 |
| **71,800** | **71,850** | 14,081 | 10,206 | 14,146 | 12,724 |
| **71,850** | **71,900** | 14,094 | 10,219 | 14,160 | 12,736 |
| **71,900** | **71,950** | 14,106 | 10,231 | 14,174 | 12,749 |
| **71,950** | **72,000** | 14,119 | 10,244 | 14,188 | 12,761 |
| **72,000** | | | | | |
| **72,000** | **72,050** | 14,131 | 10,256 | 14,202 | 12,774 |
| **72,050** | **72,100** | 14,144 | 10,269 | 14,216 | 12,786 |
| **72,100** | **72,150** | 14,156 | 10,281 | 14,230 | 12,799 |
| **72,150** | **72,200** | 14,169 | 10,294 | 14,244 | 12,811 |
| **72,200** | **72,250** | 14,181 | 10,306 | 14,258 | 12,824 |
| **72,250** | **72,300** | 14,194 | 10,319 | 14,272 | 12,836 |
| **72,300** | **72,350** | 14,206 | 10,331 | 14,286 | 12,849 |
| **72,350** | **72,400** | 14,219 | 10,344 | 14,300 | 12,861 |
| **72,400** | **72,450** | 14,231 | 10,356 | 14,314 | 12,874 |
| **72,450** | **72,500** | 14,244 | 10,369 | 14,328 | 12,886 |
| **72,500** | **72,550** | 14,256 | 10,381 | 14,342 | 12,899 |
| **72,550** | **72,600** | 14,269 | 10,394 | 14,356 | 12,911 |
| **72,600** | **72,650** | 14,281 | 10,406 | 14,370 | 12,924 |
| **72,650** | **72,700** | 14,294 | 10,419 | 14,384 | 12,936 |
| **72,700** | **72,750** | 14,306 | 10,431 | 14,398 | 12,949 |
| **72,750** | **72,800** | 14,319 | 10,444 | 14,412 | 12,961 |
| **72,800** | **72,850** | 14,331 | 10,456 | 14,426 | 12,974 |
| **72,850** | **72,900** | 14,344 | 10,469 | 14,440 | 12,986 |
| **72,900** | **72,950** | 14,356 | 10,481 | 14,454 | 12,999 |
| **72,950** | **73,000** | 14,369 | 10,494 | 14,468 | 13,011 |
| **73,000** | | | | | |
| **73,000** | **73,050** | 14,381 | 10,506 | 14,482 | 13,024 |
| **73,050** | **73,100** | 14,394 | 10,519 | 14,496 | 13,036 |
| **73,100** | **73,150** | 14,406 | 10,531 | 14,510 | 13,049 |
| **73,150** | **73,200** | 14,419 | 10,544 | 14,524 | 13,061 |
| **73,200** | **73,250** | 14,431 | 10,556 | 14,538 | 13,074 |
| **73,250** | **73,300** | 14,444 | 10,569 | 14,552 | 13,086 |
| **73,300** | **73,350** | 14,456 | 10,581 | 14,566 | 13,099 |
| **73,350** | **73,400** | 14,469 | 10,594 | 14,580 | 13,111 |
| **73,400** | **73,450** | 14,481 | 10,606 | 14,594 | 13,124 |
| **73,450** | **73,500** | 14,494 | 10,619 | 14,608 | 13,136 |
| **73,500** | **73,550** | 14,506 | 10,631 | 14,622 | 13,149 |
| **73,550** | **73,600** | 14,519 | 10,644 | 14,636 | 13,161 |
| **73,600** | **73,650** | 14,531 | 10,656 | 14,650 | 13,174 |
| **73,650** | **73,700** | 14,544 | 10,669 | 14,664 | 13,186 |
| **73,700** | **73,750** | 14,556 | 10,681 | 14,678 | 13,199 |
| **73,750** | **73,800** | 14,569 | 10,694 | 14,692 | 13,211 |
| **73,800** | **73,850** | 14,581 | 10,706 | 14,706 | 13,224 |
| **73,850** | **73,900** | 14,594 | 10,719 | 14,720 | 13,236 |
| **73,900** | **73,950** | 14,606 | 10,731 | 14,734 | 13,249 |
| **73,950** | **74,000** | 14,619 | 10,744 | 14,748 | 13,261 |

| If line 43 (taxable income) is— | | And you are— | | | |
|---|---|---|---|---|---|
| At least | But less than | Single | Married filing jointly * | Married filing sepa-rately | Head of a house-hold |
| | | Your tax is— | | | |
| **74,000** | | | | | |
| **74,000** | **74,050** | 14,631 | 10,756 | 14,762 | 13,274 |
| **74,050** | **74,100** | 14,644 | 10,769 | 14,776 | 13,286 |
| **74,100** | **74,150** | 14,656 | 10,781 | 14,790 | 13,299 |
| **74,150** | **74,200** | 14,669 | 10,794 | 14,804 | 13,311 |
| **74,200** | **74,250** | 14,681 | 10,806 | 14,818 | 13,324 |
| **74,250** | **74,300** | 14,694 | 10,819 | 14,832 | 13,336 |
| **74,300** | **74,350** | 14,706 | 10,831 | 14,846 | 13,349 |
| **74,350** | **74,400** | 14,719 | 10,844 | 14,860 | 13,361 |
| **74,400** | **74,450** | 14,731 | 10,856 | 14,874 | 13,374 |
| **74,450** | **74,500** | 14,744 | 10,869 | 14,888 | 13,386 |
| **74,500** | **74,550** | 14,756 | 10,881 | 14,902 | 13,399 |
| **74,550** | **74,600** | 14,769 | 10,894 | 14,916 | 13,411 |
| **74,600** | **74,650** | 14,781 | 10,906 | 14,930 | 13,424 |
| **74,650** | **74,700** | 14,794 | 10,919 | 14,944 | 13,436 |
| **74,700** | **74,750** | 14,806 | 10,931 | 14,958 | 13,449 |
| **74,750** | **74,800** | 14,819 | 10,944 | 14,972 | 13,461 |
| **74,800** | **74,850** | 14,831 | 10,956 | 14,986 | 13,474 |
| **74,850** | **74,900** | 14,844 | 10,969 | 15,000 | 13,486 |
| **74,900** | **74,950** | 14,856 | 10,981 | 15,014 | 13,499 |
| **74,950** | **75,000** | 14,869 | 10,994 | 15,028 | 13,511 |
| **75,000** | | | | | |
| **75,000** | **75,050** | 14,881 | 11,006 | 15,042 | 13,524 |
| **75,050** | **75,100** | 14,894 | 11,019 | 15,056 | 13,536 |
| **75,100** | **75,150** | 14,906 | 11,031 | 15,070 | 13,549 |
| **75,150** | **75,200** | 14,919 | 11,044 | 15,084 | 13,561 |
| **75,200** | **75,250** | 14,931 | 11,056 | 15,098 | 13,574 |
| **75,250** | **75,300** | 14,944 | 11,069 | 15,112 | 13,586 |
| **75,300** | **75,350** | 14,956 | 11,081 | 15,126 | 13,599 |
| **75,350** | **75,400** | 14,969 | 11,094 | 15,140 | 13,611 |
| **75,400** | **75,450** | 14,981 | 11,106 | 15,154 | 13,624 |
| **75,450** | **75,500** | 14,994 | 11,119 | 15,168 | 13,636 |
| **75,500** | **75,550** | 15,006 | 11,131 | 15,182 | 13,649 |
| **75,550** | **75,600** | 15,019 | 11,144 | 15,196 | 13,661 |
| **75,600** | **75,650** | 15,031 | 11,156 | 15,210 | 13,674 |
| **75,650** | **75,700** | 15,044 | 11,169 | 15,224 | 13,686 |
| **75,700** | **75,750** | 15,056 | 11,181 | 15,238 | 13,699 |
| **75,750** | **75,800** | 15,069 | 11,194 | 15,252 | 13,711 |
| **75,800** | **75,850** | 15,081 | 11,206 | 15,266 | 13,724 |
| **75,850** | **75,900** | 15,094 | 11,219 | 15,280 | 13,736 |
| **75,900** | **75,950** | 15,106 | 11,231 | 15,294 | 13,749 |
| **75,950** | **76,000** | 15,119 | 11,244 | 15,308 | 13,761 |
| **76,000** | | | | | |
| **76,000** | **76,050** | 15,131 | 11,256 | 15,322 | 13,774 |
| **76,050** | **76,100** | 15,144 | 11,269 | 15,336 | 13,786 |
| **76,100** | **76,150** | 15,156 | 11,281 | 15,350 | 13,799 |
| **76,150** | **76,200** | 15,169 | 11,294 | 15,364 | 13,811 |
| **76,200** | **76,250** | 15,181 | 11,306 | 15,378 | 13,824 |
| **76,250** | **76,300** | 15,194 | 11,319 | 15,392 | 13,836 |
| **76,300** | **76,350** | 15,206 | 11,331 | 15,406 | 13,849 |
| **76,350** | **76,400** | 15,219 | 11,344 | 15,420 | 13,861 |
| **76,400** | **76,450** | 15,231 | 11,356 | 15,434 | 13,874 |
| **76,450** | **76,500** | 15,244 | 11,369 | 15,448 | 13,886 |
| **76,500** | **76,550** | 15,256 | 11,381 | 15,462 | 13,899 |
| **76,550** | **76,600** | 15,269 | 11,394 | 15,476 | 13,911 |
| **76,600** | **76,650** | 15,281 | 11,406 | 15,490 | 13,924 |
| **76,650** | **76,700** | 15,294 | 11,419 | 15,504 | 13,936 |
| **76,700** | **76,750** | 15,306 | 11,431 | 15,518 | 13,949 |
| **76,750** | **76,800** | 15,319 | 11,444 | 15,532 | 13,961 |
| **76,800** | **76,850** | 15,331 | 11,456 | 15,546 | 13,974 |
| **76,850** | **76,900** | 15,344 | 11,469 | 15,560 | 13,986 |
| **76,900** | **76,950** | 15,356 | 11,481 | 15,574 | 13,999 |
| **76,950** | **77,000** | 15,369 | 11,494 | 15,588 | 14,011 |

* This column must also be used by a qualifying widow(er).

*(Continued)*

| If line 43 (taxable income) is— At least | But less than | And you are— Single | Married filing jointly * | Married filing sepa-rately | Head of a house-hold |
|---|---|---|---|---|---|
| | | Your tax is— | | | |
| **77,000** | | | | | |
| **77,000** | **77,050** | 15,381 | 11,506 | 15,602 | 14,024 |
| **77,050** | **77,100** | 15,394 | 11,519 | 15,616 | 14,036 |
| **77,100** | **77,150** | 15,406 | 11,531 | 15,630 | 14,049 |
| **77,150** | **77,200** | 15,419 | 11,544 | 15,644 | 14,061 |
| **77,200** | **77,250** | 15,431 | 11,556 | 15,658 | 14,074 |
| **77,250** | **77,300** | 15,444 | 11,569 | 15,672 | 14,086 |
| **77,300** | **77,350** | 15,456 | 11,581 | 15,686 | 14,099 |
| **77,350** | **77,400** | 15,469 | 11,594 | 15,700 | 14,111 |
| **77,400** | **77,450** | 15,481 | 11,606 | 15,714 | 14,124 |
| **77,450** | **77,500** | 15,494 | 11,619 | 15,728 | 14,136 |
| **77,500** | **77,550** | 15,506 | 11,631 | 15,742 | 14,149 |
| **77,550** | **77,600** | 15,519 | 11,644 | 15,756 | 14,161 |
| **77,600** | **77,650** | 15,531 | 11,656 | 15,770 | 14,174 |
| **77,650** | **77,700** | 15,544 | 11,669 | 15,784 | 14,186 |
| **77,700** | **77,750** | 15,556 | 11,681 | 15,798 | 14,199 |
| **77,750** | **77,800** | 15,569 | 11,694 | 15,812 | 14,211 |
| **77,800** | **77,850** | 15,581 | 11,706 | 15,826 | 14,224 |
| **77,850** | **77,900** | 15,594 | 11,719 | 15,840 | 14,236 |
| **77,900** | **77,950** | 15,606 | 11,731 | 15,854 | 14,249 |
| **77,950** | **78,000** | 15,619 | 11,744 | 15,868 | 14,261 |
| **78,000** | | | | | |
| **78,000** | **78,050** | 15,631 | 11,756 | 15,882 | 14,274 |
| **78,050** | **78,100** | 15,644 | 11,769 | 15,896 | 14,286 |
| **78,100** | **78,150** | 15,656 | 11,781 | 15,910 | 14,299 |
| **78,150** | **78,200** | 15,669 | 11,794 | 15,924 | 14,311 |
| **78,200** | **78,250** | 15,681 | 11,806 | 15,938 | 14,324 |
| **78,250** | **78,300** | 15,694 | 11,819 | 15,952 | 14,336 |
| **78,300** | **78,350** | 15,706 | 11,831 | 15,966 | 14,349 |
| **78,350** | **78,400** | 15,719 | 11,844 | 15,980 | 14,361 |
| **78,400** | **78,450** | 15,731 | 11,856 | 15,994 | 14,374 |
| **78,450** | **78,500** | 15,744 | 11,869 | 16,008 | 14,386 |
| **78,500** | **78,550** | 15,756 | 11,881 | 16,022 | 14,399 |
| **78,550** | **78,600** | 15,769 | 11,894 | 16,036 | 14,411 |
| **78,600** | **78,650** | 15,781 | 11,906 | 16,050 | 14,424 |
| **78,650** | **78,700** | 15,794 | 11,919 | 16,064 | 14,436 |
| **78,700** | **78,750** | 15,806 | 11,931 | 16,078 | 14,449 |
| **78,750** | **78,800** | 15,819 | 11,944 | 16,092 | 14,461 |
| **78,800** | **78,850** | 15,831 | 11,956 | 16,106 | 14,474 |
| **78,850** | **78,900** | 15,844 | 11,969 | 16,120 | 14,486 |
| **78,900** | **78,950** | 15,856 | 11,981 | 16,134 | 14,499 |
| **78,950** | **79,000** | 15,869 | 11,994 | 16,148 | 14,511 |
| **79,000** | | | | | |
| **79,000** | **79,050** | 15,881 | 12,006 | 16,162 | 14,524 |
| **79,050** | **79,100** | 15,894 | 12,019 | 16,176 | 14,536 |
| **79,100** | **79,150** | 15,906 | 12,031 | 16,190 | 14,549 |
| **79,150** | **79,200** | 15,919 | 12,044 | 16,204 | 14,561 |
| **79,200** | **79,250** | 15,931 | 12,056 | 16,218 | 14,574 |
| **79,250** | **79,300** | 15,944 | 12,069 | 16,232 | 14,586 |
| **79,300** | **79,350** | 15,956 | 12,081 | 16,246 | 14,599 |
| **79,350** | **79,400** | 15,969 | 12,094 | 16,260 | 14,611 |
| **79,400** | **79,450** | 15,981 | 12,106 | 16,274 | 14,624 |
| **79,450** | **79,500** | 15,994 | 12,119 | 16,288 | 14,636 |
| **79,500** | **79,550** | 16,006 | 12,131 | 16,302 | 14,649 |
| **79,550** | **79,600** | 16,019 | 12,144 | 16,316 | 14,661 |
| **79,600** | **79,650** | 16,031 | 12,156 | 16,330 | 14,674 |
| **79,650** | **79,700** | 16,044 | 12,169 | 16,344 | 14,686 |
| **79,700** | **79,750** | 16,056 | 12,181 | 16,358 | 14,699 |
| **79,750** | **79,800** | 16,069 | 12,194 | 16,372 | 14,711 |
| **79,800** | **79,850** | 16,081 | 12,206 | 16,386 | 14,724 |
| **79,850** | **79,900** | 16,094 | 12,219 | 16,400 | 14,736 |
| **79,900** | **79,950** | 16,106 | 12,231 | 16,414 | 14,749 |
| **79,950** | **80,000** | 16,119 | 12,244 | 16,428 | 14,761 |

| If line 43 (taxable income) is— At least | But less than | And you are— Single | Married filing jointly * | Married filing sepa-rately | Head of a house-hold |
|---|---|---|---|---|---|
| | | Your tax is— | | | |
| **80,000** | | | | | |
| **80,000** | **80,050** | 16,131 | 12,256 | 16,442 | 14,774 |
| **80,050** | **80,100** | 16,144 | 12,269 | 16,456 | 14,786 |
| **80,100** | **80,150** | 16,156 | 12,281 | 16,470 | 14,799 |
| **80,150** | **80,200** | 16,169 | 12,294 | 16,484 | 14,811 |
| **80,200** | **80,250** | 16,181 | 12,306 | 16,498 | 14,824 |
| **80,250** | **80,300** | 16,194 | 12,319 | 16,512 | 14,836 |
| **80,300** | **80,350** | 16,206 | 12,331 | 16,526 | 14,849 |
| **80,350** | **80,400** | 16,219 | 12,344 | 16,540 | 14,861 |
| **80,400** | **80,450** | 16,231 | 12,356 | 16,554 | 14,874 |
| **80,450** | **80,500** | 16,244 | 12,369 | 16,568 | 14,886 |
| **80,500** | **80,550** | 16,256 | 12,381 | 16,582 | 14,899 |
| **80,550** | **80,600** | 16,269 | 12,394 | 16,596 | 14,911 |
| **80,600** | **80,650** | 16,281 | 12,406 | 16,610 | 14,924 |
| **80,650** | **80,700** | 16,294 | 12,419 | 16,624 | 14,936 |
| **80,700** | **80,750** | 16,306 | 12,431 | 16,638 | 14,949 |
| **80,750** | **80,800** | 16,319 | 12,444 | 16,652 | 14,961 |
| **80,800** | **80,850** | 16,331 | 12,456 | 16,666 | 14,974 |
| **80,850** | **80,900** | 16,344 | 12,469 | 16,680 | 14,986 |
| **80,900** | **80,950** | 16,356 | 12,481 | 16,694 | 14,999 |
| **80,950** | **81,000** | 16,369 | 12,494 | 16,708 | 15,011 |
| **81,000** | | | | | |
| **81,000** | **81,050** | 16,381 | 12,506 | 16,722 | 15,024 |
| **81,050** | **81,100** | 16,394 | 12,519 | 16,736 | 15,036 |
| **81,100** | **81,150** | 16,406 | 12,531 | 16,750 | 15,049 |
| **81,150** | **81,200** | 16,419 | 12,544 | 16,764 | 15,061 |
| **81,200** | **81,250** | 16,431 | 12,556 | 16,778 | 15,074 |
| **81,250** | **81,300** | 16,444 | 12,569 | 16,792 | 15,086 |
| **81,300** | **81,350** | 16,456 | 12,581 | 16,806 | 15,099 |
| **81,350** | **81,400** | 16,469 | 12,594 | 16,820 | 15,111 |
| **81,400** | **81,450** | 16,481 | 12,606 | 16,834 | 15,124 |
| **81,450** | **81,500** | 16,494 | 12,619 | 16,848 | 15,136 |
| **81,500** | **81,550** | 16,506 | 12,631 | 16,862 | 15,149 |
| **81,550** | **81,600** | 16,519 | 12,644 | 16,876 | 15,161 |
| **81,600** | **81,650** | 16,531 | 12,656 | 16,890 | 15,174 |
| **81,650** | **81,700** | 16,544 | 12,669 | 16,904 | 15,186 |
| **81,700** | **81,750** | 16,556 | 12,681 | 16,918 | 15,199 |
| **81,750** | **81,800** | 16,569 | 12,694 | 16,932 | 15,211 |
| **81,800** | **81,850** | 16,581 | 12,706 | 16,946 | 15,224 |
| **81,850** | **81,900** | 16,594 | 12,719 | 16,960 | 15,236 |
| **81,900** | **81,950** | 16,606 | 12,731 | 16,974 | 15,249 |
| **81,950** | **82,000** | 16,619 | 12,744 | 16,988 | 15,261 |
| **82,000** | | | | | |
| **82,000** | **82,050** | 16,631 | 12,756 | 17,002 | 15,274 |
| **82,050** | **82,100** | 16,644 | 12,769 | 17,016 | 15,286 |
| **82,100** | **82,150** | 16,656 | 12,781 | 17,030 | 15,299 |
| **82,150** | **82,200** | 16,669 | 12,794 | 17,044 | 15,311 |
| **82,200** | **82,250** | 16,681 | 12,806 | 17,058 | 15,324 |
| **82,250** | **82,300** | 16,694 | 12,819 | 17,072 | 15,336 |
| **82,300** | **82,350** | 16,706 | 12,831 | 17,086 | 15,349 |
| **82,350** | **82,400** | 16,719 | 12,844 | 17,100 | 15,361 |
| **82,400** | **82,450** | 16,731 | 12,856 | 17,114 | 15,374 |
| **82,450** | **82,500** | 16,744 | 12,869 | 17,128 | 15,386 |
| **82,500** | **82,550** | 16,756 | 12,881 | 17,142 | 15,399 |
| **82,550** | **82,600** | 16,769 | 12,894 | 17,156 | 15,411 |
| **82,600** | **82,650** | 16,781 | 12,906 | 17,170 | 15,424 |
| **82,650** | **82,700** | 16,794 | 12,919 | 17,184 | 15,436 |
| **82,700** | **82,750** | 16,806 | 12,931 | 17,198 | 15,449 |
| **82,750** | **82,800** | 16,819 | 12,944 | 17,212 | 15,461 |
| **82,800** | **82,850** | 16,831 | 12,956 | 17,226 | 15,474 |
| **82,850** | **82,900** | 16,844 | 12,969 | 17,240 | 15,486 |
| **82,900** | **82,950** | 16,856 | 12,981 | 17,254 | 15,499 |
| **82,950** | **83,000** | 16,869 | 12,994 | 17,268 | 15,511 |

| If line 43 (taxable income) is— At least | But less than | And you are— Single | Married filing jointly * | Married filing sepa-rately | Head of a house-hold |
|---|---|---|---|---|---|
| | | Your tax is— | | | |
| **83,000** | | | | | |
| **83,000** | **83,050** | 16,881 | 13,006 | 17,282 | 15,524 |
| **83,050** | **83,100** | 16,894 | 13,019 | 17,296 | 15,536 |
| **83,100** | **83,150** | 16,906 | 13,031 | 17,310 | 15,549 |
| **83,150** | **83,200** | 16,919 | 13,044 | 17,324 | 15,561 |
| **83,200** | **83,250** | 16,931 | 13,056 | 17,338 | 15,574 |
| **83,250** | **83,300** | 16,944 | 13,069 | 17,352 | 15,586 |
| **83,300** | **83,350** | 16,956 | 13,081 | 17,366 | 15,599 |
| **83,350** | **83,400** | 16,969 | 13,094 | 17,380 | 15,611 |
| **83,400** | **83,450** | 16,981 | 13,106 | 17,394 | 15,624 |
| **83,450** | **83,500** | 16,994 | 13,119 | 17,408 | 15,636 |
| **83,500** | **83,550** | 17,006 | 13,131 | 17,422 | 15,649 |
| **83,550** | **83,600** | 17,019 | 13,144 | 17,436 | 15,661 |
| **83,600** | **83,650** | 17,032 | 13,156 | 17,450 | 15,674 |
| **83,650** | **83,700** | 17,046 | 13,169 | 17,464 | 15,686 |
| **83,700** | **83,750** | 17,060 | 13,181 | 17,478 | 15,699 |
| **83,750** | **83,800** | 17,074 | 13,194 | 17,492 | 15,711 |
| **83,800** | **83,850** | 17,088 | 13,206 | 17,506 | 15,724 |
| **83,850** | **83,900** | 17,102 | 13,219 | 17,520 | 15,736 |
| **83,900** | **83,950** | 17,116 | 13,231 | 17,534 | 15,749 |
| **83,950** | **84,000** | 17,130 | 13,244 | 17,548 | 15,761 |
| **84,000** | | | | | |
| **84,000** | **84,050** | 17,144 | 13,256 | 17,562 | 15,774 |
| **84,050** | **84,100** | 17,158 | 13,269 | 17,576 | 15,786 |
| **84,100** | **84,150** | 17,172 | 13,281 | 17,590 | 15,799 |
| **84,150** | **84,200** | 17,186 | 13,294 | 17,604 | 15,811 |
| **84,200** | **84,250** | 17,200 | 13,306 | 17,618 | 15,824 |
| **84,250** | **84,300** | 17,214 | 13,319 | 17,632 | 15,836 |
| **84,300** | **84,350** | 17,228 | 13,331 | 17,646 | 15,849 |
| **84,350** | **84,400** | 17,242 | 13,344 | 17,660 | 15,861 |
| **84,400** | **84,450** | 17,256 | 13,356 | 17,674 | 15,874 |
| **84,450** | **84,500** | 17,270 | 13,369 | 17,688 | 15,886 |
| **84,500** | **84,550** | 17,284 | 13,381 | 17,702 | 15,899 |
| **84,550** | **84,600** | 17,298 | 13,394 | 17,716 | 15,911 |
| **84,600** | **84,650** | 17,312 | 13,406 | 17,730 | 15,924 |
| **84,650** | **84,700** | 17,326 | 13,419 | 17,744 | 15,936 |
| **84,700** | **84,750** | 17,340 | 13,431 | 17,758 | 15,949 |
| **84,750** | **84,800** | 17,354 | 13,444 | 17,772 | 15,961 |
| **84,800** | **84,850** | 17,368 | 13,456 | 17,786 | 15,974 |
| **84,850** | **84,900** | 17,382 | 13,469 | 17,800 | 15,986 |
| **84,900** | **84,950** | 17,396 | 13,481 | 17,814 | 15,999 |
| **84,950** | **85,000** | 17,410 | 13,494 | 17,828 | 16,011 |
| **85,000** | | | | | |
| **85,000** | **85,050** | 17,424 | 13,506 | 17,842 | 16,024 |
| **85,050** | **85,100** | 17,438 | 13,519 | 17,856 | 16,036 |
| **85,100** | **85,150** | 17,452 | 13,531 | 17,870 | 16,049 |
| **85,150** | **85,200** | 17,466 | 13,544 | 17,884 | 16,061 |
| **85,200** | **85,250** | 17,480 | 13,556 | 17,898 | 16,074 |
| **85,250** | **85,300** | 17,494 | 13,569 | 17,912 | 16,086 |
| **85,300** | **85,350** | 17,508 | 13,581 | 17,926 | 16,099 |
| **85,350** | **85,400** | 17,522 | 13,594 | 17,940 | 16,111 |
| **85,400** | **85,450** | 17,536 | 13,606 | 17,954 | 16,124 |
| **85,450** | **85,500** | 17,550 | 13,619 | 17,968 | 16,136 |
| **85,500** | **85,550** | 17,564 | 13,631 | 17,982 | 16,149 |
| **85,550** | **85,600** | 17,578 | 13,644 | 17,996 | 16,161 |
| **85,600** | **85,650** | 17,592 | 13,656 | 18,010 | 16,174 |
| **85,650** | **85,700** | 17,606 | 13,669 | 18,024 | 16,186 |
| **85,700** | **85,750** | 17,620 | 13,681 | 18,038 | 16,199 |
| **85,750** | **85,800** | 17,634 | 13,694 | 18,052 | 16,211 |
| **85,800** | **85,850** | 17,648 | 13,706 | 18,066 | 16,224 |
| **85,850** | **85,900** | 17,662 | 13,719 | 18,080 | 16,236 |
| **85,900** | **85,950** | 17,676 | 13,731 | 18,094 | 16,249 |
| **85,950** | **86,000** | 17,690 | 13,744 | 18,108 | 16,261 |

* This column must also be used by a qualifying widow(er).

*(Continued)*

## 86,000

| At least | But less than | Single | Married filing jointly* | Married filing separately | Head of a household |
|---|---|---|---|---|---|
| 86,000 | 86,050 | 17,704 | 13,756 | 18,122 | 16,274 |
| 86,050 | 86,100 | 17,718 | 13,769 | 18,136 | 16,286 |
| 86,100 | 86,150 | 17,732 | 13,781 | 18,150 | 16,299 |
| 86,150 | 86,200 | 17,746 | 13,794 | 18,164 | 16,311 |
| 86,200 | 86,250 | 17,760 | 13,806 | 18,178 | 16,324 |
| 86,250 | 86,300 | 17,774 | 13,819 | 18,192 | 16,336 |
| 86,300 | 86,350 | 17,788 | 13,831 | 18,206 | 16,349 |
| 86,350 | 86,400 | 17,802 | 13,844 | 18,220 | 16,361 |
| 86,400 | 86,450 | 17,816 | 13,856 | 18,234 | 16,374 |
| 86,450 | 86,500 | 17,830 | 13,869 | 18,248 | 16,386 |
| 86,500 | 86,550 | 17,844 | 13,881 | 18,262 | 16,399 |
| 86,550 | 86,600 | 17,858 | 13,894 | 18,276 | 16,411 |
| 86,600 | 86,650 | 17,872 | 13,906 | 18,290 | 16,424 |
| 86,650 | 86,700 | 17,886 | 13,919 | 18,304 | 16,436 |
| 86,700 | 86,750 | 17,900 | 13,931 | 18,318 | 16,449 |
| 86,750 | 86,800 | 17,914 | 13,944 | 18,332 | 16,461 |
| 86,800 | 86,850 | 17,928 | 13,956 | 18,346 | 16,474 |
| 86,850 | 86,900 | 17,942 | 13,969 | 18,360 | 16,486 |
| 86,900 | 86,950 | 17,956 | 13,981 | 18,374 | 16,499 |
| 86,950 | 87,000 | 17,970 | 13,994 | 18,388 | 16,511 |

## 87,000

| At least | But less than | Single | Married filing jointly* | Married filing separately | Head of a household |
|---|---|---|---|---|---|
| 87,000 | 87,050 | 17,984 | 14,006 | 18,402 | 16,524 |
| 87,050 | 87,100 | 17,998 | 14,019 | 18,416 | 16,536 |
| 87,100 | 87,150 | 18,012 | 14,031 | 18,430 | 16,549 |
| 87,150 | 87,200 | 18,026 | 14,044 | 18,444 | 16,561 |
| 87,200 | 87,250 | 18,040 | 14,056 | 18,458 | 16,574 |
| 87,250 | 87,300 | 18,054 | 14,069 | 18,472 | 16,586 |
| 87,300 | 87,350 | 18,068 | 14,081 | 18,486 | 16,599 |
| 87,350 | 87,400 | 18,082 | 14,094 | 18,500 | 16,611 |
| 87,400 | 87,450 | 18,096 | 14,106 | 18,514 | 16,624 |
| 87,450 | 87,500 | 18,110 | 14,119 | 18,528 | 16,636 |
| 87,500 | 87,550 | 18,124 | 14,131 | 18,542 | 16,649 |
| 87,550 | 87,600 | 18,138 | 14,144 | 18,556 | 16,661 |
| 87,600 | 87,650 | 18,152 | 14,156 | 18,570 | 16,674 |
| 87,650 | 87,700 | 18,166 | 14,169 | 18,584 | 16,686 |
| 87,700 | 87,750 | 18,180 | 14,181 | 18,598 | 16,699 |
| 87,750 | 87,800 | 18,194 | 14,194 | 18,612 | 16,711 |
| 87,800 | 87,850 | 18,208 | 14,206 | 18,626 | 16,724 |
| 87,850 | 87,900 | 18,222 | 14,219 | 18,640 | 16,736 |
| 87,900 | 87,950 | 18,236 | 14,231 | 18,654 | 16,749 |
| 87,950 | 88,000 | 18,250 | 14,244 | 18,668 | 16,761 |

## 88,000

| At least | But less than | Single | Married filing jointly* | Married filing separately | Head of a household |
|---|---|---|---|---|---|
| 88,000 | 88,050 | 18,264 | 14,256 | 18,682 | 16,774 |
| 88,050 | 88,100 | 18,278 | 14,269 | 18,696 | 16,786 |
| 88,100 | 88,150 | 18,292 | 14,281 | 18,710 | 16,799 |
| 88,150 | 88,200 | 18,306 | 14,294 | 18,724 | 16,811 |
| 88,200 | 88,250 | 18,320 | 14,306 | 18,738 | 16,824 |
| 88,250 | 88,300 | 18,334 | 14,319 | 18,752 | 16,836 |
| 88,300 | 88,350 | 18,348 | 14,331 | 18,766 | 16,849 |
| 88,350 | 88,400 | 18,362 | 14,344 | 18,780 | 16,861 |
| 88,400 | 88,450 | 18,376 | 14,356 | 18,794 | 16,874 |
| 88,450 | 88,500 | 18,390 | 14,369 | 18,808 | 16,886 |
| 88,500 | 88,550 | 18,404 | 14,381 | 18,822 | 16,899 |
| 88,550 | 88,600 | 18,418 | 14,394 | 18,836 | 16,911 |
| 88,600 | 88,650 | 18,432 | 14,406 | 18,850 | 16,924 |
| 88,650 | 88,700 | 18,446 | 14,419 | 18,864 | 16,936 |
| 88,700 | 88,750 | 18,460 | 14,431 | 18,878 | 16,949 |
| 88,750 | 88,800 | 18,474 | 14,444 | 18,892 | 16,961 |
| 88,800 | 88,850 | 18,488 | 14,456 | 18,906 | 16,974 |
| 88,850 | 88,900 | 18,502 | 14,469 | 18,920 | 16,986 |
| 88,900 | 88,950 | 18,516 | 14,481 | 18,934 | 16,999 |
| 88,950 | 89,000 | 18,530 | 14,494 | 18,948 | 17,011 |

## 89,000

| At least | But less than | Single | Married filing jointly* | Married filing separately | Head of a household |
|---|---|---|---|---|---|
| 89,000 | 89,050 | 18,544 | 14,506 | 18,962 | 17,024 |
| 89,050 | 89,100 | 18,558 | 14,519 | 18,976 | 17,036 |
| 89,100 | 89,150 | 18,572 | 14,531 | 18,990 | 17,049 |
| 89,150 | 89,200 | 18,586 | 14,544 | 19,004 | 17,061 |
| 89,200 | 89,250 | 18,600 | 14,556 | 19,018 | 17,074 |
| 89,250 | 89,300 | 18,614 | 14,569 | 19,032 | 17,086 |
| 89,300 | 89,350 | 18,628 | 14,581 | 19,046 | 17,099 |
| 89,350 | 89,400 | 18,642 | 14,594 | 19,060 | 17,111 |
| 89,400 | 89,450 | 18,656 | 14,606 | 19,074 | 17,124 |
| 89,450 | 89,500 | 18,670 | 14,619 | 19,088 | 17,136 |
| 89,500 | 89,550 | 18,684 | 14,631 | 19,102 | 17,149 |
| 89,550 | 89,600 | 18,698 | 14,644 | 19,116 | 17,161 |
| 89,600 | 89,650 | 18,712 | 14,656 | 19,130 | 17,174 |
| 89,650 | 89,700 | 18,726 | 14,669 | 19,144 | 17,186 |
| 89,700 | 89,750 | 18,740 | 14,681 | 19,158 | 17,199 |
| 89,750 | 89,800 | 18,754 | 14,694 | 19,172 | 17,211 |
| 89,800 | 89,850 | 18,768 | 14,706 | 19,186 | 17,224 |
| 89,850 | 89,900 | 18,782 | 14,719 | 19,200 | 17,236 |
| 89,900 | 89,950 | 18,796 | 14,731 | 19,214 | 17,249 |
| 89,950 | 90,000 | 18,810 | 14,744 | 19,228 | 17,261 |

## 90,000

| At least | But less than | Single | Married filing jointly* | Married filing separately | Head of a household |
|---|---|---|---|---|---|
| 90,000 | 90,050 | 18,824 | 14,756 | 19,242 | 17,274 |
| 90,050 | 90,100 | 18,838 | 14,769 | 19,256 | 17,286 |
| 90,100 | 90,150 | 18,852 | 14,781 | 19,270 | 17,299 |
| 90,150 | 90,200 | 18,866 | 14,794 | 19,284 | 17,311 |
| 90,200 | 90,250 | 18,880 | 14,806 | 19,298 | 17,324 |
| 90,250 | 90,300 | 18,894 | 14,819 | 19,312 | 17,336 |
| 90,300 | 90,350 | 18,908 | 14,831 | 19,326 | 17,349 |
| 90,350 | 90,400 | 18,922 | 14,844 | 19,340 | 17,361 |
| 90,400 | 90,450 | 18,936 | 14,856 | 19,354 | 17,374 |
| 90,450 | 90,500 | 18,950 | 14,869 | 19,368 | 17,386 |
| 90,500 | 90,550 | 18,964 | 14,881 | 19,382 | 17,399 |
| 90,550 | 90,600 | 18,978 | 14,894 | 19,396 | 17,411 |
| 90,600 | 90,650 | 18,992 | 14,906 | 19,410 | 17,424 |
| 90,650 | 90,700 | 19,006 | 14,919 | 19,424 | 17,436 |
| 90,700 | 90,750 | 19,020 | 14,931 | 19,438 | 17,449 |
| 90,750 | 90,800 | 19,034 | 14,944 | 19,452 | 17,461 |
| 90,800 | 90,850 | 19,048 | 14,956 | 19,466 | 17,474 |
| 90,850 | 90,900 | 19,062 | 14,969 | 19,480 | 17,486 |
| 90,900 | 90,950 | 19,076 | 14,981 | 19,494 | 17,499 |
| 90,950 | 91,000 | 19,090 | 14,994 | 19,508 | 17,511 |

## 91,000

| At least | But less than | Single | Married filing jointly* | Married filing separately | Head of a household |
|---|---|---|---|---|---|
| 91,000 | 91,050 | 19,104 | 15,006 | 19,522 | 17,524 |
| 91,050 | 91,100 | 19,118 | 15,019 | 19,536 | 17,536 |
| 91,100 | 91,150 | 19,132 | 15,031 | 19,550 | 17,549 |
| 91,150 | 91,200 | 19,146 | 15,044 | 19,564 | 17,561 |
| 91,200 | 91,250 | 19,160 | 15,056 | 19,578 | 17,574 |
| 91,250 | 91,300 | 19,174 | 15,069 | 19,592 | 17,586 |
| 91,300 | 91,350 | 19,188 | 15,081 | 19,606 | 17,599 |
| 91,350 | 91,400 | 19,202 | 15,094 | 19,620 | 17,611 |
| 91,400 | 91,450 | 19,216 | 15,106 | 19,634 | 17,624 |
| 91,450 | 91,500 | 19,230 | 15,119 | 19,648 | 17,636 |
| 91,500 | 91,550 | 19,244 | 15,131 | 19,662 | 17,649 |
| 91,550 | 91,600 | 19,258 | 15,144 | 19,676 | 17,661 |
| 91,600 | 91,650 | 19,272 | 15,156 | 19,690 | 17,674 |
| 91,650 | 91,700 | 19,286 | 15,169 | 19,704 | 17,686 |
| 91,700 | 91,750 | 19,300 | 15,181 | 19,718 | 17,699 |
| 91,750 | 91,800 | 19,314 | 15,194 | 19,732 | 17,711 |
| 91,800 | 91,850 | 19,328 | 15,206 | 19,746 | 17,724 |
| 91,850 | 91,900 | 19,342 | 15,219 | 19,760 | 17,736 |
| 91,900 | 91,950 | 19,356 | 15,231 | 19,774 | 17,749 |
| 91,950 | 92,000 | 19,370 | 15,244 | 19,788 | 17,761 |

## 92,000

| At least | But less than | Single | Married filing jointly* | Married filing separately | Head of a household |
|---|---|---|---|---|---|
| 92,000 | 92,050 | 19,384 | 15,256 | 19,802 | 17,774 |
| 92,050 | 92,100 | 19,398 | 15,269 | 19,816 | 17,786 |
| 92,100 | 92,150 | 19,412 | 15,281 | 19,830 | 17,799 |
| 92,150 | 92,200 | 19,426 | 15,294 | 19,844 | 17,811 |
| 92,200 | 92,250 | 19,440 | 15,306 | 19,858 | 17,824 |
| 92,250 | 92,300 | 19,454 | 15,319 | 19,872 | 17,836 |
| 92,300 | 92,350 | 19,468 | 15,331 | 19,886 | 17,849 |
| 92,350 | 92,400 | 19,482 | 15,344 | 19,900 | 17,861 |
| 92,400 | 92,450 | 19,496 | 15,356 | 19,914 | 17,874 |
| 92,450 | 92,500 | 19,510 | 15,369 | 19,928 | 17,886 |
| 92,500 | 92,550 | 19,524 | 15,381 | 19,942 | 17,899 |
| 92,550 | 92,600 | 19,538 | 15,394 | 19,956 | 17,911 |
| 92,600 | 92,650 | 19,552 | 15,406 | 19,970 | 17,924 |
| 92,650 | 92,700 | 19,566 | 15,419 | 19,984 | 17,936 |
| 92,700 | 92,750 | 19,580 | 15,431 | 19,998 | 17,949 |
| 92,750 | 92,800 | 19,594 | 15,444 | 20,012 | 17,961 |
| 92,800 | 92,850 | 19,608 | 15,456 | 20,026 | 17,974 |
| 92,850 | 92,900 | 19,622 | 15,469 | 20,040 | 17,986 |
| 92,900 | 92,950 | 19,636 | 15,481 | 20,054 | 17,999 |
| 92,950 | 93,000 | 19,650 | 15,494 | 20,068 | 18,011 |

## 93,000

| At least | But less than | Single | Married filing jointly* | Married filing separately | Head of a household |
|---|---|---|---|---|---|
| 93,000 | 93,050 | 19,664 | 15,506 | 20,082 | 18,024 |
| 93,050 | 93,100 | 19,678 | 15,519 | 20,096 | 18,036 |
| 93,100 | 93,150 | 19,692 | 15,531 | 20,110 | 18,049 |
| 93,150 | 93,200 | 19,706 | 15,544 | 20,124 | 18,061 |
| 93,200 | 93,250 | 19,720 | 15,556 | 20,138 | 18,074 |
| 93,250 | 93,300 | 19,734 | 15,569 | 20,152 | 18,086 |
| 93,300 | 93,350 | 19,748 | 15,581 | 20,166 | 18,099 |
| 93,350 | 93,400 | 19,762 | 15,594 | 20,180 | 18,111 |
| 93,400 | 93,450 | 19,776 | 15,606 | 20,194 | 18,124 |
| 93,450 | 93,500 | 19,790 | 15,619 | 20,208 | 18,136 |
| 93,500 | 93,550 | 19,804 | 15,631 | 20,222 | 18,149 |
| 93,550 | 93,600 | 19,818 | 15,644 | 20,236 | 18,161 |
| 93,600 | 93,650 | 19,832 | 15,656 | 20,250 | 18,174 |
| 93,650 | 93,700 | 19,846 | 15,669 | 20,264 | 18,186 |
| 93,700 | 93,750 | 19,860 | 15,681 | 20,278 | 18,199 |
| 93,750 | 93,800 | 19,874 | 15,694 | 20,292 | 18,211 |
| 93,800 | 93,850 | 19,888 | 15,706 | 20,306 | 18,224 |
| 93,850 | 93,900 | 19,902 | 15,719 | 20,320 | 18,236 |
| 93,900 | 93,950 | 19,916 | 15,731 | 20,334 | 18,249 |
| 93,950 | 94,000 | 19,930 | 15,744 | 20,348 | 18,261 |

## 94,000

| At least | But less than | Single | Married filing jointly* | Married filing separately | Head of a household |
|---|---|---|---|---|---|
| 94,000 | 94,050 | 19,944 | 15,756 | 20,362 | 18,274 |
| 94,050 | 94,100 | 19,958 | 15,769 | 20,376 | 18,286 |
| 94,100 | 94,150 | 19,972 | 15,781 | 20,390 | 18,299 |
| 94,150 | 94,200 | 19,986 | 15,794 | 20,404 | 18,311 |
| 94,200 | 94,250 | 20,000 | 15,806 | 20,418 | 18,324 |
| 94,250 | 94,300 | 20,014 | 15,819 | 20,432 | 18,336 |
| 94,300 | 94,350 | 20,028 | 15,831 | 20,446 | 18,349 |
| 94,350 | 94,400 | 20,042 | 15,844 | 20,460 | 18,361 |
| 94,400 | 94,450 | 20,056 | 15,856 | 20,474 | 18,374 |
| 94,450 | 94,500 | 20,070 | 15,869 | 20,488 | 18,386 |
| 94,500 | 94,550 | 20,084 | 15,881 | 20,502 | 18,399 |
| 94,550 | 94,600 | 20,098 | 15,894 | 20,516 | 18,411 |
| 94,600 | 94,650 | 20,112 | 15,906 | 20,530 | 18,424 |
| 94,650 | 94,700 | 20,126 | 15,919 | 20,544 | 18,436 |
| 94,700 | 94,750 | 20,140 | 15,931 | 20,558 | 18,449 |
| 94,750 | 94,800 | 20,154 | 15,944 | 20,572 | 18,461 |
| 94,800 | 94,850 | 20,168 | 15,956 | 20,586 | 18,474 |
| 94,850 | 94,900 | 20,182 | 15,969 | 20,600 | 18,486 |
| 94,900 | 94,950 | 20,196 | 15,981 | 20,614 | 18,499 |
| 94,950 | 95,000 | 20,210 | 15,994 | 20,628 | 18,511 |

* This column must also be used by a qualifying widow(er).

(Continued)

## 95,000

| At least | But less than | Single | Married filing jointly* | Married filing separately | Head of a household |
|---|---|---|---|---|---|
| 95,000 | 95,050 | 20,224 | 16,006 | 20,642 | 18,524 |
| 95,050 | 95,100 | 20,238 | 16,019 | 20,656 | 18,536 |
| 95,100 | 95,150 | 20,252 | 16,031 | 20,670 | 18,549 |
| 95,150 | 95,200 | 20,266 | 16,044 | 20,684 | 18,561 |
| 95,200 | 95,250 | 20,280 | 16,056 | 20,698 | 18,574 |
| 95,250 | 95,300 | 20,294 | 16,069 | 20,712 | 18,586 |
| 95,300 | 95,350 | 20,308 | 16,081 | 20,726 | 18,599 |
| 95,350 | 95,400 | 20,322 | 16,094 | 20,740 | 18,611 |
| 95,400 | 95,450 | 20,336 | 16,106 | 20,754 | 18,624 |
| 95,450 | 95,500 | 20,350 | 16,119 | 20,768 | 18,636 |
| 95,500 | 95,550 | 20,364 | 16,131 | 20,782 | 18,649 |
| 95,550 | 95,600 | 20,378 | 16,144 | 20,796 | 18,661 |
| 95,600 | 95,650 | 20,392 | 16,156 | 20,810 | 18,674 |
| 95,650 | 95,700 | 20,406 | 16,169 | 20,824 | 18,686 |
| 95,700 | 95,750 | 20,420 | 16,181 | 20,838 | 18,699 |
| 95,750 | 95,800 | 20,434 | 16,194 | 20,852 | 18,711 |
| 95,800 | 95,850 | 20,448 | 16,206 | 20,866 | 18,724 |
| 95,850 | 95,900 | 20,462 | 16,219 | 20,880 | 18,736 |
| 95,900 | 95,950 | 20,476 | 16,231 | 20,894 | 18,749 |
| 95,950 | 96,000 | 20,490 | 16,244 | 20,908 | 18,761 |

## 96,000

| At least | But less than | Single | Married filing jointly* | Married filing separately | Head of a household |
|---|---|---|---|---|---|
| 96,000 | 96,050 | 20,504 | 16,256 | 20,922 | 18,774 |
| 96,050 | 96,100 | 20,518 | 16,269 | 20,936 | 18,786 |
| 96,100 | 96,150 | 20,532 | 16,281 | 20,950 | 18,799 |
| 96,150 | 96,200 | 20,546 | 16,294 | 20,964 | 18,811 |
| 96,200 | 96,250 | 20,560 | 16,306 | 20,978 | 18,824 |
| 96,250 | 96,300 | 20,574 | 16,319 | 20,992 | 18,836 |
| 96,300 | 96,350 | 20,588 | 16,331 | 21,006 | 18,849 |
| 96,350 | 96,400 | 20,602 | 16,344 | 21,020 | 18,861 |
| 96,400 | 96,450 | 20,616 | 16,356 | 21,034 | 18,874 |
| 96,450 | 96,500 | 20,630 | 16,369 | 21,048 | 18,886 |
| 96,500 | 96,550 | 20,644 | 16,381 | 21,062 | 18,899 |
| 96,550 | 96,600 | 20,658 | 16,394 | 21,076 | 18,911 |
| 96,600 | 96,650 | 20,672 | 16,406 | 21,090 | 18,924 |
| 96,650 | 96,700 | 20,686 | 16,419 | 21,104 | 18,936 |
| 96,700 | 96,750 | 20,700 | 16,431 | 21,118 | 18,949 |
| 96,750 | 96,800 | 20,714 | 16,444 | 21,132 | 18,961 |
| 96,800 | 96,850 | 20,728 | 16,456 | 21,146 | 18,974 |
| 96,850 | 96,900 | 20,742 | 16,469 | 21,160 | 18,986 |
| 96,900 | 96,950 | 20,756 | 16,481 | 21,174 | 18,999 |
| 96,950 | 97,000 | 20,770 | 16,494 | 21,188 | 19,011 |

## 97,000

| At least | But less than | Single | Married filing jointly* | Married filing separately | Head of a household |
|---|---|---|---|---|---|
| 97,000 | 97,050 | 20,784 | 16,506 | 21,202 | 19,024 |
| 97,050 | 97,100 | 20,798 | 16,519 | 21,216 | 19,036 |
| 97,100 | 97,150 | 20,812 | 16,531 | 21,230 | 19,049 |
| 97,150 | 97,200 | 20,826 | 16,544 | 21,244 | 19,061 |
| 97,200 | 97,250 | 20,840 | 16,556 | 21,258 | 19,074 |
| 97,250 | 97,300 | 20,854 | 16,569 | 21,272 | 19,086 |
| 97,300 | 97,350 | 20,868 | 16,581 | 21,286 | 19,099 |
| 97,350 | 97,400 | 20,882 | 16,594 | 21,300 | 19,111 |
| 97,400 | 97,450 | 20,896 | 16,606 | 21,314 | 19,124 |
| 97,450 | 97,500 | 20,910 | 16,619 | 21,328 | 19,136 |
| 97,500 | 97,550 | 20,924 | 16,631 | 21,342 | 19,149 |
| 97,550 | 97,600 | 20,938 | 16,644 | 21,356 | 19,161 |
| 97,600 | 97,650 | 20,952 | 16,656 | 21,370 | 19,174 |
| 97,650 | 97,700 | 20,966 | 16,669 | 21,384 | 19,186 |
| 97,700 | 97,750 | 20,980 | 16,681 | 21,398 | 19,199 |
| 97,750 | 97,800 | 20,994 | 16,694 | 21,412 | 19,211 |
| 97,800 | 97,850 | 21,008 | 16,706 | 21,426 | 19,224 |
| 97,850 | 97,900 | 21,022 | 16,719 | 21,440 | 19,236 |
| 97,900 | 97,950 | 21,036 | 16,731 | 21,454 | 19,249 |
| 97,950 | 98,000 | 21,050 | 16,744 | 21,468 | 19,261 |

## 98,000

| At least | But less than | Single | Married filing jointly* | Married filing separately | Head of a household |
|---|---|---|---|---|---|
| 98,000 | 98,050 | 21,064 | 16,756 | 21,482 | 19,274 |
| 98,050 | 98,100 | 21,078 | 16,769 | 21,496 | 19,286 |
| 98,100 | 98,150 | 21,092 | 16,781 | 21,510 | 19,299 |
| 98,150 | 98,200 | 21,106 | 16,794 | 21,524 | 19,311 |
| 98,200 | 98,250 | 21,120 | 16,806 | 21,538 | 19,324 |
| 98,250 | 98,300 | 21,134 | 16,819 | 21,552 | 19,336 |
| 98,300 | 98,350 | 21,148 | 16,831 | 21,566 | 19,349 |
| 98,350 | 98,400 | 21,162 | 16,844 | 21,580 | 19,361 |
| 98,400 | 98,450 | 21,176 | 16,856 | 21,594 | 19,374 |
| 98,450 | 98,500 | 21,190 | 16,869 | 21,608 | 19,386 |
| 98,500 | 98,550 | 21,204 | 16,881 | 21,622 | 19,399 |
| 98,550 | 98,600 | 21,218 | 16,894 | 21,636 | 19,411 |
| 98,600 | 98,650 | 21,232 | 16,906 | 21,650 | 19,424 |
| 98,650 | 98,700 | 21,246 | 16,919 | 21,664 | 19,436 |
| 98,700 | 98,750 | 21,260 | 16,931 | 21,678 | 19,449 |
| 98,750 | 98,800 | 21,274 | 16,944 | 21,692 | 19,461 |
| 98,800 | 98,850 | 21,288 | 16,956 | 21,706 | 19,474 |
| 98,850 | 98,900 | 21,302 | 16,969 | 21,720 | 19,486 |
| 98,900 | 98,950 | 21,316 | 16,981 | 21,734 | 19,499 |
| 98,950 | 99,000 | 21,330 | 16,994 | 21,748 | 19,511 |

## 99,000

| At least | But less than | Single | Married filing jointly* | Married filing separately | Head of a household |
|---|---|---|---|---|---|
| 99,000 | 99,050 | 21,344 | 17,006 | 21,762 | 19,524 |
| 99,050 | 99,100 | 21,358 | 17,019 | 21,776 | 19,536 |
| 99,100 | 99,150 | 21,372 | 17,031 | 21,790 | 19,549 |
| 99,150 | 99,200 | 21,386 | 17,044 | 21,804 | 19,561 |
| 99,200 | 99,250 | 21,400 | 17,056 | 21,818 | 19,574 |
| 99,250 | 99,300 | 21,414 | 17,069 | 21,832 | 19,586 |
| 99,300 | 99,350 | 21,428 | 17,081 | 21,846 | 19,599 |
| 99,350 | 99,400 | 21,442 | 17,094 | 21,860 | 19,611 |
| 99,400 | 99,450 | 21,456 | 17,106 | 21,874 | 19,624 |
| 99,450 | 99,500 | 21,470 | 17,119 | 21,888 | 19,636 |
| 99,500 | 99,550 | 21,484 | 17,131 | 21,902 | 19,649 |
| 99,550 | 99,600 | 21,498 | 17,144 | 21,916 | 19,661 |
| 99,600 | 99,650 | 21,512 | 17,156 | 21,930 | 19,674 |
| 99,650 | 99,700 | 21,526 | 17,169 | 21,944 | 19,686 |
| 99,700 | 99,750 | 21,540 | 17,181 | 21,958 | 19,699 |
| 99,750 | 99,800 | 21,554 | 17,194 | 21,972 | 19,711 |
| 99,800 | 99,850 | 21,568 | 17,206 | 21,986 | 19,724 |
| 99,850 | 99,900 | 21,582 | 17,219 | 22,000 | 19,736 |
| 99,900 | 99,950 | 21,596 | 17,231 | 22,014 | 19,749 |
| 99,950 | 100,000 | 21,610 | 17,244 | 22,028 | 19,761 |

$100,000 or over — use the Tax Computation Worksheet

* This column must also be used by a qualifying widow(er)

# 2011 Tax Computation Worksheet—Line 44

 See the instructions for line 44 to see if you must use the worksheet below to figure your tax.

**Note.** If you are required to use this worksheet to figure the tax on an amount from another form or worksheet, such as the Qualified Dividends and Capital Gain Tax Worksheet, the Schedule D Tax Worksheet, Schedule J, Form 8615, or the Foreign Earned Income Tax Worksheet, enter the amount from that form or worksheet in column (a) of the row that applies to the amount you are looking up. Enter the result on the appropriate line of the form or worksheet that you are completing.

**Section A**—Use if your filing status is **Single.** Complete the row below that applies to you.

| Taxable income. If line 43 is— | (a) Enter the amount from line 43 | (b) Multiplication amount | (c) Multiply (a) by (b) | (d) Subtraction amount | Tax. Subtract (d) from (c). Enter the result here and on Form 1040, line 44 |
|---|---|---|---|---|---|
| At least $100,000 but not over $174,400 | $ | × 28% (.28) | $ | $ 6,383.00 | $ |
| Over $174,400 but not over $379,150 | $ | × 33% (.33) | $ | $ 15,103.00 | $ |
| Over $379,150 | $ | × 35% (.35) | $ | $22,686.00 | $ |

**Section B**—Use if your filing status is **Married filing jointly** or **Qualifying widow(er).** Complete the row below that applies to you.

| Taxable income. If line 43 is— | (a) Enter the amount from line 43 | (b) Multiplication amount | (c) Multiply (a) by (b) | (d) Subtraction amount | Tax. Subtract (d) from (c). Enter the result here and on Form 1040, line 44 |
|---|---|---|---|---|---|
| At least $100,000 but not over $139,350 | $ | × 25% (.25) | $ | $ 7,750.00 | $ |
| Over $139,350 but not over $212,300 | $ | × 28% (.28) | $ | $ 11,930.50 | $ |
| Over $212,300 but not over $379,150 | $ | × 33% (.33) | $ | $ 22,545.50 | $ |
| Over $379,150 | $ | × 35% (.35) | $ | $ 30,128.50 | $ |

**Section C**—Use if your filing status is **Married filing separately.** Complete the row below that applies to you.

| Taxable income. If line 43 is— | (a) Enter the amount from line 43 | (b) Multiplication amount | (c) Multiply (a) by (b) | (d) Subtraction amount | Tax. Subtract (d) from (c). Enter the result here and on Form 1040, line 44 |
|---|---|---|---|---|---|
| At least $100,000 but not over $106,150 | $ | × 28% (.28) | $ | $ 5,965.25 | $ |
| Over $106,150 but not over $189,575 | $ | × 33% (.33) | $ | $ 11,272.75 | $ |
| Over $189,575 | $ | × 35% (.35) | $ | $ 15,064.25 | $ |

**Section D**—Use if your filing status is **Head of household.** Complete the row below that applies to you.

| Taxable income. If line 43 is— | (a) Enter the amount from line 43 | (b) Multiplication amount | (c) Multiply (a) by (b) | (d) Subtraction amount | Tax. Subtract (d) from (c). Enter the result here and on Form 1040, line 44 |
|---|---|---|---|---|---|
| At least $100,000 but not over $119,400 | $ | × 25% (.25) | $ | $ 5,232.50 | $ |
| Over $119,400 but not over $193,350 | $ | × 28% (.28) | $ | $ 8,814.50 | $ |
| Over $193,350 but not over $379,150 | $ | × 33% (.33) | $ | $ 18,432.00 | $ |
| Over $379,150 | $ | × 35% (.35) | $ | $ 26,065.00 | $ |

# Appendix B - Optional Sales Tax Tables

# 2011 Optional State and Certain Local Sales Tax Tables

| Income | | Exemptions | | | | | | Exemptions | | | | | | Exemptions | | | | | | Exemptions | | | | | | Exemptions | | | | | |
|---|---|---|---|---|---|---|---|---|---|---|---|---|---|---|---|---|---|---|---|---|---|---|---|---|---|---|---|---|---|---|---|
| At least | But less than | 1 | 2 | 3 | 4 | 5 | Over 5 | 1 | 2 | 3 | 4 | 5 | Over 5 | 1 | 2 | 3 | 4 | 5 | Over 5 | 1 | 2 | 3 | 4 | 5 | Over 5 | 1 | 2 | 3 | 4 | 5 | Over 5 |
| | | **Alabama** | | | | | **4.0000%** | **Arizona** | | | | | **6.6000%** | **Arkansas** | | | | | **6.0000%** | **California[1,2]** | | | | | **7.7459%** | **Colorado** | | | | | **2.9000%** |
| $0 | $20,000 | 226 | 267 | 295 | 317 | 335 | 361 | 260 | 288 | 305 | 319 | 329 | 344 | 290 | 326 | 348 | 366 | 380 | 399 | 289 | 316 | 333 | 346 | 356 | 370 | 117 | 129 | 137 | 143 | 148 | 155 |
| 20,000 | 30,000 | 333 | 392 | 432 | 464 | 490 | 527 | 429 | 473 | 502 | 524 | 541 | 566 | 464 | 521 | 557 | 584 | 607 | 637 | 479 | 522 | 550 | 571 | 588 | 612 | 182 | 201 | 213 | 223 | 230 | 240 |
| 30,000 | 40,000 | 385 | 452 | 499 | 535 | 564 | 607 | 516 | 569 | 604 | 630 | 651 | 680 | 553 | 619 | 663 | 695 | 722 | 758 | 577 | 629 | 663 | 688 | 709 | 737 | 215 | 237 | 252 | 262 | 271 | 283 |
| 40,000 | 50,000 | 428 | 503 | 554 | 593 | 626 | 673 | 591 | 652 | 691 | 721 | 745 | 778 | 628 | 704 | 753 | 790 | 820 | 862 | 662 | 722 | 761 | 790 | 813 | 845 | 243 | 268 | 284 | 296 | 306 | 320 |
| 50,000 | 60,000 | 466 | 547 | 602 | 645 | 681 | 731 | 659 | 726 | 770 | 803 | 830 | 867 | 696 | 779 | 834 | 875 | 908 | 954 | 738 | 806 | 849 | 881 | 907 | 942 | 268 | 295 | 313 | 326 | 337 | 352 |
| 60,000 | 70,000 | 500 | 587 | 646 | 691 | 730 | 783 | 721 | 795 | 843 | 879 | 908 | 948 | 757 | 848 | 907 | 952 | 988 | 1038 | 809 | 882 | 929 | 964 | 993 | 1032 | 291 | 320 | 339 | 353 | 365 | 381 |
| 70,000 | 80,000 | 532 | 624 | 686 | 734 | 775 | 832 | 779 | 859 | 911 | 950 | 982 | 1025 | 815 | 913 | 976 | 1025 | 1064 | 1118 | 875 | 955 | 1005 | 1043 | 1074 | 1116 | 312 | 343 | 364 | 379 | 391 | 409 |
| 80,000 | 90,000 | 562 | 658 | 723 | 774 | 816 | 876 | 834 | 919 | 974 | 1016 | 1050 | 1096 | 868 | 973 | 1041 | 1092 | 1133 | 1191 | 937 | 1022 | 1076 | 1117 | 1150 | 1195 | 332 | 365 | 386 | 403 | 416 | 434 |
| 90,000 | 100,000 | 589 | 689 | 757 | 811 | 855 | 918 | 885 | 976 | 1035 | 1079 | 1115 | 1164 | 919 | 1029 | 1101 | 1155 | 1199 | 1260 | 996 | 1086 | 1144 | 1187 | 1222 | 1269 | 350 | 385 | 408 | 425 | 439 | 458 |
| 100,000 | 120,000 | 625 | 731 | 803 | 859 | 906 | 972 | 953 | 1051 | 1114 | 1162 | 1200 | 1253 | 985 | 1104 | 1181 | 1239 | 1286 | 1351 | 1073 | 1170 | 1233 | 1279 | 1317 | 1368 | 374 | 412 | 436 | 454 | 469 | 489 |
| 120,000 | 140,000 | 673 | 786 | 863 | 924 | 974 | 1044 | 1047 | 1154 | 1223 | 1276 | 1318 | 1376 | 1076 | 1206 | 1289 | 1353 | 1405 | 1476 | 1180 | 1287 | 1355 | 1406 | 1447 | 1504 | 407 | 448 | 474 | 494 | 510 | 532 |
| 140,000 | 160,000 | 715 | 834 | 916 | 979 | 1032 | 1107 | 1129 | 1245 | 1319 | 1375 | 1421 | 1484 | 1155 | 1294 | 1384 | 1452 | 1508 | 1584 | 1274 | 1389 | 1462 | 1517 | 1562 | 1622 | 436 | 479 | 507 | 528 | 545 | 569 |
| 160,000 | 180,000 | 756 | 882 | 967 | 1034 | 1090 | 1169 | 1211 | 1335 | 1415 | 1475 | 1524 | 1591 | 1234 | 1382 | 1479 | 1551 | 1610 | 1692 | 1367 | 1490 | 1569 | 1628 | 1676 | 1741 | 465 | 510 | 540 | 562 | 580 | 605 |
| 180,000 | 200,000 | 793 | 924 | 1013 | 1083 | 1141 | 1223 | 1285 | 1416 | 1501 | 1565 | 1617 | 1688 | 1305 | 1462 | 1563 | 1640 | 1703 | 1789 | 1452 | 1582 | 1666 | 1729 | 1779 | 1848 | 490 | 539 | 570 | 593 | 612 | 638 |
| 200,000 or more | | 971 | 1129 | 1237 | 1321 | 1390 | 1489 | 1656 | 1824 | 1933 | 2014 | 2081 | 2172 | 1656 | 1855 | 1984 | 2081 | 2160 | 2270 | 1875 | 2044 | 2151 | 2232 | 2297 | 2386 | 617 | 677 | 715 | 744 | 768 | 800 |
| **Income** | | **Connecticut[1]** | | | | | **6.1764%** | **District of Columbia** | | | | | **6.0000%** | **Florida** | | | | | **6.0000%** | **Georgia** | | | | | **4.0000%** | **Hawaii[5]** | | | | | **4.0000%** |
| $0 | $20,000 | 250 | 271 | 285 | 295 | 303 | 314 | 191 | 204 | 213 | 220 | 225 | 232 | 253 | 277 | 292 | 303 | 313 | 325 | 160 | 177 | 189 | 197 | 204 | 214 | 253 | 291 | 317 | 336 | 352 | 374 |
| 20,000 | 30,000 | 411 | 446 | 469 | 485 | 498 | 516 | 315 | 337 | 352 | 362 | 371 | 383 | 416 | 455 | 480 | 498 | 514 | 534 | 252 | 279 | 296 | 309 | 320 | 335 | 393 | 451 | 490 | 520 | 544 | 578 |
| 30,000 | 40,000 | 495 | 537 | 563 | 583 | 599 | 621 | 379 | 406 | 423 | 436 | 446 | 460 | 500 | 547 | 577 | 599 | 617 | 642 | 298 | 330 | 350 | 366 | 378 | 396 | 462 | 531 | 576 | 611 | 640 | 680 |
| 40,000 | 50,000 | 566 | 615 | 645 | 668 | 686 | 711 | 434 | 466 | 485 | 500 | 512 | 528 | 572 | 626 | 660 | 686 | 706 | 735 | 338 | 373 | 396 | 414 | 428 | 447 | 521 | 598 | 650 | 689 | 721 | 766 |
| 50,000 | 60,000 | 631 | 685 | 719 | 745 | 765 | 793 | 484 | 519 | 541 | 557 | 571 | 588 | 637 | 697 | 735 | 764 | 787 | 819 | 373 | 412 | 437 | 456 | 472 | 493 | 573 | 658 | 714 | 758 | 793 | 842 |
| 60,000 | 70,000 | 690 | 749 | 787 | 815 | 837 | 867 | 530 | 568 | 592 | 610 | 624 | 644 | 697 | 762 | 804 | 835 | 861 | 895 | 405 | 447 | 475 | 495 | 512 | 535 | 620 | 712 | 773 | 820 | 858 | 911 |
| 70,000 | 80,000 | 746 | 810 | 851 | 881 | 905 | 938 | 573 | 615 | 641 | 660 | 675 | 696 | 754 | 824 | 869 | 903 | 930 | 967 | 435 | 480 | 509 | 532 | 550 | 575 | 664 | 763 | 828 | 878 | 919 | 976 |
| 80,000 | 90,000 | 798 | 867 | 910 | 942 | 968 | 1003 | 614 | 658 | 685 | 706 | 723 | 745 | 806 | 881 | 929 | 966 | 995 | 1035 | 463 | 511 | 542 | 565 | 584 | 611 | 705 | 809 | 878 | 931 | 975 | 1035 |
| 90,000 | 100,000 | 848 | 920 | 966 | 1001 | 1028 | 1065 | 652 | 699 | 728 | 750 | 768 | 792 | 856 | 936 | 987 | 1025 | 1056 | 1098 | 489 | 539 | 572 | 597 | 617 | 645 | 743 | 853 | 926 | 982 | 1028 | 1091 |
| 100,000 | 120,000 | 913 | 991 | 1041 | 1078 | 1107 | 1147 | 702 | 753 | 784 | 808 | 827 | 853 | 921 | 1007 | 1062 | 1104 | 1137 | 1183 | 523 | 577 | 612 | 639 | 660 | 690 | 793 | 911 | 988 | 1048 | 1097 | 1164 |
| 120,000 | 140,000 | 1002 | 1088 | 1143 | 1183 | 1216 | 1260 | 772 | 827 | 862 | 888 | 909 | 937 | 1012 | 1106 | 1166 | 1212 | 1248 | 1298 | 570 | 629 | 667 | 696 | 719 | 751 | 862 | 989 | 1073 | 1138 | 1190 | 1264 |
| 140,000 | 160,000 | 1081 | 1174 | 1232 | 1276 | 1311 | 1359 | 832 | 892 | 930 | 958 | 980 | 1011 | 1091 | 1192 | 1257 | 1306 | 1345 | 1399 | 611 | 674 | 714 | 745 | 770 | 804 | 921 | 1057 | 1147 | 1215 | 1272 | 1350 |
| 160,000 | 180,000 | 1159 | 1259 | 1322 | 1369 | 1406 | 1457 | 893 | 957 | 997 | 1027 | 1051 | 1084 | 1169 | 1278 | 1348 | 1400 | 1442 | 1500 | 652 | 718 | 761 | 794 | 821 | 857 | 979 | 1124 | 1219 | 1292 | 1352 | 1436 |
| 180,000 | 200,000 | 1229 | 1335 | 1402 | 1452 | 1492 | 1546 | 948 | 1016 | 1059 | 1090 | 1116 | 1151 | 1241 | 1356 | 1430 | 1485 | 1530 | 1591 | 688 | 758 | 804 | 838 | 866 | 904 | 1032 | 1184 | 1284 | 1361 | 1425 | 1513 |
| 200,000 or more | | 1583 | 1720 | 1806 | 1870 | 1922 | 1992 | 1222 | 1310 | 1365 | 1406 | 1439 | 1483 | 1597 | 1745 | 1840 | 1911 | 1968 | 2047 | 869 | 956 | 1013 | 1056 | 1090 | 1138 | 1290 | 1479 | 1604 | 1700 | 1779 | 1888 |
| **Income** | | **Idaho** | | | | | **6.0000%** | **Illinois** | | | | | **6.2500%** | **Indiana** | | | | | **7.0000%** | **Iowa** | | | | | **6.0000%** | **Kansas** | | | | | **6.3000%** |
| $0 | $20,000 | 339 | 400 | 441 | 473 | 500 | 538 | 262 | 294 | 314 | 330 | 343 | 361 | 299 | 332 | 353 | 370 | 383 | 401 | 259 | 288 | 306 | 320 | 331 | 346 | 369 | 435 | 480 | 515 | 544 | 585 |
| 20,000 | 30,000 | 505 | 594 | 654 | 700 | 739 | 794 | 403 | 450 | 481 | 505 | 525 | 552 | 462 | 514 | 547 | 571 | 592 | 619 | 427 | 474 | 505 | 528 | 546 | 571 | 560 | 659 | 726 | 778 | 822 | 883 |
| 30,000 | 40,000 | 586 | 688 | 757 | 810 | 855 | 918 | 472 | 527 | 563 | 591 | 614 | 646 | 544 | 604 | 643 | 672 | 695 | 728 | 514 | 571 | 608 | 635 | 657 | 688 | 653 | 768 | 846 | 907 | 957 | 1028 |
| 40,000 | 50,000 | 654 | 767 | 843 | 902 | 952 | 1022 | 531 | 592 | 633 | 664 | 689 | 725 | 613 | 680 | 724 | 756 | 783 | 819 | 589 | 654 | 696 | 728 | 754 | 789 | 732 | 861 | 948 | 1015 | 1072 | 1151 |
| 50,000 | 60,000 | 714 | 836 | 919 | 984 | 1037 | 1113 | 583 | 650 | 694 | 728 | 756 | 795 | 674 | 748 | 796 | 832 | 861 | 901 | 657 | 730 | 777 | 812 | 840 | 880 | 801 | 942 | 1037 | 1111 | 1172 | 1259 |
| 60,000 | 70,000 | 768 | 898 | 987 | 1056 | 1114 | 1195 | 629 | 702 | 750 | 786 | 816 | 858 | 729 | 810 | 861 | 900 | 931 | 974 | 719 | 799 | 850 | 889 | 920 | 963 | 864 | 1015 | 1117 | 1197 | 1263 | 1356 |
| 70,000 | 80,000 | 818 | 957 | 1051 | 1124 | 1185 | 1271 | 673 | 751 | 802 | 841 | 873 | 917 | 781 | 867 | 922 | 964 | 997 | 1043 | 777 | 864 | 919 | 961 | 995 | 1041 | 922 | 1083 | 1192 | 1277 | 1348 | 1447 |
| 80,000 | 90,000 | 864 | 1010 | 1109 | 1186 | 1250 | 1340 | 714 | 796 | 850 | 891 | 925 | 971 | 829 | 920 | 978 | 1022 | 1058 | 1107 | 832 | 924 | 984 | 1029 | 1065 | 1115 | 976 | 1146 | 1261 | 1351 | 1425 | 1530 |
| 90,000 | 100,000 | 907 | 1060 | 1163 | 1244 | 1311 | 1406 | 752 | 838 | 894 | 938 | 973 | 1022 | 874 | 970 | 1031 | 1078 | 1115 | 1166 | 884 | 982 | 1045 | 1093 | 1131 | 1184 | 1027 | 1205 | 1326 | 1420 | 1498 | 1608 |
| 100,000 | 120,000 | 964 | 1125 | 1235 | 1320 | 1391 | 1491 | 801 | 893 | 953 | 999 | 1037 | 1089 | 933 | 1035 | 1101 | 1150 | 1190 | 1245 | 952 | 1058 | 1126 | 1177 | 1219 | 1276 | 1092 | 1282 | 1410 | 1510 | 1593 | 1710 |
| 120,000 | 140,000 | 1040 | 1213 | 1331 | 1422 | 1499 | 1606 | 869 | 968 | 1033 | 1083 | 1123 | 1180 | 1013 | 1124 | 1195 | 1248 | 1292 | 1351 | 1046 | 1162 | 1237 | 1294 | 1339 | 1402 | 1182 | 1386 | 1525 | 1633 | 1722 | 1848 |
| 140,000 | 160,000 | 1106 | 1290 | 1414 | 1511 | 1591 | 1705 | 928 | 1033 | 1102 | 1155 | 1198 | 1258 | 1083 | 1201 | 1277 | 1334 | 1380 | 1443 | 1128 | 1254 | 1335 | 1395 | 1445 | 1512 | 1259 | 1477 | 1624 | 1738 | 1834 | 1967 |
| 160,000 | 180,000 | 1172 | 1365 | 1496 | 1598 | 1683 | 1803 | 985 | 1097 | 1170 | 1226 | 1272 | 1336 | 1152 | 1277 | 1358 | 1418 | 1467 | 1534 | 1210 | 1345 | 1432 | 1497 | 1550 | 1623 | 1335 | 1566 | 1721 | 1843 | 1943 | 2085 |
| 180,000 | 200,000 | 1230 | 1432 | 1569 | 1676 | 1764 | 1890 | 1037 | 1154 | 1231 | 1290 | 1338 | 1405 | 1213 | 1345 | 1430 | 1494 | 1545 | 1616 | 1284 | 1428 | 1520 | 1589 | 1645 | 1723 | 1403 | 1645 | 1809 | 1936 | 2042 | 2190 |
| 200,000 or more | | 1514 | 1758 | 1924 | 2053 | 2161 | 2312 | 1291 | 1435 | 1530 | 1602 | 1662 | 1744 | 1516 | 1681 | 1786 | 1865 | 1929 | 2017 | 1655 | 1841 | 1960 | 2050 | 2122 | 2222 | 1736 | 2033 | 2234 | 2390 | 2520 | 2702 |
| **Income** | | **Kentucky** | | | | | **6.0000%** | **Louisiana** | | | | | **4.0000%** | **Maine** | | | | | **5.0000%** | **Maryland** | | | | | **6.0000%** | **Massachusetts** | | | | | **6.2500%** |
| $0 | $20,000 | 243 | 269 | 286 | 298 | 308 | 322 | 169 | 184 | 194 | 201 | 207 | 215 | 160 | 173 | 181 | 187 | 192 | 198 | 233 | 257 | 273 | 285 | 295 | 309 | 207 | 223 | 233 | 241 | 247 | 256 |
| 20,000 | 30,000 | 388 | 428 | 454 | 474 | 489 | 511 | 278 | 303 | 319 | 331 | 340 | 353 | 261 | 282 | 295 | 305 | 313 | 323 | 379 | 418 | 444 | 464 | 480 | 502 | 325 | 350 | 365 | 377 | 387 | 400 |
| 30,000 | 40,000 | 461 | 508 | 539 | 562 | 581 | 607 | 334 | 364 | 383 | 398 | 409 | 425 | 314 | 338 | 354 | 365 | 375 | 387 | 453 | 501 | 532 | 556 | 575 | 601 | 384 | 413 | 432 | 446 | 457 | 472 |
| 40,000 | 50,000 | 524 | 577 | 612 | 638 | 659 | 688 | 383 | 417 | 439 | 456 | 469 | 487 | 359 | 387 | 404 | 418 | 428 | 443 | 518 | 572 | 607 | 634 | 656 | 687 | 435 | 467 | 488 | 504 | 516 | 533 |
| 50,000 | 60,000 | 580 | 639 | 677 | 706 | 729 | 761 | 427 | 465 | 490 | 508 | 522 | 542 | 399 | 430 | 450 | 465 | 476 | 492 | 575 | 636 | 675 | 705 | 730 | 763 | 480 | 515 | 538 | 555 | 569 | 588 |
| 60,000 | 70,000 | 630 | 695 | 736 | 767 | 793 | 827 | 467 | 509 | 536 | 555 | 571 | 593 | 436 | 470 | 491 | 507 | 520 | 538 | 628 | 694 | 737 | 770 | 796 | 833 | 521 | 559 | 584 | 602 | 617 | 637 |
| 70,000 | 80,000 | 678 | 747 | 792 | 825 | 852 | 890 | 505 | 550 | 579 | 601 | 618 | 642 | 471 | 508 | 531 | 548 | 562 | 581 | 678 | 749 | 795 | 831 | 859 | 899 | 559 | 600 | 627 | 646 | 662 | 684 |
| 80,000 | 90,000 | 723 | 796 | 843 | 879 | 908 | 947 | 541 | 589 | 620 | 643 | 661 | 686 | 504 | 543 | 567 | 586 | 600 | 621 | 724 | 800 | 850 | 887 | 918 | 960 | 595 | 638 | 666 | 687 | 704 | 727 |
| 90,000 | 100,000 | 765 | 842 | 892 | 929 | 960 | 1002 | 574 | 625 | 658 | 682 | 702 | 729 | 534 | 576 | 602 | 621 | 637 | 658 | 768 | 848 | 901 | 941 | 973 | 1018 | 628 | 674 | 703 | 725 | 743 | 767 |
| 100,000 | 120,000 | 820 | 902 | 956 | 996 | 1028 | 1073 | 618 | 673 | 709 | 735 | 756 | 785 | 575 | 619 | 647 | 668 | 685 | 708 | 825 | 912 | 968 | 1011 | 1046 | 1094 | 672 | 721 | 752 | 776 | 794 | 820 |
| 120,000 | 140,000 | 895 | 985 | 1043 | 1087 | 1122 | 1171 | 679 | 740 | 778 | 807 | 830 | 862 | 631 | 679 | 710 | 733 | 751 | 776 | 904 | 999 | 1061 | 1108 | 1146 | 1199 | 732 | 785 | 819 | 844 | 865 | 893 |
| 140,000 | 160,000 | 961 | 1057 | 1119 | 1166 | 1204 | 1256 | 732 | 798 | 839 | 870 | 895 | 930 | 680 | 732 | 765 | 789 | 809 | 836 | 973 | 1075 | 1142 | 1193 | 1234 | 1291 | 784 | 841 | 877 | 904 | 926 | 956 |
| 160,000 | 180,000 | 1026 | 1129 | 1195 | 1245 | 1285 | 1341 | 785 | 855 | 900 | 933 | 960 | 997 | 728 | 784 | 819 | 845 | 867 | 895 | 1042 | 1151 | 1223 | 1277 | 1321 | 1382 | 836 | 896 | 934 | 963 | 986 | 1018 |
| 180,000 | 200,000 | 1085 | 1193 | 1263 | 1315 | 1358 | 1417 | 833 | 908 | 955 | 990 | 1019 | 1058 | 772 | 831 | 868 | 896 | 919 | 949 | 1104 | 1220 | 1295 | 1353 | 1400 | 1464 | 883 | 946 | 986 | 1016 | 1041 | 1074 |
| 200,000 or more | | 1377 | 1512 | 1600 | 1666 | 1720 | 1793 | 1074 | 1169 | 1230 | 1275 | 1312 | 1362 | 992 | 1067 | 1114 | 1150 | 1178 | 1217 | 1413 | 1561 | 1658 | 1731 | 1791 | 1874 | 1113 | 1191 | 1241 | 1279 | 1309 | 1350 |
| **Income** | | **Michigan** | | | | | **6.0000%** | **Minnesota** | | | | | **6.8750%** | **Mississippi** | | | | | **7.0000%** | **Missouri** | | | | | **4.2250%** | **Nebraska** | | | | | **5.5000%** |
| $0 | $20,000 | 232 | 256 | 272 | 283 | 293 | 306 | 245 | 265 | 278 | 287 | 295 | 305 | 424 | 493 | 539 | 575 | 604 | 645 | 181 | 206 | 222 | 234 | 244 | 258 | 239 | 264 | 279 | 291 | 301 | 314 |
| 20,000 | 30,000 | 368 | 405 | 429 | 447 | 461 | 481 | 409 | 443 | 464 | 480 | 493 | 511 | 651 | 755 | 825 | 879 | 924 | 986 | 286 | 323 | 348 | 367 | 382 | 404 | 391 | 431 | 457 | 477 | 492 | 514 |
| 30,000 | 40,000 | 436 | 479 | 508 | 529 | 546 | 570 | 494 | 535 | 561 | 581 | 597 | 618 | 762 | 884 | 966 | 1029 | 1081 | 1154 | 338 | 382 | 411 | 433 | 451 | 477 | 469 | 517 | 549 | 572 | 591 | 616 |
| 40,000 | 50,000 | 494 | 543 | 575 | 599 | 618 | 645 | 568 | 616 | 646 | 668 | 686 | 711 | 856 | 993 | 1085 | 1156 | 1214 | 1295 | 383 | 432 | 465 | 490 | 510 | 539 | 536 | 592 | 627 | 654 | 676 | 705 |
| 50,000 | 60,000 | 546 | 600 | 635 | 662 | 683 | 712 | 635 | 688 | 722 | 747 | 768 | 795 | 940 | 1090 | 1190 | 1267 | 1331 | 1420 | 423 | 477 | 513 | 540 | 563 | 594 | 597 | 659 | 698 | 728 | 752 | 785 |
| 60,000 | 70,000 | 593 | 652 | 690 | 718 | 742 | 773 | 696 | 755 | 792 | 820 | 842 | 873 | 1015 | 1177 | 1285 | 1368 | 1437 | 1533 | 459 | 518 | 556 | 586 | 610 | 644 | 652 | 720 | 763 | 795 | 822 | 858 |
| 70,000 | 80,000 | 638 | 701 | 741 | 772 | 797 | 831 | 755 | 818 | 859 | 889 | 913 | 946 | 1086 | 1258 | 1374 | 1463 | 1536 | 1639 | 493 | 556 | 597 | 629 | 655 | 691 | 704 | 778 | 824 | 859 | 888 | 926 |
| 80,000 | 90,000 | 679 | 746 | 789 | 821 | 848 | 884 | 809 | 877 | 921 | 953 | 979 | 1015 | 1150 | 1333 | 1455 | 1549 | 1627 | 1736 | 524 | 591 | 635 | 669 | 696 | 735 | 753 | 831 | 881 | 919 | 949 | 990 |
| [illegible] | 100,[illegible] | 716 | [illegible] | [illegible] | [illegible] | 886 | [illegible] | [illegible] | [illegible] | [illegible] | [illegible] | [illegible] | [illegible] | [illegible] | 1404 | 1532 | 1631 | [illegible] | [illegible] | [illegible] | [illegible] | [illegible] | 706 | [illegible] | 770 | [illegible] | [illegible] | [illegible] | [illegible] | [illegible] | [illegible] |
| 100,000 | 120,000 | 769 | 844 | 892 | 929 | 959 | 999 | 929 | 1008 | 1058 | 1095 | 1125 | 1166 | 1291 | 1496 | 1632 | 1738 | 1825 | 1946 | 593 | 668 | 717 | 755 | 787 | 830 | 859 | 949 | 1006 | 1049 | 1084 | 1131 |
| 120,000 | 140,000 | 839 | 920 | 973 | 1013 | 1045 | 1089 | 1023 | 1110 | 1165 | 1206 | 1239 | 1285 | 1399 | 1621 | 1768 | 1882 | 1977 | 2108 | 646 | 728 | 781 | 823 | 856 | 903 | 943 | 1041 | 1104 | 1151 | 1189 | 1241 |
| 140,000 | 160,000 | 899 | 987 | 1043 | 1085 | 1120 | 1167 | 1105 | 1200 | 1260 | 1304 | 1340 | 1389 | 1493 | 1729 | 1886 | 2008 | 2108 | 2248 | 692 | 779 | 837 | 881 | 917 | 967 | 1016 | 1121 | 1189 | 1240 | 1281 | 1337 |
| 160,000 | 180,000 | 960 | 1053 | 1112 | 1157 | 1194 | 1244 | 1188 | 1290 | 1354 | 1402 | 1441 | 1493 | 1585 | 1836 | 2003 | 2131 | 2238 | 2386 | 738 | 831 | 892 | 939 | 977 | 1030 | 1088 | 1202 | 1274 | 1328 | 1372 | 1432 |
| 180,000 | 200,000 | 1014 | 1112 | 1175 | 1222 | 1261 | 1314 | 1263 | 1371 | 1439 | 1491 | 1532 | 1588 | 1668 | 1931 | 2107 | 2242 | 2354 | 2510 | 780 | 877 | 941 | 991 | 1031 | 1087 | 1154 | 1274 | 1351 | 1409 | 1455 | 1519 |
| 200,000 or more | | 1283 | 1405 | 1484 | 1543 | 1591 | 1658 | 1639 | 1780 | 1870 | 1936 | 1990 | 2063 | 2074 | 2399 | 2616 | 2783 | 2922 | 3114 | 984 | 1105 | 1186 | 1247 | 1297 | 1367 | 1481 | 1636 | 1735 | 1809 | 1869 | 1950 |

(Continued)

## 2011 Optional State and Certain Local Sales Tax Tables *(Continued)*

| Income | | Nevada[3] 6.8500% | | | | | | New Jersey[4] 7.0000% | | | | | | New Mexico 5.1250% | | | | | | New York 4.0000% | | | | | | North Carolina[1] 5.2459% | | | | | |
|---|---|---|---|---|---|---|---|---|---|---|---|---|---|---|---|---|---|---|---|---|---|---|---|---|---|---|---|---|---|---|---|
| At least | But less than | Exemptions 1 | 2 | 3 | 4 | 5 | Over 5 | Exemptions 1 | 2 | 3 | 4 | 5 | Over 5 | Exemptions 1 | 2 | 3 | 4 | 5 | Over 5 | Exemptions 1 | 2 | 3 | 4 | 5 | Over 5 | Exemptions 1 | 2 | 3 | 4 | 5 | Over 5 |
| $0 | $20,000 | 266 | 293 | 311 | 324 | 334 | 349 | 263 | 282 | 294 | 303 | 310 | 320 | 235 | 252 | 262 | 270 | 276 | 284 | 155 | 167 | 174 | 180 | 185 | 191 | 254 | 289 | 313 | 331 | 345 | 366 |
| 20,000 | 30,000 | 420 | 462 | 488 | 509 | 525 | 547 | 436 | 467 | 487 | 502 | 514 | 530 | 391 | 419 | 436 | 449 | 459 | 473 | 255 | 275 | 287 | 296 | 304 | 314 | 397 | 452 | 488 | 516 | 539 | 570 |
| 30,000 | 40,000 | 498 | 546 | 578 | 601 | 621 | 647 | 525 | 563 | 587 | 605 | 619 | 639 | 472 | 506 | 527 | 542 | 554 | 571 | 307 | 330 | 345 | 356 | 365 | 378 | 468 | 533 | 576 | 608 | 635 | 672 |
| 40,000 | 50,000 | 564 | 619 | 654 | 681 | 702 | 732 | 603 | 646 | 674 | 694 | 711 | 733 | 542 | 581 | 605 | 623 | 637 | 656 | 352 | 378 | 396 | 408 | 419 | 433 | 528 | 602 | 650 | 687 | 717 | 759 |
| 50,000 | 60,000 | 623 | 683 | 722 | 751 | 775 | 807 | 673 | 721 | 752 | 775 | 793 | 818 | 605 | 649 | 676 | 696 | 711 | 733 | 392 | 422 | 441 | 455 | 467 | 482 | 582 | 663 | 716 | 756 | 790 | 835 |
| 60,000 | 70,000 | 676 | 742 | 784 | 815 | 841 | 876 | 737 | 790 | 823 | 848 | 868 | 896 | 663 | 711 | 741 | 762 | 780 | 803 | 429 | 462 | 482 | 498 | 510 | 528 | 631 | 718 | 776 | 820 | 855 | 905 |
| 70,000 | 80,000 | 727 | 797 | 841 | 875 | 903 | 940 | 797 | 855 | 891 | 918 | 940 | 969 | 718 | 770 | 802 | 826 | 844 | 870 | 464 | 499 | 522 | 538 | 552 | 570 | 677 | 770 | 832 | 879 | 917 | 970 |
| 80,000 | 90,000 | 773 | 847 | 895 | 931 | 960 | 1000 | 853 | 915 | 954 | 983 | 1006 | 1038 | 769 | 825 | 859 | 885 | 905 | 932 | 496 | 534 | 558 | 576 | 590 | 610 | 719 | 818 | 883 | 933 | 974 | 1031 |
| 90,000 | 100,000 | 817 | 895 | 946 | 983 | 1014 | 1056 | 907 | 972 | 1014 | 1045 | 1069 | 1103 | 818 | 877 | 914 | 940 | 962 | 991 | 527 | 567 | 593 | 612 | 627 | 648 | 759 | 863 | 932 | 985 | 1028 | 1087 |
| 100,000 | 120,000 | 875 | 958 | 1012 | 1052 | 1085 | 1130 | 978 | 1048 | 1093 | 1126 | 1153 | 1189 | 882 | 946 | 985 | 1014 | 1038 | 1069 | 568 | 611 | 638 | 659 | 675 | 698 | 811 | 923 | 996 | 1052 | 1098 | 1162 |
| 120,000 | 140,000 | 954 | 1044 | 1102 | 1146 | 1182 | 1230 | 1075 | 1152 | 1202 | 1238 | 1267 | 1307 | 971 | 1041 | 1084 | 1116 | 1142 | 1176 | 623 | 671 | 701 | 724 | 742 | 767 | 882 | 1003 | 1083 | 1144 | 1194 | 1263 |
| 140,000 | 160,000 | 1022 | 1119 | 1181 | 1228 | 1266 | 1318 | 1160 | 1244 | 1297 | 1336 | 1368 | 1411 | 1048 | 1124 | 1171 | 1206 | 1233 | 1270 | 672 | 723 | 756 | 780 | 800 | 827 | 944 | 1073 | 1159 | 1224 | 1277 | 1351 |
| 160,000 | 180,000 | 1091 | 1193 | 1259 | 1309 | 1349 | 1405 | 1245 | 1335 | 1392 | 1434 | 1468 | 1515 | 1126 | 1207 | 1258 | 1295 | 1325 | 1365 | 721 | 776 | 811 | 837 | 858 | 887 | 1005 | 1143 | 1233 | 1303 | 1359 | 1438 |
| 180,000 | 200,000 | 1152 | 1260 | 1330 | 1382 | 1424 | 1483 | 1322 | 1418 | 1478 | 1523 | 1559 | 1608 | 1196 | 1283 | 1336 | 1376 | 1407 | 1450 | 765 | 823 | 860 | 888 | 910 | 941 | 1060 | 1205 | 1301 | 1373 | 1433 | 1516 |
| 200,000 or more | | 1455 | 1590 | 1677 | 1742 | 1795 | 1868 | 1707 | 1831 | 1909 | 1967 | 2014 | 2078 | 1548 | 1661 | 1730 | 1782 | 1822 | 1878 | 986 | 1061 | 1108 | 1144 | 1172 | 1212 | 1330 | 1511 | 1631 | 1722 | 1796 | 1900 |

| Income | | North Dakota 5.0000% | | | | | | Ohio 5.5000% | | | | | | Oklahoma 4.5000% | | | | | | Pennsylvania 6.0000% | | | | | | Rhode Island 7.0000% | | | | | |
|---|---|---|---|---|---|---|---|---|---|---|---|---|---|---|---|---|---|---|---|---|---|---|---|---|---|---|---|---|---|---|---|
| $0 | $20,000 | 194 | 218 | 233 | 245 | 255 | 268 | 234 | 255 | 269 | 279 | 287 | 299 | 247 | 288 | 315 | 337 | 354 | 379 | 214 | 230 | 240 | 248 | 254 | 262 | 260 | 283 | 297 | 308 | 316 | 328 |
| 20,000 | 30,000 | 303 | 339 | 363 | 382 | 397 | 417 | 382 | 417 | 439 | 456 | 469 | 488 | 382 | 444 | 486 | 519 | 546 | 584 | 348 | 374 | 391 | 403 | 413 | 427 | 404 | 438 | 460 | 476 | 489 | 507 |
| 30,000 | 40,000 | 358 | 400 | 428 | 450 | 467 | 492 | 459 | 500 | 527 | 547 | 563 | 585 | 448 | 521 | 571 | 609 | 641 | 686 | 417 | 448 | 468 | 483 | 495 | 511 | 475 | 515 | 541 | 560 | 575 | 596 |
| 40,000 | 50,000 | 404 | 452 | 483 | 507 | 527 | 555 | 524 | 572 | 602 | 625 | 644 | 669 | 505 | 587 | 642 | 685 | 721 | 771 | 476 | 512 | 535 | 552 | 566 | 584 | 535 | 580 | 609 | 631 | 648 | 672 |
| 50,000 | 60,000 | 445 | 498 | 532 | 559 | 580 | 611 | 584 | 637 | 670 | 696 | 716 | 744 | 555 | 645 | 706 | 753 | 792 | 847 | 530 | 569 | 595 | 614 | 629 | 649 | 589 | 638 | 670 | 694 | 713 | 739 |
| 60,000 | 70,000 | 482 | 539 | 576 | 605 | 629 | 661 | 638 | 695 | 732 | 760 | 782 | 813 | 601 | 698 | 763 | 814 | 856 | 916 | 578 | 622 | 649 | 670 | 687 | 709 | 637 | 691 | 725 | 751 | 771 | 799 |
| 70,000 | 80,000 | 517 | 578 | 618 | 649 | 674 | 709 | 689 | 751 | 791 | 821 | 845 | 877 | 643 | 747 | 817 | 871 | 917 | 980 | 624 | 671 | 701 | 723 | 741 | 765 | 682 | 740 | 776 | 804 | 826 | 856 |
| 80,000 | 90,000 | 550 | 614 | 656 | 689 | 715 | 752 | 736 | 803 | 845 | 877 | 903 | 938 | 682 | 792 | 866 | 924 | 972 | 1039 | 667 | 717 | 749 | 773 | 792 | 818 | 724 | 785 | 824 | 853 | 876 | 908 |
| 90,000 | 100,000 | 580 | 648 | 692 | 727 | 755 | 794 | 781 | 852 | 897 | 930 | 958 | 995 | 719 | 835 | 913 | 974 | 1024 | 1095 | 707 | 761 | 794 | 819 | 840 | 867 | 763 | 828 | 869 | 899 | 924 | 957 |
| 100,000 | 120,000 | 620 | 692 | 740 | 776 | 806 | 848 | 840 | 916 | 965 | 1001 | 1030 | 1070 | 768 | 891 | 974 | 1038 | 1092 | 1168 | 761 | 818 | 854 | 881 | 903 | 932 | 815 | 883 | 927 | 959 | 986 | 1021 |
| 120,000 | 140,000 | 674 | 752 | 804 | 844 | 876 | 921 | 922 | 1005 | 1058 | 1098 | 1130 | 1174 | 833 | 966 | 1057 | 1127 | 1185 | 1266 | 834 | 896 | 936 | 966 | 989 | 1022 | 885 | 959 | 1006 | 1042 | 1070 | 1109 |
| 140,000 | 160,000 | 721 | 805 | 860 | 902 | 937 | 985 | 993 | 1083 | 1140 | 1182 | 1217 | 1264 | 890 | 1032 | 1128 | 1203 | 1265 | 1352 | 898 | 965 | 1008 | 1040 | 1065 | 1100 | 946 | 1025 | 1075 | 1113 | 1143 | 1185 |
| 160,000 | 180,000 | 768 | 857 | 915 | 960 | 997 | 1048 | 1064 | 1160 | 1221 | 1267 | 1304 | 1354 | 946 | 1097 | 1199 | 1278 | 1344 | 1437 | 962 | 1034 | 1079 | 1113 | 1141 | 1178 | 1006 | 1090 | 1144 | 1183 | 1216 | 1259 |
| 180,000 | 200,000 | 810 | 903 | 965 | 1012 | 1051 | 1105 | 1128 | 1230 | 1294 | 1343 | 1382 | 1435 | 997 | 1155 | 1263 | 1346 | 1415 | 1513 | 1019 | 1095 | 1144 | 1180 | 1209 | 1248 | 1060 | 1148 | 1205 | 1247 | 1281 | 1327 |
| 200,000 or more | | 1016 | 1132 | 1209 | 1268 | 1316 | 1383 | 1448 | 1578 | 1661 | 1723 | 1773 | 1841 | 1245 | 1441 | 1574 | 1678 | 1764 | 1884 | 1306 | 1403 | 1465 | 1511 | 1548 | 1599 | 1325 | 1435 | 1505 | 1557 | 1599 | 1656 |

| Income | | South Carolina 6.0000% | | | | | | South Dakota 4.0000% | | | | | | Tennessee 7.0000% | | | | | | Texas 6.2500% | | | | | | Utah 4.7000% | | | | | |
|---|---|---|---|---|---|---|---|---|---|---|---|---|---|---|---|---|---|---|---|---|---|---|---|---|---|---|---|---|---|---|---|
| $0 | $20,000 | 249 | 273 | 288 | 300 | 309 | 322 | 238 | 278 | 304 | 325 | 342 | 366 | 389 | 446 | 485 | 514 | 538 | 572 | 269 | 299 | 318 | 332 | 344 | 360 | 246 | 280 | 303 | 320 | 335 | 355 |
| 20,000 | 30,000 | 406 | 445 | 471 | 489 | 505 | 525 | 368 | 429 | 470 | 501 | 528 | 564 | 604 | 692 | 751 | 796 | 833 | 885 | 439 | 488 | 519 | 542 | 561 | 588 | 387 | 440 | 476 | 503 | 525 | 556 |
| 30,000 | 40,000 | 486 | 534 | 564 | 587 | 605 | 630 | 432 | 504 | 552 | 589 | 619 | 662 | 711 | 814 | 883 | 936 | 980 | 1040 | 526 | 585 | 622 | 650 | 673 | 705 | 457 | 521 | 562 | 594 | 621 | 657 |
| 40,000 | 50,000 | 556 | 610 | 645 | 670 | 691 | 720 | 486 | 567 | 621 | 663 | 697 | 745 | 802 | 918 | 995 | 1055 | 1104 | 1172 | 602 | 668 | 711 | 743 | 770 | 805 | 518 | 589 | 636 | 672 | 702 | 743 |
| 50,000 | 60,000 | 618 | 678 | 717 | 746 | 769 | 800 | 535 | 623 | 682 | 728 | 766 | 819 | 883 | 1010 | 1095 | 1160 | 1214 | 1289 | 669 | 744 | 791 | 827 | 856 | 896 | 572 | 650 | 702 | 742 | 774 | 820 |
| 60,000 | 70,000 | 675 | 741 | 783 | 814 | 840 | 874 | 578 | 674 | 738 | 787 | 828 | 885 | 956 | 1094 | 1185 | 1255 | 1313 | 1394 | 731 | 812 | 864 | 904 | 935 | 979 | 620 | 705 | 761 | 804 | 840 | 889 |
| 70,000 | 80,000 | 728 | 800 | 845 | 879 | 907 | 944 | 619 | 721 | 790 | 842 | 886 | 947 | 1025 | 1172 | 1269 | 1345 | 1407 | 1493 | 789 | 877 | 933 | 976 | 1010 | 1057 | 666 | 757 | 817 | 864 | 901 | 954 |
| 80,000 | 90,000 | 778 | 855 | 903 | 939 | 969 | 1008 | 657 | 765 | 837 | 893 | 940 | 1005 | 1088 | 1244 | 1347 | 1427 | 1492 | 1584 | 844 | 937 | 997 | 1043 | 1079 | 1130 | 709 | 805 | 869 | 918 | 958 | 1014 |
| 90,000 | 100,000 | 826 | 907 | 958 | 997 | 1027 | 1070 | 692 | 806 | 882 | 941 | 990 | 1058 | 1147 | 1311 | 1420 | 1504 | 1573 | 1670 | 895 | 994 | 1058 | 1106 | 1145 | 1199 | 749 | 851 | 918 | 969 | 1012 | 1071 |
| 100,000 | 120,000 | 888 | 975 | 1030 | 1072 | 1105 | 1151 | 739 | 860 | 941 | 1004 | 1056 | 1129 | 1226 | 1400 | 1516 | 1606 | 1679 | 1782 | 963 | 1069 | 1138 | 1190 | 1232 | 1289 | 801 | 910 | 982 | 1037 | 1082 | 1145 |
| 120,000 | 140,000 | 973 | 1069 | 1130 | 1175 | 1212 | 1261 | 802 | 933 | 1021 | 1089 | 1146 | 1225 | 1332 | 1521 | 1647 | 1744 | 1824 | 1935 | 1055 | 1173 | 1248 | 1305 | 1351 | 1414 | 873 | 991 | 1069 | 1129 | 1178 | 1247 |
| 140,000 | 160,000 | 1048 | 1151 | 1216 | 1265 | 1305 | 1358 | 857 | 997 | 1091 | 1163 | 1223 | 1308 | 1424 | 1626 | 1760 | 1864 | 1949 | 2067 | 1137 | 1263 | 1344 | 1405 | 1455 | 1523 | 935 | 1061 | 1145 | 1209 | 1262 | 1335 |
| 160,000 | 180,000 | 1123 | 1233 | 1303 | 1355 | 1397 | 1455 | 911 | 1060 | 1159 | 1236 | 1300 | 1390 | 1516 | 1730 | 1873 | 1982 | 2073 | 2198 | 1217 | 1353 | 1440 | 1506 | 1559 | 1631 | 997 | 1131 | 1220 | 1288 | 1344 | 1422 |
| 180,000 | 200,000 | 1190 | 1307 | 1381 | 1436 | 1481 | 1542 | 959 | 1116 | 1221 | 1302 | 1369 | 1463 | 1598 | 1823 | 1973 | 2089 | 2184 | 2316 | 1291 | 1434 | 1526 | 1596 | 1652 | 1730 | 1053 | 1194 | 1288 | 1360 | 1419 | 1501 |
| 200,000 or more | | 1525 | 1675 | 1770 | 1841 | 1899 | 1977 | 1197 | 1392 | 1522 | 1623 | 1706 | 1823 | 2002 | 2282 | 2468 | 2611 | 2729 | 2893 | 1655 | 1839 | 1958 | 2047 | 2119 | 2219 | 1327 | 1504 | 1621 | 1711 | 1785 | 1887 |

| Income | | Vermont 6.0000% | | | | | | Virginia 4.0000% | | | | | | Washington 6.5000% | | | | | | West Virginia 6.0000% | | | | | | Wisconsin 5.0000% | | | | | |
|---|---|---|---|---|---|---|---|---|---|---|---|---|---|---|---|---|---|---|---|---|---|---|---|---|---|---|---|---|---|---|---|
| $0 | $20,000 | 169 | 177 | 182 | 185 | 188 | 192 | 175 | 199 | 214 | 227 | 237 | 250 | 268 | 294 | 311 | 324 | 335 | 349 | 304 | 348 | 377 | 399 | 417 | 443 | 222 | 244 | 259 | 269 | 278 | 290 |
| 20,000 | 30,000 | 265 | 278 | 286 | 291 | 296 | 302 | 268 | 304 | 328 | 346 | 361 | 381 | 444 | 488 | 517 | 538 | 555 | 579 | 484 | 554 | 599 | 635 | 663 | 703 | 361 | 398 | 422 | 439 | 453 | 473 |
| 30,000 | 40,000 | 313 | 328 | 338 | 344 | 350 | 357 | 314 | 356 | 383 | 405 | 422 | 446 | 536 | 589 | 623 | 649 | 670 | 698 | 575 | 657 | 712 | 753 | 787 | 835 | 433 | 477 | 505 | 526 | 543 | 566 |
| 40,000 | 50,000 | 355 | 372 | 382 | 390 | 396 | 404 | 353 | 400 | 431 | 454 | 474 | 500 | 615 | 676 | 715 | 745 | 769 | 802 | 652 | 746 | 807 | 855 | 893 | 947 | 495 | 545 | 577 | 601 | 620 | 647 |
| 50,000 | 60,000 | 391 | 410 | 421 | 430 | 436 | 445 | 388 | 439 | 472 | 498 | 519 | 549 | 686 | 755 | 799 | 832 | 858 | 895 | 721 | 825 | 893 | 945 | 988 | 1048 | 550 | 606 | 642 | 668 | 690 | 719 |
| 60,000 | 70,000 | 425 | 445 | 457 | 466 | 473 | 483 | 419 | 474 | 510 | 538 | 561 | 592 | 752 | 827 | 875 | 911 | 940 | 981 | 784 | 897 | 971 | 1027 | 1074 | 1139 | 601 | 662 | 701 | 730 | 753 | 786 |
| 70,000 | 80,000 | 456 | 477 | 491 | 500 | 508 | 518 | 449 | 507 | 545 | 575 | 599 | 633 | 814 | 895 | 947 | 986 | 1018 | 1061 | 843 | 964 | 1044 | 1105 | 1155 | 1224 | 648 | 714 | 756 | 788 | 813 | 848 |
| 80,000 | 90,000 | 485 | 508 | 522 | 532 | 540 | 551 | 476 | 537 | 578 | 609 | 635 | 670 | 872 | 959 | 1014 | 1056 | 1090 | 1137 | 898 | 1027 | 1111 | 1176 | 1230 | 1304 | 693 | 763 | 808 | 842 | 869 | 906 |
| 90,000 | 100,000 | 512 | 536 | 551 | 562 | 570 | 582 | 501 | 566 | 609 | 641 | 668 | 705 | 927 | 1019 | 1078 | 1123 | 1159 | 1208 | 950 | 1086 | 1175 | 1244 | 1300 | 1378 | 735 | 809 | 857 | 893 | 922 | 961 |
| 100,000 | 120,000 | 547 | 573 | 589 | 601 | 610 | 622 | 535 | 603 | 649 | 683 | 712 | 751 | 999 | 1099 | 1162 | 1210 | 1249 | 1303 | 1018 | 1163 | 1259 | 1333 | 1393 | 1477 | 790 | 870 | 922 | 960 | 991 | 1034 |
| 120,000 | 140,000 | 596 | 624 | 641 | 654 | 664 | 678 | 580 | 654 | 703 | 740 | 771 | 814 | 1099 | 1208 | 1278 | 1331 | 1374 | 1433 | 1110 | 1269 | 1374 | 1454 | 1520 | 1611 | 866 | 954 | 1010 | 1053 | 1087 | 1133 |
| 140,000 | 160,000 | 638 | 668 | 687 | 700 | 711 | 726 | 620 | 698 | 750 | 790 | 823 | 868 | 1187 | 1304 | 1380 | 1437 | 1483 | 1547 | 1191 | 1361 | 1473 | 1559 | 1630 | 1728 | 932 | 1027 | 1088 | 1133 | 1170 | 1220 |
| 160,000 | 180,000 | 680 | 712 | 732 | 746 | 758 | 773 | 659 | 742 | 797 | 839 | 873 | 922 | 1274 | 1401 | 1482 | 1543 | 1593 | 1661 | 1271 | 1453 | 1572 | 1664 | 1739 | 1844 | 998 | 1100 | 1165 | 1214 | 1253 | 1306 |
| 180,000 | 200,000 | 718 | 752 | 772 | 787 | 800 | 816 | 694 | 781 | 838 | 883 | 919 | 970 | 1353 | 1487 | 1574 | 1639 | 1691 | 1764 | 1343 | 1535 | 1661 | 1758 | 1838 | 1948 | 1058 | 1166 | 1235 | 1286 | 1328 | 1385 |
| 200,000 or more | | 903 | 945 | 972 | 991 | 1006 | 1026 | 866 | 973 | 1043 | 1098 | 1142 | 1204 | 1750 | 1923 | 2035 | 2119 | 2187 | 2280 | 1700 | 1942 | 2102 | 2224 | 2325 | 2464 | 1355 | 1494 | 1582 | 1648 | 1701 | 1774 |

| Income | | Wyoming 4.0000% | | | | | |
|---|---|---|---|---|---|---|---|
| $0 | $20,000 | 166 | 181 | 191 | 198 | 204 | 211 |
| 20,000 | 30,000 | 274 | 299 | 314 | 326 | 336 | 349 |
| 30,000 | 40,000 | 330 | 360 | 378 | 393 | 404 | 420 |
| 40,000 | 50,000 | 378 | 412 | 434 | 450 | 463 | 481 |
| 50,000 | 60,000 | 422 | 460 | 484 | 502 | 516 | 536 |
| 60,000 | 70,000 | 461 | 503 | 529 | 549 | 565 | 587 |
| 70,000 | 80,000 | 499 | 544 | 573 | 594 | 611 | 635 |
| 80,000 | 90,000 | 534 | 582 | 613 | 636 | 654 | 679 |
| 90,000 | 100,000 | 567 | 618 | 651 | 675 | 695 | 722 |
| 100,000 | 120,000 | 611 | 666 | 701 | 727 | 748 | 777 |
| 120,000 | 140,000 | 672 | 732 | 770 | 799 | 822 | 854 |
| 140,000 | 160,000 | 724 | 789 | 831 | 862 | 887 | 921 |
| 160,000 | 180,000 | 777 | 847 | 891 | 925 | 952 | 988 |
| 180,000 | 200,000 | 825 | 899 | 946 | 981 | 1010 | 1049 |
| 200,000 or more | | 1064 | 1159 | 1220 | 1265 | 1302 | 1352 |

**Note. Alaska** does not have a state sales tax. Alaska residents should follow the instructions on the next page to determine their local sales tax amount.

1 The rates for California, Connecticut, and North Carolina increased during 2011, so the rates given are averaged over the year.

2 The California table includes the 1.25% uniform local sales tax rate in addition to the 6.4959% blended state sales tax rate for a total of 7.7459%.

3 The Nevada table includes the 2.25% uniform local sales tax rate in addition to the 4.6000% state sales tax rate.

4 Residents of Salem County should deduct only half of the amount in the state table.

5 The 4.0% rate for Hawaii is actually an excise tax but is treated as a sales tax for purpose of this deduction.

# Which Optional Local Sales Tax Table Should I Use?

| IF you live in the state of... | AND you live in... | THEN use Local Table... |
|---|---|---|
| Alaska | Any locality | C |
| Arizona | Mesa or Tucson | A |
| | Chandler, Gilbert, Glendale, Peoria, Phoenix, Scottsdale, Tempe, Yuma, or any other locality | B |
| Arkansas | Any locality | B |
| California | Los Angeles County | A |
| Colorado | Adams County, Arapahoe County, Boulder County, Centennial, Colorado Springs, Denver City/Denver County, El Paso County, Jefferson County, Larimer County, Pueblo County, or any other locality | A |
| | Arvada, Aurora, City of Boulder, Fort Collins, Greeley, Lakewood, Longmont, City of Pueblo, or Westminster | B |
| | Thornton | C |
| Georgia | Any locality | B |
| Illinois | Any locality | A |
| Louisiana | One of the following parishes: Ascension, Bossier, Caddo, Calcasieu, East Baton Rouge, Iberia, Jefferson, Lafayette, Lafourche, Livingston, Orleans, Ouachita, Rapides, St. Bernard, St. Landry, St. Tammany, Tangipahoa, or Terrebonne | C |
| | Any other locality | B |
| Missouri | Any locality | B |
| New York | Chautauqua County, Chenango County, Columbia County, Delaware County, Greene County, Hamilton County, Madison County, Tioga County, Wayne County, New York City, or Norwich City | A |
| | One of the following counties: Albany, Allegany, Broome, Cattaraugus, Cayuga, Chemung, Clinton, Cortland, Dutchess, Erie, Essex, Franklin, Fulton, Genesee, Herkimer, Jefferson, Lewis, Livingston, Monroe, Montgomery, Nassau, Niagara, Oneida, Onondaga, Ontario, Orange, Orleans, Oswego, Otsego, Putnam, Rensselaer, Rockland, St. Lawrence, Saratoga, Schenectady, Schoharie, Schuyler, Seneca, Steuben, Suffolk, Sullivan, Tompkins, Ulster, Warren, Washington, Westchester, Wyoming, or Yates Or the City of Oneida | B |
| | Any other locality | D |
| North Carolina | Any locality | A |
| South Carolina | Cherokee County, Chesterfield County, Darlington County, Dillon County, Horry County, Jasper County, Lee County, Lexington County, or Myrtle Beach | A |
| | Charleston County or any other locality | B |
| Tennessee | Any locality | B |
| Utah | Any locality | A |
| Virginia | Any locality | B |

# 2011 Optional Local Sales Tax Tables for Certain Local Jurisdictions
## (Based on a local sales tax rate of 1 percent)*

| Income | | Local Table A | | | | | | Local Table B | | | | | | Local Table C | | | | | | Local Table D | | | | | |
|---|---|---|---|---|---|---|---|---|---|---|---|---|---|---|---|---|---|---|---|---|---|---|---|---|---|
| At least | But less than | Exemptions | | | | | | Exemptions | | | | | | Exemptions | | | | | | Exemptions | | | | | |
| | | 1 | 2 | 3 | 4 | 5 | Over 5 | 1 | 2 | 3 | 4 | 5 | Over 5 | 1 | 2 | 3 | 4 | 5 | Over 5 | 1 | 2 | 3 | 4 | 5 | Over 5 |
| $0 | $20,000 | 41 | 46 | 49 | 51 | 53 | 55 | 50 | 58 | 63 | 67 | 71 | 75 | 60 | 69 | 75 | 80 | 84 | 89 | 39 | 42 | 44 | 45 | 46 | 48 |
| 20,000 | 30,000 | 64 | 71 | 76 | 79 | 82 | 86 | 76 | 88 | 96 | 102 | 107 | 114 | 92 | 106 | 115 | 122 | 128 | 136 | 64 | 69 | 72 | 74 | 76 | 79 |
| 30,000 | 40,000 | 75 | 84 | 89 | 93 | 96 | 101 | 89 | 103 | 112 | 119 | 125 | 133 | 108 | 124 | 135 | 143 | 150 | 159 | 77 | 83 | 86 | 89 | 91 | 95 |
| 40,000 | 50,000 | 85 | 94 | 100 | 105 | 109 | 114 | 100 | 116 | 126 | 134 | 140 | 149 | 121 | 139 | 151 | 161 | 168 | 179 | 88 | 95 | 99 | 102 | 105 | 108 |
| 50,000 | 60,000 | 94 | 104 | 110 | 115 | 119 | 125 | 110 | 127 | 138 | 147 | 154 | 164 | 133 | 153 | 166 | 176 | 184 | 196 | 98 | 106 | 110 | 114 | 117 | 121 |
| 60,000 | 70,000 | 101 | 112 | 119 | 125 | 129 | 135 | 119 | 137 | 149 | 158 | 166 | 176 | 144 | 165 | 179 | 190 | 199 | 211 | 107 | 116 | 121 | 125 | 128 | 132 |
| 70,000 | 80,000 | 109 | 120 | 128 | 134 | 138 | 145 | 127 | 146 | 159 | 169 | 177 | 188 | 154 | 177 | 192 | 203 | 213 | 226 | 116 | 125 | 131 | 135 | 138 | 143 |
| 80,000 | 90,000 | 115 | 128 | 136 | 142 | 147 | 154 | 135 | 155 | 168 | 179 | 187 | 199 | 163 | 187 | 203 | 215 | 225 | 239 | 124 | 134 | 140 | 144 | 148 | 153 |
| 90,000 | 100,000 | 122 | 135 | 143 | 150 | 155 | 162 | 142 | 163 | 177 | 188 | 197 | 210 | 172 | 197 | 214 | 227 | 237 | 252 | 132 | 142 | 148 | 153 | 157 | 162 |
| 100,000 | 120,000 | 130 | 144 | 153 | 160 | 165 | 173 | 151 | 174 | 189 | 200 | 210 | 223 | 183 | 210 | 228 | 241 | 253 | 268 | 142 | 153 | 160 | 165 | 169 | 175 |
| 120,000 | 140,000 | 141 | 156 | 166 | 174 | 180 | 188 | 164 | 188 | 204 | 217 | 227 | 241 | 199 | 228 | 247 | 262 | 274 | 291 | 156 | 168 | 175 | 181 | 186 | 192 |
| 140,000 | 160,000 | 151 | 167 | 178 | 186 | 192 | 201 | 175 | 200 | 218 | 231 | 242 | 257 | 212 | 243 | 263 | 279 | 292 | 310 | 168 | 181 | 189 | 195 | 200 | 207 |
| 160,000 | 180,000 | 161 | 178 | 189 | 197 | 204 | 213 | 185 | 213 | 231 | 245 | 257 | 273 | 225 | 258 | 280 | 297 | 310 | 329 | 180 | 194 | 202 | 209 | 214 | 222 |
| 180,000 | 200,000 | 170 | 188 | 199 | 208 | 215 | 225 | 195 | 224 | 243 | 258 | 270 | 287 | 237 | 272 | 294 | 312 | 326 | 346 | 191 | 206 | 215 | 222 | 228 | 235 |
| 200,000 or more | | 213 | 235 | 249 | 260 | 269 | 282 | 242 | 278 | 301 | 319 | 334 | 355 | 295 | 338 | 366 | 387 | 405 | 430 | 247 | 265 | 277 | 286 | 293 | 303 |

*If your local rate is different from 1 percent, the local portion of your deduction for sales tax will be proportionally larger or smaller. See the instructions for line 3 of the State and Local General Sales Tax Deduction Worksheet.

# Appendix C - Depreciation Tables

## Table B-1. Table of Class Lives and Recovery Periods

| Asset class | Description of assets included | Class Life (in years) | Recovery Periods (in years) GDS (MACRS) | Recovery Periods (in years) ADS |
|---|---|---|---|---|
| | SPECIFIC DEPRECIABLE ASSETS USED IN ALL BUSINESS ACTIVITIES, EXCEPT AS NOTED: | | | |
| 00.11 | **Office Furniture, Fixtures, and Equipment:** Includes furniture and fixtures that are not a structural component of a building. Includes such assets as desks, files, safes, and communications equipment. Does not include communications equipment that is included in other classes. | 10 | 7 | 10 |
| 00.12 | **Information Systems:** Includes computers and their peripheral equipment used in administering normal business transactions and the maintenance of business records, their retrieval and analysis. Information systems are defined as: 1) Computers: A computer is a programmable electronically activated device capable of accepting information, applying prescribed processes to the information, and supplying the results of these processes with or without human intervention. It usually consists of a central processing unit containing extensive storage, logic, arithmetic, and control capabilities. Excluded from this category are adding machines, electronic desk calculators, etc., and other equipment described in class 00.13. 2) Peripheral equipment consists of the auxiliary machines which are designed to be placed under control of the central processing unit. Nonlimiting examples are: Card readers, card punches, magnetic tape feeds, high speed printers, optical character readers, tape cassettes, mass storage units, paper tape equipment, keypunches, data entry devices, teleprinters, terminals, tape drives, disc drives, disc files, disc packs, visual image projector tubes, card sorters, plotters, and collators. Peripheral equipment may be used on-line or off-line. Does not incude equipment that is an integral part of other capital equipment that is included in other classes of economic activity, i.e., computers used primarily for process or production control, switching, channeling, and automating distributive trades and services such as point of sale (POS) computer systems. Also, does not include equipment of a kind used primarily for amusement or entertainment of the user. | 6 | 5 | 5 |
| 00.13 | **Data Handling Equipment; except Computers:** Includes only typewriters, calculators, adding and accounting machines, copiers, and duplicating equipment. | 6 | 5 | 6 |
| 00.21 | **Airplanes (airframes and engines), except those used in commercial or contract carrying of passengers or freight, and all helicopters (airframes and engines)** | 6 | 5 | 6 |
| 00.22 | **Automobiles, Taxis** | 3 | 5 | 5 |
| 00.23 | **Buses** | 9 | 5 | 9 |
| 00.241 | **Light General Purpose Trucks:** Includes trucks for use over the road (actual weight less than 13,000 pounds) | 4 | 5 | 5 |
| 00.242 | **Heavy General Purpose Trucks:** Includes heavy general purpose trucks, concrete ready mix-trucks, and ore trucks, for use over the road (actual unloaded weight 13,000 pounds or more) | 6 | 5 | 6 |
| 00.25 | **Railroad Cars and Locomotives, except those owned by railroad transportation companies** | 15 | 7 | 15 |
| 00.26 | **Tractor Units for Use Over-The-Road** | 4 | 3 | 4 |
| 00.27 | **Trailers and Trailer-Mounted Containers** | 6 | 5 | 6 |
| 00.28 | **Vessels, Barges, Tugs, and Similar Water Transportation Equipment, except those used in marine construction** | 18 | 10 | 18 |
| 00.3 | **Land Improvements:** Includes improvements directly to or added to land, whether such improvements are section 1245 property or section 1250 property, provided such improvements are depreciable. Examples of such assets might include sidewalks, roads, canals, waterways, drainage facilities, sewers (not including municipal sewers in Class 51), wharves and docks, bridges, fences, landscaping shrubbery, or radio and television transmitting towers. Does not include land improvements that are explicitly included in any other class, and buildings and structural components as defined in section 1.48-1(e) of the regulations. Excludes public utility initial clearing and grading land improvements as specified in Rev. Rul. 72-403, 1972-2 C.B. 102. | 20 | 15 | 20 |
| 00.4 | **Industrial Steam and Electric Generation and/or Distribution Systems:** Includes assets, whether such assets are section 1245 property or 1250 property, providing such assets are depreciable, used in the production and/or distribution of electricity with rated total capacity in excess of 500 Kilowatts and/or assets used in the production and/or distribution of steam with rated total capacity in excess of 12,500 pounds per hour for use by the taxpayer in its industrial manufacturing process or plant activity and not ordinarily available for sale to others. Does not include buildings and structural components as defined in section 1.48-1(e) of the regulations. Assets used to generate and/or distribute electricity or steam of the type described above, but of lesser rated capacity, are not included, but are included in the appropriate manufacturing equipment classes elsewhere specified. Also includes electric generating and steam distribution assets, which may utilize steam produced by a waste reduction and resource recovery plant, used by the taxpayer in its industrial manufacturing process or plant activity. Steam and chemical recovery boiler systems used for the recovery and regeneration of chemicals used in manufacturing, with rated capacity in excess of that described above, with specifically related distribution and return systems are not included but are included in appropriate manufacturing equipment classes elsewhere specified. An example of an excluded steam and chemical recovery boiler system is that used in the pulp and paper manufacturing equipment classes elsewhere specified. An example of an excluded steam and chemical recovery boiler system is that used in the pulp and paper manufacturing industry. | 22 | 15 | 22 |

Table B-2. **Table of Class Lives and Recovery Periods**

| Asset class | Description of assets included | Class Life (in years) | GDS (MACRS) | ADS |
|---|---|---|---|---|
| | | | Recovery Periods (in years) | |
| | *DEPRECIABLE ASSETS USED IN THE FOLLOWING ACTIVITIES:* | | | |
| 01.1 | **Agriculture:** Includes machinery and equipment, grain bins, and fences but no other land improvements, that are used in the production of crops or plants, vines, and trees; livestock; the operation of farm dairies, nurseries, greenhouses, sod farms, mushroom cellars, cranberry bogs, apiaries, and fur farms; the performance of agriculture, animal husbandry, and horticultural services. | 10 | 7 | 10 |
| 01.11 | **Cotton Ginning Assets** | 12 | 7 | 12 |
| 01.21 | **Cattle, Breeding or Dairy** | 7 | 5 | 7 |
| 01.221 | **Any breeding or work horse that is 12 years old or less at the time it is placed in service**** | 10 | 7 | 10 |
| 01.222 | **Any breeding or work horse that is more than 12 years old at the time it is placed in service**** | 10 | 3 | 10 |
| 01.223 | **Any race horse that is more than 2 years old at the time it is placed in service**** | * | 3 | 12 |
| 01.224 | **Any horse that is more than 12 years old at the time it is placed in service and that is neither a race horse nor a horse described in class 01.222**** | * | 3 | 12 |
| 01.225 | **Any horse not described in classes 01.221, 01.222, 01.223, or 01.224** | * | 7 | 12 |
| 01.23 | **Hogs, Breeding** | 3 | 3 | 3 |
| 01.24 | **Sheep and Goats, Breeding** | 5 | 5 | 5 |
| 01.3 | **Farm buildings except structures included in Class 01.4** | 25 | 20 | 25 |
| 01.4 | **Single purpose agricultural or horticultural structures (within the meaning of section 168(i)(13) of the Code)** | 15 | 10*** | 15 |
| 10.0 | **Mining:** Includes assets used in the mining and quarrying of metallic and nonmetallic minerals (including sand, gravel, stone, and clay) and the milling, beneficiation and other primary preparation of such materials. | 10 | 7 | 10 |
| 13.0 | **Offshore Drilling:** Includes assets used in offshore drilling for oil and gas such as floating, self-propelled and other drilling vessels, barges, platforms, and drilling equipment and support vessels such as tenders, barges, towboats and crewboats. Excludes oil and gas production assets. | 7.5 | 5 | 7.5 |
| 13.1 | **Drilling of Oil and Gas Wells:** Includes assets used in the drilling of onshore oil and gas wells and the provision of geophysical and other exploration services; and the provision of such oil and gas field services as chemical treatment, plugging and abandoning of wells and cementing or perforating well casings. Does not include assets used in the performance of any of these activities and services by integrated petroleum and natural gas producers for their own account. | 6 | 5 | 6 |
| 13.2 | **Exploration for and Production of Petroleum and Natural Gas Deposits:** Includes assets used by petroleum and natural gas producers for drilling of wells and production of petroleum and natural gas, including gathering pipelines and related storage facilities. Also includes petroleum and natural gas offshore transportation facilities used by producers and others consisting of platforms (other than drilling platforms classified in Class 13.0), compression or pumping equipment, and gathering and transmission lines to the first onshore transshipment facility. The assets used in the first onshore transshipment facility are also included and consist of separation equipment (used for separation of natural gas, liquids, and in Class 49.23), and liquid holding or storage facilities (other than those classified in Class 49.25). Does not include support vessels. | 14 | 7 | 14 |
| 13.3 | **Petroleum Refining:** Includes assets used for the distillation, fractionation, and catalytic cracking of crude petroleum into gasoline and its other components. | 16 | 10 | 16 |
| 15.0 | **Construction:** Includes assets used in construction by general building, special trade, heavy and marine construction contractors, operative and investment builders, real estate subdividers and developers, and others except railroads. | 6 | 5 | 6 |
| 20.1 | **Manufacture of Grain and Grain Mill Products:** Includes assets used in the production of flours, cereals, livestock feeds, and other grain and grain mill products. | 17 | 10 | 17 |
| 20.2 | **Manufacture of Sugar and Sugar Products:** Includes assets used in the production of raw sugar, syrup, or finished sugar from sugar cane or sugar beets. | 18 | 10 | 18 |
| 20.3 | **Manufacture of Vegetable Oils and Vegetable Oil Products:** Includes assets used in the production of oil from vegetable materials and the manufacture of related vegetable oil products. | 18 | 10 | 18 |
| 20.4 | **Manufacture of Other Food and Kindred Products:** Includes assets used in the production of foods and beverages not included in classes 20.1, 20.2 and 20.3. | 12 | 7 | 12 |
| 20.5 | **Manufacture of Food and Beverages—Special Handling Devices:** Includes assets defined as specialized materials handling devices such as returnable pallets, palletized containers, and fish processing equipment including boxes, baskets, carts, and flaking trays used in activities as defined in classes 20.1, 20.2, 20.3 and 20.4. Does not include general purpose small tools such as wrenches and drills, both hand and power-driven, and other general purpose equipment such as conveyors, transfer equipment, and materials handling devices. | 4 | 3 | 4 |

\* Property described in asset classes 01.223, 01.224, and 01.225 are assigned recovery periods but have no class lives.

\*\* A horse is more than 2 (or 12) years old after the day that is 24 (or 144) months after its actual birthdate.

\*\*\* 7 If property was placed in service before 1989.

## Table B-2. Table of Class Lives and Recovery Periods

| Asset class | Description of assets included | Class Life (in years) | Recovery Periods (in years) GDS (MACRS) | ADS |
|---|---|---|---|---|
| 21.0 | **Manufacture of Tobacco and Tobacco Products:** Includes assets used in the production of cigarettes, cigars, smoking and chewing tobacco, snuff, and other tobacco products. | 15 | 7 | 15 |
| 22.1 | **Manufacture of Knitted Goods:** Includes assets used in the production of knitted and netted fabrics and lace. Assets used in yarn preparation, bleaching, dyeing, printing, and other similar finishing processes, texturing, and packaging, are elsewhere classified. | 7.5 | 5 | 7.5 |
| 22.2 | **Manufacture of Yarn, Thread, and Woven Fabric:** Includes assets used in the production of spun yarns including the preparing, blending, spinning, and twisting of fibers into yarns and threads, the preparation of yarns such as twisting, warping, and winding, the production of covered elastic yarn and thread, cordage, woven fabric, tire fabric, braided fabric, twisted jute for packaging, mattresses, pads, sheets, and industrial belts, and the processing of textile mill waste to recover fibers, flocks, and shoddies. Assets used to manufacture carpets, man-made fibers, and nonwovens, and assets used in texturing, bleaching, dyeing, printing, and other similar finishing processes, are elsewhere classified. | 11 | 7 | 11 |
| 22.3 | **Manufacture of Carpets and Dyeing, Finishing, and Packaging of Textile Products and Manufacture of Medical and Dental Supplies:** Includes assets used in the production of carpets, rugs, mats, woven carpet backing, chenille, and other tufted products, and assets used in the joining together of backing with carpet yarn or fabric. Includes assets used in washing, scouring, bleaching, dyeing, printing, drying, and similar finishing processes applied to textile fabrics, yarns, threads, and other textile goods. Includes assets used in the production and packaging of textile products, other than apparel, by creasing, forming, trimming, cutting, and sewing, such as the preparation of carpet and fabric samples, or similar joining together processes (other than the production of scrim reinforced paper products and laminated paper products) such as the sewing and folding of hosiery and panty hose, and the creasing, folding, trimming, and cutting of fabrics to produce nonwoven products, such as disposable diapers and sanitary products. Also includes assets used in the production of medical and dental supplies other than drugs and medicines. Assets used in the manufacture of nonwoven carpet backing, and hard surface floor covering such as tile, rubber, and cork, are elsewhere classified. | 9 | 5 | 9 |
| 22.4 | **Manufacture of Textile Yarns:** Includes assets used in the processing of yarns to impart bulk and/or stretch properties to the yarn. The principal machines involved are falsetwist, draw, beam-to-beam, and stuffer box texturing equipment and related highspeed twisters and winders. Assets, as described above, which are used to further process man-made fibers are elsewhere classified when located in the same plant in an integrated operation with man-made fiber producing assets. Assets used to manufacture man-made fibers and assets used in bleaching, dyeing, printing, and other similar finishing processes, are elsewhere classified. | 8 | 5 | 8 |
| 22.5 | **Manufacture of Nonwoven Fabrics:** Includes assets used in the production of nonwoven fabrics, felt goods including felt hats, padding, batting, wadding, oakum, and fillings, from new materials and from textile mill waste. Nonwoven fabrics are defined as fabrics (other than reinforced and laminated composites consisting of nonwovens and other products) manufactured by bonding natural and/or synthetic fibers and/or filaments by means of induced mechanical interlocking, fluid entanglement, chemical adhesion, thermal or solvent reaction, or by combination thereof other than natural hydration bonding as ocurs with natural cellulose fibers. Such means include resin bonding, web bonding, and melt bonding. Specifically includes assets used to make flocked and needle punched products other than carpets and rugs. Assets, as described above, which are used to manufacture nonwovens are elsewhere classified when located in the same plant in an integrated operation with man-made fiber producing assets. Assets used to manufacture man-made fibers and assets used in bleaching, dyeing, printing, and other similar finishing processes, are elsewhere classified. | 10 | 7 | 10 |
| 23.0 | **Manufacture of Apparel and Other Finished Products:** Includes assets used in the production of clothing and fabricated textile products by the cutting and sewing of woven fabrics, other textile products, and furs; but does not include assets used in the manufacture of apparel from rubber and leather. | 9 | 5 | 9 |
| 24.1 | **Cutting of Timber:** Includes logging machinery and equipment and roadbuilding equipment used by logging and sawmill operators and pulp manufacturers for their own account. | 6 | 5 | 6 |
| 24.2 | **Sawing of Dimensional Stock from Logs:** Includes machinery and equipment installed in permanent or well established sawmills. | 10 | 7 | 10 |
| 24.3 | **Sawing of Dimensional Stock from Logs:** Includes machinery and equipment in sawmills characterized by temporary foundations and a lack, or minimum amount, of lumberhandling, drying, and residue disposal equipment and facilities. | 6 | 5 | 6 |
| 24.4 | **Manufacture of Wood Products, and Furniture:** Includes assets used in the production of plywood, hardboard, flooring, veneers, furniture, and other wood products, including the treatment of poles and timber. | 10 | 7 | 10 |
| 26.1 | **Manufacture of Pulp and Paper:** Includes assets for pulp materials handling and storage, pulp mill processing, bleach processing, paper and paperboard manufacturing, and on-line finishing. Includes pollution control assets and all land improvements associated with the factory site or production process such as effluent ponds and canals, provided such improvements are depreciable but does not include buildings and structural components as defined in section 1.48-1(e)(1) of the regulations. Includes steam and chemical recovery boiler systems, with any rated capacity, used for the recovery and regeneration of chemicals used in manufacturing. Does not include assets used either in pulpwood logging, or in the manufacture of hardboard. | 13 | 7 | 13 |

Table B-2. **Table of Class Lives and Recovery Periods**

| Asset class | Description of assets included | Class Life (in years) | Recovery Periods (in years) GDS (MACRS) | ADS |
|---|---|---|---|---|
| 26.2 | **Manufacture of Converted Paper, Paperboard, and Pulp Products:** Includes assets used for modification, or remanufacture of paper and pulp into converted products, such as paper coated off the paper machine, paper bags, paper boxes, cartons and envelopes. Does not include assets used for manufacture of nonwovens that are elsewhere classified. | 10 | 7 | 10 |
| 27.0 | **Printing, Publishing, and Allied Industries:** Includes assets used in printing by one or more processes, such as letter-press, lithography, gravure, or screen; the performance of services for the printing trade, such as bookbinding, typesetting, engraving, photo-engraving, and electrotyping; and the publication of newspapers, books, and periodicals. | 11 | 7 | 11 |
| 28.0 | **Manufacture of Chemicals and Allied Products:** Includes assets used to manufacture basic organic and inorganic chemicals; chemical products to be used in further manufacture, such as synthetic fibers and plastics materials; and finished chemical products. Includes assets used to further process man-made fibers, to manufacture plastic film, and to manufacture nonwoven fabrics, when such assets are located in the same plant in an integrated operation with chemical products producing assets. Also includes assets used to manufacture photographic supplies, such as film, photographic paper, sensitized photographic paper, and developing chemicals. Includes all land improvements associated with plant site or production processes, such as effluent ponds and canals, provided such land improvements are depreciable but does not include buildings and structural components as defined in section 1.48-1(e) of the regulations. Does not include assets used in the manufacture of finished rubber and plastic products or in the production of natural gas products, butane, propane, and by-products of natural gas production plants. | 9.5 | 5 | 9.5 |
| 30.1 | **Manufacture of Rubber Products:** Includes assets used for the production of products from natural, synthetic, or reclaimed rubber, gutta percha, balata, or gutta siak, such as tires, tubes, rubber footwear, mechanical rubber goods, heels and soles, flooring, and rubber sundries; and in the recapping, retreading, and rebuilding of tires. | 14 | 7 | 14 |
| 30.11 | **Manufacture of Rubber Products—Special Tools and Devices:** Includes assets defined as special tools, such as jigs, dies, mandrels, molds, lasts, patterns, specialty containers, pallets, shells; and tire molds, and accessory parts such as rings and insert plates used in activities as defined in class 30.1. Does not include tire building drums and accessory parts and general purpose small tools such as wrenches and drills, both power and hand-driven, and other general purpose equipment such as conveyors and transfer equipment. | 4 | 3 | 4 |
| 30.2 | **Manufacture of Finished Plastic Products:** Includes assets used in the manufacture of plastics products and the molding of primary plastics for the trade. Does not include assets used in the manufacture of basic plastics materials nor the manufacture of phonograph records. | 11 | 7 | 11 |
| 30.21 | **Manufacture of Finished Plastic Products—Special Tools:** Includes assets defined as special tools, such as jigs, dies, fixtures, molds, patterns, gauges, and specialty transfer and shipping devices, used in activities as defined in class 30.2. Special tools are specifically designed for the production or processing of particular parts and have no significant utilitarian value and cannot be adapted to further or different use after changes or improvements are made in the model design of the particular part produced by the special tools. Does not include general purpose small tools such as wrenches and drills, both hand and power-driven, and other general purpose equipment such as conveyors, transfer equipment, and materials handling devices. | 3.5 | 3 | 3.5 |
| 31.0 | **Manufacture of Leather and Leather Products:** Includes assets used in the tanning, currying, and finishing of hides and skins; the processing of fur pelts; and the manufacture of finished leather products, such as footwear, belting, apparel, and luggage. | 11 | 7 | 11 |
| 32.1 | **Manufacture of Glass Products:** Includes assets used in the production of flat, blown, or pressed products of glass, such as float and window glass, glass containers, glassware and fiberglass. Does not include assets used in the manufacture of lenses. | 14 | 7 | 14 |
| 32.11 | **Manufacture of Glass Products—Special Tools:** Includes assets defined as special tools such as molds, patterns, pallets, and specialty transfer and shipping devices such as steel racks to transport automotive glass, used in activities as defined in class 32.1. Special tools are specifically designed for the production or processing of particular parts and have no significant utilitarian value and cannot be adapted to further or different use after changes or improvements are made in the model design of the particular part produced by the special tools. Does not include general purpose small tools such as wrenches and drills, both hand and power-driven, and other general purpose equipment such as conveyors, transfer equipment, and materials handling devices. | 2.5 | 3 | 2.5 |
| 32.2 | **Manufacture of Cement:** Includes assets used in the production of cement, but does not include assets used in the manufacture of concrete and concrete products nor in any mining or extraction process. | 20 | 15 | 20 |
| 32.3 | **Manufacture of Other Stone and Clay Products:** Includes assets used in the manufacture of products from materials in the form of clay and stone, such as brick, tile, and pipe; pottery and related products, such as vitreous-china, plumbing fixtures, earthenware and ceramic insulating materials; and also includes assets used in manufacture of concrete and concrete products. Does not include assets used in any mining or extraction processes. | 15 | 7 | 15 |

## Table B-2. Table of Class Lives and Recovery Periods

| Asset class | Description of assets included | Class Life (in years) | Recovery Periods (in years) | |
|---|---|---|---|---|
| | | | GDS (MACRS) | ADS |
| 33.2 | **Manufacture of Primary Nonferrous Metals:** Includes assets used in the smelting, refining, and electrolysis of nonferrous metals from ore, pig, or scrap, the rolling, drawing, and alloying of nonferrous metals; the manufacture of castings, forgings, and other basic products of nonferrous metals; and the manufacture of nails, spikes, structural shapes, tubing, wire, and cable. | 14 | 7 | 14 |
| 33.21 | **Manufacture of Primary Nonferrous Metals—Special Tools:** Includes assets defined as special tools such as dies, jigs, molds, patterns, fixtures, gauges, and drawings concerning such special tools used in the activities as defined in class 33.2, Manufacture of Primary Nonferrous Metals. Special tools are specifically designed for the production or processing of particular products or parts and have no significant utilitarian value and cannot be adapted to further or different use after changes or improvements are made in the model design of the particular part produced by the special tools. Does not include general purpose small tools such as wrenches and drills, both hand and power-driven, and other general purpose equipment such as conveyors, transfer equipment, and materials handling devices. Rolls, mandrels and refractories are not included in class 33.21 but are included in class 33.2. | 6.5 | 5 | 6.5 |
| 33.3 | **Manufacture of Foundry Products:** Includes assets used in the casting of iron and steel, including related operations such as molding and coremaking. Also includes assets used in the finishing of castings and patternmaking when performed at the foundry, all special tools and related land improvements. | 14 | 7 | 14 |
| 33.4 | **Manufacture of Primary Steel Mill Products:** Includes assets used in the smelting, reduction, and refining of iron and steel from ore, pig, or scrap; the rolling, drawing and alloying of steel; the manufacture of nails, spikes, structural shapes, tubing, wire, and cable. Includes assets used by steel service centers, ferrous metal forges, and assets used in coke production, regardless of ownership. Also includes related land improvements and all special tools used in the above activities. | 15 | 7 | 15 |
| 34.0 | **Manufacture of Fabricated Metal Products:** Includes assets used in the production of metal cans, tinware, fabricated structural metal products, metal stampings, and other ferrous and nonferrous metal and wire products not elsewhere classified. Does not include assets used to manufacture non-electric heating apparatus. | 12 | 7 | 12 |
| 34.01 | **Manufacture of Fabricated Metal Products—Special Tools:** Includes assets defined as special tools such as dies, jigs, molds, patterns, fixtures, gauges, and returnable containers and drawings concerning such special tools used in the activities as defined in class 34.0. Special tools are specifically designed for the production or processing of particular machine components, products, or parts, and have no significant utilitarian value and cannot be adapted to further or different use after changes or improvements are made in the model design of the particular part produced by the special tools. Does not include general small tools such as wrenches and drills, both hand and power-driven, and other general purpose equipment such as conveyors, transfer equipment, and materials handling devices. | 3 | 3 | 3 |
| 35.0 | **Manufacture of Electrical and Non-Electrical Machinery and Other Mechanical Products:** Includes assets used to manufacture or rebuild finished machinery and equipment and replacement parts thereof such as machine tools, general industrial and special industry machinery, electrical power generation, transmission, and distribution systems, space heating, cooling, and refrigeration systems, commercial and home appliances, farm and garden machinery, construction machinery, mining and oil field machinery, internal combustion engines (except those elsewhere classified), turbines (except those that power airborne vehicles), batteries, lamps and lighting fixtures, carbon and graphite products, and electromechanical and mechanical products including business machines, instruments, watches and clocks, vending and amusement machines, photographic equipment, medical and dental equipment and appliances, and ophthalmic goods. Includes assets used by manufacturers or rebuilders of such finished machinery and equipment in activities elsewhere classified such as the manufacture of castings, forgings, rubber and plastic products, electronic subassemblies or other manufacturing activities if the interim products are used by the same manufacturer primarily in the manufacture, assembly, or rebuilding of such finished machinery and equipment. Does not include assets used in mining, assets used in the manufacture of primary ferrous and nonferrous metals, assets included in class 00.11 through 00.4 and assets elsewhere classified. | 10 | 7 | 10 |
| 36.0 | **Manufacture of Electronic Components, Products, and Systems:** Includes assets used in the manufacture of electronic communication, computation, instrumentation and control system, including airborne applications; also includes assets used in the manufacture of electronic products such as frequency and amplitude modulated transmitters and receivers, electronic switching stations, television cameras, video recorders, record players and tape recorders, computers and computer peripheral machines, and electronic instruments, watches, and clocks; also includes assets used in the manufacture of components, provided their primary use is products and systems defined above such as electron tubes, capacitors, coils, resistors, printed circuit substrates, switches, harness cables, lasers, fiber optic devices, and magnetic media devices. Specifically excludes assets used to manufacture electronic products and components, photocopiers, typewriters, postage meters and other electromechanical and mechanical business machines and instruments that are elsewhere classified. Does not include semiconductor manufacturing equipment included in class 36.1. | 6 | 5 | 6 |
| 36.1 | **Any Semiconductor Manufacturing Equipment** | 5 | 5 | 5 |

Table B-2. **Table of Class Lives and Recovery Periods**

| Asset class | Description of assets included | Class Life (in years) | Recovery Periods (in years) GDS (MACRS) | ADS |
|---|---|---|---|---|
| 37.11 | **Manufacture of Motor Vehicles:** Includes assets used in the manufacture and assembly of finished automobiles, trucks, trailers, motor homes, and buses. Does not include assets used in mining, printing and publishing, production of primary metals, electricity, or steam, or the manufacture of glass, industrial chemicals, batteries, or rubber products, which are classified elsewhere. Includes assets used in manufacturing activities elsewhere classified other than those excluded above, where such activities are incidental to and an integral part of the manufacture and assembly of finished motor vehicles such as the manufacture of parts and subassemblies of fabricated metal products, electrical equipment, textiles, plastics, leather, and foundry and forging operations. Does not include any assets not classified in manufacturing activity classes, e.g., does not include any assets classified in asset guideline classes 00.11 through 00.4. Activities will be considered incidental to the manufacture and assembly of finished motor vehicles only if 75 percent or more of the value of the products produced under one roof are used for the manufacture and assembly of finished motor vehicles. Parts that are produced as a normal replacement stock complement in connection with the manufacture and assembly of finished motor vehicles are considered used for the manufacture assembly of finished motor vehicles. Does not include assets used in the manufacture of component parts if these assets are used by taxpayers not engaged in the assembly of finished motor vehicles. | 12 | 7 | 12 |
| 37.12 | **Manufacture of Motor Vehicles—Special Tools:** Includes assets defined as special tools, such as jigs, dies, fixtures, molds, patterns, gauges, and specialty transfer and shipping devices, owned by manufacturers of finished motor vehicles and used in qualified activities as defined in class 37.11. Special tools are specifically designed for the production or processing of particular motor vehicle components and have no significant utilitarian value, and cannot be adapted to further or different use, after changes or improvements are made in the model design of the particular part produced by the special tools. Does not include general purpose small tools such as wrenches and drills, both hand and powerdriven, and other general purpose equipment such as conveyors, transfer equipment, and materials handling devices. | 3 | 3 | 3 |
| 37.2 | **Manufacture of Aerospace Products:** Includes assets used in the manufacture and assembly of airborne vehicles and their component parts including hydraulic, pneumatic, electrical, and mechanical systems. Does not include assets used in the production of electronic airborne detection, guidance, control, radiation, computation, test, navigation, and communication equipment or the components thereof. | 10 | 7 | 10 |
| 37.31 | **Ship and Boat Building Machinery and Equipment:** Includes assets used in the manufacture and repair of ships, boats, caissons, marine drilling rigs, and special fabrications not included in asset classes 37.32 and 37.33. Specifically includes all manufacturing and repairing machinery and equipment, including machinery and equipment used in the operation of assets included in asset class 37.32. Excludes buildings and their structural components. | 12 | 7 | 12 |
| 37.32 | **Ship and Boat Building Dry Docks and Land Improvements:** Includes assets used in the manufacture and repair of ships, boats, caissons, marine drilling rigs, and special fabrications not included in asset classes 37.31 and 37.33. Specifically includes floating and fixed dry docks, ship basins, graving docks, shipways, piers, and all other land improvements such as water, sewer, and electric systems. Excludes buildings and their structural components. | 16 | 10 | 16 |
| 37.33 | **Ship and Boat Building—Special Tools:** Includes assets defined as special tools such as dies, jigs, molds, patterns, fixtures, gauges, and drawings concerning such special tools used in the activities defined in classes 37.31 and 37.32. Special tools are specifically designed for the production or processing of particular machine components, products, or parts, and have no significant utilitarian value and cannot be adapted to further or different use after changes or improvements are made in the model design of the particular part produced by the special tools. Does not include general purpose small tools such as wrenches and drills, both hand and power-driven, and other general purpose equipment such as conveyors, transfer equipment, and materials handling devices. | 6.5 | 5 | 6.5 |
| 37.41 | **Manufacture of Locomotives:** Includes assets used in building or rebuilding railroad locomotives (including mining and industrial locomotives). Does not include assets of railroad transportation companies or assets of companies which manufacture components of locomotives but do not manufacture finished locomotives. | 11.5 | 7 | 11.5 |
| 37.42 | **Manufacture of Railroad Cars:** Includes assets used in building or rebuilding railroad freight or passenger cars (including rail transit cars). Does not include assets of railroad transportation companies or assets of companies which manufacture components of railroad cars but do not manufacture finished railroad cars. | 12 | 7 | 12 |
| 39.0 | **Manufacture of Athletic, Jewelry, and Other Goods:** Includes assets used in the production of jewelry; musical instruments; toys and sporting goods; motion picture and television films and tapes; and pens, pencils, office and art supplies, brooms, brushes, caskets, etc. **Railroad Transportation:** Classes with the prefix 40 include the assets identified below that are used in the commercial and contract carrying of passengers and freight by rail. Assets of electrified railroads will be classified in a manner corresponding to that set forth below for railroads not independently operated as electric lines. Excludes the assets included in classes with the prefix beginning 00.1 and 00.2 above, and also excludes any non-depreciable assets included in Interstate Commerce Commission accounts enumerated for this class. | 12 | 7 | 12 |

Table B-2. **Table of Class Lives and Recovery Periods**

| Asset class | Description of assets included | Class Life (in years) | Recovery Periods (in years) GDS (MACRS) | ADS |
|---|---|---|---|---|
| 40.1 | **Railroad Machinery and Equipment:** Includes assets classified in the following Interstate Commerce Commission accounts: **Roadway accounts:** (16) Station and office buildings (freight handling machinery and equipment only) (25) TOFC/COFC terminals (freight handling machinery and equipment only) (26) Communication systems (27) Signals and interlockers (37) Roadway machines (44) Shop machinery **Equipment accounts:** (52) Locomotives (53) Freight train cars (54) Passenger train cars (57) Work equipment | 14 | 7 | 14 |
| 40.2 | **Railroad Structures and Similar Improvements:** Includes assets classified in the following Interstate Commerce Commission road accounts: (6) Bridges, trestles, and culverts (7) Elevated structures (13) Fences, snowsheds, and signs (16) Station and office buildings (stations and other operating structures only) (17) Roadway buildings (18) Water stations (19) Fuel stations (20) Shops and enginehouses (25) TOFC/COFC terminals (operating structures only) (31) Power transmission systems (35) Miscellaneous structures (39) Public improvements construction | 30 | 20 | 30 |
| 40.3 | **Railroad Wharves and Docks:** Includes assets classified in the following Interstate Commission Commerce accounts: (23) Wharves and docks (24) Coal and ore wharves | 20 | 15 | 20 |
| 40.4 | **Railroad Track** | 10 | 7 | 10 |
| 40.51 | **Railroad Hydraulic Electric Generating Equipment** | 50 | 20 | 50 |
| 40.52 | **Railroad Nuclear Electric Generating Equipment** | 20 | 15 | 20 |
| 40.53 | **Railroad Steam Electric Generating Equipment** | 28 | 20 | 28 |
| 40.54 | **Railroad Steam, Compressed Air, and Other Power Plan Equipment** | 28 | 20 | 28 |
| 41.0 | **Motor Transport—Passengers:** Includes assets used in the urban and interurban commercial and contract carrying of passengers by road, except the transportation assets included in classes with the prefix 00.2. | 8 | 5 | 8 |
| 42.0 | **Motor Transport—Freight:** Includes assets used in the commercial and contract carrying of freight by road, except the transportation assets included in classes with the prefix 00.2. | 8 | 5 | 8 |
| 44.0 | **Water Transportation:** Includes assets used in the commercial and contract carrying of freight and passengers by water except the transportation assets included in classes with the prefix 00.2. Includes all related land improvements. | 20 | 15 | 20 |
| 45.0 | **Air Transport:** Includes assets (except helicopters) used in commercial and contract carrying of passengers and freight by air. For purposes of section 1.167(a)-11(d)(2)(iv)(a) of the regulations, expenditures for "repair, maintenance, rehabilitation, or improvement," shall consist of direct maintenance expenses (irrespective of airworthiness provisions or charges) as defined by Civil Aeronautics Board uniform accounts 5200, maintenance burden (exclusive of expenses pertaining to maintenance buildings and improvements) as defined by Civil Aeronautics Board accounts 5300, and expenditures which are not "excluded additions" as defined in section 1.167(a)-11(d)(2)(vi) of the regulations and which would be charged to property and equipment accounts in the Civil Aeronautics Board uniform system of accounts. | 12 | 7 | 12 |
| 45.1 | **Air Transport (restricted):** Includes each asset described in the description of class 45.0 which was held by the taxpayer on April 15, 1976, or is acquired by the taxpayer pursuant to a contract which was, on April 15, 1976, and at all times thereafter, binding on the taxpayer. This criterion of classification based on binding contract concept is to be applied in the same manner as under the general rules expressed in section 49(b)(1), (4), (5) and (8) of the Code (as in effect prior to its repeal by the Revenue Act of 1978, section 312(c)(1), (d), 1978-3 C.B. 1, 60). | 6 | 5 | 6 |
| 46.0 | **Pipeline Transportation:** Includes assets used in the private, commercial, and contract carrying of petroleum, gas and other products by means of pipes and conveyors. The trunk lines and related storage facilities of integrated petroleum and natural gas producers are included in this class. Excludes initial clearing and grading land improvements as specified in Rev. Rul. 72-403, 1972-2; C.B. 102, but includes all other related land improvements. | 22 | 15 | 22 |

Table B-2. **Table of Class Lives and Recovery Periods**

| Asset class | Description of assets included | Class Life (in years) | Recovery Periods (in years) GDS (MACRS) | ADS |
|---|---|---|---|---|
| 48.11 | **Telephone Communications:**<br>Includes the assets classified below and that are used in the provision of commercial and contract telephonic services such as:<br>**Telephone Central Office Buildings:**<br>Includes assets intended to house central office equipment, as defined in Federal Communications Commission Part 31 Account No. 212 whether section 1245 or section 1250 property. | 45 | 20 | 45 |
| 48.12 | **Telephone Central Office Equipment:**<br>Includes central office switching and related equipment as defined in Federal Communications Commission Part 31 Account No. 221.<br>Does not include computer-based telephone central office switching equipment included in class 48.121. Does not include private branch exchange (PBX) equipment. | 18 | 10 | 18 |
| 48.121 | **Computer-based Telephone Central Office Switching Equipment:**<br>Includes equipment whose functions are those of a computer or peripheral equipment (as defined in section 168(i)(2)(B) of the Code) used in its capacity as telephone central office equipment. Does not include private exchange (PBX) equipment. | 9.5 | 5 | 9.5 |
| 48.13 | **Telephone Station Equipment:**<br>Includes such station apparatus and connections as teletypewriters, telephones, booths, private exchanges, and comparable equipment as defined in Federal Communications Commission Part 31 Account Nos. 231, 232, and 234. | 10 | 7* | 10* |
| 48.14 | **Telephone Distribution Plant:**<br>Includes such assets as pole lines, cable, aerial wire, underground conduits, and comparable equipment, and related land improvements as defined in Federal Communications Commission Part 31 Account Nos. 241, 242.1, 242.2, 242.3, 242.4, 243, and 244. | 24 | 15 | 24 |
| 48.2 | **Radio and Television Broadcastings:**<br>Includes assets used in radio and television broadcasting, except transmitting towers.<br>**Telegraph, Ocean Cable, and Satellite Communications (TOCSC)** includes communications-related assets used to provide domestic and international radio-telegraph, wire-telegraph, ocean-cable, and satellite communications services; also includes related land improvements. If property described in Classes 48.31–48.45 is comparable to telephone distribution plant described in Class 48.14 and used for 2-way exchange of voice and data communication which is the equivalent of telephone communication, such property is assigned a class life of 24 years under this revenue procedure. Comparable equipment does not include cable television equipment used primarily for 1-way communication. | 6 | 5 | 6 |
| 48.31 | **TOCSC—Electric Power Generating and Distribution Systems:**<br>Includes assets used in the provision of electric power by generation, modulation, rectification, channelization, control, and distribution. Does not include these assets when they are installed on customers premises. | 19 | 10 | 19 |
| 48.32 | **TOCSC—High Frequency Radio and Microwave Systems:**<br>Includes assets such as transmitters and receivers, antenna supporting structures, antennas, transmission lines from equipment to antenna, transmitter cooling systems, and control and amplification equipment. Does not include cable and long-line systems. | 13 | 7 | 13 |
| 48.33 | **TOCSC—Cable and Long-line Systems:**<br>Includes assets such as transmission lines, pole lines, ocean cables, buried cable and conduit, repeaters, repeater stations, and other related assets. Does not include high frequency radio or microwave systems. | 26.5 | 20 | 26.5 |
| 48.34 | **TOCSC—Central Office Control Equipment:**<br>Includes assets for general control, switching, and monitoring of communications signals including electromechanical switching and channeling apparatus, multiplexing equipment patching and monitoring facilities, in-house cabling, teleprinter equipment, and associated site improvements. | 16.5 | 10 | 16.5 |
| 48.35 | **TOCSC—Computerized Switching, Channeling, and Associated Control Equipment:**<br>Includes central office switching computers, interfacing computers, other associated specialized control equipment, and site improvements. | 10.5 | 7 | 10.5 |
| 48.36 | **TOCSC—Satellite Ground Segment Property:**<br>Includes assets such as fixed earth station equipment, antennas, satellite communications equipment, and interface equipment used in satellite communications. Does not include general purpose equipment or equipment used in satellite space segment property. | 10 | 7 | 10 |
| 48.37 | **TOCSC—Satellite Space Segment Property:**<br>Includes satellites and equipment used for telemetry, tracking, control, and monitoring when used in satellite communications. | 8 | 5 | 8 |
| 48.38 | **TOCSC—Equipment Installed on Customer's Premises:**<br>Includes assets installed on customer's premises, such as computers, terminal equipment, power generation and distribution systems, private switching center, teleprinters, facsimile equipment and other associated and related equipment. | 10 | 7 | 10 |
| 48.39 | **TOCSC—Support and Service Equipment:**<br>Includes assets used to support but not engage in communications. Includes store, warehouse and shop tools, and test and laboratory assets.<br>**Cable Television (CATV):** Includes communications-related assets used to provide cable television community antenna television services. Does not include assets used to provide subscribers with two-way communications services. | 13.5 | 7 | 13.5 |

\* Property described in asset guideline class 48.13 which is qualified technological equipment as defined in section 168(i)(2) is assigned a 5-year recovery period.

Table B-2. **Table of Class Lives and Recovery Periods**

| Asset class | Description of assets included | Class Life (in years) | Recovery Periods (in years) GDS (MACRS) | ADS |
|---|---|---|---|---|
| 48.41 | **CATV—Headend:** Includes assets such as towers, antennas, preamplifiers, converters, modulation equipment, and program non-duplication systems. Does not include headend buildings and program origination assets. | 11 | 7 | 11 |
| 48.42 | **CATV—Subscriber Connection and Distribution Systems:** Includes assets such as trunk and feeder cable, connecting hardware, amplifiers, power equipment, passive devices, directional taps, pedestals, pressure taps, drop cables, matching transformers, multiple set connector equipment, and convertors. | 10 | 7 | 10 |
| 48.43 | **CATV—Program Origination:** Includes assets such as cameras, film chains, video tape recorders, lighting, and remote location equipment excluding vehicles. Does not include buildings and their structural components. | 9 | 5 | 9 |
| 48.44 | **CATV—Service and Test:** Includes assets such as oscilloscopes, field strength meters, spectrum analyzers, and cable testing equipment, but does not include vehicles. | 8.5 | 5 | 8.5 |
| 48.45 | **CATV—Microwave Systems:** Inlcudes assets such as towers, antennas, transmitting and receiving equipment, and broad band microwave assets is used in the provision of cable television services. Does not include assets used in the provision of common carrier services. | 9.5 | 5 | 9.5 |
| 49.11 | **Electric, Gas, Water and Steam, Utility Services:** Includes assets used in the production, transmission and distribution of electricity, gas, steam, or water for sale including related land improvements. **Electric Utility Hydraulic Production Plant:** Includes assets used in the hydraulic power production of electricity for sale, including related land improvements, such as dams, flumes, canals, and waterways. | 50 | 20 | 50 |
| 49.12 | **Electric Utility Nuclear Production Plant:** Includes assets used in the nuclear power production and electricity for sale and related land improvements. Does not include nuclear fuel assemblies. | 20 | 15 | 20 |
| 49.121 | **Electric Utility Nuclear Fuel Assemblies:** Includes initial core and replacement core nuclear fuel assemblies (i.e., the composite of fabricated nuclear fuel and container) when used in a boiling water, pressurized water, or high temperature gas reactor used in the production of electricity. Does not include nuclear fuel assemblies used in breader reactors. | 5 | 5 | 5 |
| 49.13 | **Electric Utility Steam Production Plant:** Includes assets used in the steam power production of electricity for sale, combusion turbines operated in a combined cycle with a conventional steam unit and related land improvements. Also includes package boilers, electric generators and related assets such as electricity and steam distribution systems as used by a waste reduction and resource recovery plant if the steam or electricity is normally for sale to others. | 28 | 20 | 28 |
| 49.14 | **Electric Utility Transmission and Distribution Plant:** Includes assets used in the transmission and distribution of electricity for sale and related land improvements. Excludes initial clearing and grading land improvements as specified in Rev. Rul. 72-403, 1972-2 C.B. 102. | 30 | 20 | 30 |
| 49.15 | **Electric Utility Combustion Turbine Production Plant:** Includes assets used in the production of electricity for sale by the use of such prime movers as jet engines, combustion turbines, diesel engines, gasoline engines, and other internal combustion engines, their associated power turbines and/or generators, and related land improvements. Does not include combustion turbines operated in a combined cycle with a conventional steam unit. | 20 | 15 | 20 |
| 49.21 | **Gas Utility Distribution Facilities:** Includes gas water heaters and gas conversion equipment installed by utility on customers' premises on a rental basis. | 35 | 20 | 35 |
| 49.221 | **Gas Utility Manufactured Gas Production Plants:** Includes assets used in the manufacture of gas having chemical and/or physical properties which do not permit complete interchangeability with domestic natural gas. Does not include gas-producing systems and related systems used in waste reduction and resource recovery plants which are elsewhere classified. | 30 | 20 | 30 |
| 49.222 | **Gas Utility Substitute Natural Gas (SNG) Production Plant (naphtha or lighter hydrocarbon feedstocks):** Includes assets used in the catalytic conversion of feedstocks or naphtha or lighter hydrocarbons to a gaseous fuel which is completely interchangeable with domestic natural gas. | 14 | 7 | 14 |
| 49.223 | **Substitute Natural Gas—Coal Gasification:** Includes assets used in the manufacture and production of pipeline quality gas from coal using the basic Lurgi process with advanced methanation. Includes all process plant equipment and structures used in this coal gasification process and all utility assets such as cooling systems, water supply and treatment facilities, and assets used in the production and distribution of electricity and steam for use by the taxpayer in a gasification plant and attendant coal mining site processes but not for assets used in the production and distribution of electricity and steam for sale to others. Also includes all other related land improvements. Does not include assets used in the direct mining and treatment of coal prior to the gasification process itself. | 18 | 10 | 18 |
| 49.23 | **Natural Gas Production Plant** | 14 | 7 | 14 |
| 49.24 | **Gas Utility Trunk Pipelines and Related Storage Facilities:** Excluding initial clearing and grading land improvements as specified in Rev. Rul. 72-40. | 22 | 15 | 22 |
| 49.25 | **Liquefied Natural Gas Plant:** Includes assets used in the liquefaction, storage, and regasification of natural gas including loading and unloading connections, instrumentation equipment and controls, pumps, vaporizers and odorizers, tanks, and related land improvements. Also includes pipeline interconnections with gas transmission lines and distribution systems and marine terminal facilities. | 22 | 15 | 22 |

## Table B-2. Table of Class Lives and Recovery Periods

| Asset class | Description of assets included | Class Life (in years) | GDS (MACRS) | ADS |
|---|---|---|---|---|
| | | | **Recovery Periods (in years)** | |
| 49.3 | **Water Utilities:** Includes assets used in the gathering, treatment, and commercial distribution of water. | 50 | 20*** | 50 |
| 49.4 | **Central Steam Utility Production and Distribution:** Includes assets used in the production and distribution of steam for sale. Does not include assets used in waste reduction and resource recovery plants which are elsewhere classified. | 28 | 20 | 28 |
| 49.5 | **Waste Reduction and Resource Recovery Plants:** Includes assets used in the conversion of refuse or other solid waste or biomass to heat or to a solid, liquid, or gaseous fuel. Also includes all process plant equipment and structures at the site used to receive, handle, collect, and process refuse or other solid waste or biomass in a waterwall, combustion system, oil or gas pyrolysis system, or refuse derived fuel system to create hot water, gas, steam and electricity. Includes material recovery and support assets used in refuse or solid refuse or solid waste receiving, collecting, handling, sorting, shredding, classifying, and separation systems. Does not include any package boilers, or electric generators and related assets such as electricity, hot water, steam and manufactured gas production plants classified in classes 00.4, 49.13, 49.221, and 49.4. Does include, however, all other utilities such as water supply and treatment facilities, ash handling and other related land improvements of a waste reduction and resource recovery plant. | 10 | 7 | 10 |
| 50. | **Municipal Wastewater Treatment Plant** | 24 | 15 | 24 |
| 51. | **Municipal Sewer** | 50 | 20*** | 50 |
| 57.0 | **Distributive Trades and Services:** Includes assets used in wholesale and retail trade, and personal and professional services. Includes section 1245 assets used in marketing petroleum and petroleum products. | 9 | 5 | 9* |
| 57.1 | **Distributive Trades and Services—Billboard, Service Station Buildings and Petroleum Marketing Land Improvements:** Includes section 1250 assets, including service station buildings and depreciable land improvements, whether section 1250 property or section 1245 property, used in the marketing of petroleum and petroleum products, but not including any of these facilities related to petroleum and natural gas trunk pipelines. Includes car wash buildings and related land improvements. Includes billboards, whether such assets are section 1245 property or section 1250 property. Excludes all other land improvements, buildings and structural components as defined in section 1.48-1(e) of the regulations. See *Gas station convenience stores* in chapter 3. | 20 | 15 | 20 |
| 79.0 | **Recreation:** Includes assets used in the provision of entertainment services on payment of a fee or admission charge, as in the operation of bowling alleys, billiard and pool establishments, theaters, concert halls, and miniature golf courses. Does not include amusement and theme parks and assets which consist primarily of specialized land improvements or structures, such as golf courses, sports stadia, race tracks, ski slopes, and buildings which house the assets used in entertainment services. | 10 | 7 | 10 |
| 80.0 | **Theme and Amusement Parks:** Includes assets used in the provision of rides, attractions, and amusements in activities defined as theme and amusement parks, and includes appurtenances associated with a ride, attraction, amusement or theme setting within the park such as ticket booths, facades, shop interiors, and props, special purpose structures, and buildings other than warehouses, administration buildings, hotels, and motels. Includes all land improvements for or in support of park activities (e.g., parking lots, sidewalks, waterways, bridges, fences, landscaping, etc.), and support functions (e.g., food and beverage retailing, souvenir vending and other nonlodging accommodations) if owned by the park and provided exclusively for the benefit of park patrons. Theme and amusement parks are defined as combinations of amusements, rides, and attractions which are permanently situated on park land and open to the public for the price of admission. This guideline class is a composite of all assets used in this industry except transportation equipment (general purpose trucks, cars, airplanes, etc., which are included in asset guideline classes with the prefix 00.2), assets used in the provision of administrative services (asset classes with the prefix 00.1) and warehouses, administration buildings, hotels and motels. | 12.5 | 7 | 12.5 |
| | **Certain Property for Which Recovery Periods Assigned** A. Personal Property With No Class Life Section 1245 Real Property With No Class Life | | 7 7 | 12 40 |
| | B. Qualified Technological Equipment, as defined in section 168(i)(2). | ** | 5 | 5 |
| | C. Property Used in Connection with Research and Experimentation referred to in section 168(e)(3)(B). | ** | 5 | class life if no class life—12 |
| | D. Alternative energy property described in sections 48(l)(3)(A)(ix) (as in effect on the day before the date of enactment (11/5/90) of the Revenue Reconciliation Act of 1990). | ** | 5 | class life if no class life—12 |
| | E. Biomass property described in section 48(l)(15) (as in effect on the day before the date of enactment (11/5/90) of the Revenue Reconciliation Act of 1990) and is a qualifying small production facility within the meaning of section 3(17)(c) of the Federal Power Act (16 U.S.C. 796(17)(C)), as in effect on September 1, 1986. | ** | 5 | class life if no class life—12 |
| | F. Energy property described in section 48(a)(3)(A) (or would be described if "solar or wind energy" were substituted for "solar energy" in section 48(a)(3)(A)(i)). | ** | 5 | class life if no class life—12 |

\* Any high technology medical equipment as defined in section 168(i)(2)(C) which is described in asset guideline class 57.0 is assigned a 5-year recovery period for the alternate MACRS method.

\*\* The class life (if any) of property described in classes B, C, D, E, or F is determined by reference to the asset guideline classes. If an item of property described in paragraphs B, C, D, E, or F is not described in any asset guideline class, such item of property has no class life.

\*\*\* Use straight line over 25 years if placed in service after June 12, 1996, unless placed in service under a binding contract in effect before June 10, 1996, and at all times until placed in service.

**Table A-1.** **3-, 5-, 7-, 10-, 15-, and 20-Year Property**
**Half-Year Convention**

| Year | Depreciation rate for recovery period | | | | | |
|------|--------|--------|--------|---------|---------|---------|
|      | 3-year | 5-year | 7-year | 10-year | 15-year | 20-year |
| 1  | 33.33% | 20.00% | 14.29% | 10.00% | 5.00% | 3.750% |
| 2  | 44.45  | 32.00  | 24.49  | 18.00  | 9.50  | 7.219  |
| 3  | 14.81  | 19.20  | 17.49  | 14.40  | 8.55  | 6.677  |
| 4  | 7.41   | 11.52  | 12.49  | 11.52  | 7.70  | 6.177  |
| 5  |        | 11.52  | 8.93   | 9.22   | 6.93  | 5.713  |
| 6  |        | 5.76   | 8.92   | 7.37   | 6.23  | 5.285  |
| 7  |        |        | 8.93   | 6.55   | 5.90  | 4.888  |
| 8  |        |        | 4.46   | 6.55   | 5.90  | 4.522  |
| 9  |        |        |        | 6.56   | 5.91  | 4.462  |
| 10 |        |        |        | 6.55   | 5.90  | 4.461  |
| 11 |        |        |        | 3.28   | 5.91  | 4.462  |
| 12 |        |        |        |        | 5.90  | 4.461  |
| 13 |        |        |        |        | 5.91  | 4.462  |
| 14 |        |        |        |        | 5.90  | 4.461  |
| 15 |        |        |        |        | 5.91  | 4.462  |
| 16 |        |        |        |        | 2.95  | 4.461  |
| 17 |        |        |        |        |       | 4.462  |
| 18 |        |        |        |        |       | 4.461  |
| 19 |        |        |        |        |       | 4.462  |
| 20 |        |        |        |        |       | 4.461  |
| 21 |        |        |        |        |       | 2.231  |

**Table A-2.** **3-, 5-, 7-, 10-, 15-, and 20-Year Property**
**Mid-Quarter Convention**
**Placed in Service in First Quarter**

| Year | Depreciation rate for recovery period | | | | | |
|------|--------|--------|--------|---------|---------|---------|
|      | 3-year | 5-year | 7-year | 10-year | 15-year | 20-year |
| 1  | 58.33% | 35.00% | 25.00% | 17.50% | 8.75% | 6.563% |
| 2  | 27.78  | 26.00  | 21.43  | 16.50  | 9.13  | 7.000  |
| 3  | 12.35  | 15.60  | 15.31  | 13.20  | 8.21  | 6.482  |
| 4  | 1.54   | 11.01  | 10.93  | 10.56  | 7.39  | 5.996  |
| 5  |        | 11.01  | 8.75   | 8.45   | 6.65  | 5.546  |
| 6  |        | 1.38   | 8.74   | 6.76   | 5.99  | 5.130  |
| 7  |        |        | 8.75   | 6.55   | 5.90  | 4.746  |
| 8  |        |        | 1.09   | 6.55   | 5.91  | 4.459  |
| 9  |        |        |        | 6.56   | 5.90  | 4.459  |
| 10 |        |        |        | 6.55   | 5.91  | 4.459  |
| 11 |        |        |        | 0.82   | 5.90  | 4.459  |
| 12 |        |        |        |        | 5.91  | 4.460  |
| 13 |        |        |        |        | 5.90  | 4.459  |
| 14 |        |        |        |        | 5.91  | 4.460  |
| 15 |        |        |        |        | 5.90  | 4.459  |
| 16 |        |        |        |        | 0.74  | 4.460  |
| 17 |        |        |        |        |       | 4.459  |
| 18 |        |        |        |        |       | 4.460  |
| 19 |        |        |        |        |       | 4.459  |
| 20 |        |        |        |        |       | 4.460  |
| 21 |        |        |        |        |       | 0.565  |

## Table A-3.  3-, 5-, 7-, 10-, 15-, and 20-Year Property
### Mid-Quarter Convention
### Placed in Service in Second Quarter

| Year | Depreciation rate for recovery period | | | | | |
|------|--------|--------|--------|---------|---------|---------|
| | 3-year | 5-year | 7-year | 10-year | 15-year | 20-year |
| 1 | 41.67% | 25.00% | 17.85% | 12.50% | 6.25% | 4.688% |
| 2 | 38.89 | 30.00 | 23.47 | 17.50 | 9.38 | 7.148 |
| 3 | 14.14 | 18.00 | 16.76 | 14.00 | 8.44 | 6.612 |
| 4 | 5.30 | 11.37 | 11.97 | 11.20 | 7.59 | 6.116 |
| 5 | | 11.37 | 8.87 | 8.96 | 6.83 | 5.658 |
| 6 | | 4.26 | 8.87 | 7.17 | 6.15 | 5.233 |
| 7 | | | 8.87 | 6.55 | 5.91 | 4.841 |
| 8 | | | 3.34 | 6.55 | 5.90 | 4.478 |
| 9 | | | | 6.56 | 5.91 | 4.463 |
| 10 | | | | 6.55 | 5.90 | 4.463 |
| 11 | | | | 2.46 | 5.91 | 4.463 |
| 12 | | | | | 5.90 | 4.463 |
| 13 | | | | | 5.91 | 4.463 |
| 14 | | | | | 5.90 | 4.463 |
| 15 | | | | | 5.91 | 4.462 |
| 16 | | | | | 2.21 | 4.463 |
| 17 | | | | | | 4.462 |
| 18 | | | | | | 4.463 |
| 19 | | | | | | 4.462 |
| 20 | | | | | | 4.463 |
| 21 | | | | | | 1.673 |

## Table A-4.  3-, 5-, 7-, 10-, 15-, and 20-Year Property
### Mid-Quarter Convention
### Placed in Service in Third Quarter

| Year | Depreciation rate for recovery period | | | | | |
|------|--------|--------|--------|---------|---------|---------|
| | 3-year | 5-year | 7-year | 10-year | 15-year | 20-year |
| 1 | 25.00% | 15.00% | 10.71% | 7.50% | 3.75% | 2.813% |
| 2 | 50.00 | 34.00 | 25.51 | 18.50 | 9.63 | 7.289 |
| 3 | 16.67 | 20.40 | 18.22 | 14.80 | 8.66 | 6.742 |
| 4 | 8.33 | 12.24 | 13.02 | 11.84 | 7.80 | 6.237 |
| 5 | | 11.30 | 9.30 | 9.47 | 7.02 | 5.769 |
| 6 | | 7.06 | 8.85 | 7.58 | 6.31 | 5.336 |
| 7 | | | 8.86 | 6.55 | 5.90 | 4.936 |
| 8 | | | 5.53 | 6.55 | 5.90 | 4.566 |
| 9 | | | | 6.56 | 5.91 | 4.460 |
| 10 | | | | 6.55 | 5.90 | 4.460 |
| 11 | | | | 4.10 | 5.91 | 4.460 |
| 12 | | | | | 5.90 | 4.460 |
| 13 | | | | | 5.91 | 4.461 |
| 14 | | | | | 5.90 | 4.460 |
| 15 | | | | | 5.91 | 4.461 |
| 16 | | | | | 3.69 | 4.460 |
| 17 | | | | | | 4.461 |
| 18 | | | | | | 4.460 |
| 19 | | | | | | 4.461 |
| 20 | | | | | | 4.460 |
| 21 | | | | | | 2.788 |

## Table A-5.  3-, 5-, 7-, 10-, 15-, and 20-Year Property
### Mid-Quarter Convention
### Placed in Service in Fourth Quarter

| Year | Depreciation rate for recovery period | | | | | |
|---|---|---|---|---|---|---|
| | 3-year | 5-year | 7-year | 10-year | 15-year | 20-year |
| 1 | 8.33% | 5.00% | 3.57% | 2.50% | 1.25% | 0.938% |
| 2 | 61.11 | 38.00 | 27.55 | 19.50 | 9.88 | 7.430 |
| 3 | 20.37 | 22.80 | 19.68 | 15.60 | 8.89 | 6.872 |
| 4 | 10.19 | 13.68 | 14.06 | 12.48 | 8.00 | 6.357 |
| 5 | | 10.94 | 10.04 | 9.98 | 7.20 | 5.880 |
| 6 | | 9.58 | 8.73 | 7.99 | 6.48 | 5.439 |
| 7 | | | 8.73 | 6.55 | 5.90 | 5.031 |
| 8 | | | 7.64 | 6.55 | 5.90 | 4.654 |
| 9 | | | | 6.56 | 5.90 | 4.458 |
| 10 | | | | 6.55 | 5.91 | 4.458 |
| 11 | | | | 5.74 | 5.90 | 4.458 |
| 12 | | | | | 5.91 | 4.458 |
| 13 | | | | | 5.90 | 4.458 |
| 14 | | | | | 5.91 | 4.458 |
| 15 | | | | | 5.90 | 4.458 |
| 16 | | | | | 5.17 | 4.458 |
| 17 | | | | | | 4.458 |
| 18 | | | | | | 4.459 |
| 19 | | | | | | 4.458 |
| 20 | | | | | | 4.459 |
| 21 | | | | | | 3.901 |

## Table A-6.  Residential Rental Property
### Mid-Month Convention
### Straight Line—27.5 Years

| Year | Month property placed in service | | | | | | | | | | | |
|---|---|---|---|---|---|---|---|---|---|---|---|---|
| | 1 | 2 | 3 | 4 | 5 | 6 | 7 | 8 | 9 | 10 | 11 | 12 |
| 1 | 3.485% | 3.182% | 2.879% | 2.576% | 2.273% | 1.970% | 1.667% | 1.364% | 1.061% | 0.758% | 0.455% | 0.152% |
| 2–9 | 3.636 | 3.636 | 3.636 | 3.636 | 3.636 | 3.636 | 3.636 | 3.636 | 3.636 | 3.636 | 3.636 | 3.636 |
| 10 | 3.637 | 3.637 | 3.637 | 3.637 | 3.637 | 3.637 | 3.636 | 3.636 | 3.636 | 3.636 | 3.636 | 3.636 |
| 11 | 3.636 | 3.636 | 3.636 | 3.636 | 3.636 | 3.636 | 3.637 | 3.637 | 3.637 | 3.637 | 3.637 | 3.637 |
| 12 | 3.637 | 3.637 | 3.637 | 3.637 | 3.637 | 3.637 | 3.636 | 3.636 | 3.636 | 3.636 | 3.636 | 3.636 |
| 13 | 3.636 | 3.636 | 3.636 | 3.636 | 3.636 | 3.636 | 3.637 | 3.637 | 3.637 | 3.637 | 3.637 | 3.637 |
| 14 | 3.637 | 3.637 | 3.637 | 3.637 | 3.637 | 3.637 | 3.636 | 3.636 | 3.636 | 3.636 | 3.636 | 3.636 |
| 15 | 3.636 | 3.636 | 3.636 | 3.636 | 3.636 | 3.636 | 3.637 | 3.637 | 3.637 | 3.637 | 3.637 | 3.637 |
| 16 | 3.637 | 3.637 | 3.637 | 3.637 | 3.637 | 3.637 | 3.636 | 3.636 | 3.636 | 3.636 | 3.636 | 3.636 |
| 17 | 3.636 | 3.636 | 3.636 | 3.636 | 3.636 | 3.636 | 3.637 | 3.637 | 3.637 | 3.637 | 3.637 | 3.637 |
| 18 | 3.637 | 3.637 | 3.637 | 3.637 | 3.637 | 3.637 | 3.636 | 3.636 | 3.636 | 3.636 | 3.636 | 3.636 |
| 19 | 3.636 | 3.636 | 3.636 | 3.636 | 3.636 | 3.636 | 3.637 | 3.637 | 3.637 | 3.637 | 3.637 | 3.637 |
| 20 | 3.637 | 3.637 | 3.637 | 3.637 | 3.637 | 3.637 | 3.636 | 3.636 | 3.636 | 3.636 | 3.636 | 3.636 |
| 21 | 3.636 | 3.636 | 3.636 | 3.636 | 3.636 | 3.636 | 3.637 | 3.637 | 3.637 | 3.637 | 3.637 | 3.637 |
| 22 | 3.637 | 3.637 | 3.637 | 3.637 | 3.637 | 3.637 | 3.636 | 3.636 | 3.636 | 3.636 | 3.636 | 3.636 |
| 23 | 3.636 | 3.636 | 3.636 | 3.636 | 3.636 | 3.636 | 3.637 | 3.637 | 3.637 | 3.637 | 3.637 | 3.637 |
| 24 | 3.637 | 3.637 | 3.637 | 3.637 | 3.637 | 3.637 | 3.636 | 3.636 | 3.636 | 3.636 | 3.636 | 3.636 |
| 25 | 3.636 | 3.636 | 3.636 | 3.636 | 3.636 | 3.636 | 3.637 | 3.637 | 3.637 | 3.637 | 3.637 | 3.637 |
| 26 | 3.637 | 3.637 | 3.637 | 3.637 | 3.637 | 3.637 | 3.636 | 3.636 | 3.636 | 3.636 | 3.636 | 3.636 |
| 27 | 3.636 | 3.636 | 3.636 | 3.636 | 3.636 | 3.636 | 3.637 | 3.637 | 3.637 | 3.637 | 3.637 | 3.637 |
| 28 | 1.97 | 2.273 | 2.576 | 2.879 | 3.182 | 3.485 | 3.636 | 3.636 | 3.636 | 3.636 | 3.636 | 3.636 |
| 29 | | | | | | | 0.152 | 0.455 | 0.758 | 1.061 | 1.364 | 1.667 |

Table A-7.    **Nonresidential Real Property**
**Mid-Month Convention**
**Straight Line—31.5 Years**

| Year | Month property placed in service | | | | | | | | | | | |
|---|---|---|---|---|---|---|---|---|---|---|---|---|
| | 1 | 2 | 3 | 4 | 5 | 6 | 7 | 8 | 9 | 10 | 11 | 12 |
| 1 | 3.042% | 2.778% | 2.513% | 2.249% | 1.984% | 1.720% | 1.455% | 1.190% | 0.926% | 0.661% | 0.397% | 0.132% |
| 2–7 | 3.175 | 3.175 | 3.175 | 3.175 | 3.175 | 3.175 | 3.175 | 3.175 | 3.175 | 3.175 | 3.175 | 3.175 |
| 8 | 3.175 | 3.174 | 3.175 | 3.174 | 3.175 | 3.174 | 3.175 | 3.175 | 3.175 | 3.175 | 3.175 | 3.175 |
| 9 | 3.174 | 3.175 | 3.174 | 3.175 | 3.174 | 3.175 | 3.174 | 3.175 | 3.174 | 3.175 | 3.174 | 3.175 |
| 10 | 3.175 | 3.174 | 3.175 | 3.174 | 3.175 | 3.174 | 3.175 | 3.174 | 3.175 | 3.174 | 3.175 | 3.174 |
| 11 | 3.174 | 3.175 | 3.174 | 3.175 | 3.174 | 3.175 | 3.174 | 3.175 | 3.174 | 3.175 | 3.174 | 3.175 |
| 12 | 3.175 | 3.174 | 3.175 | 3.174 | 3.175 | 3.174 | 3.175 | 3.174 | 3.175 | 3.174 | 3.175 | 3.174 |
| 13 | 3.174 | 3.175 | 3.174 | 3.175 | 3.174 | 3.175 | 3.174 | 3.175 | 3.174 | 3.175 | 3.174 | 3.175 |
| 14 | 3.175 | 3.174 | 3.175 | 3.174 | 3.175 | 3.174 | 3.175 | 3.174 | 3.175 | 3.174 | 3.175 | 3.174 |
| 15 | 3.174 | 3.175 | 3.174 | 3.175 | 3.174 | 3.175 | 3.174 | 3.175 | 3.174 | 3.175 | 3.174 | 3.175 |
| 16 | 3.175 | 3.174 | 3.175 | 3.174 | 3.175 | 3.174 | 3.175 | 3.174 | 3.175 | 3.174 | 3.175 | 3.174 |
| 17 | 3.174 | 3.175 | 3.174 | 3.175 | 3.174 | 3.175 | 3.174 | 3.175 | 3.174 | 3.175 | 3.174 | 3.175 |
| 18 | 3.175 | 3.174 | 3.175 | 3.174 | 3.175 | 3.174 | 3.175 | 3.174 | 3.175 | 3.174 | 3.175 | 3.174 |
| 19 | 3.174 | 3.175 | 3.174 | 3.175 | 3.174 | 3.175 | 3.174 | 3.175 | 3.174 | 3.175 | 3.174 | 3.175 |
| 20 | 3.175 | 3.174 | 3.175 | 3.174 | 3.175 | 3.174 | 3.175 | 3.174 | 3.175 | 3.174 | 3.175 | 3.174 |
| 21 | 3.174 | 3.175 | 3.174 | 3.175 | 3.174 | 3.175 | 3.174 | 3.175 | 3.174 | 3.175 | 3.174 | 3.175 |
| 22 | 3.175 | 3.174 | 3.175 | 3.174 | 3.175 | 3.174 | 3.175 | 3.174 | 3.175 | 3.174 | 3.175 | 3.174 |
| 23 | 3.174 | 3.175 | 3.174 | 3.175 | 3.174 | 3.175 | 3.174 | 3.175 | 3.174 | 3.175 | 3.174 | 3.175 |
| 24 | 3.175 | 3.174 | 3.175 | 3.174 | 3.175 | 3.174 | 3.175 | 3.174 | 3.175 | 3.174 | 3.175 | 3.174 |
| 25 | 3.174 | 3.175 | 3.174 | 3.175 | 3.174 | 3.175 | 3.174 | 3.175 | 3.174 | 3.175 | 3.174 | 3.175 |
| 26 | 3.175 | 3.174 | 3.175 | 3.174 | 3.175 | 3.174 | 3.175 | 3.174 | 3.175 | 3.174 | 3.175 | 3.174 |
| 27 | 3.174 | 3.175 | 3.174 | 3.175 | 3.174 | 3.175 | 3.174 | 3.175 | 3.174 | 3.175 | 3.174 | 3.175 |
| 28 | 3.175 | 3.174 | 3.175 | 3.174 | 3.175 | 3.174 | 3.175 | 3.174 | 3.175 | 3.174 | 3.175 | 3.174 |
| 29 | 3.174 | 3.175 | 3.174 | 3.175 | 3.174 | 3.175 | 3.174 | 3.175 | 3.174 | 3.175 | 3.174 | 3.175 |
| 30 | 3.175 | 3.174 | 3.175 | 3.174 | 3.175 | 3.174 | 3.175 | 3.174 | 3.175 | 3.174 | 3.175 | 3.174 |
| 31 | 3.174 | 3.175 | 3.174 | 3.175 | 3.174 | 3.175 | 3.174 | 3.175 | 3.174 | 3.175 | 3.174 | 3.175 |
| 32 | 1.720 | 1.984 | 2.249 | 2.513 | 2.778 | 3.042 | 3.175 | 3.174 | 3.175 | 3.174 | 3.175 | 3.174 |
| 33 | | | | | | | 0.132 | 0.397 | 0.661 | 0.926 | 1.190 | 1.455 |

Table A-7a.    **Nonresidential Real Property**
**Mid-Month Convention**
**Straight Line—39 Years**

| Year | Month property placed in service | | | | | | | | | | | |
|---|---|---|---|---|---|---|---|---|---|---|---|---|
| | 1 | 2 | 3 | 4 | 5 | 6 | 7 | 8 | 9 | 10 | 11 | 12 |
| 1 | 2.461% | 2.247% | 2.033% | 1.819% | 1.605% | 1.391% | 1.177% | 0.963% | 0.749% | 0.535% | 0.321% | 0.107% |
| 2–39 | 2.564 | 2.564 | 2.564 | 2.564 | 2.564 | 2.564 | 2.564 | 2.564 | 2.564 | 2.564 | 2.564 | 2.564 |
| 40 | 0.107 | 0.321 | 0.535 | 0.749 | 0.963 | 1.177 | 1.391 | 1.605 | 1.819 | 2.033 | 2.247 | 2.461 |

# Appendix D– Answer Guide

# *Chapter 1 Review*

1) List three things that are added to the basis of a property.

**Sales tax**
**Freight**
**Installation and testing**
**Excise taxes**
**Legal and accounting fees that must be capitalized (added to the basis)**
**Revenue stamps**
**Recording fees**
**Real estate taxes that were assumed for the seller**

2) List three types of settlement fees that are not added to the basis.

**Fire insurance premiums**
**Rent for occupancy of the property before closing**
**Charges for utilities or other services related to occupancy of the property before closing**
**Charges connected with getting a loan**
**Fees for refinancing a mortgage**

3) List three things that decrease a property's basis.

**Exclusion from income of subsidies for energy conservation measures**
**Casualty or theft loss deductions and insurance reimbursements**
**Credit for qualified electric vehicles**
**Section 179 deduction**
**Deduction for clean-fuel vehicles and clean-fuel vehicle refueling property**
**Depreciation or Amortization**
**Nontaxable corporate distributions**
**Deferred gains**
**Investment credit**
**Rebates from a manufacturer or seller**
**Easements**

4) What is the depreciable basis of converted property?

**The basis for depreciation is the lesser of the fair market value of the property on the date of the conversion, or the adjusted basis on the date of the conversion.**

5) What is the depreciable basis of a gift?

**The taxpayer's basis in the property for depreciation is the donor's adjusted basis, plus or minus any required adjustments while the taxpayer holds the property.**

6) What are the two qualifications that have to be met for an expense to be classified as a start-up cost?

**To qualify as a start-up cost, it must meet both of the following tests:**

- **It is a cost that could be deducted if it is paid or incurred to operate an existing active trade or business (in the same field as the one the taxpayer entered into).**
- **It is a cost paid or incurred before the day the active trade or business begins.**

## *Exercises*

1) Find the adjusted basis. Eddie Miller bought an office building for $67,000 in 2005. The land was $12,500 and the building was $54,500. His settlement costs, at the time of the purchase, were $3,824. He made some major improvements to the interior of the building in 2007, for a total cost of $5,676. He has claimed the allowable depreciation deduction of $12,322. What is the adjusted basis for the building and the land separately?

**The land is 18.66% of the full cost (12,500 ÷ 67,000)**
**Land Basis: 3,824 x 18.66% = 714; 12,500 + 714=13,214**
   **The adjusted basis of the land is $13,214.**
**Building Basis: 3,824 – 714 = 3,110; 54,500 + 3,110 + 5,676 – 12,322 = 50,964**
   **The adjusted basis of the building is $50,964.**

2) Jenny Monroe bought a house on a lot in 1996 for a total of $74,000. The land was $11,750. She put a new roof on the house in 2000 for $3,200 and repainted some of the rooms for $325. She moved out of the house and began renting it out in 2004. The FMV at that time was $83,000 for the house and $17,500 for the land. She has since added on a room for $4,250 and claimed depreciation deductions in the amount of $13,900. What is her basis for depreciation? Her basis if she sold it at a gain? Her basis if she sold it at a loss?

**The adjusted basis of the House at the time of conversion: $62,250 + 3,200 = $65,450.**

**The adjusted basis of the land at the time of conversion is $11,750.**

**The basis for depreciation is $65,450;**
**The basis if sold at a gain: 65,450 + 4,250 – 13,900 = 55,800; 55,800 + 11,750 = 67,550**
   **The basis is $67,550.**
**The basis if sold at a loss is $67,550.**

3) Billy Martin's dad gave him a truck. Billy's dad had an adjusted basis of $22,000. The FMV of the truck when he gave it to Billy was $14,300. What is Billy's basis for depreciation, gain, and loss?
**The basis for depreciation is $14,300.**
**The basis if sold at a gain is $22,000.**
**The basis if sold at a loss is $14,300.**

4) Billy's dad also gave him a piece of land. Billy's dad had an adjusted basis of $13,000. The FMV of the land when he gave it to Billy was $26,000. What is Billy's basis for depreciation, gain, and loss?

**The basis for depreciation is $13,000.**
**The basis if sold at a gain is $13,000.**
**The basis if sold at a loss is $13,000.**

# Chapter 2 Review

1) The hybrid method of accounting is a combination of what two methods?

   **The hybrid method of accounting is a combination of the cash and accrual methods.**

2) The taxpayer has to keep what to have a cost of goods sold?

   **The taxpayer has to keep inventory to have a cost of goods sold.**

3) What are the two methods of inventory valuation?

   **The two methods of inventory valuation are cost and the lower of cost or market.**

4) Define FIFO.

   **FIFO (First in first out) – This is a method of valuing inventory in which the first items purchased or produced are the first items sold.**

5) Define LIFO.

   **LIFO (Last in first out) – This is a method of valuing inventory in which the last items purchased or produced are the first items sold.**

6) What is the standard mileage rate for 2011?

   **The standard mileage rate is 51 cents per business mile driven before July 1$^{st}$, 2011, and 55.5 cents per business mile driven after June 30$^{th}$, 2011.**

7) If the taxpayer pays a contractor $600 or more, what must they do?

   **If the taxpayer pays anyone $600 or more, the taxpayer must file a Form 1099-MISC with the IRS, as well as the payee.**

8) What is the federal MI&E rate for 2011?

   **The federal MI&E rate is $46 per day for travel within the United States for 2011.**

9) What are indirect expenses on a Form 8829?

   **Indirect expenses are expenses that relate to the entire home.**

10) What two taxes make up SE tax?

   **Self employment taxes are the social security and Medicare taxes the self employed taxpayer must pay on their business income.**

Form **1040**
Department of the Treasury—Internal Revenue Service (99)

**U.S. Individual Income Tax Return** 2011   OMB No. 1545-0074   IRS Use Only—Do not write or staple in this space.

For the year Jan. 1–Dec. 31, 2011, or other tax year beginning _____ , 2011, ending _____ , 20 ___ | See separate instructions.

| Your first name and initial | Last name | | Your social security number |
|---|---|---|---|
| TIMOTHY | THOMPSON | | 5 6 7 8 7 4 3 2 1 |
| If a joint return, spouse's first name and initial | Last name | | Spouse's social security number |
| | | | |

Home address (number and street). If you have a P.O. box, see instructions. | Apt. no. | ▲ Make sure the SSN(s) above and on line 6c are correct.

453 ROBIN STREET

City, town or post office, state, and ZIP code. If you have a foreign address, also complete spaces below (see instructions).

YOUR CITY, YOUR STATE, YOUR ZIP CODE

**Presidential Election Campaign**
Check here if you, or your spouse if filing jointly, want $3 to go to this fund. Checking a box below will not change your tax or refund. ☐ You ☐ Spouse

| Foreign country name | Foreign province/county | Foreign postal code |
|---|---|---|
| | | |

**Filing Status**

Check only one box.

1. ☐ Single
2. ☐ Married filing jointly (even if only one had income)
3. ☐ Married filing separately. Enter spouse's SSN above and full name here. ▶
4. ☑ Head of household (with qualifying person). (See instructions.) If the qualifying person is a child but not your dependent, enter this child's name here. ▶ _____
5. ☐ Qualifying widow(er) with dependent child

**Exemptions**

6a ☑ **Yourself.** If someone can claim you as a dependent, **do not** check box 6a . . . . .
b ☐ **Spouse** . . . . . . . . . . .

| c Dependents: | (2) Dependent's social security number | (3) Dependent's relationship to you | (4) ✓ if child under age 17 qualifying for child tax credit (see instructions) |
|---|---|---|---|
| (1) First name   Last name | | | |
| LENA THOMPSON | 4 3 9 5 1 5 8 8 2 | DAUGHTER | ☑ |
| | | | ☐ |
| | | | ☐ |
| | | | ☐ |

If more than four dependents, see instructions and check here ▶ ☐

| Boxes checked on 6a and 6b | 1 |
|---|---|
| No. of children on 6c who: • lived with you | 1 |
| • did not live with you due to divorce or separation (see instructions) | 0 |
| Dependents on 6c not entered above | 0 |
| Add numbers on lines above ▶ | 2 |

d Total number of exemptions claimed . . . . . . . . . . . . . . . . . .

**Income**

Attach Form(s) W-2 here. Also attach Forms W-2G and 1099-R if tax was withheld.

If you did not get a W-2, see instructions.

Enclose, but do not attach, any payment. Also, please use Form 1040-V.

| | | | |
|---|---|---|---|
| 7 | Wages, salaries, tips, etc. Attach Form(s) W-2 . . . . . . . | 7 | |
| 8a | **Taxable** interest. Attach Schedule B if required . . . . . . . | 8a | 532 |
| b | **Tax-exempt** interest. **Do not** include on line 8a . . . 8b | | |
| 9a | Ordinary dividends. Attach Schedule B if required . . . . . | 9a | |
| b | Qualified dividends . . . . . . . 9b | | |
| 10 | Taxable refunds, credits, or offsets of state and local income taxes . . . . . | 10 | |
| 11 | Alimony received . . . . . . . . . . . . . . . . | 11 | |
| 12 | Business income or (loss). Attach Schedule C or C-EZ . . . . . . . . | 12 | 45,207 |
| 13 | Capital gain or (loss). Attach Schedule D if required. If not required, check here ▶ ☐ | 13 | |
| 14 | Other gains or (losses). Attach Form 4797 . . . . . . . . . | 14 | |
| 15a | IRA distributions . 15a _____ b Taxable amount . . . | 15b | |
| 16a | Pensions and annuities 16a _____ b Taxable amount . . . | 16b | |
| 17 | Rental real estate, royalties, partnerships, S corporations, trusts, etc. Attach Schedule E | 17 | |
| 18 | Farm income or (loss). Attach Schedule F . . . . . . . . . | 18 | |
| 19 | Unemployment compensation . . . . . . . . . . . . | 19 | |
| 20a | Social security benefits 20a _____ b Taxable amount . . . | 20b | |
| 21 | Other income. List type and amount   GAMBLING WINNINGS | 21 | 550 |
| 22 | Combine the amounts in the far right column for lines 7 through 21. This is your **total income** ▶ | 22 | 46,289 |

**Adjusted Gross Income**

| | | | |
|---|---|---|---|
| 23 | Educator expenses . . . . . . . . . . | 23 | |
| 24 | Certain business expenses of reservists, performing artists, and fee-basis government officials. Attach Form 2106 or 2106-EZ | 24 | |
| 25 | Health savings account deduction. Attach Form 8889 . | 25 | |
| 26 | Moving expenses. Attach Form 3903 . . . . . . | 26 | |
| 27 | Deductible part of self-employment tax. Attach Schedule SE . | 27 | 3,193 |
| 28 | Self-employed SEP, SIMPLE, and qualified plans . . | 28 | |
| 29 | Self-employed health insurance deduction . . . . | 29 | |
| 30 | Penalty on early withdrawal of savings . . . . . . | 30 | |
| 31a | Alimony paid  b Recipient's SSN ▶ _____ | 31a | |
| 32 | IRA deduction . . . . . . . . . . | 32 | |
| 33 | Student loan interest deduction . . . . . . . | 33 | |
| 34 | Tuition and fees. Attach Form 8917 . . . . . . | 34 | |
| 35 | Domestic production activities deduction. Attach Form 8903 | 35 | |
| 36 | Add lines 23 through 35 . . . . . . . . . . . . . . . . . . | 36 | 3,193 |
| 37 | Subtract line 36 from line 22. This is your **adjusted gross income** . . . . . ▶ | 37 | 43,096 |

**For Disclosure, Privacy Act, and Paperwork Reduction Act Notice, see separate instructions.**   Cat. No. 11320B   Form **1040** (2011)

| | | | | | |
|---|---|---|---|---|---|
| **Tax and Credits** | 38 | Amount from line 37 (adjusted gross income) . . . . . . . . . . | | 38 | 43,096 |
| | 39a | Check if: ☐ **You** were born before January 2, 1947, ☐ **Spouse** was born before January 2, 1947, ☐ Blind. ☐ Blind. } **Total boxes** checked ▶ 39a | | | |
| **Standard Deduction for—** | b | If your spouse itemizes on a separate return or you were a dual-status alien, check here ▶ 39b ☐ | | | |
| • People who check any box on line 39a or 39b **or** who can be claimed as a dependent, see instructions. | 40 | **Itemized deductions** (from Schedule A) **or** your **standard deduction** (see left margin) . . | | 40 | 8,500 |
| | 41 | Subtract line 40 from line 38 . . . . . . . . . . . . . | | 41 | 34,596 |
| | 42 | **Exemptions.** Multiply $3,700 by the number on line 6d. . . . . . . | | 42 | 7,400 |
| | 43 | **Taxable income.** Subtract line 42 from line 41. If line 42 is more than line 41, enter -0- . . | | 43 | 27,196 |
| | 44 | **Tax** (see instructions). Check if any from: **a** ☐ Form(s) 8814 **b** ☐ Form 4972 **c** ☐ 962 election | | 44 | 3,469 |
| • All others: Single or Married filing separately, $5,800 | 45 | **Alternative minimum tax** (see instructions). Attach Form 6251 . . . . . . | | 45 | |
| | 46 | Add lines 44 and 45 . . . . . . . . . . . . . . . . . ▶ | | 46 | 3,469 |
| | 47 | Foreign tax credit. Attach Form 1116 if required . . . . | 47 | | |
| Married filing jointly or Qualifying widow(er), $11,600 | 48 | Credit for child and dependent care expenses. Attach Form 2441 | 48 | 280 | |
| | 49 | Education credits from Form 8863, line 23 . . . . | 49 | | |
| | 50 | Retirement savings contributions credit. Attach Form 8880 | 50 | | |
| Head of household, $8,500 | 51 | Child tax credit (see instructions) . . . . . . . | 51 | 1,000 | |
| | 52 | Residential energy credits. Attach Form 5695 . . . | 52 | | |
| | 53 | Other credits from Form: **a** ☐ 3800 **b** ☐ 8801 **c** ☐ | 53 | | |
| | 54 | Add lines 47 through 53. These are your **total credits** . . . . . . . | | 54 | 1,280 |
| | 55 | Subtract line 54 from line 46. If line 54 is more than line 46, enter -0- . . . . . . ▶ | | 55 | 2,189 |
| **Other Taxes** | 56 | Self-employment tax. Attach Schedule SE . . . . . . . . . . | | 56 | 5,553 |
| | 57 | Unreported social security and Medicare tax from Form: **a** ☐ 4137 **b** ☐ 8919 . . | | 57 | |
| | 58 | Additional tax on IRAs, other qualified retirement plans, etc. Attach Form 5329 if required . . | | 58 | |
| | 59a | Household employment taxes from Schedule H . . . . . . . . . | | 59a | |
| | b | First-time homebuyer credit repayment. Attach Form 5405 if required . . . . . | | 59b | |
| | 60 | Other taxes. Enter code(s) from instructions | | 60 | |
| | 61 | Add lines 55 through 60. This is your **total tax** . . . . . . . . . . ▶ | | 61 | 7,742 |
| **Payments** | 62 | Federal income tax withheld from Forms W-2 and 1099 . . | 62 | | |
| | 63 | 2011 estimated tax payments and amount applied from 2010 return | 63 | 8,000 | |
| If you have a qualifying child, attach Schedule EIC. | 64a | **Earned income credit (EIC)** . . . . . . . . . | 64a | | |
| | b | Nontaxable combat pay election | 64b | | |
| | 65 | Additional child tax credit. Attach Form 8812 . . . . . | 65 | | |
| | 66 | American opportunity credit from Form 8863, line 14 . . . | 66 | | |
| | 67 | First-time homebuyer credit from Form 5405, line 10 . . . | 67 | | |
| | 68 | Amount paid with request for extension to file . . . . | 68 | | |
| | 69 | Excess social security and tier 1 RRTA tax withheld . . . . | 69 | | |
| | 70 | Credit for federal tax on fuels. Attach Form 4136 . . . . | 70 | | |
| | 71 | Credits from Form: **a** ☐ 2439 **b** ☐ 8839 **c** ☐ 8801 **d** ☐ 8885 | 71 | | |
| | 72 | Add lines 62, 63, 64a, and 65 through 71. These are your **total payments** . . . . . ▶ | | 72 | 8,000 |
| **Refund** | 73 | If line 72 is more than line 61, subtract line 61 from line 72. This is the amount you **overpaid** | | 73 | 258 |
| | 74a | Amount of line 73 you want **refunded to you**. If Form 8888 is attached, check here . ▶ ☐ | | 74a | 258 |
| Direct deposit? See instructions. | ▶ b | Routing number | ▶ c Type: ☐ Checking ☐ Savings | | |
| | ▶ d | Account number | | | |
| | 75 | Amount of line 73 you want **applied to your 2012 estimated tax** ▶ | 75 | | |
| **Amount You Owe** | 76 | **Amount you owe.** Subtract line 72 from line 61. For details on how to pay, see instructions ▶ | | 76 | |
| | 77 | Estimated tax penalty (see instructions) . . . . . . . . | 77 | | |

**Third Party Designee**

Do you want to allow another person to discuss this return with the IRS (see instructions)? ☐ **Yes.** Complete below. ☐ **No**

| Designee's name ▶ | Phone no. ▶ | Personal identification number (PIN) ▶ |
|---|---|---|

**Sign Here**

Under penalties of perjury, I declare that I have examined this return and accompanying schedules and statements, and to the best of my knowledge and belief, they are true, correct, and complete. Declaration of preparer (other than taxpayer) is based on all information of which preparer has any knowledge.

Joint return? See instructions. Keep a copy for your records.

| Your signature | Date | Your occupation SELF EMPLOYED | Daytime phone number |
|---|---|---|---|
| Spouse's signature. If a joint return, **both** must sign. | Date | Spouse's occupation | If the IRS sent you an Identity Protection PIN, enter it here (see inst.) |

**Paid Preparer Use Only**

| Print/Type preparer's name JANE DOE | Preparer's signature | Date | Check ☐ if self-employed | PTIN P00000000 |
|---|---|---|---|---|
| Firm's name ▶ MY TAX SERVICE | | | Firm's EIN ▶ | 63-5555555 |
| Firm's address ▶ 100 MAIN ST., YOUR CITY, YOUR STATE, YOUR ZIP CODE | | Phone no. | | (555)555-5555 |

Form **1040** (2011)

# SCHEDULE C
## (Form 1040)

Department of the Treasury
Internal Revenue Service (99)

# Profit or Loss From Business
## (Sole Proprietorship)

► **For information on Schedule C and its instructions, go to** *www.irs.gov/schedulec*
► **Attach to Form 1040, 1040NR, or 1041; partnerships generally must file Form 1065.**

OMB No. 1545-0074

**2011**

Attachment
Sequence No. **09**

| Name of proprietor | Social security number (SSN) |
|---|---|
| TIMOTHY THOMPSON | 567-87-4321 |

**A** Principal business or profession, including product or service (see instructions)
PLUMBING

**B** Enter code from instructions ► 2 3 8 2 2 0

**C** Business name. If no separate business name, leave blank.
PLUMBERS R US

**D** Employer ID number (EIN), (see instr.)

**E** Business address (including suite or room no.) ► 453 ROBIN STREET
City, town or post office, state, and ZIP code    YOUR CITY, YOUR STATE, YOUR ZIP CODE

**F** Accounting method: **(1)** ✔ Cash **(2)** ☐ Accrual **(3)** ☐ Other (specify) ►

**G** Did you "materially participate" in the operation of this business during 2011? If "No," see instructions for limit on losses . ✔ Yes ☐ No

**H** If you started or acquired this business during 2011, check here . . . . . . . . . . . ► ☐

**I** Did you make any payments in 2011 that would require you to file Form(s) 1099? (see instructions) . . . . . . . ☐ Yes ✔ No

**J** If "Yes," did you or will you file all required Forms 1099? . . . . . . . . . . . . . ☐ Yes ☐ No

## Part I  Income

| | | | | |
|---|---|---|---|---|
| 1a | Merchant card and third party payments. For 2011, enter -0- . . . | 1a | | |
| b | Gross receipts or sales not entered on line 1a (see instructions) . . | 1b | 87,890 | |
| c | Income reported to you on Form W-2 if the "Statutory Employee" box on that form was checked. **Caution.** See instr. before completing this line | 1c | | |
| d | **Total gross receipts.** Add lines 1a through 1c . . . . . . . . . . . | 1d | | 87,890 |
| 2 | Returns and allowances plus any other adjustments (see instructions) . . . . . . . | 2 | | |
| 3 | Subtract line 2 from line 1d . . . . . . . . . . . . . . . . . . | 3 | | 87,890 |
| 4 | Cost of goods sold (from line 42) . . . . . . . . . . . . . . . | 4 | | |
| 5 | **Gross profit.** Subtract line 4 from line 3 . . . . . . . . . . . . | 5 | | 87,890 |
| 6 | Other income, including federal and state gasoline or fuel tax credit or refund (see instructions) . . . . | 6 | | |
| 7 | **Gross income.** Add lines 5 and 6 . . . . . . . . . . . . . . . . ► | 7 | | 87,890 |

## Part II  Expenses   Enter expenses for business use of your home only on line 30.

| | | | | | | | |
|---|---|---|---|---|---|---|---|
| 8 | Advertising . . . . . | 8 | 1,594 | 18 | Office expense (see instructions) | 18 | 2,655 |
| 9 | Car and truck expenses (see instructions). . . . . | 9 | 10,141 | 19 | Pension and profit-sharing plans . | 19 | |
| | | | | 20 | Rent or lease (see instructions): | | |
| 10 | Commissions and fees . | 10 | | a | Vehicles, machinery, and equipment | 20a | 12,000 |
| 11 | Contract labor (see instructions) | 11 | | b | Other business property . . . | 20b | |
| 12 | Depletion . . . . . | 12 | | 21 | Repairs and maintenance . . . | 21 | 2,313 |
| 13 | Depreciation and section 179 expense deduction (not included in Part III) (see instructions). . . . . | 13 | | 22 | Supplies (not included in Part III) . | 22 | 5,688 |
| | | | | 23 | Taxes and licenses . . . . . | 23 | 856 |
| | | | | 24 | Travel, meals, and entertainment: | | |
| 14 | Employee benefit programs (other than on line 19) . . | 14 | | a | Travel . . . . . . . . . | 24a | |
| 15 | Insurance (other than health) | 15 | 2,433 | b | Deductible meals and entertainment (see instructions) . | 24b | |
| 16 | Interest: | | | 25 | Utilities . . . . . . . . | 25 | |
| a | Mortgage (paid to banks, etc.) | 16a | | 26 | Wages (less employment credits) . | 26 | |
| b | Other . . . . . . | 16b | | 27a | Other expenses (from line 48) . . | 27a | |
| 17 | Legal and professional services | 17 | 3,500 | b | **Reserved for future use** . . . | 27b | |

| | | | |
|---|---|---|---|
| 28 | **Total expenses** before expenses for business use of home. Add lines 8 through 27a . . . . . . . ► | 28 | 41,180 |
| 29 | Tentative profit or (loss). Subtract line 28 from line 7 . . . . . . . . . . . . . . . | 29 | 46,710 |
| 30 | Expenses for business use of your home. Attach **Form 8829.** Do **not** report such expenses elsewhere . . | 30 | 1,503 |
| 31 | **Net profit or (loss).** Subtract line 30 from line 29.<br>• If a profit, enter on both **Form 1040, line 12** (or **Form 1040NR, line 13**) and on **Schedule SE, line 2.** If you entered an amount on line 1c, see instr. Estates and trusts, enter on **Form 1041, line 3.**<br>• If a loss, you **must** go to line 32. | 31 | 45,207 |
| 32 | If you have a loss, check the box that describes your investment in this activity (see instructions).<br>• If you checked 32a, enter the loss on both **Form 1040, line 12,** (or **Form 1040NR, line 13**) and on **Schedule SE, line 2.** If you entered an amount on line 1c, see the instructions for line 31. Estates and trusts, enter on **Form 1041, line 3.**<br>• If you checked 32b, you **must** attach **Form 6198.** Your loss may be limited. | 32a ☐ All investment is at risk.<br>32b ☐ Some investment is not at risk. |

**For Paperwork Reduction Act Notice, see your tax return instructions.**    Cat. No. 11334P    Schedule C (Form 1040) 2011

**Part III**    **Cost of Goods Sold**   (see instructions)

**33**   Method(s) used to value closing inventory:    **a** ☐ Cost     **b** ☐ Lower of cost or market     **c** ☐ Other (attach explanation)

**34**   Was there any change in determining quantities, costs, or valuations between opening and closing inventory? If "Yes," attach explanation   . . . . . . . . . . . . . . . . . . . . .    ☐ **Yes**    ☐ **No**

| | | |
|---|---|---|
| **35** Inventory at beginning of year. If different from last year's closing inventory, attach explanation . . . | **35** | |
| **36** Purchases less cost of items withdrawn for personal use . . . . . . . | **36** | |
| **37** Cost of labor. Do not include any amounts paid to yourself . . . . . . . | **37** | |
| **38** Materials and supplies . . . . . . . . . . | **38** | |
| **39** Other costs . . . . . . . . . . . . . | **39** | |
| **40** Add lines 35 through 39 . . . . . . . . . | **40** | |
| **41** Inventory at end of year . . . . . . . . . | **41** | |
| **42** **Cost of goods sold.** Subtract line 41 from line 40. Enter the result here and on line 4 . . . . . | **42** | |

**Part IV**    **Information on Your Vehicle.** Complete this part **only** if you are claiming car or truck expenses on line 9 and are not required to file Form 4562 for this business. See the instructions for line 13 to find out if you must file Form 4562.

**43**   When did you place your vehicle in service for business purposes? (month, day, year)   ▶   01 / 01 / 2008

**44**   Of the total number of miles you drove your vehicle during 2011, enter the number of miles you used your vehicle for:

   **a**   Business    18,977     **b** Commuting (see instructions)     **c** Other    6,689

**45**   Was your vehicle available for personal use during off-duty hours?   . . . . . . . . . . . . . . . . . ☑ **Yes**    ☐ **No**

**46**   Do you (or your spouse) have another vehicle available for personal use?.   . . . . . . . . . . . . . . ☑ **Yes**    ☐ **No**

**47a**   Do you have evidence to support your deduction?   . . . . . . . . . . . . . . . . . . . . ☑ **Yes**    ☐ **No**

   **b**   If "Yes," is the evidence written?   . . . . . . . . . . . . . . . . . . . . . . . . ☑ **Yes**    ☐ **No**

**Part V**    **Other Expenses.** List below business expenses not included on lines 8–26 or line 30.

| | | |
|---|---|---|
| | | |
| | | |
| | | |
| | | |
| | | |
| | | |
| | | |
| | | |
| **48**   **Total other expenses.** Enter here and on line 27a . . . . . . . . . . . . . . . . . | **48** | |

# Self-Employment Tax

►Attach to Form 1040 or Form 1040NR. ►See separate instructions.

OMB No. 1545-0074

2011

Attachment
Sequence No. 17

| Name of person with **self-employment** income (as shown on Form 1040) | Social security number of person with **self-employment** income ► |
|---|---|
| TIMOTHY THOMPSON | 567-87-4321 |

***Before you begin:*** To determine if you must file Schedule SE, see the instructions.

## May I Use Short Schedule SE or Must I Use Long Schedule SE?

**Note.** Use this flowchart **only if** you must file Schedule SE. If unsure, see *Who Must File Schedule SE* in the instructions.

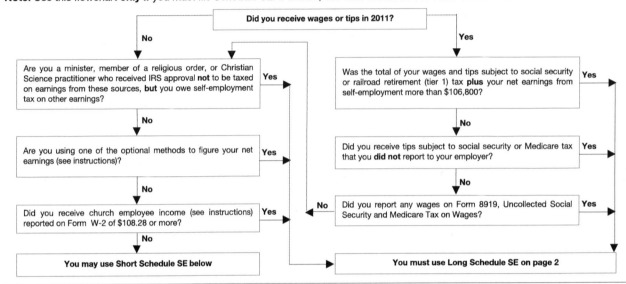

## Section A—Short Schedule SE. Caution. Read above to see if you can use Short Schedule SE.

| | | | |
|---|---|---|---:|
| **1a** | Net farm profit or (loss) from Schedule F, line 34, and farm partnerships, Schedule K-1 (Form 1065), box 14, code A . . . . . . . . . . . . . . . . . . | **1a** | |
| **b** | If you received social security retirement or disability benefits, enter the amount of Conservation Reserve Program payments included on Schedule F, line 4b, or listed on Schedule K-1 (Form 1065), box 20, code Y | **1b** ( | ) |
| **2** | Net profit or (loss) from Schedule C, line 31; Schedule C-EZ, line 3; Schedule K-1 (Form 1065), box 14, code A (other than farming); and Schedule K-1 (Form 1065-B), box 9, code J1. Ministers and members of religious orders, see instructions for types of income to report on this line. See instructions for other income to report . . . . . . . . . . . . . . | **2** | 45,207 |
| **3** | Combine lines 1a, 1b, and 2 . . . . . . . . . . . . . . . . . . | **3** | 45,207 |
| **4** | Multiply line 3 by 92.35% (.9235). If less than $400, you do not owe self-employment tax; **do not** file this schedule unless you have an amount on line 1b . . . . . . . . . . . ► | **4** | 41,749 |
| | **Note.** If line 4 is less than $400 due to Conservation Reserve Program payments on line 1b, see instructions. | | |
| **5** | **Self-employment tax.** If the amount on line 4 is: <br> • $106,800 or less, multiply line 4 by 13.3% (.133). Enter the result here and on **Form 1040, line 56,** or **Form 1040NR, line 54** <br> • More than $106,800, multiply line 4 by 2.9% (.029). Then, add $11,107.20 to the result. Enter the total here and on **Form 1040, line 56,** or **Form 1040NR, line 54** . . . . . . . | **5** | 5,553 |
| **6** | **Deduction for employer-equivalent portion of self-employment tax.** <br> If the amount on line 5 is: <br> • $14,204.40 or less, multiply line 5 by 57.51% (.5751) <br> • More than $14,204.40, multiply line 5 by 50% (.50) and add $1,067 to the result. <br> Enter the result here and on **Form 1040, line 27,** or **Form 1040NR, line 27** . . . . . . . . . . . . . . . . . . | **6** | 3,193 |

**For Paperwork Reduction Act Notice, see your tax return instructions.** Cat. No. 11358Z **Schedule SE (Form 1040) 2011**

Form **2441**

Department of the Treasury
Internal Revenue Service (99)

# Child and Dependent Care Expenses

▶ Attach to Form 1040, Form 1040A, or Form 1040NR.
▶ See separate instructions.

1040
1040A
1040NR
2441

OMB No. 1545-0074

**2011**

Attachment
Sequence No. **21**

Name(s) shown on return

TIMOTHY THOMPSON

Your social security number

567-87-4321

**Part I** Persons or Organizations Who Provided the Care—You **must** complete this part.
(If you have more than two care providers, see the instructions.)

| 1 | (a) Care provider's name | (b) Address (number, street, apt. no., city, state, and ZIP code) | (c) Identifying number (SSN or EIN) | (d) Amount paid (see instructions) |
|---|---|---|---|---|
| | WE LOVE KIDS | 222 TODDLER LANE<br>YOUR CITY, YOUR STATE, YOUR ZIP CODE | 39-5392431 | 1,398 |
| | | | | |

Did you receive **dependent care benefits?**

**No** ▶ Complete only Part II below.

**Yes** ▶ Complete Part III on the back next.

**Caution.** If the care was provided in your home, you may owe employment taxes. If you do, you cannot file Form 1040A. For details, see the instructions for Form 1040, line 59a, or Form 1040NR, line 58a.

**Part II** Credit for Child and Dependent Care Expenses

2  Information about your **qualifying person(s)**. If you have more than two qualifying persons, see the instructions.

| (a) Qualifying person's name | | (b) Qualifying person's social security number | (c) **Qualified expenses** you incurred and paid in 2011 for the person listed in column (a) |
|---|---|---|---|
| First | Last | | |
| LENA | THOMPSON | 439-51-5882 | 1,398 |
| | | | |

3  Add the amounts in column (c) of line 2. **Do not** enter more than $3,000 for one qualifying person or $6,000 for two or more persons. If you completed Part III, enter the amount from line 31 . . . **3** — 1,398

4  Enter your **earned income**. See instructions . . . . . . . . . . . . . **4** — 42,014

5  If married filing jointly, enter your spouse's earned income (if your spouse was a student or was disabled, see the instructions); **all others**, enter the amount from line 4 . . . . . **5** — 42,014

6  Enter the **smallest** of line 3, 4, or 5 . . . . . . . . . . . . . **6** — 1,398

7  Enter the amount from Form 1040, line 38; Form 1040A, line 22; or Form 1040NR, line 37. . . . . **7** — 43,096

8  Enter on line 8 the decimal amount shown below that applies to the amount on line 7

| If line 7 is: | | | If line 7 is: | | |
|---|---|---|---|---|---|
| Over | But not over | Decimal amount is | Over | But not over | Decimal amount is |
| $0—15,000 | | .35 | $29,000—31,000 | | .27 |
| 15,000—17,000 | | .34 | 31,000—33,000 | | .26 |
| 17,000—19,000 | | .33 | 33,000—35,000 | | .25 |
| 19,000—21,000 | | .32 | 35,000—37,000 | | .24 |
| 21,000—23,000 | | .31 | 37,000—39,000 | | .23 |
| 23,000—25,000 | | .30 | 39,000—41,000 | | .22 |
| 25,000—27,000 | | .29 | 41,000—43,000 | | .21 |
| 27,000—29,000 | | .28 | 43,000—No limit | | .20 |

**8** — X . 20

9  Multiply line 6 by the decimal amount on line 8. If you paid 2010 expenses in 2011, see the instructions . . . . . . . . . . . . . . . . **9** — 280

10  Tax liability limit. Enter the amount from the Credit Limit Worksheet in the instructions. . . . . . | **10** | 3,469 |

11  Credit for child and dependent care expenses. Enter the smaller of line 9 or line 10 here and on Form 1040, line 48; Form 1040A, line 29; or Form 1040NR, line 46 . . . . **11** — 280

**For Paperwork Reduction Act Notice, see your tax return instructions.**      Cat. No. 11862M      Form **2441** (2011)

Form **8829**

Department of the Treasury
Internal Revenue Service (99)

## Expenses for Business Use of Your Home

▶ File only with Schedule C (Form 1040). Use a separate Form 8829 for each home you used for business during the year.
▶ See separate instructions.

OMB No. 1545-0074

**2011**

Attachment
Sequence No. **176**

Name(s) of proprietor(s)

TIMOTHY THOMPSON

Your social security number

567-87-4321

### Part I   Part of Your Home Used for Business

| | | |
|---|---|---:|
| 1 | Area used regularly and exclusively for business, regularly for daycare, or for storage of inventory or product samples (see instructions) . . . . . . . . . . . . . . . **1** | 165 |
| 2 | Total area of home  . . . . . . . . . . . . . . . . . . **2** | 1,825 |
| 3 | Divide line 1 by line 2. Enter the result as a percentage  . . . . . . . . . **3** | 9.04 % |

For daycare facilities not used exclusively for business, go to line 4. All others go to line 7.

| | | | | |
|---|---|---|---|---:|
| 4 | Multiply days used for daycare during year by hours used per day | **4** | | hr. |
| 5 | Total hours available for use during the year (365 days x 24 hours) (see instructions) | **5** | 8,760 hr. | |
| 6 | Divide line 4 by line 5. Enter the result as a decimal amount . . . | **6** | . | |
| 7 | Business percentage. For daycare facilities not used exclusively for business, multiply line 6 by line 3 (enter the result as a percentage). All others, enter the amount from line 3 . . . . . ▶ | **7** | | 9.04 % |

### Part II   Figure Your Allowable Deduction

| | | | | | |
|---|---|---|---|---|---:|
| 8 | Enter the amount from Schedule C, line 29, **plus** any gain derived from the business use of your home and shown on Schedule D or Form 4797, minus any loss from the trade or business not derived from the business use of your home and shown on Schedule D or Form 4797.  See instructions  . . | | | **8** | 46,710 |

See instructions for columns (a) and (b) before completing lines 9–21.

| | | | (a) Direct expenses | (b) Indirect expenses | | |
|---|---|---|---|---|---|---:|
| 9 | Casualty losses (see instructions). . . . | **9** | | | | |
| 10 | Deductible mortgage interest (see instructions) | **10** | | 3,229 | | |
| 11 | Real estate taxes (see instructions) . . . . | **11** | | 289 | | |
| 12 | Add lines 9, 10, and 11 . . . . . . . | **12** | | 3,518 | | |
| 13 | Multiply line 12, column (b) by line 7 . . . . | | **13** | 318 | | |
| 14 | Add line 12, column (a) and line 13 . . . . | | | | **14** | 318 |
| 15 | Subtract line 14 from line 8. If zero or less, enter -0- | | | | **15** | 46,392 |
| 16 | Excess mortgage interest (see instructions) . | **16** | | | | |
| 17 | Insurance . . . . . . . . . . . | **17** | | 2,566 | | |
| 18 | Rent . . . . . . . . . . . . . | **18** | | | | |
| 19 | Repairs and maintenance . . . . . . . | **19** | 450 | | | |
| 20 | Utilities . . . . . . . . . . . . | **20** | 312 | 2,112 | | |
| 21 | Other expenses (see instructions). . . . . | **21** | | | | |
| 22 | Add lines 16 through 21 . . . . . . . . | **22** | 762 | 4,678 | | |
| 23 | Multiply line 22, column (b) by line 7 . . . . . . . . . . | | **23** | 423 | | |
| 24 | Carryover of operating expenses from 2010 Form 8829, line 42 . . | | **24** | | | |
| 25 | Add line 22 column (a), line 23, and line 24. . . . . . . . . . . . | | | | **25** | 1,185 |
| 26 | Allowable operating expenses. Enter the **smaller** of line 15 or line 25 . . . . . . . | | | | **26** | 1,185 |
| 27 | Limit on excess casualty losses and depreciation. Subtract line 26 from line 15 . . . . . | | | | **27** | 45,207 |
| 28 | Excess casualty losses (see instructions) . . . . . . . . . . | | **28** | | | |
| 29 | Depreciation of your home from line 41 below . . . . . . . | | **29** | | | |
| 30 | Carryover of excess casualty losses and depreciation from 2010 Form 8829, line 43 | | **30** | | | |
| 31 | Add lines 28 through 30 . . . . . . . . . . . . . . . . . | | | | **31** | |
| 32 | Allowable excess casualty losses and depreciation. Enter the **smaller** of line 27 or line 31 . . | | | | **32** | |
| 33 | Add lines 14, 26, and 32. . . . . . . . . . . . . . . . . . | | | | **33** | 1,503 |
| 34 | Casualty loss portion, if any, from lines 14 and 32. Carry amount to **Form 4684** (see instructions) | | | | **34** | |
| 35 | **Allowable expenses for business use of your home.** Subtract line 34 from line 33. Enter here and on Schedule C, line 30. If your home was used for more than one business, see instructions ▶ | | | | **35** | 1,503 |

### Part III   Depreciation of Your Home

| | | | |
|---|---|---|---:|
| 36 | Enter the **smaller** of your home's adjusted basis or its fair market value (see instructions) . . | **36** | |
| 37 | Value of land included on line 36 . . . . . . . . . . . . . . . . . . . | **37** | |
| 38 | Basis of building. Subtract line 37 from line 36 . . . . . . . . . . . . . . | **38** | |
| 39 | Business basis of building. Multiply line 38 by line 7. . . . . . . . . . . . . | **39** | |
| 40 | Depreciation percentage (see instructions). . . . . . . . . . . . . . . . | **40** | % |
| 41 | Depreciation allowable (see instructions). Multiply line 39 by line 40. Enter here and on line 29 above | **41** | |

### Part IV   Carryover of Unallowed Expenses to 2012

| | | | |
|---|---|---|---:|
| 42 | Operating expenses. Subtract line 26 from line 25. If less than zero, enter -0- . . . . . . | **42** | |
| 43 | Excess casualty losses and depreciation. Subtract line 32 from line 31. If less than zero, enter -0- | **43** | |

**For Paperwork Reduction Act Notice, see your tax return instructions.**

Cat. No. 13232M

Form **8829** (2011)

**CAUTION**

- To be a qualifying child for the child tax credit, the child must be your dependent, **under age 17** at the end of 2011, and meet all the conditions in Steps 1 through 3 in the instructions for line 6c.
- If you do not have a qualifying child, you cannot claim the child tax credit.
- **Do not** use this worksheet if you answered "Yes" to question 1 or 2 of *Who Must Use Pub. 972*, earlier. Instead, use Pub. 972

**Part 1**

1. Number of qualifying children: _____1_____ × $1,000.
   Enter the result.

   | 1 | 1,000 |

2. Enter the amount from Form 1040, line 38.

   | 2 | 43,098 |

3. Enter the amount shown below for your filing status.

   - Married filing jointly — $110,000
   - Single, head of household, or qualifying widow(er) — $75,000
   - Married filing separately — $55,000

   | 3 | 75,000 |

4. Is the amount on line 2 more than the amount on line 3?

   [X] **No.** Leave line 4 blank. Enter -0- on line 5, and go to line 6.

   [ ] **Yes.** Subtract line 3 from line 2.

   | 4 | |

   If the result is not a multiple of $1,000, increase it to the next multiple of $1,000. For example, increase $425 to $1,000, increase $1,025 to $2,000, etc.

5. Multiply the amount on line 4 by 5% (.05). Enter the result.

   | 5 | 0 |

6. Is the amount on line 1 more than the amount on line 5?

   [ ] **No.** [STOP]

   You cannot take the child tax credit on Form 1040, line 51. You also cannot take the additional child tax credit on Form 1040, line 65. Complete the rest of your Form 1040.

   [X] **Yes.** Subtract line 5 from line 1. Enter the result.
   *Go to Part 2.*

   | 6 | 1,000 |

***Before you begin Part 2:*** √ Figure the amount of any credits you are claiming on Form 5695, Part I; Form 8834, Part I; Form 8910; Form 8936; or Schedule R.

**Part 2**

7.  Enter the amount from Form 1040, line 46.

    **7** | 3,469

8.  Add any amounts from:

    Form 1040, line 47 _____

    Form 1040, line 48 + ___280___

    Form 1040, line 49 + _____

    Form 1040, line 50 + _____

    Form 5695, line 14 + _____

    Form 8834, line 23 + _____

    Form 8910, line 22 + _____

    Form 8936, line 15 + _____

    Schedule R, line 22 + _____

    Enter the total.   **8** | 280

9.  Are the amounts on lines 7 and 8 the same?

    ☐ **Yes.** |STOP|
    You cannot take this credit because there is no tax to reduce. However, you may be able to take the **additional child tax credit.** See the **TIP** below.

    ☒ **No.** Subtract line 8 from line 7.

    **9** | 3,189

10. Is the amount on line 6 more than the amount on line 9?

    ☐ **Yes.** Enter the amount from line 9.
    Also, you may be able to take the **additional child tax credit.** See the **TIP** below.   } **This is your child tax credit.**

    ☒ **No.** Enter the amount from line 6.

    **10** | 1,000

    Enter this amount on Form 1040, line 51.

    1040

    **TIP**
    You may be able to take the **additional child tax credit** on Form 1040, line 65, if you answered "Yes" on line 9 **or** line 10 above.

    • First, complete your Form 1040 through lines 64a and 64b.

    • Then, use Form 8812 to figure any additional child tax credit.

## 2012 Estimated Tax Worksheet

*Keep for Your Records*

| | | | |
|---|---|---|---|
| 1 | Adjusted gross income you expect in 2012 (see instructions) . . . . . . . . . . . | **1** | 53,096 |
| 2 | • If you plan to itemize deductions, enter the estimated total of your itemized deductions. } | | |
| | • If you do not plan to itemize deductions, enter your standard deduction. | **2** | 8,700 |
| 3 | Subtract line 2 from line 1. . . . . . . . . . . . . . . . . . . . . | **3** | 44,396 |
| 4 | Exemptions. Multiply $3,800 by the number of personal exemptions . . . . . . . . | **4** | 7,600 |
| 5 | Subtract line 4 from line 3. . . . . . . . . . . . . . . . . . . . . | **5** | 36,796 |
| 6 | **Tax.** Figure your tax on the amount on line 5 by using the **2012 Tax Rate Schedules.** **Caution:** *If you will have qualified dividends or a net capital gain, or expect to exclude or deduct foreign earned income or housing, see chapter 2 of Pub. 505 to figure the tax* . . . . . . . . | **6** | 4,896 |
| 7 | Alternative minimum tax from **Form 6251** . . . . . . . . . . . . . . . . | **7** | |
| 8 | Add lines 6 and 7. Add to this amount any other taxes you expect to include in the total on Form 1040, line 44 . . . . . . . . . . . . . . . . . . . . . . | **8** | 4,896 |
| 9 | Credits (see instructions). **Do not** include any income tax withholding on this line . . . . . . | **9** | |
| 10 | Subtract line 9 from line 8. If zero or less, enter -0- . . . . . . . . . . . . . | **10** | 4,896 |
| 11 | Self-employment tax (see instructions) . . . . . . . . . . . . . . . . . | **11** | 7,801 |
| 12 | Other taxes (see instructions) . . . . . . . . . . . . . . . . . . . . | **12** | |
| 13a | Add lines 10 through 12 . . . . . . . . . . . . . . . . . . . . . . | **13a** | 12,697 |
| b | Earned income credit, additional child tax credit, fuel tax credit, refundable American opportunity credit, and refundable credits from **Forms 8801** and **8885**. . . . . . . . . . ▶ | **13b** | |
| c | **Total 2012 estimated tax.** Subtract line 13b from line 13a. If zero or less, enter -0- . . . ▶ | **13c** | 12,697 |

| | | | | | |
|---|---|---|---|---|---|
| 14a | Multiply line 13c by 90% (66²/₃% for farmers and fishermen) . . . . | **14a** | 11,427 | | |
| b | Required annual payment based on prior year's tax (see instructions) . | **14b** | 7,742 | | |
| c | **Required annual payment to avoid a penalty.** Enter the **smaller** of line 14a or 14b . . . ▶ | | | **14c** | 7,742 |

**Caution:** *Generally, if you do not prepay (through income tax withholding and estimated tax payments) at least the amount on line 14c, you may owe a penalty for not paying enough estimated tax. To avoid a penalty, make sure your estimate on line 13c is as accurate as possible. Even if you pay the required annual payment, you may still owe tax when you file your return. If you prefer, you can pay the amount shown on line 13c. For details, see chapter 2 of Pub. 505.*

| | | | |
|---|---|---|---|
| 15 | Income tax withheld and estimated to be withheld during 2012 (including income tax withholding on pensions, annuities, certain deferred income, etc.) . . . . . . . . . . . . | **15** | |

| | | | | |
|---|---|---|---|---|
| 16a | Subtract line 15 from line 14c . . . . . . . . . . . . . | **16a** | 7,742 |
| | Is the result zero or less? | | |
| | ☐ **Yes.** Stop here. You are not required to make estimated tax payments. | | |
| | ☒ **No.** Go to line 16b. | | |
| b | Subtract line 15 from line 13c . . . . . . . . . . . . . | **16b** | 12,697 |
| | Is the result less than $1,000? | | |
| | ☐ **Yes.** Stop here. You are not required to make estimated tax payments. | | |
| | ☒ **No.** Go to line 17 to figure your required payment. | | |

| | | | |
|---|---|---|---|
| 17 | If the first payment you are required to make is due April 17, 2012, enter ¼ of line 16a (minus any 2011 overpayment that you are applying to this installment) here, and on your estimated tax payment voucher(s) if you are paying by check or money order. . . . . . . . . . . | **17** | 3,174 |

# Chapter 3 Review

1) What four requirements must property meet to be considered depreciable property?

- **It must be property the taxpayer owns.**
- **It must be used in the taxpayer's business or income-producing activity.**
- **It must have a determinable useful life.**
- **It must be expected to last more than one year.**

2) List three types of tangible property.

**Tangible property includes furniture, tools, and vehicles.**

3) List three types of intangible property.

**Intangible properties include insurance policies, stocks, and bonds.**

4) What method is used to depreciate most personal property? What about real property?

**The 200% Declining Balance method is used for most personal property.**
**The Straight Line method is used to depreciate real property.**

5) What information do you need to calculate prior depreciation?

**The type of property, basis of the property, and the date placed in service is needed to calculate prior depreciation.**

6) What requirements must property meet to qualify for the section 179 deduction?

- **It must be eligible property,**
- **It must be acquired for business use,**
- **It must have been acquired by purchase, and**
- **It must not be property that does not qualify.**

7) What is the special depreciation allowance for 2011 and when can it be taken?

**The taxpayer can take a special depreciation deduction allowance of 100% during 2011. The allowance is taken after any Section 179 deduction, and before the regular depreciation is calculated.**

8) What is listed property and when is it depreciated using the MACRS alternative depreciation system?

**Listed property is any of the following:**

- **Passenger automobiles weighing 6,000 pounds or less.**
- **Any other property used for transportation, unless it is an excepted vehicle.**
- **Property generally used for entertainment, recreation, or amusement (including photographic, communication, and video-recording equipment).**
- **Computers and related peripheral equipment, unless used only at a regular business establishment and owned or leased by the person operating the establishment. A regular business establishment includes a portion of a dwelling unit that is used both regularly and exclusively for business.**
- **Cellular telephones (or similar telecommunication equipment).**

**If the taxpayer is depreciating listed property and the business use of the property is 50% or less, the property must be depreciated using MACRS alternative depreciation system.**

# Chapter 3 Exercise #1

| Description of Property | Date Placed in Service | Cost or other Basis | Business/ Investment Use % | Business Basis (C x D) | Salvage/ Land Value | Section 179 Deduction or Bonus Depreciation | Depreciation Basis [E – (F + G)] | Method/ Convention | Recovery Period | Prior Depreciation | Depreciation Percentage | Depreciation Deduction (K x L) |
|---|---|---|---|---|---|---|---|---|---|---|---|---|
| A | B | C | D | E | F | G | H | I | J | K | L | M |
| Rental House | 10/2002 | 27,500 | 100% | 27,500 | 10,000 | | 17,500 | SL/MM | 27.5yrs | 5,221 | 3.636% | 636 |
| Computer | 07/05/09 | 1,309 | 100% | 1,309 | | | 1,309 | 200DB/HY | 5yrs | 681 | 19.20% | 251 |
| Copy Machine | 08/07/11 | 599 | 100% | 599 | | | 599 | 200DB/HY | 5 yrs | | 20.00% | 120 |
| Heavy Truck | 08/19/10 | 17,289 | 100% | 17,289 | | | 17,289 | 200DB/HY | 5 yrs | 3,458 | 32.00% | 5,532 |
| Sofa | 06/23/07 | 921 | 100% | 921 | | | 921 | 200DB/HY | 5 yrs | 762 | 11.52% | 106 |
| Refrigerator | 02/03/10 | 1,126 | 100% | 1,126 | | | 1,126 | 200DB/HY | 5 yrs | 225 | 32.00% | 360 |

| Description of Property | Date Placed in Service | Cost or other Basis | Business/ Investment Use % | Business Basis (C x D) | Salvage/ Land Value | Section 179 Deduction or Bonus Depreciation | Depreciation Basis [E – (F + G)] | Method/ Convention | Recovery Period | Prior Depreciation | Depreciation Percentage | Depreciation Deduction (H x L) |
|---|---|---|---|---|---|---|---|---|---|---|---|---|
| A | B | C | D | E | F | G | H | I | J | K | L | M |
| Desk | 06/03/08 | 565 | 100 | 565 | | | 565 | 200%DB/HY | 7years | 318 | 12.49 | 71 |
| Bookshelf | 05/07/06 | 123 | 100 | 123 | | | 123 | 200%DB/HY | 7years | 96 | 8.92 | 11 |
| Filing Cabinet | 05/05/10 | 234 | 100 | 234 | | | 234 | 200%DB/HY | 7years | 33 | 24.49 | 57 |
| Shelves | 05/07/06 | 156 | 100 | 156 | | | 156 | 200%DB/HY | 7years | 120 | 8.92 | 14 |
| Desk | 08/21/07 | 723 | 100 | 723 | | | 723 | 200%DB/HY | 7years | 496 | 8.93 | 65 |
| Office Building | 05/07/06 | 89,633 | 100 | 89,633 | 13,500 | | 76,133 | SL/ MM | 39years | 9,030 | 2.564 | 1,952 |
| | | | | | | | | | | | | |
| | | | | | | | | | | | | |
| | | | | | | | | | | | | |
| | | | | | | | | | | | | |
| | | | | | | | | | | | | |

# Chapter 4 Review

1) What is the difference between realized gains and losses, and recognized gains and losses?

   **The realized gain or loss is the amount realized from the sale or exchange of property compared with the adjusted basis of that property.**
   **The recognized gain or loss is the amount of gain or loss that is actually reported on the tax return.**

2) List two examples of transactions that are subject to section 1231 treatment?

   **The following transactions are subject to section 1231 treatment:**

   - **Sales or exchanges of real property or depreciable personal property used in a trade or business and held for longer than one year. Generally, property held for the production of rents or royalties is considered to be used in a trade or business.**
   - **Sales or exchanges of leaseholds used in a trade or business and held longer than one year.**
   - **Sales or exchanges of cattle and horses held for draft, breeding, dairy, or sporting purposes held for two years or longer.**
   - **Sales or exchanges of other livestock (not including poultry) held for draft, breeding, dairy, or sporting purposes and held for one year or longer.**
   - **Sales or exchanges of unharvested crops. The crop and land must be sold, exchanged, or involuntarily converted at the same time and to the same person and the land must be held longer than one year.**
   - **Cutting of timber or disposal of timber, coal, or iron ore treated as a sale.**
   - **Condemnations of a business property or a capital asset held in connection with a trade or business or a transaction entered into for profit held longer than one year.**
   - **Casualties and thefts that affected business property, property held for the production of rents and royalties, or investment property held longer than one year.**

3) What is all real property subject to an allowance for depreciation that is not, and never has been, section 1245 property?

   **Section 1250 property is any depreciable real property other than section 1245 property.**

4) What is reported on Form 4797? How many parts are there on the form?

**Form 4797 is used to report the sale of business assets. It has four parts.**

5) How do you determine the amount of excess section 179 deduction that must be recaptured?

**To determine the amount of excess section 179 deduction that must be recaptured, calculate what the allowable depreciation deduction would have been on the section 179 amount, including the current year, and deduct it from the section 179 deduction. For the following years, add the section 179 deduction back to the depreciable basis to calculate the depreciation deduction for the property.**

6) Give three examples of section 280F property.

**Section 280F property includes items such as automobiles, computers, cellular telephones, and property generally used for purposes of entertainment and amusement.**

7) What do you do to the basis, if property that was subject to recapture is sold?

**To determine the basis of the property, first deduct all of the depreciation deductions allowed or allowable, then deduct any section 179 deductions claimed. Add any section 179 or section 280F recapture amounts to arrive at the adjusted basis. This is done to ensure the basis is reduced only by the deductions from which the taxpayer benefitted.**

# Form 1040

Department of the Treasury—Internal Revenue Service (99)

## U.S. Individual Income Tax Return  2011

OMB No. 1545-0074 | IRS Use Only—Do not write or staple in this space.

For the year Jan. 1–Dec. 31, 2011, or other tax year beginning ____ , 2011, ending ____ , 20 ____

See separate instructions.

| Your first name and initial | Last name | Your social security number |
|---|---|---|
| GEORGE | GASLOW | 5 6 4 5 5 9 8 5 5 |

| If a joint return, spouse's first name and initial | Last name | Spouse's social security number |
|---|---|---|

Home address (number and street). If you have a P.O. box, see instructions.  Apt. no.

455 OAK DRIVE

▲ Make sure the SSN(s) above and on line 6c are correct.

City, town or post office, state, and ZIP code. If you have a foreign address, also complete spaces below (see instructions).

YOUR CITY, YOUR STATE, YOUR ZIP CODE

**Presidential Election Campaign**
Check here if you, or your spouse if filing jointly, want $3 to go to this fund. Checking a box below will not change your tax or refund. ☐ You ☐ Spouse

| Foreign country name | Foreign province/county | Foreign postal code |
|---|---|---|

## Filing Status

Check only one box.

1 ☑ Single
2 ☐ Married filing jointly (even if only one had income)
3 ☐ Married filing separately. Enter spouse's SSN above and full name here. ▶
4 ☐ Head of household (with qualifying person). (See instructions.) If the qualifying person is a child but not your dependent, enter this child's name here. ▶
5 ☐ Qualifying widow(er) with dependent child

## Exemptions

6a ☑ Yourself. If someone can claim you as a dependent, **do not** check box 6a . . . . . .
b ☐ Spouse . . . . . . . . . . . . . . . . .
c Dependents:

| (1) First name   Last name | (2) Dependent's social security number | (3) Dependent's relationship to you | (4) ✓ if child under age 17 qualifying for child tax credit (see instructions) |
|---|---|---|---|
| | | | ☐ |
| | | | ☐ |
| | | | ☐ |
| | | | ☐ |

If more than four dependents, see instructions and check here ▶ ☐

d Total number of exemptions claimed

Boxes checked on 6a and 6b: **1**
No. of children on 6c who:
• lived with you: **0**
• did not live with you due to divorce or separation (see instructions): **0**
Dependents on 6c not entered above: **0**
Add numbers on lines above ▶ **1**

## Income

Attach Form(s) W-2 here. Also attach Forms W-2G and 1099-R if tax was withheld.

If you did not get a W-2, see instructions.

Enclose, but do not attach, any payment. Also, please use Form 1040-V.

| | | |
|---|---|---|
| 7 | Wages, salaries, tips, etc. Attach Form(s) W-2 | 7 |
| 8a | **Taxable** interest. Attach Schedule B if required | 8a |
| b | **Tax-exempt** interest. **Do not** include on line 8a  [8b] | |
| 9a | Ordinary dividends. Attach Schedule B if required | 9a |
| b | Qualified dividends  [9b] | |
| 10 | Taxable refunds, credits, or offsets of state and local income taxes | 10 |
| 11 | Alimony received | 11 |
| 12 | Business income or (loss). Attach Schedule C or C-EZ | 12  60,871 |
| 13 | Capital gain or (loss). Attach Schedule D if required. If not required, check here ▶ ☐ | 13  54,191 |
| 14 | Other gains or (losses). Attach Form 4797 | 14  44,567 |
| 15a | IRA distributions  [15a]  b Taxable amount | 15b |
| 16a | Pensions and annuities  [16a]  b Taxable amount | 16b |
| 17 | Rental real estate, royalties, partnerships, S corporations, trusts, etc. Attach Schedule E | 17 |
| 18 | Farm income or (loss). Attach Schedule F | 18 |
| 19 | Unemployment compensation | 19 |
| 20a | Social security benefits  [20a]  b Taxable amount | 20b |
| 21 | Other income. List type and amount | 21 |
| 22 | Combine the amounts in the far right column for lines 7 through 21. This is your **total income** ▶ | 22  159,629 |

## Adjusted Gross Income

| | | | |
|---|---|---|---|
| 23 | Educator expenses | 23 | |
| 24 | Certain business expenses of reservists, performing artists, and fee-basis government officials. Attach Form 2106 or 2106-EZ | 24 | |
| 25 | Health savings account deduction. Attach Form 8889 | 25 | |
| 26 | Moving expenses. Attach Form 3903 | 26 | |
| 27 | Deductible part of self-employment tax. Attach Schedule SE | 27 | 4,299 |
| 28 | Self-employed SEP, SIMPLE, and qualified plans | 28 | |
| 29 | Self-employed health insurance deduction | 29 | |
| 30 | Penalty on early withdrawal of savings | 30 | |
| 31a | Alimony paid  b Recipient's SSN ▶ | 31a | |
| 32 | IRA deduction | 32 | |
| 33 | Student loan interest deduction | 33 | |
| 34 | Tuition and fees. Attach Form 8917 | 34 | |
| 35 | Domestic production activities deduction. Attach Form 8903 | 35 | |
| 36 | Add lines 23 through 35 | 36 | 4,299 |
| 37 | Subtract line 36 from line 22. This is your **adjusted gross income** ▶ | 37 | 155,330 |

**For Disclosure, Privacy Act, and Paperwork Reduction Act Notice, see separate instructions.**  Cat. No. 11320B  Form **1040** (2011)

**Tax and Credits**

| | | | | |
|---|---|---|---|---|
| 38 | Amount from line 37 (adjusted gross income) | 38 | 155,330 |
| 39a | Check if: ☐ **You** were born before January 2, 1947, ☐ Blind. ☐ **Spouse** was born before January 2, 1947, ☐ Blind. } Total boxes checked ▶ 39a | | |
| **Standard Deduction for—** b | If your spouse itemizes on a separate return or you were a dual-status alien, check here ▶ 39b ☐ | | |
| • People who check any box on line 39a or 39b **or** who can be claimed as a dependent, see instructions. 40 | **Itemized deductions** (from Schedule A) **or** your **standard deduction** (see left margin) | 40 | 5,800 |
| 41 | Subtract line 40 from line 38 | 41 | 149,530 |
| 42 | **Exemptions.** Multiply $3,700 by the number on line 6d. | 42 | 3,700 |
| 43 | **Taxable income.** Subtract line 42 from line 41. If line 42 is more than line 41, enter -0- | 43 | 145,830 |
| • All others: Single or Married filing separately, $5,800 44 | **Tax** (see instructions). Check if any from: **a** ☐ Form(s) 8814 **b** ☐ Form 4972 **c** ☐ 962 election | 44 | 29,775 |
| 45 | **Alternative minimum tax** (see instructions). Attach Form 6251 | 45 | |
| Married filing jointly or Qualifying widow(er), $11,600 46 | Add lines 44 and 45 ▶ | 46 | 29,775 |
| 47 | Foreign tax credit. Attach Form 1116 if required . . . . 47 | | |
| 48 | Credit for child and dependent care expenses. Attach Form 2441 48 | | |
| 49 | Education credits from Form 8863, line 23 . . . . 49 | | |
| Head of household, $8,500 50 | Retirement savings contributions credit. Attach Form 8880 50 | | |
| 51 | Child tax credit (see instructions) . . . . . . 51 | | |
| 52 | Residential energy credits. Attach Form 5695 . . . 52 | | |
| 53 | Other credits from Form: **a** ☐ 3800 **b** ☐ 8801 **c** ☐ 53 | | |
| 54 | Add lines 47 through 53. These are your **total credits** | 54 | |
| 55 | Subtract line 54 from line 46. If line 54 is more than line 46, enter -0- ▶ | 55 | 29,775 |

**Other Taxes**

| | | | | |
|---|---|---|---|---|
| 56 | Self-employment tax. Attach Schedule SE | 56 | 7,476 |
| 57 | Unreported social security and Medicare tax from Form: **a** ☐ 4137 **b** ☐ 8919 | 57 | |
| 58 | Additional tax on IRAs, other qualified retirement plans, etc. Attach Form 5329 if required | 58 | |
| 59a | Household employment taxes from Schedule H | 59a | |
| b | First-time homebuyer credit repayment. Attach Form 5405 if required | 59b | |
| 60 | Other taxes. Enter code(s) from instructions | 60 | |
| 61 | Add lines 55 through 60. This is your **total tax** ▶ | 61 | 37,251 |

**Payments**

If you have a qualifying child, attach Schedule EIC.

| | | | | |
|---|---|---|---|---|
| 62 | Federal income tax withheld from Forms W-2 and 1099 . . 62 | | |
| 63 | 2011 estimated tax payments and amount applied from 2010 return 63 | 40,000 | |
| 64a | **Earned income credit (EIC)** . . . . . . 64a | | |
| b | Nontaxable combat pay election   64b | | |
| 65 | Additional child tax credit. Attach Form 8812 . . . . 65 | | |
| 66 | American opportunity credit from Form 8863, line 14 . . . 66 | | |
| 67 | First-time homebuyer credit from Form 5405, line 10 . . . 67 | | |
| 68 | Amount paid with request for extension to file . . . 68 | | |
| 69 | Excess social security and tier 1 RRTA tax withheld . . . 69 | | |
| 70 | Credit for federal tax on fuels. Attach Form 4136 . . . 70 | | |
| 71 | Credits from Form: **a** ☐ 2439 **b** ☐ 8839 **c** ☐ 8801 **d** ☐ 8885 71 | | |
| 72 | Add lines 62, 63, 64a, and 65 through 71. These are your **total payments** . . . . ▶ | 72 | 40,000 |

**Refund**

Direct deposit? See instructions.

| | | | | |
|---|---|---|---|---|
| 73 | If line 72 is more than line 61, subtract line 61 from line 72. This is the amount you **overpaid** | 73 | 2,749 |
| 74a | Amount of line 73 you want **refunded to you.** If Form 8888 is attached, check here . . ▶ ☐ | 74a | 2,749 |
| b | Routing number ☐☐☐☐☐☐☐☐☐ ▶ c Type: ☐ Checking ☐ Savings | | |
| d | Account number ☐☐☐☐☐☐☐☐☐☐☐☐☐☐☐☐☐ | | |
| 75 | Amount of line 73 you want **applied to your 2012 estimated tax** ▶ 75 | | |

**Amount You Owe**

| | | | | |
|---|---|---|---|---|
| 76 | **Amount you owe.** Subtract line 72 from line 61. For details on how to pay, see instructions ▶ | 76 | |
| 77 | Estimated tax penalty (see instructions) . . . . . . 77 | | |

**Third Party Designee**

Do you want to allow another person to discuss this return with the IRS (see instructions)? ☐ **Yes.** Complete below. ☐ **No**

| Designee's name ▶ | Phone no. ▶ | Personal identification number (PIN) ▶ ☐☐☐☐☐ |
|---|---|---|

**Sign Here**

Under penalties of perjury, I declare that I have examined this return and accompanying schedules and statements, and to the best of my knowledge and belief, they are true, correct, and complete. Declaration of preparer (other than taxpayer) is based on all information of which preparer has any knowledge.

Joint return? See instructions. Keep a copy for your records.

| Your signature | Date | Your occupation SELF EMPLOYED | Daytime phone number |
|---|---|---|---|
| Spouse's signature. If a joint return, **both** must sign. | Date | Spouse's occupation | If the IRS sent you an Identity Protection PIN, enter it here (see inst.) ☐☐☐☐☐☐ |

**Paid Preparer Use Only**

| Print/Type preparer's name JANE DOE | Preparer's signature | Date | Check ☐ if self-employed | PTIN P00000000 |
|---|---|---|---|---|
| Firm's name ▶ MY TAX SERVICE | | | Firm's EIN ▶ | 63-0000000 |
| Firm's address ▶ 100 MAIN ST., YOUR CITY, YOUR STATE, YOUR ZIP CODE | | Phone no. | | (555)555-5555 |

Form **1040** (2011)

# SCHEDULE C
## (Form 1040)

Department of the Treasury
Internal Revenue Service (99)

# Profit or Loss From Business
### (Sole Proprietorship)

▶ **For information on Schedule C and its instructions, go to** *www.irs.gov/schedulec*
▶ Attach to Form 1040, 1040NR, or 1041; partnerships generally must file Form 1065.

OMB No. 1545-0074

**2011**

Attachment
Sequence No. **09**

| | |
|---|---|
| Name of proprietor **GEORGE GASLOW** | Social security number (SSN) **564-55-9855** |

**A** Principal business or profession, including product or service (see instructions)
**AUTOMOTIVE REPAIR**

**B** Enter code from instructions ▶ 8 1 1 1 1 0

**C** Business name. If no separate business name, leave blank.
**GEORGE'S AUTOMOTIVE**

**D** Employer ID number (EIN), (see instr.)

**E** Business address (including suite or room no.) ▶ 453 MAGNOLIA DRIVE
City, town or post office, state, and ZIP code    YOUR CITY, YOUR STATE, YOUR ZIP CODE

**F** Accounting method:   (1) ✔ Cash   (2) ☐ Accrual   (3) ☐ Other (specify) ▶

**G** Did you "materially participate" in the operation of this business during 2011? If "No," see instructions for limit on losses .   ✔ Yes  ☐ No

**H** If you started or acquired this business during 2011, check here   .   .   .   .   .   .   .   .   . ▶ ☐

**I** Did you make any payments in 2011 that would require you to file Form(s) 1099? (see instructions) .   .   .   .   .   .   .   ☐ Yes  ✔ No

**J** If "Yes," did you or will you file all required Forms 1099? .   .   .   .   .   .   .   .   .   .   .   .   .   . ☐ Yes  ☐ No

## Part I   Income

| | | | |
|---|---|---|---|
| **1a** Merchant card and third party payments. For 2011, enter -0- . . . | 1a | | |
| **b** Gross receipts or sales not entered on line 1a (see instructions) . . | 1b | 96,234 | |
| **c** Income reported to you on Form W-2 if the "Statutory Employee" box on that form was checked. **Caution.** See instr. before completing this line | 1c | | |
| **d** **Total gross receipts.** Add lines 1a through 1c . . . . . . . . . . . . . . . | 1d | 96,234 |
| **2** Returns and allowances plus any other adjustments (see instructions) . . . . . . . . . | 2 | |
| **3** Subtract line 2 from line 1d . . . . . . . . . . . . . . . . . . . . | 3 | 96,234 |
| **4** Cost of goods sold (from line 42) . . . . . . . . . . . . . . . . . | 4 | |
| **5** **Gross profit.** Subtract line 4 from line 3 . . . . . . . . . . . . . . . . | 5 | 96,234 |
| **6** Other income, including federal and state gasoline or fuel tax credit or refund (see instructions) . . . . | 6 | 1,069 |
| **7** **Gross income.** Add lines 5 and 6 . . . . . . . . . . . . . . . . . ▶ | 7 | 97,303 |

## Part II   Expenses      Enter expenses for business use of your home only on line 30.

| | | | | | | |
|---|---|---|---|---|---|---|
| **8** Advertising . . . . . | 8 | 856 | **18** Office expense (see instructions) | 18 | 433 |
| **9** Car and truck expenses (see instructions). . . . . | 9 | | **19** Pension and profit-sharing plans . | 19 | |
| **10** Commissions and fees . | 10 | | **20** Rent or lease (see instructions): | | |
| **11** Contract labor (see instructions) | 11 | | **a** Vehicles, machinery, and equipment | 20a | |
| **12** Depletion . . . . . | 12 | | **b** Other business property . . . | 20b | |
| **13** Depreciation and section 179 expense deduction (not included in Part III) (see instructions). . . . . | 13 | 6,088 | **21** Repairs and maintenance . . . | 21 | |
| | | | **22** Supplies (not included in Part III) . | 22 | 23,499 |
| | | | **23** Taxes and licenses . . . . . | 23 | 1,135 |
| | | | **24** Travel, meals, and entertainment: | | |
| **14** Employee benefit programs (other than on line 19) . . | 14 | | **a** Travel . . . . . . . . . | 24a | |
| **15** Insurance (other than health) | 15 | 3,522 | **b** Deductible meals and entertainment (see instructions) . | 24b | |
| **16** Interest: | | | **25** Utilities . . . . . . . . | 25 | |
| **a** Mortgage (paid to banks, etc.) | 16a | | **26** Wages (less employment credits) . | 26 | |
| **b** Other . . . . . . | 16b | | **27a** Other expenses (from line 48) . . | 27a | |
| **17** Legal and professional services | 17 | 899 | **b** Reserved for future use . . . | 27b | |

| | | |
|---|---|---|
| **28** **Total expenses** before expenses for business use of home. Add lines 8 through 27a . . . . . . ▶ | 28 | 36,432 |
| **29** Tentative profit or (loss). Subtract line 28 from line 7 . . . . . . . . . . . . . . . . | 29 | 60,871 |
| **30** Expenses for business use of your home. Attach **Form 8829.** Do **not** report such expenses elsewhere . . | 30 | |
| **31** **Net profit or (loss).** Subtract line 30 from line 29. | | |

• If a profit, enter on both **Form 1040, line 12** (or **Form 1040NR, line 13**) and on **Schedule SE, line 2.**
If you entered an amount on line 1c, see instr. Estates and trusts, enter on **Form 1041, line 3.**

• If a loss, you **must** go to line 32.

| | |
|---|---|
| 31 | 60,871 |

**32** If you have a loss, check the box that describes your investment in this activity (see instructions).

• If you checked 32a, enter the loss on both **Form 1040, line 12,** (or **Form 1040NR, line 13**) and on **Schedule SE, line 2.** If you entered an amount on line 1c, see the instructions for line 31. Estates and trusts, enter on **Form 1041, line 3.**

• If you checked 32b, you **must** attach **Form 6198.** Your loss may be limited.

**32a** ☐ All investment is at risk.
**32b** ☐ Some investment is not at risk.

**For Paperwork Reduction Act Notice, see your tax return instructions.**     Cat. No. 11334P     Schedule C (Form 1040) 2011

| SCHEDULE D (Form 1040) | Capital Gains and Losses | OMB No. 1545-0074 |
|---|---|---|

**Capital Gains and Losses**

Department of the Treasury
Internal Revenue Service (99)

► Attach to Form 1040 or Form 1040NR. ► See Instructions for Schedule D (Form 1040).
► Use Form 8949 to list your transactions for lines 1, 2, 3, 8, 9, and 10.

**2011**

Attachment Sequence No. **12**

Name(s) shown on return

GEORGE GASLOW

Your social security number

564-55-9855

## Part I — Short-Term Capital Gains and Losses—Assets Held One Year or Less

Complete Form 8949 before completing line 1, 2, or 3.

This form may be easier to complete if you round off cents to whole dollars.

| | | **(e)** Sales price from Form(s) 8949, line 2, column (e) | **(f)** Cost or other basis from Form(s) 8949, line 2, column (f) | **(g)** Adjustments to gain or loss from Form(s) 8949, line 2, column (g) | **(h)** Gain or (loss) Combine columns (e), (f), and (g) |
|---|---|---|---|---|---|
| 1 | Short-term totals from all Forms 8949 with **box A** checked in **Part I** . . . . . . . . . . . . | | ( ) | | |
| 2 | Short-term totals from all Forms 8949 with **box B** checked in **Part I** . . . . . . . . . . . . | | ( ) | | |
| 3 | Short-term totals from all Forms 8949 with **box C** checked in **Part I** . . . . . . . . . . . . | | ( ) | | |

| | | | |
|---|---|---|---|
| 4 | Short-term gain from Form 6252 and short-term gain or (loss) from Forms 4684, 6781, and 8824 . | **4** | |
| 5 | Net short-term gain or (loss) from partnerships, S corporations, estates, and trusts from Schedule(s) K-1 . . . . . . . . . . . . . . . . . | **5** | |
| 6 | Short-term capital loss carryover. Enter the amount, if any, from line 8 of your **Capital Loss Carryover Worksheet** in the instructions . . . . . . . . . . . . . . . | **6** | ( ) |
| 7 | **Net short-term capital gain or (loss).** Combine lines 1 through 6 in column (h). If you have any long-term capital gains or losses, go to Part II below. Otherwise, go to Part III on the back . . . | **7** | |

## Part II — Long-Term Capital Gains and Losses—Assets Held More Than One Year

Complete Form 8949 before completing line 8, 9, or 10.

This form may be easier to complete if you round off cents to whole dollars.

| | | **(e)** Sales price from Form(s) 8949, line 4, column (e) | **(f)** Cost or other basis from Form(s) 8949, line 4, column (f) | **(g)** Adjustments to gain or loss from Form(s) 8949, line 4, column (g) | **(h)** Gain or (loss) Combine columns (e), (f), and (g) |
|---|---|---|---|---|---|
| 8 | Long-term totals from all Forms 8949 with **box A** checked in **Part II** . . . . . . . . . . | | ( ) | | |
| 9 | Long-term totals from all Forms 8949 with **box B** checked in **Part II** . . . . . . . . . . | | ( ) | | |
| 10 | Long-term totals from all Forms 8949 with **box C** checked in **Part II** . . . . . . . . . . | | ( ) | | |

| | | | |
|---|---|---|---|
| 11 | Gain from Form 4797, Part I; long-term gain from Forms 2439 and 6252; and long-term gain or (loss) from Forms 4684, 6781, and 8824 . . . . . . . . . . . . . . . . . | **11** | 54,191 |
| 12 | Net long-term gain or (loss) from partnerships, S corporations, estates, and trusts from Schedule(s) K-1 | **12** | |
| 13 | Capital gain distributions. See the instructions . . . . . . . . . . . . . . | **13** | |
| 14 | Long-term capital loss carryover. Enter the amount, if any, from line 13 of your **Capital Loss Carryover Worksheet** in the instructions . . . . . . . . . . . . . . . | **14** | ( ) |
| 15 | **Net long-term capital gain or (loss).** Combine lines 8 through 14 in column (h). Then go to Part III on the back . . . . . . . . . . . . . . . . . . . . . . | **15** | 54,191 |

For Paperwork Reduction Act Notice, see your tax return instructions.      Cat. No. 11338H      Schedule D (Form 1040) 2011

**Part III**   **Summary**

| | | | |
|---|---|---|---|
| **16** | Combine lines 7 and 15 and enter the result   . . . . . . . . . . . . . . | **16** | 54,191 |

    • If line 16 is a **gain**, enter the amount from line 16 on Form 1040, line 13, or Form 1040NR, line 14. Then go to line 17 below.

    • If line 16 is a **loss**, skip lines 17 through 20 below. Then go to line 21. Also be sure to complete line 22.

    • If line 16 is **zero**, skip lines 17 through 21 below and enter -0- on Form 1040, line 13, or Form 1040NR, line 14. Then go to line 22.

**17**  Are lines 15 and 16 **both** gains?
    ☑ **Yes.** Go to line 18.
    ☐ **No.** Skip lines 18 through 21, and go to line 22.

| | | | |
|---|---|---|---|
| **18** | Enter the amount, if any, from line 7 of the **28% Rate Gain Worksheet** in the instructions  . . ► | **18** | |
| **19** | Enter the amount, if any, from line 18 of the **Unrecaptured Section 1250 Gain Worksheet** in the instructions  . . . . . . . . . . . . . . . . . . . . . . . . . ► | **19** | 23,743 |

**20**  Are lines 18 and 19 **both** zero or blank?
    ☐ **Yes.** Complete Form 1040 through line 43, or Form 1040NR through line 41. Then complete the **Qualified Dividends and Capital Gain Tax Worksheet** in the instructions for Form 1040, line 44 (or in the instructions for Form 1040NR, line 42). **Do not** complete lines 21 and 22 below.

    ☑ **No.** Complete Form 1040 through line 43, or Form 1040NR through line 41. Then complete the **Schedule D Tax Worksheet** in the instructions. **Do not** complete lines 21 and 22 below.

**21**  If line 16 is a loss, enter here and on Form 1040, line 13, or Form 1040NR, line 14, the **smaller** of:

    • The loss on line 16 or
    • ($3,000), or if married filing separately, ($1,500)   . . . . . . . . . . . . . . 

| | |
|---|---|
| **21** ( | ) |

    **Note.**  When figuring which amount is smaller, treat both amounts as positive numbers.

**22**  Do you have qualified dividends on Form 1040, line 9b, or Form 1040NR, line 10b?

    ☐ **Yes.** Complete Form 1040 through line 43, or Form 1040NR through line 41. Then complete the **Qualified Dividends and Capital Gain Tax Worksheet** in the instructions for Form 1040, line 44 (or in the instructions for Form 1040NR, line 42).
    ☐ **No.** Complete the rest of Form 1040 or Form 1040NR.

## SCHEDULE SE
### (Form 1040)

Department of the Treasury
Internal Revenue Service (99)

# Self-Employment Tax

▶ **Attach to Form 1040 or Form 1040NR.**     ▶ **See separate instructions.**

**2011**

Attachment
Sequence No. **17**

| Name of person with **self-employment** income (as shown on Form 1040) | Social security number of person with **self-employment** income ▶ |
|---|---|
| GEORGE GASLOW | 564-55-9855 |

**Before you begin:** To determine if you must file Schedule SE, see the instructions.

## May I Use Short Schedule SE or Must I Use Long Schedule SE?

**Note.** Use this flowchart **only if** you must file Schedule SE. If unsure, see *Who Must File Schedule SE* in the instructions.

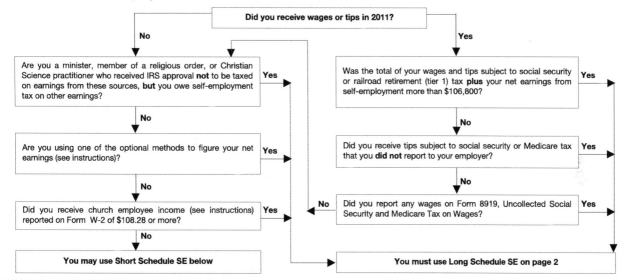

**Section A—Short Schedule SE. Caution.** Read above to see if you can use Short Schedule SE.

| | | | |
|---|---|---|---|
| **1a** | Net farm profit or (loss) from Schedule F, line 34, and farm partnerships, Schedule K-1 (Form 1065), box 14, code A . . . . . . . . . . . . . . . . . . . | **1a** | |
| **b** | If you received social security retirement or disability benefits, enter the amount of Conservation Reserve Program payments included on Schedule F, line 4b, or listed on Schedule K-1 (Form 1065), box 20, code Y | **1b** ( | ) |
| **2** | Net profit or (loss) from Schedule C, line 31; Schedule C-EZ, line 3; Schedule K-1 (Form 1065), box 14, code A (other than farming); and Schedule K-1 (Form 1065-B), box 9, code J1. Ministers and members of religious orders, see instructions for types of income to report on this line. See instructions for other income to report . . . . . . . . . . . . . . . | **2** | 60,871 |
| **3** | Combine lines 1a, 1b, and 2 . . . . . . . . . . . . . . . . . . . | **3** | 60,871 |
| **4** | Multiply line 3 by 92.35% (.9235). If less than $400, you do not owe self-employment tax; **do not** file this schedule unless you have an amount on line 1b . . . . . . . . . . . ▶ | **4** | 56,214 |
| | **Note.** If line 4 is less than $400 due to Conservation Reserve Program payments on line 1b, see instructions. | | |
| **5** | **Self-employment tax.** If the amount on line 4 is: <br> • $106,800 or less, multiply line 4 by 13.3% (.133). Enter the result here and on **Form 1040, line 56,** or **Form 1040NR, line 54** <br> • More than $106,800, multiply line 4 by 2.9% (.029). Then, add $11,107.20 to the result. Enter the total here and on **Form 1040, line 56,** or **Form 1040NR, line 54** . . . . . . . . | **5** | 7,476 |
| **6** | **Deduction for employer-equivalent portion of self-employment tax.** If the amount on line 5 is: <br> • $14,204.40 or less, multiply line 5 by 57.51% (.5751) <br> • More than $14,204.40, multiply line 5 by 50% (.50) and add $1,067 to the result. Enter the result here and on **Form 1040, line 27,** or **Form 1040NR, line 27** . . . . . . . . . . . | **6** | 4,299 |

**For Paperwork Reduction Act Notice, see your tax return instructions.**     Cat. No. 11358Z     **Schedule SE (Form 1040) 2011**

D-27

Form **4797**

Department of the Treasury
Internal Revenue Service (99)

## Sales of Business Property
**(Also Involuntary Conversions and Recapture Amounts Under Sections 179 and 280F(b)(2))**

▶ Attach to your tax return.　　▶ See separate instructions.

OMB No. 1545-0184

20**11**

Attachment
Sequence No. **27**

| Name(s) shown on return | Identifying number |
|---|---|
| GEORGE GASLOW | 564-55-9855 |

**1** Enter the gross proceeds from sales or exchanges reported to you for 2011 on Form(s) 1099-B or 1099-S (or substitute statement) that you are including on line 2, 10, or 20 (see instructions) . . . . . . . . | **1** |

### Part I — Sales or Exchanges of Property Used in a Trade or Business and Involuntary Conversions From Other Than Casualty or Theft—Most Property Held More Than 1 Year (see instructions)

| **2** | (a) Description of property | (b) Date acquired (mo., day, yr.) | (c) Date sold (mo., day, yr.) | (d) Gross sales price | (e) Depreciation allowed or allowable since acquisition | (f) Cost or other basis, plus improvements and expense of sale | (g) Gain or (loss) Subtract (f) from the sum of (d) and (e) |
|---|---|---|---|---|---|---|---|
| | LAND | 02/05/2001 | 07/05/2011 | 11,926 | | 9,612 | 2,314 |
| | | | | | | | |
| | | | | | | | |
| | | | | | | | |

| | | |
|---|---|---|
| **3** Gain, if any, from Form 4684, line 39 . . . . . . . . . . . . . . . . . . | **3** | |
| **4** Section 1231 gain from installment sales from Form 6252, line 26 or 37 . . . . . . . . . . | **4** | |
| **5** Section 1231 gain or (loss) from like-kind exchanges from Form 8824 . . . . . . . . . . | **5** | |
| **6** Gain, if any, from line 32, from other than casualty or theft. . . . . . . . . . . . | **6** | 51,877 |
| **7** Combine lines 2 through 6. Enter the gain or (loss) here and on the appropriate line as follows: . . . . . . | **7** | 54,191 |

**Partnerships (except electing large partnerships) and S corporations.** Report the gain or (loss) following the instructions for Form 1065, Schedule K, line 10, or Form 1120S, Schedule K, line 9. Skip lines 8, 9, 11, and 12 below.

**Individuals, partners, S corporation shareholders, and all others.** If line 7 is zero or a loss, enter the amount from line 7 on line 11 below and skip lines 8 and 9. If line 7 is a gain and you did not have any prior year section 1231 losses, or they were recaptured in an earlier year, enter the gain from line 7 as a long-term capital gain on the Schedule D filed with your return and skip lines 8, 9, 11, and 12 below.

| | | |
|---|---|---|
| **8** Nonrecaptured net section 1231 losses from prior years (see instructions) . . . . . . . . . | **8** | |
| **9** Subtract line 8 from line 7. If zero or less, enter -0-. If line 9 is zero, enter the gain from line 7 on line 12 below. If line 9 is more than zero, enter the amount from line 8 on line 12 below and enter the gain from line 9 as a long-term capital gain on the Schedule D filed with your return (see instructions) . . . . . . . . . . . . . . . | **9** | |

### Part II — Ordinary Gains and Losses (see instructions)

**10** Ordinary gains and losses not included on lines 11 through 16 (include property held 1 year or less):

| | | | | | | |
|---|---|---|---|---|---|---|
| | | | | | | |
| | | | | | | |
| | | | | | | |
| | | | | | | |

| | | |
|---|---|---|
| **11** Loss, if any, from line 7 . . . . . . . . . . . . . . . . . . . . . | **11** ( ) |
| **12** Gain, if any, from line 7 or amount from line 8, if applicable . . . . . . . . . . . | **12** | |
| **13** Gain, if any, from line 31 . . . . . . . . . . . . . . . . . . . | **13** | 44,567 |
| **14** Net gain or (loss) from Form 4684, lines 31 and 38a . . . . . . . . . . . . | **14** | |
| **15** Ordinary gain from installment sales from Form 6252, line 25 or 36 . . . . . . . . . | **15** | |
| **16** Ordinary gain or (loss) from like-kind exchanges from Form 8824. . . . . . . . . . | **16** | |
| **17** Combine lines 10 through 16 . . . . . . . . . . . . . . . . . . . | **17** | 44,567 |

**18** For all except individual returns, enter the amount from line 17 on the appropriate line of your return and skip lines a and b below. For individual returns, complete lines a and b below:

**a** If the loss on line 11 includes a loss from Form 4684, line 35, column (b)(ii), enter that part of the loss here. Enter the part of the loss from income-producing property on Schedule A (Form 1040), line 28, and the part of the loss from property used as an employee on Schedule A (Form 1040), line 23. Identify as from "Form 4797, line 18a." See instructions . . | **18a** | |

**b** Redetermine the gain or (loss) on line 17 excluding the loss, if any, on line 18a. Enter here and on Form 1040, line 14 | **18b** | 44,567 |

**For Paperwork Reduction Act Notice, see separate instructions.**　　Cat. No. 13086I　　Form **4797** (2011)

## Part III   Gain From Disposition of Property Under Sections 1245, 1250, 1252, 1254, and 1255 (see instructions)

| 19 | (a) Description of section 1245, 1250, 1252, 1254, or 1255 property: | (b) Date acquired (mo., day, yr.) | (c) Date sold (mo., day, yr.) |
|---|---|---|---|
| A | SHOP | 02/05/2001 | 07/05/2011 |
| B | MACHINE 1 | 02/16/2006 | 07/05/2011 |
| C | MACHINE 2 | 03/19/2006 | 07/05/2011 |
| D | | | |

| | These columns relate to the properties on lines 19A through 19D. ▶ | | Property A | Property B | Property C | Property D |
|---|---|---|---|---|---|---|
| 20 | Gross sales price (**Note:** See line 1 before completing.) | 20 | 114,007 | 32,899 | 28,950 | |
| 21 | Cost or other basis plus expense of sale | 21 | 91,878 | 26,894 | 34,018 | |
| 22 | Depreciation (or depletion) allowed or allowable | 22 | 23,743 | 21,737 | 27,898 | |
| 23 | Adjusted basis. Subtract line 22 from line 21 | 23 | 68,135 | 5,157 | 6,120 | |
| 24 | Total gain. Subtract line 23 from line 20 | 24 | 45,872 | 27,742 | 22,830 | |
| 25 | **If section 1245 property:** | | | | | |
| a | Depreciation allowed or allowable from line 22 | 25a | | 21,737 | 27,898 | |
| b | Enter the **smaller** of line 24 or 25a | 25b | | 21,737 | 22,830 | |
| 26 | **If section 1250 property:** If straight line depreciation was used, enter -0- on line 26g, except for a corporation subject to section 291. | | | | | |
| a | Additional depreciation after 1975 (see instructions) | 26a | | | | |
| b | Applicable percentage multiplied by the **smaller** of line 24 or line 26a (see instructions) | 26b | | | | |
| c | Subtract line 26a from line 24. If residential rental property **or** line 24 is not more than line 26a, skip lines 26d and 26e | 26c | | | | |
| d | Additional depreciation after 1969 and before 1976 | 26d | | | | |
| e | Enter the **smaller** of line 26c or 26d | 26e | | | | |
| f | Section 291 amount (corporations only) | 26f | | | | |
| g | Add lines 26b, 26e, and 26f | 26g | | | | |
| 27 | **If section 1252 property:** Skip this section if you did not dispose of farmland or if this form is being completed for a partnership (other than an electing large partnership). | | | | | |
| a | Soil, water, and land clearing expenses | 27a | | | | |
| b | Line 27a multiplied by applicable percentage (see instructions) | 27b | | | | |
| c | Enter the **smaller** of line 24 or 27b | 27c | | | | |
| 28 | **If section 1254 property:** | | | | | |
| a | Intangible drilling and development costs, expenditures for development of mines and other natural deposits, mining exploration costs, and depletion (see instructions) | 28a | | | | |
| b | Enter the **smaller** of line 24 or 28a | 28b | | | | |
| 29 | **If section 1255 property:** | | | | | |
| a | Applicable percentage of payments excluded from income under section 126 (see instructions) | 29a | | | | |
| b | Enter the **smaller** of line 24 or 29a (see instructions) | 29b | | | | |

**Summary of Part III Gains.** Complete property columns A through D through line 29b before going to line 30.

| 30 | Total gains for all properties. Add property columns A through D, line 24 | 30 | 96,444 |
|---|---|---|---|
| 31 | Add property columns A through D, lines 25b, 26g, 27c, 28b, and 29b. Enter here and on line 13 | 31 | 44,567 |
| 32 | Subtract line 31 from line 30. Enter the portion from casualty or theft on Form 4684, line 33. Enter the portion from other than casualty or theft on Form 4797, line 6 | 32 | 51,877 |

## Part IV   Recapture Amounts Under Sections 179 and 280F(b)(2) When Business Use Drops to 50% or Less (see instructions)

| | | | (a) Section 179 | (b) Section 280F(b)(2) |
|---|---|---|---|---|
| 33 | Section 179 expense deduction or depreciation allowable in prior years | 33 | | 1,650 |
| 34 | Recomputed depreciation (see instructions) | 34 | | 581 |
| 35 | Recapture amount. Subtract line 34 from line 33. See the instructions for where to report | 35 | | 1,069 |

Form **4797** (2011)

# Form **4562**

Department of the Treasury
Internal Revenue Service  (99)

## Depreciation and Amortization
### (Including Information on Listed Property)

▶ See separate instructions.          ▶ Attach to your tax return.

OMB No. 1545-0172

**2011**

Attachment
Sequence No. **179**

| Name(s) shown on return | Business or activity to which this form relates | Identifying number |
|---|---|---|
| GEORGE GASLOW | GEORGE'S AUTOMOTIVE | 564-55-9855 |

## Part I   Election To Expense Certain Property Under Section 179
**Note:** *If you have any listed property, complete Part V before you complete Part I.*

| | | | |
|---|---|---|---|
| 1 | Maximum amount (see instructions) . . . . . . . . . . . . . . . . | **1** | 500,000 |
| 2 | Total cost of section 179 property placed in service (see instructions) . . . . . . . . . | **2** | |
| 3 | Threshold cost of section 179 property before reduction in limitation (see instructions) . . . . . . | **3** | 2,000,000 |
| 4 | Reduction in limitation. Subtract line 3 from line 2. If zero or less, enter -0- . . . . . . . | **4** | |
| 5 | Dollar limitation for tax year. Subtract line 4 from line 1. If zero or less, enter -0-. If married filing separately, see instructions | **5** | |

| **6** | (a) Description of property | (b) Cost (business use only) | (c) Elected cost | |
|---|---|---|---|---|
| | | | | |
| | | | | |

| | | | |
|---|---|---|---|
| 7 | Listed property. Enter the amount from line 29 . . . . . . . . . | **7** | |
| 8 | Total elected cost of section 179 property. Add amounts in column (c), lines 6 and 7 . . . . . . | **8** | |
| 9 | Tentative deduction. Enter the **smaller** of line 5 or line 8 . . . . . . . | **9** | |
| 10 | Carryover of disallowed deduction from line 13 of your 2010 Form 4562 . . | **10** | |
| 11 | Business income limitation. Enter the smaller of business income (not less than zero) or line 5 (see instructions) | **11** | |
| 12 | Section 179 expense deduction. Add lines 9 and 10, but do not enter more than line 11 . . . . . | **12** | |
| 13 | Carryover of disallowed deduction to 2012. Add lines 9 and 10, less line 12 ▶ | **13** | |

**Note:** *Do not use Part II or Part III below for listed property. Instead, use Part V.*

## Part II   Special Depreciation Allowance and Other Depreciation (Do not include listed property.) (See instructions.)

| | | | |
|---|---|---|---|
| 14 | Special depreciation allowance for qualified property (other than listed property) placed in service during the tax year (see instructions) . . . . . . . . . . . . . . . | **14** | |
| 15 | Property subject to section 168(f)(1) election . . . . . . . . . . . . . . | **15** | |
| 16 | Other depreciation (including ACRS) . . . . . . . . . . . . . . . . | **16** | |

## Part III   MACRS Depreciation (Do not include listed property.) (See instructions.)

### Section A

| | | | |
|---|---|---|---|
| 17 | MACRS deductions for assets placed in service in tax years beginning before 2011 . . . . . . | **17** | 4,583 |
| 18 | If you are electing to group any assets placed in service during the tax year into one or more general asset accounts, check here . . . . . . . . . . . . . . . . ▶ ☐ | | |

### Section B—Assets Placed in Service During 2011 Tax Year Using the General Depreciation System

| (a) Classification of property | (b) Month and year placed in service | (c) Basis for depreciation (business/investment use only—see instructions) | (d) Recovery period | (e) Convention | (f) Method | (g) Depreciation deduction |
|---|---|---|---|---|---|---|
| **19a** 3-year property | | | | | | |
| **b** 5-year property | | | | | | |
| **c** 7-year property | | | | | | |
| **d** 10-year property | | | | | | |
| **e** 15-year property | | | | | | |
| **f** 20-year property | | | | | | |
| **g** 25-year property | | | 25 yrs. | | S/L | |
| **h** Residential rental property | | | 27.5 yrs. | MM | S/L | |
| | | | 27.5 yrs. | MM | S/L | |
| **i** Nonresidential real property | 06/2011 | 99,300 | 39 yrs. | MM | S/L | 1,379 |
| | | | | MM | S/L | |

### Section C—Assets Placed in Service During 2011 Tax Year Using the Alternative Depreciation System

| | | | | | | |
|---|---|---|---|---|---|---|
| **20a** Class life | | | | | S/L | |
| **b** 12-year | | | 12 yrs. | | S/L | |
| **c** 40-year | | | 40 yrs. | MM | S/L | |

## Part IV   Summary (See instructions.)

| | | | |
|---|---|---|---|
| 21 | Listed property. Enter amount from line 28 . . . . . . . . . . . . . . | **21** | 126 |
| 22 | **Total.** Add amounts from line 12, lines 14 through 17, lines 19 and 20 in column (g), and line 21. Enter here and on the appropriate lines of your return. Partnerships and S corporations—see instructions . . . . . | **22** | 6,088 |
| 23 | For assets shown above and placed in service during the current year, enter the portion of the basis attributable to section 263A costs . . . . . . . | **23** | |

**For Paperwork Reduction Act Notice, see separate instructions.**          Cat. No. 12906N          Form **4562** (2011)

D-30

## Part V — Listed Property (Include automobiles, certain other vehicles, certain computers, and property used for entertainment, recreation, or amusement.)

**Note:** *For any vehicle for which you are using the standard mileage rate or deducting lease expense, complete **only** 24a, 24b, columns (a) through (c) of Section A, all of Section B, and Section C if applicable.*

### Section A—Depreciation and Other Information (Caution: *See the instructions for limits for passenger automobiles.*)

**24a** Do you have evidence to support the business/investment use claimed?  ☑ **Yes** ☐ **No**   **24b** If "Yes," is the evidence written?  ☑ **Yes** ☐ **No**

| (a) Type of property (list vehicles first) | (b) Date placed in service | (c) Business/ investment use percentage | (d) Cost or other basis | (e) Basis for depreciation (business/investment use only) | (f) Recovery period | (g) Method/ Convention | (h) Depreciation deduction | (i) Elected section 179 cost |
|---|---|---|---|---|---|---|---|---|
| **25** Special depreciation allowance for qualified listed property placed in service during the tax year and used more than 50% in a qualified business use (see instructions) . **25** | | | | | | | | |
| **26** Property used more than 50% in a qualified business use: | | | | | | | | |
| | | % | | | | | | |
| | | % | | | | | | |
| | | % | | | | | | |
| **27** Property used 50% or less in a qualified business use: | | | | | | | | |
| FAX MACHINE | 7/13/08 | 43 % | 2,931 | 1,260 | 10 | S/L – HY | 126 | |
| | | % | | | | S/L – | | |
| | | % | | | | S/L – | | |
| **28** Add amounts in column (h), lines 25 through 27. Enter here and on line 21, page 1 . **28** | | | | | | | 126 | |
| **29** Add amounts in column (i), line 26. Enter here and on line 7, page 1 . . . . . . . . . . . . . **29** | | | | | | | | |

### Section B—Information on Use of Vehicles

Complete this section for vehicles used by a sole proprietor, partner, or other "more than 5% owner," or related person. If you provided vehicles to your employees, first answer the questions in Section C to see if you meet an exception to completing this section for those vehicles.

| | (a) Vehicle 1 | | (b) Vehicle 2 | | (c) Vehicle 3 | | (d) Vehicle 4 | | (e) Vehicle 5 | | (f) Vehicle 6 | |
|---|---|---|---|---|---|---|---|---|---|---|---|---|
| **30** Total business/investment miles driven during the year (**do not** include commuting miles) . | | | | | | | | | | | | |
| **31** Total commuting miles driven during the year | | | | | | | | | | | | |
| **32** Total other personal (noncommuting) miles driven . . . . . . . . . . | | | | | | | | | | | | |
| **33** Total miles driven during the year. Add lines 30 through 32 . . . . . . . . . | | | | | | | | | | | | |
| **34** Was the vehicle available for personal use during off-duty hours? . . . . . . . | Yes | No | Yes | No | Yes | No | Yes | No | Yes | No | Yes | No |
| **35** Was the vehicle used primarily by a more than 5% owner or related person? . . . | | | | | | | | | | | | |
| **36** Is another vehicle available for personal use? | | | | | | | | | | | | |

### Section C—Questions for Employers Who Provide Vehicles for Use by Their Employees

Answer these questions to determine if you meet an exception to completing Section B for vehicles used by employees who **are not** more than 5% owners or related persons (see instructions).

| | Yes | No |
|---|---|---|
| **37** Do you maintain a written policy statement that prohibits all personal use of vehicles, including commuting, by your employees? . . . . . . . . . . . . | | |
| **38** Do you maintain a written policy statement that prohibits personal use of vehicles, except commuting, by your employees? See the instructions for vehicles used by corporate officers, directors, or 1% or more owners . . . . | | |
| **39** Do you treat all use of vehicles by employees as personal use? . . . . . . . . . . . | | |
| **40** Do you provide more than five vehicles to your employees, obtain information from your employees about the use of the vehicles, and retain the information received? . . . . . . . . . . . . | | |
| **41** Do you meet the requirements concerning qualified automobile demonstration use? (See instructions.) . . . | | |

**Note:** *If your answer to 37, 38, 39, 40, or 41 is "Yes," do not complete Section B for the covered vehicles.*

## Part VI — Amortization

| (a) Description of costs | (b) Date amortization begins | (c) Amortizable amount | (d) Code section | (e) Amortization period or percentage | (f) Amortization for this year |
|---|---|---|---|---|---|
| **42** Amortization of costs that begins during your 2011 tax year (see instructions): | | | | | |
| | | | | | |
| | | | | | |
| **43** Amortization of costs that began before your 2011 tax year . . . . . . . . . . . **43** | | | | | |
| **44 Total.** Add amounts in column (f). See the instructions for where to report . . . . . . . . **44** | | | | | |

Form **4562** (2011)

| Description of Property | Date Placed in Service | Cost or other Basis | Business/ Investment Use % | Business Basis (C x D) | Salvage/ Land Value | Section 179 Deduction or Bonus Depreciation | Depreciation Basis [E – (F + G)] | Method/ Convention | Recovery Period | Prior Depreciation | Depreciation Percentage | Depreciation Deduction (H x L) |
|---|---|---|---|---|---|---|---|---|---|---|---|---|
| A | B | C | D | E | F | G | H | I | J | K | L | M |
| Fax Machine | 07/13/08 | 2931 | 43% | 1260 | | | 1260 | SL/HY | 10yrs | 950 | 10 | 126 |
| Computer | 07/16/09 | 1895 | 100 | 1895 | | | 1895 | 200%DB/ HY | 5yrs | 985 | 19.20 | 364 |
| Machine 1 | 02/16/06 | 26459 | 100 | 26459 | | | 26459 | 200%DB/HY | 7yrs | 20557 | 8.92 | 1180 |
| Machine 2 | 03/19/06 | 33959 | 100 | 33959 | | | 33959 | 200%DB/HY | 7yrs | 26383 | 8.92 | 1515 |
| Shelves | 09/26/08 | 2325 | 100 | 2325 | | | 2325 | 200%DB/HY | 7yrs | 1308 | 12.49 | 290 |
| Shop | 02/05/01 | 98200 | 100 | 98200 | 9300 | | 88900 | SL/MM | 39yrs | 22509 | 2.564 | 1234 |
| Shop | 06/30/1 | 112500 | 100 | 112500 | 13200 | | 99300 | SL/MM | 39yrs | | 1.391 | 1379 |

# Schedule D Tax Worksheet

**Complete this worksheet only if line 18 or line 19 of Schedule D is more than zero. Otherwise, complete the Qualified Dividends and Capital Gain Tax Worksheet in the Instructions for Form 1040, line 44 (or in the Instructions for Form 1040NR, line 42) to figure your tax.**

**Exception: Do not** use the Qualified Dividends and Capital Gain Tax Worksheet **or** this worksheet to figure your tax if:
- Line 15 or line 16 of Schedule D is zero or less **and** you have no qualified dividends on Form 1040, line 9b (or Form 1040NR, line 10b); **or**
- Form 1040, line 43 (or Form 1040NR, line 41) is zero or less.

Instead, see the instructions for Form 1040, line 44 (or Form 1040NR, line 42).

| | | | |
|---|---|---:|---:|
| 1. | Enter your taxable income from Form 1040, line 43 (or Form 1040NR, line 41). (However, if you are filing Form 2555 or 2555-EZ (relating to foreign earned income), enter instead the amount from line 3 of the Foreign Earned Income Tax Worksheet in the Instructions for Form 1040, line 44) . . . . . . . . . . . . . . . . | **1.** | 145,878 |
| 2. | Enter your qualified dividends from Form 1040, line 9b (or Form 1040NR, line 10b) . . . . . . . . . . . . . . . . . . . **2.** | | |
| 3. | Enter the amount from Form 4952 (used to figure investment interest expense deduction), line 4g . . . . . . . . . . . . . . **3.** | | |
| 4. | Enter the amount from Form 4952, line 4e* **4.** | | |
| 5. | Subtract line 4 from line 3. If zero or less, enter -0- . . . . . . . . . **5.** | | |
| 6. | Subtract line 5 from line 2. If zero or less, enter -0-** . . . . . . . . . **6.** | | |
| 7. | Enter the **smaller** of line 15 or line 16 of Schedule D . . . . . . . **7.** 54,191 | | |
| 8. | Enter the **smaller** of line 3 or line 4 . . . . . . . . . . . . . . **8.** | | |
| 9. | Subtract line 8 from line 7. If zero or less, enter -0-** . . . . . . . . . . . . . . . . . . . **9.** 54,191 | | |
| 10. | Add lines 6 and 9 . . . . . . . . . . . . . . . . . . . . . . . . . . | **10.** | 54,191 |
| 11. | Add lines 18 and 19 of Schedule D** . . . . . . . . . . . . . . . . . . . **11.** 23,743 | | |
| 12. | Enter the **smaller** of line 9 or line 11 . . . . . . . . . . . . . . . . . . **12.** 23,743 | | |
| 13. | Subtract line 12 from line 10 . . . . . . . . . . . . . . . . . . . . . . . | **13.** | 30,448 |
| 14. | Subtract line 13 from line 1. If zero or less, enter -0- . . . . . . . . . . . . . . . . . . . | **14.** | 115,430 |
| 15. | Enter: | | |
| | • $34,500 if single or married filing separately; | | |
| | • $69,000 if married filing jointly or qualifying widow(er); or | | |
| | • $46,250 if head of household . . . . . . . . **15.** 34,500 | | |
| 16. | Enter the **smaller** of line 1 or line 15 . . . . . . . . . . . . . . . . . . . . . . **16.** | 34,500 | |
| 17. | Enter the **smaller** of line 14 or line 16 . . . . . . . . . . . . . . . . . . . **17.** 34,500 | | |
| 18. | Subtract line 10 from line 1. If zero or less, enter -0- . . . . . . . **18.** 91,687 | | |
| 19. | Enter the **larger** of line 17 or line 18 . . . . . . . . . . . . . . . . . ▶ **19.** 91,687 | | |
| 20. | Subtract line 17 from line 16. This amount is taxed at 0%. . . . . . ▶ **20.** | | |
| | **If lines 1 and 16 are the same, skip lines 21 through 33 and go to line 34. Otherwise, go to line 21.** | | |
| 21. | Enter the **smaller** of line 1 or line 13 . . . . . . . . . . . . . . . . . **21.** 30,448 | | |
| 22. | Enter the amount from line 20 (if line 20 is blank, enter -0-) . . . . . . . . . . **22.** | | |
| 23. | Subtract line 22 from line 21. If zero or less, enter -0- . . . . . . . . . . ▶ **23.** | 30,448 | |
| 24. | Multiply line 23 by 15% (.15) . . . . . . . . . . . . . . . . . . . . . . | **24.** | 4,567 |
| | **If Schedule D, line 19, is zero or blank, skip lines 25 through 30 and go to line 31. Otherwise, go to line 25.** | | |
| 25. | Enter the **smaller** of line 9 above or Schedule D, line 19 . . . . . . . . . **25.** 23,743 | | |
| 26. | Add lines 10 and 19 . . . . . . . . . . . . . . . . . . **26.** 145,878 | | |
| 27. | Enter the amount from line 1 above . . . . . . . . . . . **27.** 145,878 | | |
| 28. | Subtract line 27 from line 26. If zero or less, enter -0- . . . . . . . . . . . . . **28.** | | |
| 29. | Subtract line 28 from line 25. If zero or less, enter -0- . . . . . . . . . . . . . . ▶ **29.** | 23,743 | |
| 30. | Multiply line 29 by 25% (.25) . . . . . . . . . . . . . . . . . . . . . . | **30.** | 5,936 |
| | **If Schedule D, line 18, is zero or blank, skip lines 31 through 33 and go to line 34. Otherwise, go to line 31.** | | |
| 31. | Add lines 19, 20, 23, and 29 . . . . . . . . . . . . . . . . . . **31.** | | |
| 32. | Subtract line 31 from line 1 . . . . . . . . . . . . . . . . . . **32.** | | |
| 33. | Multiply line 32 by 28% (.28) . . . . . . . . . . . . . . . . . . . . . . | **33.** | |
| 34. | Figure the tax on the amount on **line 19**. If the amount on line 19 is less than $100,000, use the Tax Table to figure the tax. If the amount on line 19 is $100,000 or more, use the Tax Computation Worksheet . . . . . . . . . . . . . . . . | **34.** | 19,286 |
| 35. | Add lines 24, 30, 33, and 34 . . . . . . . . . . . . . . . . . . | **35.** | 29,789 |
| 36. | Figure the tax on the amount on **line 1**. If the amount on line 1 is less than $100,000, use the Tax Table to figure the tax. If the amount on line 1 is $100,000 or more, use the Tax Computation Worksheet . . . . . . . . . . . . . . . . | **36.** | 34,463 |
| 37. | **Tax on all taxable income (including capital gains and qualified dividends).** Enter the **smaller** of line 35 or line 36. Also include this amount on Form 1040, line 44 (or Form 1040NR, line 42). (If you are filing Form 2555 or 2555-EZ, do not enter this amount on Form 1040, line 44. Instead, enter it on line 4 of the Foreign Earned Income Tax Worksheet in the Form 1040 instructions) . . . | **37.** | 29,789 |

*If applicable, enter instead the smaller amount you entered on the dotted line next to line 4e of Form 4952.

**If you are filing Form 2555 or 2555-EZ, see the footnote in the Foreign Earned Income Tax Worksheet in the Instructions for Form 1040, line 44, before completing this line.